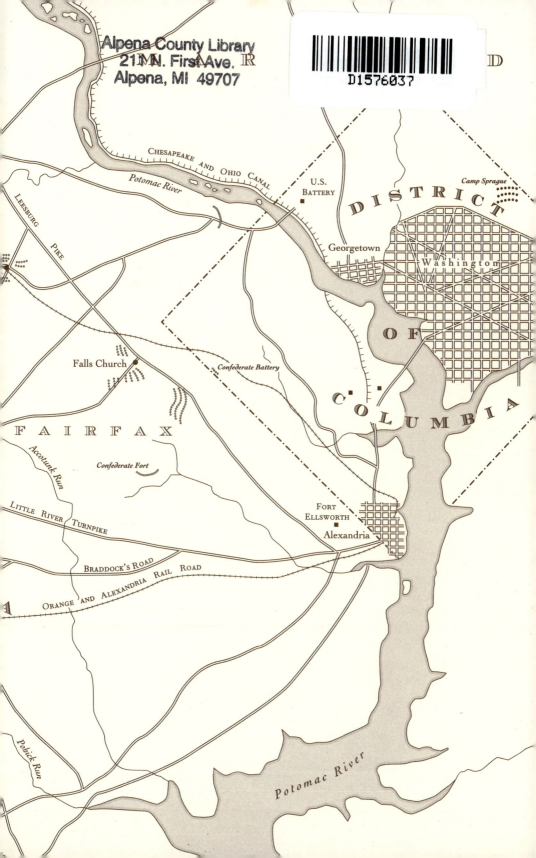

CHESAPEAKE AND OHIO CANAL

Potomac River

U.S.
BATTERY

Camp Sprague

D I S T R I C T

Georgetown

Washington

LEESBURG PIKE

O F

Falls Church

Confederate Battery

C O L U M B I A

F A I R F A X

Accotunk Run

Confederate Fort

LITTLE RIVER TURNPIKE

FORT
ELLSWORTH

Alexandria

BRADDOCK'S ROAD

ORANGE AND ALEXANDRIA RAIL ROAD

A

Pohick Run

Potomac River

DONNYBROOK

★★★★★

DONNYBROOK

★★★★★

THE BATTLE OF BULL RUN, 1861

★★★★★

David Detzer

973.7
DETZ
c.1

Harcourt, Inc.

Orlando   Austin   New York   San Diego   Toronto   London

www.HarcourtBooks.com

Library of Congress Cataloging-in-Publication Data
Detzer, David.
Donnybrook: the Battle of Bull Run, 1861/David Detzer. — 1st ed.
          p.   cm.
Includes bibliographical references and index.
ISBN 0-15-100889-2
1. Bull Run, 1st Battle of, Va., 1861. I. Title.
E472.18.D48 2004
973.7'31 — dc22   2004005227

Text set in Cochin
Designed by Suzanne Fridley

Printed in the United States of America

First edition
A C E G I K J H F D B

For Melanie, of course,
the tender of my cloud forest —
and for her two kids, my pals, Calvin
and Oliver Gillette, who claim, perhaps correctly,
they understand the Civil War far better than I.

CONTENTS

Book Three: Agley

Foreword

When the Civil War started, Nathan Bedford Forrest, with no formal education, volunteered for Confederate service as a private. During the war he rose to become one of the most famous cavalry leaders in history. Forrest, a good soldier and a hard man, was not much for fancy words; he preferred straight talk. He once defined the meaning of warfare this way: "War means fighting." And he added, "And fighting means killing."

In the first months of the Civil War, many Americans did not yet realize the truth of those words. Few understood how *ugly* the war would become. At the railroad stations, North and South, as men left to "fight," there was much naïve laughter and gaiety. Tears were shed, of course, but sweet tears mostly, not the bitter weeping that would later come. Few Americans yet had any sense of what an actual battlefield would be like. They would get their first important lesson in July 1861, when a great Union army and a major Confederate force clashed near a Virginia stream called Bull Run.

After that terrible day it would be impossible for thinking people—on either side—to feel so casual about war. Bloodier battles would be fought in the next few years at places like Shiloh and Antietam and Gettysburg, but none would be quite as educational.

What circumstances brought the two armies there that hot July day?

On April 12, 1861, dozens of Confederate cannon opened fire on Fort Sumter, a small Federal fortification inside Charleston Harbor, South Carolina. The following afternoon, after more than thirty hours of steady bombardment, Major Robert Anderson, the fort's commander, surrendered. Within a few hours the new president of the United States, Abraham Lincoln, called his cabinet together to discuss their options. Personally, he was determined not to accept the insult to the flag. He wished to raise an army immediately to show the firm resolve of his government. His cabinet concurred. It agreed he should issue a proclamation calling on the states to raise 75,000 volunteers who would serve for three months. It seemed like an appropriate number of men: large enough to show the Federal government's seriousness, small enough that all the volunteers could be fairly easily clothed and armed. As to their three-month term of service, it seemed possible there would be little or no fighting—once the administration had revealed its determination. Besides, the Treasury was empty and Congress was not in session. Lincoln's thinking reflected the fact that he had been a lawyer: He wished to keep the matter as simple, as controlled, as possible. At the moment, there seemed no point in raising an unnecessarily huge and cumbersome and expensive force.

Then, during the next few days, it became clear that Washington, D.C., itself was in danger. Just to its south, in Virginia, armed bands sprang up and grabbed critical places not far from the capital. North of Washington, in Baltimore and in the Maryland countryside, angry and desperate mobs cut transportation and communication between the capital and the North. It became instantly obvious that Washington must have military protection, and quickly. Several states, already raising volunteers, forwarded them. It was touch and go for a while. There were clashes in Maryland. But after two or three weeks, the first great crisis of the war subsided. Maryland seemed relatively secure.

There remained, however, the matter of Virginia—especially that region of it a short mile away from the District of Columbia, just across the Potomac River. If the Confederates brought artillery to the hills across the way, the guns could easily blast the White House and other Federal structures. Lincoln and his advisers considered their options. Since the District now contained a garrison of thousands of volunteers who had rushed there to protect it, whose numbers were still growing almost daily, the administration decided to push a portion of these troops across the river, as a defensive measure if nothing else. In late May, more than 10,000 Union soldiers marched into Virginia, and started to build fortifications. Lincoln now had to consider whether to move them forward from this bridgehead.

Virginia's leaders, meanwhile, invited Jefferson Davis to bring his Confederate government up from Montgomery, Alabama. Davis agreed to accept the offer, saying that Richmond would be an appropriate capital city. In June, as Lincoln's soldiers were entrenching themselves into the hills of northern Virginia, the Confederate leadership was settling down a hundred miles away. By itself, this would have created almost unbearable tension. But Southern troops were also pouring into this region. Davis and his military advisers—men like Robert E. Lee—wanted to do what Lincoln had done with Washington: to defend their capital, Richmond, by pushing troops well ahead of the city. By mid-June Confederate regiments were camping only a few miles from Lincoln's army. The central axis of these advanced Confederate positions was a tiny railroad station called Manassas Junction. Robert E. Lee went there to examine the situation, and, concluding it was an important spot that must be defended, he ordered more soldiers there.

Washington noticed the change. At the end of June, Lincoln decided to challenge the growing Confederate position at Manassas Junction. He told his generals to make preparations.

In mid-July a Union army—the largest in American history up to this moment—started forward. The Confederates at Manassas Junction flexed their muscles—and waited.

This is the story.

This book has three sections. Book One describes how both sides prepared for the battle. It speaks of the various plans and the men who formulated them, and about how the two sides maneuvered their forces and got themselves ready. There were optimists and pessimists on each side, but most people, North and South, believed their cause was just and their foes would prove weak. Average Americans, unacquainted with the chaos of battle, could not imagine what the coming war—which would consist of more than 10,000 battles and skirmishes—would involve. They assumed that the approaching fight near Manassas Junction would be the only real battle, or at least that there would be only a handful more. Book Two describes how the two armies positioned themselves near the stream called Bull Run and prepared to do battle. Book Three describes what happened once the armies entered the actual conflict on July 21, 1861, and how so many of the neat plans quickly fell apart.

The first part of our story, therefore, is mostly about leaders: high-ranking politicians and generals, and their analyses and schemes. The second and third parts focus on those individuals—of high rank and low—who were expected to follow the blueprints. This section describes their initial enthusiasms and naïveté, their sore feet and aching shoulders in the hot July sun, and their heroism and confusion and cowardice in battle. Or, to put it a different way, the opening sections deal with *why* a battle was fought near Bull Run; the last section tells what happened there—so far as can be known from the confusing and contradictory accounts.

A couple of things are clear about the battle: It was hard fought, and it could have gone either way. For a number of reasons, as we will see, the Union army would begin to withdraw late in the afternoon. Since the Federal force had not won, and since its supply line was long and inefficient, and since many of the troops were worn out, the army's leaders decided to pull all the way back to Washington.

Many Northerners had assumed their soldiers would be victorious. Now they demanded to know what went wrong. Who was at fault? Editors pointed fingers at this person and that. On December 20, 1861, a new congressional committee, the Joint Committee on the Conduct of the Present War, held its first session inside a room in the basement of the Capitol. The official purpose was to investigate why the Union armies had not been more successful. Congress had granted this seven-man committee the power to call witnesses, who were required, in secret session, to respond to any questions the Committee asked. On this December morning the committee agreed on its first order of business: "to investigate the disaster to our arms at Bull Run, Virginia." The resulting investigation constituted the first broad, organized effort to analyze the battle, but the results were unconvincing. After six months the Committee could not really make sense of it. Since then, a number of historians have also tried to clarify the events of that day, with varying degrees of success. After almost a century and a half, a cloud of confusion still lingers over that battlefield.

This book is not an attempt to lay blame on any individual. Far too many people contributed to the unfortunate events of that day, including two American icons—Abraham Lincoln and Robert E. Lee.

Instead, this story is intended as a cautionary tale—a glimpse of the chasm between military planning and reality.

AUTHOR'S NOTE

A matter of names: During the war the two sides generally disagreed about the names of battles, partly out of pride. They would even disagree on what to call the war itself, though both Jefferson Davis and Robert E. Lee generally thought "civil war" was satisfactory. After the fighting was over, many folks on both sides refused to use whichever names their enemies adopted, which has made things complicated for historians.

When the two armies that we are about to focus on had a small skirmish at Blackburn's Ford on July 18, 1861, Southern newspapers reported the "victory" in almost biblical terms, hysterically describing the enemy as having attacked with at least 15,000 men and having littered the ground with thousands of their dead. What should such a great victory be called? (Northern reports decided to call the incident "the Battle of Blackburn's Ford"—an inaccurate label for the clash since, among other things, the fighting had also involved a nearby spot called Mitchell's Ford.) Within a few days most Southern press reports settled on "the Battle of Bull Run"—a not unreasonable designation since the stream really was an important physical feature in the skirmish.

Having adopted that name for the incident near Blackburn's Ford, Southerners had to choose a label other than "Bull Run" when the far greater battle took place three days later. They finally agreed on "Manassas." (Unfortunately, this name was inappropriate since none of that huge battle took place near the station—though the railroad depot was not far from Beauregard's headquarters.) Ever since July 21, 1861, Southern loyalists have insisted on using "Manassas" rather than "Bull Run"—as much as anything, it would seem, to indicate their fervent independence.

I have decided to use "Blackburn's Ford" for the skirmish and "Bull Run" for the important battle because, outside the South, those are the most recognizable names, the ones used in textbooks.

The mildly disparaging labels "rebel" and "Yankee" were often used during the war's first weeks as terms of opprobrium. I have occasionally utilized them here merely to indicate the sentiments of the side I am, at that moment, focusing on.

CAST OF MAJOR CHARACTERS

★★ *Union* ★★

ABRAHAM LINCOLN

SIMON CAMERON, *Secretary of War*

LIEUTENANT GENERAL WINFIELD SCOTT, *General in Chief*

Major General Robert Patterson *(Commander of the Army in the Shenandoah Valley)*

Brigadier General Irvin McDowell *(Commander of the Army at Bull Run)*

Major John Gross Barnard *(Chief Engineer, Responsible for Mapping and Planning Details)*

Major William Barry *(Chief of Artillery)*

Captain Charles Griffin *(Battery D, Fifth Artillery)*

Captain James B. Ricketts *(Battery 1, First Artillery)*

Brigadier General Daniel Tyler *(First Division)*

Colonel Erasmus Keyes *(First Brigade)*

Brigadier General Robert C. Schenck *(Second Brigade)*

Colonel William T. Sherman *(Third Brigade)*

Colonel Israel B. Richardson *(Fourth Brigade)*

Colonel David Hunter *(Second Division)*

Colonel Andrew Porter *(First Brigade)*

Major George Sykes *(Commander of the Battalion of Regular Infantry)*

Colonel Ambrose Burnside *(Second Brigade)*

Colonel Samuel P. Heintzelman *(Third Division)*

Colonel William B. Franklin *(First Brigade)*

Colonel Orlando B. Willcox *(Second Brigade)*

Colonel Oliver O. Howard *(Third Brigade)*

Colonel Dixon S. Miles *(Fifth Division)*

Colonel Louis Blenker *(First Brigade)*

Colonel Thomas A. Davies *(Second Brigade)*

★★ *Confederate* ★★

JEFFERSON DAVIS
MAJOR GENERAL ROBERT E. LEE *(Chief Military Advisor)*
Brigadier General Joseph E. Johnston *(Commander of the
Army of the Shenandoah)*
Major William H. C. Whiting *(Chief Engineer)*
Colonel William N. Pendleton *(Chief of Artillery)*
Captain John D. Imboden
Colonel J. E. B. Stuart *(First Cavalry)*
Brigadier General Thomas J. Jackson *(First Brigade)*
Lieutenant Colonel John Echols *(Twenty-seventh Virginia)*
Captain Thomas McAllister *("Alleghany Roughs")*
Colonel Francis S. Bartow *(Second Brigade)*
Lieutenant Colonel William Montgomery Gardner
(Eighth Georgia)
Brigadier General Barnard Bee *(Third Brigade)*
Brigadier General Kirby Smith *(Fourth Brigade)*
Brigadier General P. G. T. Beauregard *(Commander of the
Army at Manassas Junction)*
Colonel Thomas Jordan *(Acting Assistant Adjutant
General)*
Colonel Alexander R. Chisolm, *Aide-de-Camp*
Colonel James Chesnut, *Aide-de-Camp*
Captain E. Porter Alexander *(Chief Signal Officer)*
Brigadier General Milledge L. Bonham *(First Brigade)*
Brigadier General Richard S. Ewell *(Second Brigade)*
Brigadier General David R. Jones *(Third Brigade)*
Brigadier General James Longstreet *(Fourth Brigade)*
Colonel P. St. George Cocke *(Fifth Brigade)*
Colonel Jubal P. Early *(Sixth Brigade)*
Brigadier General Nathan B. ("Shanks") Evans *(Seventh
Brigade)*
Major Roberdeau Wheat *(First Louisiana)*
Colonel Wade Hampton *("Hampton's Legion," unbrigaded)*
Colonel Charles Fisher *(Sixth North Carolina, unbrigaded)*

DONNYBROOK

BOOK ONE

PLANS AND ILLUSIONS

*All wars are planned by old men
In council rooms apart,
Who plan for greater armament
And map the battle chart.*
—GRANTLAND RICE

The Sacred Soil

*The sacred soil of Virginia, in which repose the ashes of so
many of the illustrious patriots who gave independence to their
country, has been desecrated by the hostile tread of an armed enemy,
who proclaims his malignant hatred of Virginia because she will not
bow her proud neck to the humiliating yoke of Yankee rule.*
—RICHMOND ENQUIRER, MAY 25, 1861

On April 17, 1861, a special convention of Virginians
voted on a resolution about whether their state should secede.
The mood in the chamber was emotional and caustic. The final
tally was far from overwhelming for either side. Of the 143 dele-
gates present that day, only 88 accepted secession — 62.5 percent.
The opposition, many from the western counties of the state, remained adamantly opposed. The convention's leaders concluded
it would be prudent to involve the state's citizenry in such a critical matter. They decided on a popular referendum, to take place
five weeks later. On May 23, 1861, Virginia's voters lined up at
polling places; a majority agreed that their state must secede.

Late that night a Federal army crossed the Potomac from the
District of Columbia. Before the sun rose on May 24, Arlington,
Virginia — part of "the sacred soil" — was controlled by Lincoln's
troops. When, a few hours later, Federal soldiers arrived in
Alexandria, five miles downriver, a battalion of Virginia militiamen began to slip out of town. Moving nervously through the
morning's shadows, they eluded the Union troops and marched

quickly out along the railroad tracks. On most mornings a train made a regular run westward from Alexandria. On this day it was halted before it even reached town, and the battalion clambered aboard its flatcars. Some citizens, roused by the morning's events, were on hand to watch them leave, and a few civilians, frightened by the unknown, joined the troops on the train. A Virginia soldier noted that many of these citizens were prosperous gentlemen who were leaving behind full warehouses or well-stocked shops or barns packed with grain. In their misguided dementia, or at least their impulsiveness, they were fleeing without thought of their unprotected families still at home.

As the train chugged away, its civilian passengers, peering back toward Alexandria, spontaneously began to sing an old hymn. The soldiers joined in. One of them would recall: "It was madness, it is true, but yet a transcendent madness, in which greed, envy, and malice had no part, and so these elderly fellows — deacons, vestrymen, and communicants — sat in the crowded flats, and as their homes, their families, and their fortunes were left behind, they joined in the jubilant chorus, 'We'll be gay and happy still.'" The train shuddered westward.

Late that morning, the locomotive arrived at the tiny depot, Manassas Junction. The battalion alighted, wondering: Would Lincoln's army follow them?[1]

During that day and the next, as Southerners became aware of the "invasion" of northern Virginia, their reaction bordered on hysteria. Their newspapers expressed shock and rage. Their correspondents rifled their memory banks for appropriate terms. Part of this ranting reflected genuine hatred, part was simple literary tap dancing, the kind of riff journalists in 1861 played when they had the spotlight and could indicate, among other things, how well educated they were, sprinkling their paragraphs with multiple allusions drawn from ancient history and the Bible. Union troops, they said, were rapists: "The monsters have been hunting married females from house to house, for the gratification of their brutal lusts." They were urban scum: "thieves, pickpockets, loafers, and scoundrels," or "greasy mudsills," or "swinish groundlings," or "lewd fellows of the baser sort," or "barefoot, dirty and degraded." They were depicted as mindless savages: as "minions," "brutes," "barbarians," "hordes," "myrmidons," and "diabolical fiends." As money-grubbing thugs: "mercenaries," "hirelings," "pirates," "Vandals," "plunderers," and "Hessians." Southern reporters linked the "invasion" to abolitionism and "Black Republicans," and especially to "the despot" Lincoln: "that Baboon in the White House," "that wicked tyrant," "that corrupt and arrogant creature in power." And so on.

These Union murderers had just defiled Virginia—and they seemed certain to be thrusting soon toward Richmond.

Several weeks earlier, on April 27, 1861, the leaders of Virginia had written Jefferson Davis that they would welcome becoming the home of the Confederate capital. Davis and his colleagues were receptive. The benefits of moving from Montgomery, Alabama—the Confederacy's temporary capital—were many. Montgomery was a small city and something of an eyesore. Besides, summer was approaching and central Alabama was likely to be stifling. On the other hand, transferring the Confederate capital to Richmond had certain drawbacks. Ever since the bombardment of Fort Sumter, Union troops had been pouring into Washington, only 123 miles away. The land between the two cities would almost certainly become bloody. But the advantages were also manifest. Among other things, the transfer would cement the Upper South to the Deep South.

On May 20, the Confederate congress voted to relocate to Richmond and agreed to reconvene there two months later, on July 20. Jefferson Davis began his own move to Virginia within a week, along with a thousand civil servants. Before his departure, Davis's wife, Varina, had lunch in Montgomery with Mary Chesnut, the wife of James Chesnut, one of South Carolina's most prominent politicians. The two women were intelligent, strong willed, charming, and clever. Over their meal, they shared with each other their relief about the transfer. The hotels here, they agreed, were ghastly. So was the food. But Mary mentioned that her husband was opposed to the move because he considered Montgomery more central. Varina Davis shrugged off that concern. "The Yankees will make it hot for us," she said, "go where we will. And if war comes..."

Mary Chesnut interrupted, "And it has come?"

"Yes," Mrs. Davis replied, and peered around the dining room. "I fancy these dainty folks may live to regret the fare of the Montgomery hotels, even."

"Never," snorted Mary Chesnut.[2]

Jefferson Davis was a person with many fine qualities. Of middle height, he seemed taller because he was slender and held himself stiffly erect. An intelligent man, he had read broadly and deeply. He had few bad habits. He drank little, worked hard, and always strived to be at his best. He was proud and stubborn. He would need these qualities to hold together his new "country," based as it was on the concept of states' rights. His weaknesses were not immediately evident. He was not blessed with wit or humor or empathy for others, and he could be a devout hater of anyone who provoked him. He himself admitted it. "I have an infirmity of which I am heartily ashamed," he said. "When I am aroused in a matter, I lose control of my feelings and become personal." Perhaps his efforts to rein in his emotions made him suffer an extraordinary menu of ailments that tortured him with long bouts of pain, aching joints, and intestinal problems. He drove himself hard, striving to work through the searing headaches and the dizziness. Sometimes he succeeded, other times they laid him low. His most troublesome illness was trigeminal neuralgia, sometimes called tic douloureux, a disorder of the fifth cranial nerve. The condition may have resulted from a bout of shingles (an infection caused by the varicella-zoster virus — essentially a recurrence of childhood chicken pox). Shingles can lead to postherpetic neuralgia, a nasty and painful reaction, and when PHN attacks the trigeminal nerve, the resulting agonies can be excruciating, and those suffering from it often commit suicide. (Davis's facial neuralgia caused him to lose the sight in his left eye, which became covered with a whitish film.) Stress tended to trigger his attacks. The previous few weeks had drained his energies and emotions. By the time he left Montgomery on May 26, he was so unwell he hoped the long train trip would allow him a period of relative tranquility and leisure to recuperate. Along the way, however, as word spread of his passing through, mobs gathered by the tracks to see him and to hear his words. Over and over, he dragged himself erect and stepped from the train to speak to the curious listeners, maintaining a strong and confident countenance.

On the morning of May 29, less than a week after the Yankee "invasion," he arrived in Richmond. Predictably, he was greeted by a cheering mass. Bands played "Dixie" and other lively tunes. Cannon gave him a fifteen-gun salute, one for each "Southern" (that is, "slave") state. He was exhausted. When offered the use of a large carriage, drawn by four bays, he accepted. It took him to the Spotswood, the city's newest and grandest hostelry, past throngs who lined the way, who were laughing, shouting, weeping, reaching out to grasp his hand. At the hotel he was shown his suite, number 83, whose door had been thoughtfully decorated with the Confederate coat of arms and a flag. He glanced around his accommodations, opened one of its windows, and gave a brief address to the thousands of spectators who had gathered to gawk at him. He closed the window and told his aides to announce that the next day he would personally receive visitors: ladies from eleven to noon, gentlemen from noon to one-thirty. In five days he would be fifty-four.

Three days later Varina arrived. She had brought their three children with her, and she was ten weeks pregnant with their fourth. Davis met her at the railroad station. On their ride back to the Spotswood, someone threw her a bouquet, but it missed and tumbled into the street. Observers noticed with pleasure that Davis stopped the carriage, picked up the bouquet, and gallantly handed it to his wife. Definitions of beauty change, but photographs of Varina show her to be a remarkably handsome woman and by some standards strikingly lovely. Some Richmond matrons tut-tutted about the olive tone of her complexion, but all agreed she had fine, deep, dark eyes and full lips. Well-to-do Virginians considered it essential to possess the proper forebears, and some thought Jefferson Davis's illiterate Welsh grandfather a trifle too recent to permit an aura of aristocracy. A few were even put off because Varina's grandfather had been New Jersey's governor during the Revolution—though they were pleased to learn that one branch of her family owned a presentable plantation near Manassas Gap. She pretended not to notice the gossip, or mind it. As to the Spotswood, she was used to hotel existence. When her husband had been a senator in Washington, they had resided in hotels, and she had shown herself to be a polished hostess. She continued that tradition with the ladies of the government and those of Richmond.[3]

Once he settled in, President Davis spent little time schmoozing. His main concern, quite simply, was war. He had studied the subject as a youth; he had graduated from West Point and served for years in the army. Even after he eventually resigned his military commission, he read constantly about battles. When the Mexican War began, he led Mississippi's volunteers to a reasonable share of glory, and when he was seriously wounded and returned home, his state rewarded him with a seat in the Senate, where he chaired the Committee on Military Affairs. In the 1850s President Franklin Pierce selected him as secretary of war; and after that, he served more years in the Senate, continuing to specialize in military matters. In 1861, except for Lieutenant General Winfield Scott, Jefferson Davis was America's most famous military expert. He was in Washington, sitting in the Senate, when Mississippi, his home state, seceded, and he returned there, expecting to be chosen to command its volunteers. He suspected the split in the United States would likely erupt in a "civil war," as he recently had termed such a conflict. He was stunned, and apparently disappointed, when the Confederacy picked him to be its first president. But once officially in that office, he never revealed a secret hunger to act as a politician-on-horseback, a Napoleon Bonaparte. If such thoughts lingered, he kept them to himself.

Even before Virginia's referendum on secession, and before Davis arrived in Richmond, he had been pressed for advice about the state's precarious military situation. Governor John Letcher had appointed a local man, Robert E. Lee, to take charge of the state's military, but now, with the May 24 takeover of Arlington and Alexandria, many citizens wanted the assistance of Jefferson Davis, a more respected military personage. The Yankee move into northern Virginia, by itself, was not of military importance, but it indicated a change in Lincoln's policy—from a passive-defensive stance to one of aggression. Anyone looking at rough maps of the northern portion of Virginia, printed in most newspapers, could see a fact that jumped out: Railroad lines connected Alexandria to Richmond.

Any innovation, especially something that can transport goods or people, inevitably is considered for its military potential. By 1833 Prussians had constructed railways for strategic reasons, and in 1859, for the first time, soldiers had been transported by rail for specific military purposes when French troops chuffed across Italy at almost fifteen miles per hour. In early 1861 South Carolina had used railroads to carry its troops to the siege of Fort Sumter. In mid-April Virginians had used trains to capture Harpers Ferry, and Lincoln's secretary of war, Simon Cameron, had wired the governor of Massachusetts to forward volunteers to Washington by rail. In other words, men making military plans now had to consider this new form of transportation—with all its promise, and headaches. They scrutinized maps of rail lines, and they made particular note of junctions where lines came together—like the obscure spot not far west of Alexandria: Manassas Junction.

Few Americans had yet ridden a train. A certain romantic aura still clung to the image of racing through the countryside on one of those metal beasts. But the railroads galumphing through the South provided no grandeur. Locomotives were cinder spewing, noisy, palsied, and often dangerous. Travelers, trudging aboard passenger cars, required a certain hardihood. "Whatever may be the normal comforts of American railway cars," said William Russell, a British journalist who had experienced a wide range of transport during his career, "they are certainly most unpleasant conveyances when the war spirit is abroad, and the heat of the day, which is excessive, did not contribute to diminish the annoyance of foul air—the odour of whiskey, tobacco, and the like, combined with innumerable flies." He might also have mentioned the overflowing cuspidors and the greasy kerosene lanterns that hung above the aisles.

Russell's experiences on America's railroads would have been luxurious compared to those of most Confederate soldiers who were being jostled in the spring of 1861 from one Southern crisis point to another. "We had to ride all the way from Columbia on open platform cars," a South Carolina boy wrote his mother, "and the smoke blowing in my face produced such a soreness in my eyes that I was almost blinded when I got to Petersburg. We had to ride out in a tremendous storm, and had that night to sleep in the open air, on the benches and floor of the car, perfectly wet." Normally, Southern soldiers squeezed themselves into stinking baggage cars, along with fifty or sixty others. If lucky, they found themselves perched on rude backless benches. There they were forced to crouch, hour after hour, for days. Each car generally had one or two pails that soldiers with firm stomachs could use as toilets. Luckily, trains usually halted rather often, to take on water for their steam engines and logs from massive piles left along the tracks by local farmers. Whenever a train halted, cramped soldiers tumbled out, stretched their muscles, urinated in relief, and breathed in air that wasn't contaminated with foul odors or the soot from the smokestack. When a train restarted, some troops often decided to clamber onto the roofs of the cars. It seemed at first a splendid idea—offering fresh breezes and a bit of adventure. But they soon regretted the notion. Being atop a moving train was uncomfortable because of the smoke of the engine; it was also dangerous, as unexpected bumps and jerks threw precarious soldiers off and low bridges crushed the skulls of lads taking their first trip away from home.

A passenger train could, when conditions were perfect, attain speeds of sixty miles per hour, though freight trains inevitably moved much slower. The generally dependable freight train that traveled the 170 miles from Alexandria to Lynchburg, Virginia, was typical of the better sort. In good summer weather, carrying light loads, it took eight hours to make the trip—averaging, therefore, less than twenty-five miles per hour. The railroad "system" in the Confederacy was in fact quite unsystematic. A few lines stretched several hundred miles, but many spanned only a dozen miles or less. Virginia boasted the most modern "system" in the Confederacy, and yet she was serviced by *seventeen* different railroad companies. Some of the tracks laid by these firms were made of relatively good "T-bar" iron, which could last, if properly maintained, for ten or fifteen years. Other companies had only rusty, flat "strap" rails, laid across deteriorating wooden ties. Such tracks fell apart frequently. So did many of the flimsy wooden bridges in Virginia—to say nothing of the rest of the Confederacy. In the best of times, accidents had been common, but the Panic of 1857 had chased money from the economy, and many rail lines had deteriorated. The United States led the world in railroad accidents, at a rate ten times higher per passenger mile than France and forty times higher than England.

Now, in 1861, the weakened Southern railroads were expected to move large numbers of men and enormous quantities of goods—and to do so at a relatively rapid pace. Some individuals understood how impossible that expectation was; most did not. They glanced at maps of the South, saw grids of tracks, and felt confident that vast armies could now be moved swiftly. They did not stop to consider that Southern railroads had not yet adopted a standard gauge. An engine that traveled from point A to point B could move no farther because the track from B to C was either wider or narrower. Even where gauges were of the same width, railroad lines frequently did not touch each other—a phenomenon that was intentional. When a city's leaders invested in a railroad, they wanted it to benefit *their* town, not some other place farther down the track. Profit, as many saw it, derived from passengers who were forced to alight and eat at the city's restaurants and perhaps sleep in its hostelries, along with goods that had to be unloaded from a train whenever a track ceased, and had to be carted by draymen from one place to another, and sometimes stored inside city warehouses. More profit.

So far as transportation was concerned, Richmond's leaders had been energetic for decades; the city was the terminus for five railroads. Yet no two of them were linked together. Military men responsible for moving soldiers found the situation a quagmire. Sleepy troops might be persuaded to wobble from one train station to another, but maneuvering masses of cavalry and artillery horses, to say nothing of mountains of military equipment and ammunition, was a quartermaster's nightmare.

Coordinating the movement of men and provisions and tents and ammunition was always immensely complicated, but particularly in a society that had prided itself on not being rigid about schedules, not being "Yankee." For example, before the war, passenger trains seldom traveled after dark. With war upon them, one might assume their tempo would have speeded up, but old patterns were hard to change. In June a train carrying troops to Richmond halted in Lynchburg because the railroad company refused to operate on the Sabbath.[4]

West and southwest of Alexandria, Virginia, in Fairfax and Prince William Counties, the topography is as softly undulating as an unmade bed. The region had once been somewhat prosperous, but its alluvial soil had proved resistant to long-term tobacco growing, and most of the land was sinking back to nature. A few forests were thick and older than envy, but most of the area's trees were scrawny pines and oaks, clumped in copses of a dozen acres or so.

Each county had a courthouse, with a nearby tavern and a few residences. Sprinkled along the railroad lines were numerous small stations, and next to many depots stood places for wayfarers to eat and drink and rest a while. Highways of sorts—mostly poorly maintained—also linked the towns. Farms nestled against these roads. Clustered around the rural residences—large or small—were barns and chicken coops, springhouses (for cooling fresh milk and eggs), outhouses, kitchens, wells, and perhaps shacks for slaves. Farmers hereabouts produced foodstuffs—wheat and corn, beef and pork and eggs. Many marked their property lines with rude log fences, which also served to keep cattle and wandering hogs from trampling the produce. When a farmer was ready to sell something, several times a year he would put the stuff in a wagon—unless he intended to sell cattle, which he herded to market. In either case he did not need fine turnpikes. He could simply trail along obscure, grown-over paths through the woods. He and his family might follow these "roads" on Sundays to attend some rustic church. But he had no reason to improve them or mark them on a map. They served him when he needed them and that was sufficient. Some market towns had also evolved, where farmers could buy and sell things and socialize together, discussing the fickle weather and the dubious behavior of their children. Between such towns, roads were generally somewhat better, and except after heavy storms, one could maneuver a carriage or a surrey on them with some confidence.

Fairfax and Prince William Counties were also veined by countless creeks and streams, as rainwater whispered downhill toward the ocean. Local folks usually called these rivulets "runs." The closer these streams were to the Atlantic, the deeper they tended to be. A man on horseback seldom had problems crossing them anywhere, except during spring rains. But a farmer with a packed wagon or a drover herding his beeves had to search out shallows. Such fording places tended to acquire the name of a local farmer: McLean's Ford, Gates' Ford, Blackburn's Ford. Paths, often virtually invisible, trailed to these crossings, then beyond. One of the longest of such streams was Bull Run, muscular enough to serve as the boundary between the two counties.

By the time Jefferson Davis arrived in Richmond, Robert E. Lee had already been thinking deeply for weeks about the military situation of these two counties. Early in the year he had written, "I can only see that a fearful calamity is upon us, & fear that the country will have to pass through for its sins a fearful ordeal." He said he considered the South's complaints about Northern aggression to be just, "but I see no cause of disunion, strife & civil war & pray it may be averted." But he wrestled with where his "honor" lay. He felt that he loved the Union. "I am willing to sacrifice everything but honor for its preservation." On the other hand, "a Union that can only be maintained by swords and bayonets, and in which strife and civil war are to take the place of brotherly love and kindness, has no charm for me." If it came to war, he would, he said, "draw my sword" only in defense of Virginia. On April 19, when he officially learned that Virginia's convention had voted to secede, he could not deceive himself. His state — his "country," he sometimes called it — would soon be at war; his "honor" demanded he join it. He sent his resignation to Secretary of War Cameron and made arrangements to go to Richmond to confer with Governor Letcher.

On the morning of April 22, Robert E. Lee left his house at Arlington, overlooking the Potomac and beyond it, the District of Columbia. He went to the station in Alexandria, where he boarded a train for Richmond. He would have found himself at first heading almost straight west. On a typical day this train—part of the Orange and Alexandria Railroad—stopped to take on water and logs at Springfield Station, then again at Burke's Station. Few people lived along the rail line in this section, for the soil here was stony, and forests grew close to the tracks. At Fairfax Station, a few miles farther on, Lee would have seen a few habitations, but not many. Then came Sangster's Station—again, not much more than a water tank and a large pile of wood. After this, his train would have struggled through wild country, cut by sudden ravines and ominous bogs. It would then have crossed a bridge over Bull Run, at a place called Union Mills, where that stream was wide and deep enough that it could almost be considered a river. Several miles beyond the Union Mills crossing was Manassas Junction.

By itself Manassas Junction was hardly prepossessing, not much bigger than the "stations" preceding it on the rail line. Its depot consisted of a one-story log building, about seventy-five feet long. Not far away, looking a trifle embarrassed, were an uninviting hostelry and a few sorry cottages. A quarter mile back, set apart from the unseemly rabble, stood a handsome two-and-a-half story brick house. Manassas was an almost invisible dot on any map. Only one thing set it apart. Another rail line, the Manassas Gap Railroad, coming from the breadbasket region of the Shenandoah Valley, here touched the Orange and Alexandria. This single fact was about to focus much attention onto this cluster of buildings. Robert E. Lee, whose home was not that far away, had no doubt passed through this spot many times. He was an extremely observant man, certainly one of the best military minds of the era. On the day his train passed through Manassas Junction, he was well aware that Virginia militiamen had just taken over the Federal naval yard near Norfolk and the arsenal at Harpers Ferry. Because of these two actions, this railroad junction had become a critical linchpin, linking northeast and northwest Virginia.

Lee met with Governor Letcher. Family connections were important to Virginians, and the Lees were fairly prominent, if not especially wealthy. Robert E. Lee was known to have been well respected in the American army, an excellent staff man, and Letcher put him in charge of Virginia's army and navy. Lee began issuing orders. One thing was immediately clear: He was convinced a defensive posture was best for Virginia. During the next four years, he would twice lead armies north from his state, but it can be argued that on both occasions he was trying to end the war in a single stroke, to save Virginia — his "country" — from further devastation.

Many Southerners were not so modest in their ambitions. On April 29 Jefferson Davis announced: "We seek no conquest, no aggrandizement, no concession of any kind from the States with which we were lately confederated." He added, "All we ask is to be let alone." That sounded clear enough — but the statement was a bit self-serving, and not really accurate. What exactly did Davis mean by the "we" who wished to be left alone? He really was referring to *all* fifteen slave states — even though eight were not yet part of the Confederacy and four never did join. If pressed, Davis might have also included the District of Columbia, which also allowed slavery. He was also not averse to contemplating a kind of Confederate "manifest destiny." In July he approved an invasion of the territory of New Mexico, with the goal of occupying and incorporating it into the Confederacy. And men around him eyed southern California, the northern provinces of Mexico, and Cuba — for a start. If the Confederacy had won its independence easily, one can imagine it soon contemplating a vigorous expansion.

But Robert E. Lee did not seem to share that kind of assertive imperialism. In April and May, 1861, when outlining plans for Virginia, he remained cautious. For example, on May 22 — the day before Union troops started crossing the Potomac — Lee sent an order to one of his subordinates, advising him to keep his troops under control. He added: "The policy of the State at present is strictly defensive. No attack, or provocation for attack will therefore be given." To Lee, the goal was primarily to maintain his state inviolate, or at least to rid it eventually of all invaders. Beyond that, he had no Grand Strategy — and, it would seem, he never developed one. Given this attitude, he at first saw the railways in northern Virginia not as a means of moving troops *forward*, to attack, but as avenues the enemy might use to *invade* the state. In early May he told the state's field commanders that if Federal troops crossed the Potomac, the commanders were to destroy the tracks and railroad bridges in their departments. He was particularly worried about Manassas. On May 6 he ordered Colonel Philip St. George Cocke to pay close attention to that spot. He said he considered the place vulnerable to an attack from Washington, and he wanted Cocke to keep a sizeable force there.[5]

Colonel Cocke was an enigma, then and still today. Before the year was up, he would return to his home and, on the day after Christmas, shoot himself in the head. The reasons for his suicide have never been clear. Cocke, a raffishly handsome man, had graduated from West Point in 1832, but he had resigned from the army within two years and devoted himself to managing vast plantations in Virginia and Mississippi. He was not, however, a narrow Southern nabob. He studied agriculture, wrote a good book on agronomy, and became president of Virginia's Agricultural Society. He remained interested, also, in military matters and served for nine years on the Virginia Military Institute's board. He was fifty-two, apparently quite physically fit, and was a likely candidate for a high-ranking career in Confederate service. Most observers considered him a gallant and admirable soldier. But there seemed something irregular about him. At his headquarters in Culpeper, not far from Manassas, he struck observers as "excitable" and "eccentric." A physician who met him at this time found him an honorable gentleman, but mentally scattered. "I doubted," the doctor said, "his mental balance...He was often abreacted and evidently oblivious of his surroundings, the expression of his eye was not normal." Lee did not know Cocke terribly well but must have had reservations. Other men, with military résumés far less impressive, were advanced over Cocke's head.

Before the Yankees crossed the Potomac, Cocke, replying to incessant questions from Richmond, announced that the force he had on hand was far too paltry and badly armed to defend Alexandria *and* Manassas—both of which were in his "department." To cover the region north of Richmond, almost the size of

Connecticut, he said he had less than twelve hundred men, most of whom were unarmed and without ammunition. He considered Alexandria virtually indefensible, and Manassas little better, though he thought the geography east of Manassas so rough that it might lend itself to guerrilla warfare.

On May 15, eight days prior to Virginia's referendum on secession, Lee sent Cocke a cautionary message. Though Norfolk and Harpers Ferry seemed relatively secure, Lee thought that Alexandria might be in danger, and he wanted Cocke to be ready to rush there, if necessary, to reinforce the small battalion that guarded the city.

A few days later Lee decided to make a change in commanders. He ordered Brigadier General Milledge Luke Bonham to take charge of that entire section of Virginia. Cocke would remain in position, but as one of Bonham's subordinates. Bonham, 47, was tall, somewhat strapping and graceful. He was rather good-looking, with deep-set eyes, a great mane of hair, and a full beard. Although not a West Point graduate, he had served in the regular army and had seen action in both the Seminole and Mexican Wars. He retained a kind of soldierly bearing but had a brittle temperament. He was courageous in the field, and he could be snippy with his superiors and bullying to his staff. He also had more than a trace of the same excitability that made Cocke suspect. When Lee gave Bonham the assignment, he reminded the South Carolinian that Virginia's policy "at present [was] strictly defensive." Then, Lee added that although Bonham now commanded "the Alexandria line of communications," the real key was Manassas: "As it commands the communications with Harpers Ferry, and must be firmly held."[6]

It would turn out, however, that it was not going to be either Bonham or Cocke who would ultimately be responsible for Manassas. It would be General Pierre Gustave Toutant Beauregard.

Two months earlier, Jefferson Davis had sent the Louisianan, Beauregard, to Charleston to take over the fortifications facing Fort Sumter. It was the Creole, obeying a message from Davis, who had opened fire on Fort Sumter. The easy victory over that little garrison had started the Civil War, and it had made Beauregard a hero throughout the South. On May 28, while still in transit to Virginia, Davis wired him to come to Richmond. Davis had just learned that a Federal army might move against the Confederate base at Norfolk, and he wished to utilize Beauregard's expertise to erect a defense system around the naval yard.

Beauregard left Charleston immediately, being so anxious to speak with the Confederate president that he arrived in Richmond only twenty-four hours after Davis. Like Davis, Beauregard was greeted by Richmond's population with ovations, with a large carriage, and with the offer of a fine suite at the Spotswood. He graciously thanked everyone but turned down the carriage and the suite and chose more modest digs at another hotel.

Beauregard had not yet had a chance to talk to Davis when the night train from Manassas Junction brought Lee back to the city.

The next day, May 31, General Robert E. Lee, for the first time, officially conferred with President Davis about the Civil War. The exact nature of their talk is uncertain, but it would appear that Lee expressed his opinion that Norfolk and Harpers Ferry were not, at that moment, in immediate danger, but that Manassas probably was. Lee said he had left General Bonham in charge there, with about five thousand troops, but he was still concerned.

Jefferson Davis was chewing over this opinion when Beauregard appeared. In his memoirs Beauregard says that during their meeting Davis changed his mind about sending him to Norfolk and decided to order him to Manassas instead. If Norfolk was not in immediate danger and Manassas was, Beauregard's skill at erecting defense lines, plus his popularity with South Carolinians—who formed the core of Bonham's command—made him a natural choice. That evening Beauregard repacked his luggage; he departed early the next morning, June 1.[7]

General Beauregard seemed made for this post. Of middle height and muscular, he was intelligent and energetic. With his French name, his detectable Creole accent, his dark eyes and olive complexion, he gave off more than a hint of a Napoleonic aura—though in truth he lacked Gallic flamboyance. Although invariably polite, he was normally reserved, even taciturn, and seldom smiled.

He had had a distinguished army career as an engineer, including time in the Mexican War when he had worked closely with Robert E. Lee, as part of Winfield Scott's staff.

At Manassas, Beauregard wrote Richmond that Bonham had been correct about the need here for more men and supplies. He promised, if it came to it, "to sell our lives as dearly as practicable," but more manpower, more equipment, more ammunition, and more transportation would improve his prospects. He also issued a proclamation to the people of northern Virginia. "A reckless and unprincipled tyrant has invaded your soil," it announced. "Abraham Lincoln, regardless of all moral, legal, and constitutional restraints, has thrown his abolition hosts among you." Union soldiers, he asserted, were, at that precise moment, "murdering and imprisoning your citizens, confiscating and destroying your property, and committing other acts of violence and outrage [read *rapine*] too shocking and revolting to humanity to be enumerated." He then claimed that the motto of these barbaric invaders, "by their acts, if not on their banners," was "Beauty and Booty."

This was an interesting phrase, designed to stir the breasts of all citizens. If the population did not rise up now and protect themselves, they could expect nothing less than rape and pillage. There had long been a rumor, apparently false, that when British soldiers approached New Orleans in 1815, they had placed the slogan BEAUTY AND BOOTY on their banner. Beauregard, a native of Louisiana, had certainly heard the legend. Southern journalists had lately been playing with the phrase. On May 7 a Richmond newspaper used it but merely suggested that Federal troops *might* find the notion appealing. The following day a newspaper in Charleston — where Beauregard was then stationed — repeated the Richmond story but added to it, saying, "Some of the papers in Pennsylvania, it is said, have adopted the motto 'Beauty and Booty.'" Pennsylvania troops, the Charleston newspaper declared, had begun placing skulls and crossbones on their flags. Two weeks later, when Union soldiers crossed the Potomac, Virginia's *Petersburg Express*, as rabid and undependable as any newspaper in the South, said that Federal troops in Alexandria were raping females. Such tales were believed. A Confederate soldier in Petersburg wrote his wife he had been reading that Lincoln's "lecherous hirelings" were searching out "beauty and booty." He wrote her again, a few days later from Richmond, that he had just learned that Yankee troops were raping young girls near Fort Monroe.

In other words, what had started as a single minor local story in Richmond, inaccurate at the very least, had evolved into indisputable "fact" in less than a month. One can assume that Beauregard had himself heard these lurid yarns and either believed them or decided to use them to stir the broth.[8]

In addition to erecting entrenchments and drilling his troops, reviewing the topography and worrying about inadequate water supplies, acquiring slaves and equipment, and releasing bombastic proclamations, as we will see, Beauregard began formulating some grandiose military plans, involving operations that would combine his troops with another Confederate army fifty miles west of him in the Shenandoah Valley. In his mind the two armies seemed nicely joined by the Manassas Gap Railroad. This little rail line made him dream of altering Robert E. Lee's defensive policy. He contemplated pouncing on Washington—and ending the war by this single bold act. He knew he personally did not command enough troops here at Manassas to accomplish any such goal, but if he could use the Confederate force in the Valley...

Untenable Position

Along the right shoulder of the Shenandoah River, as it flows northward, lie the Blue Ridge Mountains, a fine, protective green wall, keeping back the crowded population of the Eastern Seaboard. To its left, also stretching north and south, are the Allegheny Mountains. Together, these two gentle spines, part of the Appalachian range and separated from each other by only a few miles, create a land almost of enchantment, a breathtaking valley, as sweet and tender as a lover's dream. The Valley's soil is a bit too gnarled to be called a farming paradise, but in 1861, sprinkled along the river's edge, were splendid hamlets, surrounded by fields of wheat and corn and clover, by handsome farms, by livestock in swarms, and by orchards of luscious fruit.

A person on foot—Daniel Boone, for example—could enter the Valley rather easily, because neither mountain spine looms high enough to prevent pedestrian travel. But if one wished to move goods or drive herds, the mountains could be daunting. A few openings did break through the Blue Ridge on the eastern side, but even these, with their rocky, ungraded roads, challenged

all but the hardiest. A few years before the Civil War, several ambitious railroad men decided to lay a line through one of these
clefts, and thus was born the Manassas Gap Railroad, designed
to move grain and animals eastward, and manufactured goods
west.

At the Valley's northern end, forty miles above where that
railway poked in, the Shenandoah River links with the Potomac.
Here, where the mountains crowd together like a knuckled fist,
sits Harpers Ferry. In 1861 the little village was dark and de-
pressing, shadowed by the heights that loomed above it. Its greatest claim to fame involved the bloodshed and idealistic madness
of John Brown's raid, a year and a half before Fort Sumter.

Military planners, examining maps, inevitably focused on
Harpers Ferry. With the Shenandoah and Potomac Rivers meeting there, with a nearby canal to Washington, and with the Baltimore and Ohio Railroad as well as a telegraph trunk line passing
by, the town seemed a vital key to both Virginia and Maryland,
maybe even Pennsylvania. The next four years would lay that notion to rest; the little town would change hands over and over,
with surprisingly small strategic results. But during early 1861,
both sides remained fascinated by its apparent strategic potential.

In April, immediately after Fort Sumter fell, a cabal in Richmond, scarcely more than half-a-dozen men led by ex-Governor
Henry Wise, formulated plans to seize Harpers Ferry (and also,
though in a less-organized way, the Gosport Navy Yard near
Norfolk). Without permission from anyone in authority, simply
following their own audacity, they acted—and by doing so, they
pushed Virginia into war. Soon hundreds of volunteers approached Harpers Ferry's outskirts. A tiny Federal garrison at the
United States arsenal there destroyed what they could and fled
toward Pennsylvania. During the next few days, other volunteers
arrived, generally in "companies"—units ranging from a few
dozen men to a hundred or more. Together they formed a motley
army. Some came without weapons, most without sturdy uniforms or equipment. They had little knowledge about hygiene
and even less about diet. Some officers were competent, others
less so. As individuals, the volunteers were mostly young men of

goodwill who found "soldiering" a rather exciting, if occasionally trying, adventure. Then, a remarkable man arrived to turn them into soldiers.

In April 1861, Thomas Jonathan Jackson was a schoolteacher, and a bad one—one of those dreadful, unimaginative drones every student has tried to avoid since the pedagogues paced the Athenian agora. Jackson was born near Clarksburg, a backwater town in the hills of western Virginia. When he entered West Point, he found himself unprepared for its academics, but by diligent, ceaseless efforts, he avoided dismissal and in fact graduated seventeenth in a class of fifty-nine. He then had some ancillary battlefield experience in the Mexican War, before ill health induced him to resign from the army after only five years' service. He returned home and was hired as a professor of natural and experimental philosophy, and instructor in artillery at the Virginia Military Institute. There he applied the same technique he had used as a cadet—methodical hard work. But good teaching demands more than self-discipline. A fine teacher, by enthusiasm or wit or energy, can make any subject interesting—auto mechanics, Latin, algebraic equations. Even had Jackson possessed such attributes—and he did not—he considered them unnecessary in a classroom. He was a stern disciplinarian, a humorless, methodical twit. A friend who knew him well once said that he had a "well-nigh morbid devotion to duty." Some students found amusement in deriding his stiffness. "Tom Fool," some called him behind his back. A few considered him less comical; they thought him not merely charmless, but tactless. Because of his rigidity on matters of military decorum, he demanded the expulsion of students who, he thought, breached the rules. At least two of these, it is said, challenged him to duels. An alumni committee considered removing him from the faculty but decided not to press the point.

Professor Jackson had other attributes. His most endearing quality was his sweet-tongued love for his second wife, Mary Anna. "My *esposita*," he called her in his letters. He owned slaves and demanded their absolute obedience—hardly surprising, as he expected the same of his students (and, later, his soldiers)—and he insisted they attend morning prayers and evening devotionals with his family. On Sundays he instructed local African-Americans about the Bible, and he faithfully contributed to a local African-American church. During the 1850s he had grown into a deeply religious person. He did not swear and would not tolerate profanity or even vulgarity. On the other hand, he was neither a Bible-thumper nor, away from home, an avid proselytizer; to him, religion was a private matter.

Jackson had some countrified attitudes about health. (An acquaintance would later say about him, "He imagined that the halves of his body did not work and act in accord.") He had a habit of falling asleep during odd circumstances—while conversing, riding a horse, or walking. He may even have suffered some undiagnosed medical condition like narcolepsy, perhaps something congenital. He liked fruit, especially peaches, and was even seen on occasion sucking lemons. He avoided coffee, tea, and tobacco, apparently as a matter of taste, and intoxicants out of wisdom. A close comrade later recalled one night during the Civil War when he offered Jackson some whiskey. The ex-schoolmaster took a swig, then made a face. The friend asked, "Isn't the whiskey good?" "Yes, very," said Jackson revealingly. "I like it, and that's the reason I don't drink it."

He was moderately tall, just under six feet, and was of average build, neither slender nor heavy. He had gray blue eyes, often half-lidded and dull, a sandy hairline that was receding, and a shaggy, rust brown beard. He cared little about his appearance, so long as he remained reasonably clean and neat. He had a long, sharp nose and thin, almost invisible, lips. He looked quite like a caricature of a Virginia mountain man, and, at thirty-seven, he appeared to be what some West Point cadets had said about him two decades earlier, that he was a rough hill-person, though never a ruffian.

In the civilian world he lacked smoothness. While never quite the failure that Ulysses S. Grant had been before the war, in early 1861 Jackson was simply a lackluster, anonymous teacher. His five not terribly distinguished years in the army had provided him with little personal knowledge of fighting. Then, like Grant, when war swept across him, he brought to it certain qualities. He was honest; he was indomitable; he was methodical; he had great physical courage. In April 1861 he had an as-yet-unrecognized ability to do one thing superbly — to lead masses of infantry. No one could have imagined this unusual skill, not even he. His mind was narrow, but he had depths unplumbed, so far. An untapped capacity drowsed behind those half-lidded eyes. Virginia's secession roused him.[9]

Except for West Point, the Virginia Military Institute in Lexington was almost certainly America's best cadet school. As soon as Virginia's convention passed its resolution of secession, Governor Letcher contacted the Institute and asked the school to send specialists in the arcane science of military drilling. A slew of VMI cadets volunteered, and Jackson led them to Richmond. They set themselves up at the Fair Grounds just outside the city. Raw volunteers from throughout the state, pouring into the city, were ordered to go there to receive instruction. One of them — George Bagby, thirty-four — later recalled:

> To get up at dawn to the sound of the fife and drum, to wash my face in a hurry in a tin basin, wipe on a wet towel, and go forth with a suffocated skin, and a sense of uncleanliness to be drilled by a fat little cadet, young enough to be my son, of the Virginia Military Institute, that, indeed, was misery. How I hated that little cadet! He was always so wide-awake, so clean, so interested in the drill; his coat-tails were short and sharp, and his hands looked so big in white gloves. He made me sick.

Although Governor Letcher was pleased to have the assistance of the cadets, he was unsure what to do with Jackson, their leader. It seemed wisest to wait until Robert E. Lee arrived in town to offer advice, and Jackson's status remained murky for several days. Although exceedingly modest in many ways and despising pomposity, Jackson was driven by a purring motor of ambition and could play the military-promotion game with surprising energy, could happily write letters to powerful people, unabashedly pressing for higher rank. Lee did not know Jackson that well, but after chatting with him, he apparently saw some strength in the younger man — some *seriousness* that was especially attractive at this time of rampant emotionalism. Lee named him a colonel of the state's volunteers and sent him to Harpers Ferry. The ex-professor, extraordinarily firm with rambunctious students, was about to apply himself to the disorderly "army" in the Valley.[10]

When he arrived there, what he first observed disturbed him. Discipline was lax, the coordination among units virtually nonexistent. But he brought with him two advantages. His years in the regular army had been so brief he did not come to this task with strong reservations about volunteers, and he had spent the last decade dealing with college freshmen, a notoriously undisciplined rabble. Most soldiers at Harpers Ferry were not that different from VMI cadets. They did not need patriotic speeches; what they mainly lacked was order.

Few at Harpers Ferry were acquainted with this new arrival. One observer later said that many asked, "Who is this Colonel Jackson?"—then added that by the time "he had been in command forty-eight hours we felt his strong hand, recognized the difference between him and certain militia officers who had previously had charge of the post, and realized that we were at last under the command of a real soldier and a rigid disciplinarian."

One of Jackson's first acts was typical—of both the man and his new command. He learned that whiskey was readily available and that many volunteers had been taking deep drafts. He found some barrels, brought them out of hiding, and ordered them to be broken and their contents sloshed into the gutter. He did not stay to watch. The volunteers heard of his order and rushed to the scene with buckets. Then followed the "sound of revelry by night." The next day he had the rest of the booze poured into the nearby river. His assignment, as he was discovering, would be a challenge.[11]

Colonel Jackson also soon realized he faced more vexations than lack of discipline. His volunteers might become good soldiers in time, but his little army lacked arms, ammunition, and a variety of useful accoutrements like tents and medical supplies, knapsacks and cartridge holders and cooking utensils. Also, he began to feel that Harpers Ferry was far too vulnerable, especially from the Maryland side of the Potomac. High above the little town loomed a dark clump called Maryland Heights. If the

Yankees placed artillery there, the guns could overawe the village below it. As a disciplinarian, Jackson shared some attributes with mindless bureaucrats, but he could be a fierce and bold gambler. He eyed Maryland Heights and seriously considered crossing the Potomac and seizing them.

Word of this prospect reached Lee, who wired the surprisingly aggressive colonel. "Your intention to fortify the heights of Maryland," Lee cautioned, in his genteel way, so famous later on, "may interrupt our friendly arrangements with that State, and we have no right to intrude on her soil, unless under pressing necessity, for defense." In other words, the Confederacy was still hopeful that Maryland would soon add its star to the Southern banner, but if Jackson crossed the river — *invaded* Maryland — the Confederacy's ongoing, ticklish negotiations with that state might collapse. The fate of the District of Columbia lay in the balance. If Maryland joined the Confederacy, Lincoln almost certainly would have to abandon Washington — and, in that case, the British might immediately decide to aid the South.

On the other hand, Lee added, if Jackson ever obtained *positive evidence* that a Federal force was about to threaten his army from the Heights, he certainly had the right to defend his position. Finally, Lee said, "I know, from the spirit with which you are animated, that you will leave nothing undone to insure the defense of your post and the security of your command." Lee also, and unnecessarily, reminded the Colonel about Jackson's primary responsibility: "You will not neglect, therefore, the instruction of the troops, who ought to be constantly practicing their military exercises and prepared in every way for hard service." If Jackson felt insulted by this last jab, he gave no sign.

A few days later, he ignored the cautionary advice of Lee's message and seized the Heights. Shortly afterward, he was superseded — a decision made not by Lee, but by Jefferson Davis.[12]

In May 1861, Colonel Jackson's was still an obscure name. Another Confederate soldier seemed to have far more military promise: Joseph Eggleston Johnston.

Johnston had much going for him. He was highly intelligent, well read, energetic, and extremely fit. At fifty-four — a dozen years older than Beauregard and seventeen years older than Jackson—he had a natural demeanor of dignity and maturity. During the Revolution his father had fought with and befriended "Light Horse" Harry Lee (Robert E. Lee's father), had married a niece of Patrick Henry, had enjoyed a long and successful political career, and eventually became one of Virginia's highest judges. Joseph, the eighth son, was thus born into a prominent, respected family. But, so far as wealth and power were concerned, he would have to make his own way. He chose to attend West Point. He graduated in 1829, fourteenth in his class.

In the 1830s the army seemed a drab career to many of its brightest young officers. West Point had trained them in engineering skills, which could be much more lucrative in the vibrant civilian world of railroads and the like. Talented individuals like Robert E. Lee and Joe Johnston felt oppressed by the army's rigid system of advancement by seniority, not talent. They also felt drawn to the exciting changes sweeping America—to say nothing of the lure of earning wads of money. Lee and Johnston, childhood friends and classmates, shared with each other their frustrations. Lee, somewhat reluctantly, chose to stick it out, to remain in the army; Johnston decided to resign and become a civil engineer. By chance, however, he was only out of service a few months when fighting erupted with the Seminoles in Florida. He volunteered to help, and was sent there as a civilian topographical engineer, with an assignment to explore the coastline and waterways for locations to erect forts. The group he was with got into a skirmish. When its officers were wounded, he—although officially a civilian—took charge and helped them escape, being wounded in the process. Not long after this incident, he changed his mind about his destiny and reapplied for his commission.

During the Mexican War, he seemed everywhere, in almost every action, receiving five more wounds. Winfield Scott reportedly said, "Johnston is a great soldier, but he has an unfortunate knack of getting himself shot in nearly every engagement." Without question, he was one of America's heroes of that war.

In the following decade, the friendship between Johnston and Lee cooled. Both were ambitious. Each time an opening appeared above them, they were rivals for it. Their careers seesawed up and down, as first one, then the other, inched ahead toward the rarefied slots held by the elderly men who led the army, many of whom were veterans of the War of 1812. Someday those grizzled officers would be gone, and Johnston and Lee were poised to replace them.

Civilians often snickered at the prickly attention military men focused on matters of rank. Whenever two officers bumped together, they seemed to outsiders almost feral, sniffing each other to see who was of higher rank. But civilians did not understand. In a military world that offered paltry pay and little respect during peacetime, officers placed much emotional stock on rank— which involved, if nothing else, their livelihood. Moreover, they recognized that on a battlefield rank involved life and death. Orders must be given and followed instantaneously. In the madness and noise of battle, soldiers needed to know who outranked whom, because in the next moment the person in charge could be wiped away, and everyone had to understand who would then be in command. Under the circumstances of battlefield hysteria, one would not want two colonels debating with each other over who was in charge. The military had developed a system based on subtle distinctions—such as the *precise* date of an officer's appointment to his rank.

Lee gained some fame helping capture John Brown in 1859, but he had spent much of the 1850s in Texas, while Johnston was stationed in Washington. Johnston was a cousin, by marriage, of Secretary of War John B. Floyd, and this fact presumably helped when, in 1860, the army's quartermaster general died. Johnston was chosen to fill the vacancy over the heads of three other officers, including Lee. His new position was important, giving him the rank of brigadier general, making him the youngest general in the army. His office at the War Department was near the pleasant home he and his wife, Lydia, maintained. He walked to work; she socialized with close friends like Varina Davis.

In the army Johnston was highly respected. He was known as a valiant field officer, though like all of his age-group, he had never commanded more than a few hundred men in battle. In person, he radiated a sense of composure and confidence. He had charisma. Men were drawn to him. Later, one of the South's brightest stars, General Edward Porter Alexander, would write, "I think Gen. Jos. E. Johnston was more the soldier in looks, carriage & manner than any of our other generals." Almost a year into the Civil War, an outstanding and perceptive Union general, James S. Wadsworth, said under oath to a congressional committee: "Johnston is regarded by our officers as much superior to Beauregard; as much the ablest officer in their army." Johnston's experience as a topographical engineer, a job normally given to only the brightest officers, indicated he grasped the nature of a large landscape, permitting him to think at a higher level than simple field tactics. *Strategy*, the art of a whole campaign, is best devised by one who has enough mental capacity, as well as training, to understand the nature of the countryside, the character of the enemy, and the capacity of one's own troops. During the war Johnston would prove an excellent strategist. One can argue that in this sphere, he was Lee's superior, though Lee was far the abler tactician. But many historians have held one thing against Johnston; they have considered him overly cautious. Those who applaud Jackson's aggressiveness and Lee's willingness to win battles while sustaining great losses sniff at Joe Johnston. The truth is he was a humane general, sparing the lives of his troops. Wherever he fought, his armies suffered fewer casualties than those of other Confederate generals. He was Omar Bradley to Stonewall Jackson's George Patton. Countries are fortunate to have generals like Patton and Jackson, though preferably in positions subordinate to more measured minds, but an enlisted man might consider himself luckier to serve under a Johnston or a Bradley, who would offer less glory and a greater likelihood of survival. (One might make the argument that the Confederacy would have been better served in 1861 had Lee been sent to Harpers Ferry and Johnston given command of overall strategy, rather like Eisenhower in 1944.)[13]

During the winter of 1860–1861, Johnston remained aloof from the secessionists, but when Virginia seceded, he and Lydia packed a few things, left their Washington home and belongings, for the last time for all they knew, and crossed the Potomac. He arrived in Richmond right after Lee, in time to discover that his old rival had just been appointed to command all the state's forces. When he volunteered his services, he was assigned essentially the same duty Jackson had just left, training incoming volunteers — an important enough post, of course, but he was moody and performed this duty without enthusiasm.

Two weeks later he suddenly boarded a train for Montgomery after Davis offered him a commission as a brigadier general in the *Confederate* army and asked him to come and confer. (This CSA generalship put him, for the nonce, a step above Robert E. Lee, who held only a state position, and may partly explain Johnston's haste.) It is unclear what he and Davis talked about in Montgomery, but on May 15 Johnston was assigned to Harpers Ferry to take command. Why? Lee's cautionary message to Jackson to focus on training his troops rather than seizing Maryland Heights had been sent on May 10, about the time Johnston left Richmond for Montgomery. One can assume that Davis wanted a more experienced hand than Jackson's on the delicate helm at Harpers Ferry.

Johnston arrived at Harpers Ferry on May 23, the day of Virginia's referendum, and told Colonel Jackson he had arrived to take charge in the name of the Confederacy. Jackson, a stickler for rules, replied that he had received no official notification and refused to turn over his command until he received proper paperwork. Jackson was polite, but firm. Johnston apparently took no offense; he was far too used to army regulations.

As Johnston awaited the official orders to arrive (only a few hours), he began to examine the situation. He did not like what he saw. The Confederacy had about five thousand men on hand, but, as he later recalled, "These troops were undisciplined of course. They were also badly armed and equipped . . . and, like all new troops assembled in large bodies, they were suffering very much from sickness; nearly forty percent." He complained to his superiors that he had insufficient manpower and supplies, but he knew his problems involved more than that. He was well aware that both Davis and Lee considered Harpers Ferry a vital spot that *must* be held and "a natural fortress" that *could* be held. A quick survey of the ground and a conversation with locals convinced him — correctly — of the absurdity of their notion. Harpers

Ferry was *not* a "fortress"; it was a potential prison. Jackson had already recognized how difficult it would be to defend it unless one controlled the heights. Johnston, who permitted himself to think more strategically, concluded that his ragged, untrained, half-armed soldiers ought not get bottled up but should remain mobile. Joe Johnston was perhaps not a "great" general, but he was already conceptualizing a different approach to war, where places were not as important as soldiers. This idea set him apart from Davis, Lee, and Lincoln — and almost everyone else, North and South, military or civilian. Winfield Scott understood it, but few wanted to listen to a tired and sick old man. It would still be years before soldiers like Ulysses Grant embraced the concept — and won the war.[14]

Johnston and Lee corresponded about this matter. Lee wanted Johnston to stay at Harpers Ferry since Maryland's status remained uncertain. On the other hand, Lee indicated, if Johnston concluded he *had* to withdraw, Lee offered him reluctant permission to do so. Johnston, preferring to pass the buck on this delicate matter, pressed Richmond — which now included President Davis, who had just arrived — to accept the responsibility. Days passed. While Johnston waited for his superiors to make up their minds, he began organizing his army.

You cannot make good bread without good flour. Although Johnston did not realize it, he had under his command some of the best soldiers in American history. There was, for instance, James Ewell Brown ("Jeb") Stuart.

Stuart, 28, had graduated from West Point five years earlier. He was an interesting man, more complicated than the popular impression of him as a merry rogue on horseback, laughingly astonishing his enemies with quick cavalry antics, a kind of Errol Flynn/Robin Hood. There was, to be sure, something boyish about him. He had a ruddy complexion, sparkling blue eyes, receding auburn hair, and a vast, bushy beard that hid his lower face. Unlike most cavalrymen, he was rather large, above average height and thick in the upper body, broad-shouldered and barrel-chested. He adored eating, and had he lived longer, in a more sedate, peacetime setting, he would have likely become enormously corpulent.

But at this stage of his life, he was a hyperkinetic athlete, radiant with vast stores of animal energy, a man who found it difficult to sit still. In the summer of 1861, he said something revealing. After several days of hard riding, his men were tired and hungry and wanted to rest. "Nonsense," he told them. "You don't want to go back to camp, I know; it's stupid there, and all the fun is out here. I never go to camp if I can help it." He suggested they munch some raw ears of corn instead.

Southerners would come to love Jeb Stuart for his plumed hat and gold spurs. Such touches made him — and them, by indirect connection — a character from a novel by Walter Scott or Alexandre Dumas. But he was more than that. One of his most admirable moments came when he was a callow cadet at West Point. When he arrived there in the early 1850s, the atmosphere of the school swirled with "South versus North." Also at the school at that time was a boy from Maine, Oliver O. Howard, who almost epitomized the word *Yankee,* including an open opposition to slavery. Howard was an academic grind, who stood first or second in many of his classes. He was also quite priggish about matters of behavior, and during his plebe year he received not a single demerit — a remarkable feat that during the nineteenth century almost no other cadet matched. Many students disliked him, and most Southerners loathed him. In fact Robert E. Lee's son Custis led a pack of cadets who "shunned" him (a mean-spirited social action designed to make an individual feel isolated). Although Jeb Stuart was a prickly Virginian, proud and vain and quick to take offense, he refused to participate in this painful and cruel treatment. In fact, he befriended Howard — not casually, in some cavalier way, but genuinely and warmly. Partly, Stuart admired Howard's intelligence and hard work and strength of character. But there was something else. Both were young men of deep moral values and firm religion; both were devoted teetotalers; both were sons of families who were not well-to-do. Stuart's friendship smoothed Howard's time at West Point, which otherwise might have been unbearable. Years later, General Howard would remember Jeb Stuart with deep fondness.

When the war began, Stuart was ordered to the Valley, arriving just before Johnston. He took over the volunteer horsemen there and put them under his tutelage. They were suspicious of him at first. He was a West Point graduate, and they held that against him. But his warmth soon won most of them over. They liked, as one of them said, "the pleasant habit he had of remembering our names and faces." (Not everyone was so appreciative; Turner Ashby, later a famous Confederate cavalryman in his own right, remained jealous and aloof.)

Stuart instructed his recruits that their assumptions about cavalry work—based largely on novels and overheated journalism—were wrong. Cavalry charges, he told them, had been made largely obsolete by modern weapons. Most of their work would involve reconnaissance. They would watch the enemy, and they would block the enemy from watching them. This could be exciting, he said, because their place would be outside the safe confines of their own army's lines. They could dart about, tweaking their foes, taking enormous pleasure in baffling them.

One day he and his troopers were scouting a nearby Federal force, half a mile away. While his men lazed under the sun in a field, they were noticed by the Federals, who prepared to attack. Stuart, by himself atop a knoll, saw the enemy form for battle. One of his officers recalled, "He galloped down on us, laughing," and suggested they move back into some woods as speedily as possible. He cheerfully wrote his wife, Flora, "Look out for stirring events here."[15]

THE SCHOOL
OF THE SOLDIER

I knew no more about military law, drill, rules or tactics than a pig.
—SECOND LIEUTENANT GEORGE H. CARMICAL, SEVENTH GEORGIA[16]

*Discipline is the soul of an army, and without
the habit of obedience, an assemblage of men in battle
can never be more than a panic-stricken mob.*
—MILITARY DICTIONARY, 1861

In early 1861 Andrew G. Curtin, the extremely energetic governor of Pennsylvania, was urging President-elect Lincoln to be concerned about the secessionist South and be prepared for the possibility of war. Curtin himself began the groundwork of activating his state militia. Because Pennsylvania's southern border was the legendary Mason-Dixon Line, he had a head start over most governors. Then, four days *before* the Confederate assault on Fort Sumter, Lincoln warned him in a message, "[the] necessity of being ready increases. See to it." As soon as Fort Sumter fell, Governor Curtin put more than a dozen regiments into motion. His swift actions probably helped convince some ambivalent citizens of Maryland to eschew secession. But his exuberance had a downside. Since Lincoln's original call to arms had asked only for three-month volunteers, the terms of Curtin's original troops would end on or about July 18, which was rapidly approaching. A second problem with Governor Curtin's zeal was that neither the state of Pennsylvania nor the Federal government were ready to feed, arm, and equip these men. As a result they suffered more than regiments from most other states. They endured shoddy uniforms and outdated weapons, were promised monthly wages that were not paid (while their wives wrote them letters, complaining that rents were due, that their children were going hungry, that crops were unplanted). Some of Pennsylvania's volunteers began to feel resentful. The morale in a few regiments bordered on mutiny. Any army that depended on these early Pennsylvania warriors would show cracks. Then, in early June their commander, General Robert Patterson, was ordered to take them into Virginia and attack Joe Johnston's army at Harpers Ferry.

To appreciate the trials that Governor Curtin's and General Patterson's troops were about to endure, it is necessary to understand something of military life in 1861.

Some of Lincoln's raw volunteers were as young as twelve, some were over seventy, but the typical volunteer was in his early twenties. Some were foreign-born — German or Irish, mostly. But the great majority were native born Americans, from a society that emphasized individualism, that mostly had not yet become attuned to the merciless ticking of clocks in school and factory. The new soldiers had heard stories about the Mexican War — largely tales about America's "heroic volunteers," but little about the vast number of the troops there who had died of disease, and nothing of the many rapes those patriotic soldiers perpetrated while marching through Mexico. Americans were especially steeped in myths from the Revolution, and these, too, had been nicely burnished. Americans had heard much about George Washington crossing the Delaware, though little or nothing about General Washington becoming so exasperated with his undisciplined troops near Boston he had had some of them tied up and lashed till they were bloody. Almost every illustration of battle Americans saw in magazines and textbooks showed scenes that were nicely staged, where men died, but neatly, either in a heroic or a muted, fuzzy way. Most of 1861's volunteers, therefore, had no accurate mental images of war to draw on.[17]

The first task of the armies — on both sides — was to persuade volunteers to embrace the military world. Among other necessities, a recruit had to accept the concept of hierarchy, of ranks. An army demands immediate discipline for a subtle reason: to help the incoming soldier get past a normal rejection of all the alien aspects of military life. Many young men, after an initial period of cheerful giddiness, having left behind the strictures of home, made the painful discovery that army existence was often physically uncomfortable. It could also be psychologically jarring—since the recruits were squeezed together with men of different religions and backgrounds. It was disconcerting for a new soldier to discover that some comrades were sociopathic bullies or thieves who would steal his pants or the picture of his sweetheart, that some were shirkers who leeched off the efforts of others. Most soldiers of 1861 were literate, to one degree or another, but only a few avidly read books or magazines; a greater number could only make their marks.

Ultimately, the purpose of army discipline was to prepare a soldier for the chaos of battle, but a soldier's life began immediately. Being mustered into the army—taking one's oath—was a solemn act, but words do not make one a "warrior," any more than wearing a tuxedo makes one a gentleman. First, a new volunteer had to become familiar with the army's arcane jargon. He had to learn to differentiate between *muster* and *bivouac,* between *pickets* and *guards.* He discovered to his surprise that *windage* pertained to the diameter of a gun's bore and that a *mess* could be a convivial meeting of pals.

In 1861 the hardest task, perhaps, was to persuade the volunteer, who considered himself a civilian, only temporarily in uniform, to obey strangers. A corollary to this problem was the difficulty of teaching men—whether they had just been designated to be corporals or colonels—to *command.* In most volunteer units men were elected by comrades to their rank. Elisha Hunt Rhodes, nineteen, from Rhode Island, recalled: "I was elected First Sergeant, much to my surprise. Just what a First Sergeant's duty might be, I had no idea."

Relations between officers and enlisted men were often strained. A Massachusetts volunteer named Ike wrote home that the men of his regiment did not have much confidence in their officers. "It does not seem to us," he said, "as though there were

backbone enough to them to lead us to battle in the right shape."
A Connecticut volunteer described his colonel as "so drunk on
dress parade that he had to support himself with his saber." (In
fact, the colonel in question, George S. Burnham, was seriously
ill with neuralgia, but his men were positive his condition involved booze.) Charles Haydon, twenty-seven, member of a
Michigan regiment, wrote in his journal: "Many of the men seem
to think they should never be spoken to unless the remarks
are prefaced by some words of deferential politeness. Will the
gentlemen who comprise the first platoon have the kindness to
march forward." When the British correspondent for the *London
Times*, William Howard Russell, visited the camp of General
Irvin McDowell, he observed, as he strolled with the general,
"That not one of the many soldiers he passed in the streets
saluted him."

In the South many early volunteers happily accepted the rank
of private, considering it a matter of honor, but they often re-
sented taking orders — especially from social inferiors. "I have
known numberless cases," one of them later wrote, "in which privates have declined dinner and other invitations from officers
who had presumed upon their shoulder-straps." Orders from
such officers were often seen as impertinences, as "putting on
airs." Fistfights and even duels resulted. A South Carolinian
wrote his wife: "When we are not drilling the time is pretty much
taken up by drinking popskull, frying pan cakes, and bruising
around generally...Most of the boys here think that we are just
going to have a frolic."[18]

What Winfield Scott and McDowell and Lee and Jackson and
almost all other professional military men understood — what
civilians like Lincoln did not — was that untrained soldiers desperately need training. Professional military men considered traditional army methods the proper preparation for war. They
believed that the best thing for soldiers was *drill*. In a sense, the
drill was not simply standing or marching; it involved much of
a soldier's day, from reveille to tattoo. The physical aspects of
it strengthened the body, and the entire process indoctrinated a
raw recruit in discipline and teamwork. Without the drill, which

taught submission to orders, few reasonable men would choose to stand alone in a chilly rain for hours at night as a sentinel, or shiver on bivouac beneath a thin blanket, or carry forty or fifty pounds over long distances. And until a man could learn to accept such assignments—not happily, but as part of a team—he was unlikely to perform well on the battlefield. Only by repetition—by constant practice—could an average person acquire the necessary knowledge and skills. Army life was far more complicated than most civilians understood. A volunteer infantryman, for instance, had to learn fifteen different basic drumbeat signals and bugle calls.

The whims of a commander determined the precise format of a soldier's schedule, but a typical day began at five o'clock with reveille, with sleepy troops standing around while a sergeant took roll call. Then followed what the army called *peas on a trencher* (breakfast), then *sick call* and *fatigue call,* when those who claimed to be ailing were taken to the surgeon while the others policed the area. At eight o'clock the first sergeant of each company would announce who would be serving guard duty during the next twenty-four hours. Then came the first official drill, then lunch, and some more drilling (for those regiments with energetic colonels). In early evening was another roll call, often a *dress parade* of the entire regiment, *retreat,* supper, and *tattoo.* From that time until lights-out, those men not serving guard duty or filling out paperwork or in confinement for some infraction, could truly relax. Some wrote home, others read their Bibles. Many soldiers played games—cards often. A few would play fiddles or banjos while their comrades sang. A twenty-one-year-old volunteer from Maine wrote his sisters about what a grand time he was having: "I am just as well as a feller can be & like this life first rate, because it is a lazy life & you always called me a lazy fellow. But still, it is not a quiet life. There is plenty of noise and plenty of fun, as there is all kinds of musical instruments on the ground, fiddling, dancing, wrestling, playing cards and all sorts of amusement."[19]

Despite such moments, volunteers were often bored and hungered for distractions. Early in the morning of July 2, pickets on both sides noticed an odd thing in the sky: a distinct comet, its tail near the Big Dipper. Scientists, using telescopes, had first spotted this object early in April, but now the comet was visible to the naked eye. Whether it boded good or ill, no one could tell.

There was a bit of subdued excitement on the Fourth of July. In Washington several regiments held serious dress parades. Bands played martial music, men marched, politicians spoke, ministers invoked God's blessing. At the camp of the two Rhode Island regiments, an enlisted man, who called himself "Professor Benoni Sweet," exhibited his uncommon skills. He stretched a rope high above the ground and gave one of his civilian tightrope-walking performances. At the camp of the Second Michigan, Philo Gallup, a twenty-one-year-old private, decided to have some fun. He stole some cartridges, poured their contents into a hole, and struck a match. "It blode the ground up for fore feet around it. That is all the forth we hed here," he wrote a friend — but added with some satisfaction, "Just after the explosion I had an invitation to a dance at knite in verginaa. They todde us that it wouldent cost no eny thing if we could come. So we sed we would gow, and a nice time we had, to. There was some of the pretys girls there that I ever saw, and good danceers they was, to. I just giv myself away. They fell in love with me rite away."

The Federal Congress opened its session this day. One of Lincoln's soldiers, off duty, decided to check it out. He went to the Senate chamber but thought its activities mundane and boring. He wandered off and found himself inside the rotunda, along with a crowd of other visitors, who thronged about the massive room. Looming above them was a painting of George Washington, and next to it hung an American flag. Spontaneously, one of the tourists stopped before the flag and began to sing "The Star-Spangled Banner." Around the singer, others, moved by deep feelings, added their voices, until everyone inside the vast room had "joined in the chorus." At that juncture of American history, few exhibitions of genuine patriotism could have seemed more profound.

Confederates were uncertain whether or not to celebrate this day, which of course had also been their traditional holiday. Some commanders chose to do so, many did not. Out in the Valley,

Johnston's army remained quiet. In Richmond, some folks celebrated. "Noise of drums, tramp of marching regiments all day
long," Mary Chesnut wrote into her diary. "We ought to be miserable and anxious, and yet these are pleasant days. Perhaps we
are unnaturally exhilarated and excited."[20]

But the essence of military life had little to do with entertainment.
It involved drill, and this was a topic few new volunteers knew
much about. Volunteer units were often staffed by officers with no
other qualification than a desire to have a nifty title. But many
new officers recognized their ignorance and set about rectifying it.
They usually turned to one of several handbooks — military self-
help books, if you will. All these manuals, without exception, were
originally drawn almost word for word from French texts. (It had
been Frenchmen, after all, who had originated the modern military school at places like Saint Cyr.) Robert Anderson's *Instruction
for Field Artillery, Horse and Foot,* published in 1839, was only a version of a French handbook, yet it instructed American artillerists
so well that several battles in the Mexican War were handily won
by following the book's diagrams. In 1860 John Gibbon published
an *Artillerist's Manual,* a watered-down but slightly modernized
version of Anderson's book. Cavalrymen had a three-volume manual (1841), also taken from the French. For infantrymen, Winfield
Scott himself had turned a lengthy French text into his own three-
volume work, *Infantry Tactics* (1835). In 1861 one or the other of
such works might be found in an officer's trunk, but the most commonly read manual, *Rifle and Light Infantry Tactics,* was the product
of an army committee, chaired by William Joseph Hardee. Although Hardee himself actually did little of the work, the publica-
tion was referred to by his name, and soldiers studied "Hardee."
The book's prose was as stiff as any martinet, but in 1861 it sold
tens of thousands of copies. (Confederate and Union officers alike
stuck to their "Hardees." A Richmond newspaper announced in
July that one of the city's bookstores had already sold 20,000
copies of it and other manuals.)[21]

"Hardee" introduced readers to "The School of the Soldier." An
infantry recruit, it said, must be taught first how to do the sim-

plest things: to stand at attention, to turn, to walk, to walk fast. These sound simple enough, but new volunteers could not be expected to grasp certain essential details. For instance, a standard marching step, the book said, must be *exactly* twenty-eight inches — neither an inch more nor less. A normal marching pace must be *precisely* ninety steps per minute. Such demands sound absurdly concrete, but a thousand men — some tall, some short, some thin, some corpulent — marching in close order needed to maintain exactly the same pace, or the group tumbled into a confused clump. The manual spoke of *flank marches* and *column marches* and used unfamiliar terms like *oblique* and *countermarch.* All of these had to be learned — often by new officers and sergeants reading slowly at night by candlelight so they could describe — and demonstrate — in the morning.

And drilling became far more complicated as soon as one added the presence of a gun. Some companies had rifles; others had converted smoothbore flintlocks. Only a minority of soldiers had much acquaintance with either kind. Even farm boys who had hunted — North or South — usually had used only the family's rusty fowling piece. Now they were handed different weapons and given incredibly complex instructions on their use. On the parade ground, a lieutenant, reading from "Hardee," told the volunteers how to load — in nine (and he would insist on the importance of exactly *nine*) separate movements. Describing the first "motion," he would read:

> Grasp the piece with the left hand as high as the right elbow, and bring it vertically opposite the middle of the body, shift the right hand to the upper band, place the butt between the feet, the barrel to the front, seize it with the left hand, near the muzzle, which should be three inches from the body; carry the right hand to the cartridge box; seize the cartridge with the thumb and next two fingers and place it between the teeth.

Long before the end of that first sentence, most recruits would feel addled by confusion. The prose, theoretically well translated, hardly seemed English. (One might argue that the jargon-filled paragraphs were in fact another language: "military.") The central point of this exercise involved the recruit learning to fire his weapon with a certain amount of efficiency, in a variety of circumstances — many of them unforeseen. The marching movements themselves were based — as had always been true of almost all tactics — on the weaponry. More than two centuries earlier, the smoothbore had come into its own on the battlefield. This weapon was extremely inaccurate. With a gunpowder of uncertain consistency, its bullet might waver several feet to the right or left, or fall far short of its expected target. (There seemed little purpose in "aiming" the smoothbore; it seemed more realistic to imagine "pointing" it.) The inaccuracy of these weapons meant that troops had to learn to work together, so that their firing came at the same time. If a single soldier, pointing at an enemy, really wanted to hit that person, he would have to stand uncomfortably close to the target — a hundred feet, probably less. But if a whole mass of men fired their weapons simultaneously, their bullets would act like a giant shotgun, crisscrossing in the air and landing with devastating impact against a bunch of other soldiers. The *totality* of an army's firepower was the important thing, not an individual's skill.

Cutting a spiraled groove ("rifling") inside a gun's barrel added both distance and accuracy to the weapon, and the first "rifles" had appeared in the early 1600s, but metallurgy had been imperfect, and rifling the barrels had often weakened them so much that they often split. By the mid-nineteenth century, however, such problems had been sufficiently solved, enabling manufacturers to turn out rather dependable, relatively inexpensive rifles. The United States Army, under a tight budget, also converted many of its older smoothbores. By early 1861 North and South had thousands of each basic type — smoothbore and rifle — and within each type, dozens of subcategories. Smoothbores usually fired only round balls, but some rifles were now using conical bullets called *minié balls* (named after a Frenchman, Captain Claude Etienne Minié). A single regiment often had some soldiers carrying one kind of gun and others an entirely different kind. During a battle comrades often could not share each other's ammunition. Ordnance officers, responsible for supplying appropriate ammunition, found this situation, of course, a nightmare.

Once properly trained, a typical soldier could usually load and fire his weapon in thirty seconds. But many problems arose. Gunpowder could dirty a barrel so much that, after a few shots, an infantryman found it difficult to push the bullet easily into place. Many a soldier could be seen hammering his ramrod into the barrel, using a handy rock. And weather — rain, wind, heat, cold — influenced the way a soldier could load his gun. His own physical condition — especially exhaustion — affected his abilities. Loading a rifle or smoothbore required fine motor skills, and most soldiers arrived at a battlefield exhausted after miles of marching, after too little food, and after much sleep deprivation. Their natural excitement generally carried them along for a few minutes, but when their enthusiasm wore off, they often became clumsy and confused. Then, sometimes panic slipped its tentacles around a soldier's psyche.

Because men in groups, out of a natural animal instinct, feel a greater sense of confidence, infantry manuals emphasized the importance of keeping men close together. When soldiers advanced, whether marching four abreast in *columns* or having already wheeled into long, slender *ranks,* they were instructed to keep their right elbows — *literally* — touching the side of the man to their right. This was why textbooks demanded a specific, uniform pace. If an infantryman lagged back or stepped faster, his elbow and that of his comrade would lose this contact.

Under most battle conditions, a unit — and "Hardee" and the others focused almost solely on *companies* and *regiments* — was to form itself into two ranks, *exactly* thirteen inches apart. "Hardee" says:

> The rear rank men, in aiming, will each carry the right foot about eight inches to the right, and towards the left heel of the man next on the right, inclining the upper part of the body forward.

This way, those in the second rank would not shoot those in front. But accidents could, and did, happen.

Neither "Hardee" nor any other manual mentioned two issues. What does a soldier do when the man to his left or right feels ill and drops out of line — or gets wounded or killed? In theory one simply closed ranks, but men are not robots, and on a battlefield most people — half-trained volunteers particularly — became noticeably separated from each other. Also none of the books were clear about what to expect when a line of soldiers crossed real terrain, not some flat parade ground. The geography of northeastern France, where these manuals had gestated, was quite different from that of Virginia, with its thick forests, its fences, and its countless creeks, its steep ravines and rocky outcroppings — a land that did not lend itself to geometric lines of soldiers. In addition, there was another reality. Battlefields became lumpy with the bodies of the wounded and the dead, and with the writhing and kicking hooves of agonized horses. (A thick military dictionary, published in 1861 and designed solely for professional soldiers, was much more practical than the manuals; it urged commanders during training sessions to make their men "run in disorder, and re-form at some given point," and added: "A regiment that can pass over two hundred paces in line of battle without losing its alignment, is well instructed."[22])

The manuals also failed to describe the ambiance of a battlefield. For example, they said nothing about the noise one could expect — the explosive cacophony of thousands of muskets firing simultaneously, of artillery shells exploding, of shouting, screaming, pleading, swearing men, of conflicting bugle calls, of horses shrieking in pain, of shattering tree trunks. The crazed, stereophonic uproar of a battlefield would inevitably be unnerving. Inside its chaos many a soldier, pulling his trigger, did not realize his gun had not fired or had misfired, and he would reload and squeeze his trigger again. After every battle, guns would be found abandoned, stuffed with more than a single charge, sometimes as many as ten or more. Of the 37,000 rifles found after Gettysburg, 18,000 had more than one load pressed within.

The manuals did not provide much helpful information about many things. They virtually ignored the disturbing effects of recoil. And they hardly mentioned smoke, although it could envelop a battlefield, eliminating all sight of the enemy. The books did not suggest that putting a bayonet on one's gun weighted down the end of the barrel, making it much harder to hold the weapon up and aim it properly. And most manuals failed to tell the volunteer that a strong gust of wind would throw a musket ball twelve feet off its target at a thousand yards. Using the weapons available in 1861, a soldier was supposed to be able to calculate whether his foe was 300 yards away or 500, but unless a man was exceedingly skillful and had practiced countless times, he found it virtually impossible to judge distances with any assurance.

Cartridges had to be made by hand, and gunpowder was rather scarce. Ammunition was hard to obtain, and many commanders were reluctant to permit their volunteers too much target practice. The results showed. A soldier from Maine recalled that, when shooting, he and his comrades usually regarded themselves "safe if directly behind the man who was firing." A fellow from South Carolina wrote his wife: "We all went out yesterday to try our guns. We shot at a barrel, two or three hundred yards off, placed on a fence. Jim Lofton and myself, and one or two more, was all that hit the barrel, of my company." (Thus, at a relatively short range, less than 5 percent of that Confederate company could hit an enemy that was standing still, even though the atmospheric conditions were adequate and the soldiers did not have to worry about the confusion of battle.) A sergeant from Michigan participated in some target practice. "We had a sharp drill this afternoon and fired our first *blank* [emphasis added] cartridges. The noise seemed to confuse the men a little. We need more of it. Some of them fired almost their first guns. It all went off very well except one man shot away his ramrod at the second fire." A soldier from Mississippi, keeping a journal, noted that he and his regiment fired one afternoon at a target six feet high and two feet wide, only a hundred yards away. Two of the companies, firing together, were able to hit the target only five times. Shooting at a live person would be, of course, harder. A sergeant of the First Massachusetts drifted away from camp one evening before the password and countersign had been announced. When he returned and was unable to provide them on demand, a nervous sentinel fired at him — *at four paces* — and missed.[23]

Military professionals understood the likelihood of inaccurate shooting. This was one of the reasons they put so much emphasis on the proper use of bayonets. In theory, a soldier would fire a round or two, then charge the enemy. The headlong charge by a thousand bayonet-wielding soldiers could be terrifying to any individual trying to reload his musket. And he often ran. The concept of the bayonet charge had been around for at least two centuries. But in the years between Waterloo and Bull Run—the decades between the British Brown Bess and the Springfield rifle—guns had changed. By 1861 a decent rifle could be accurate at a distance of more than three times that of an eighteenth-century flintlock. This meant—all things being equal—that a soldier could reload his weapon and fire several times before a charging enemy could reach him. (Hardee's book took into account some of these changes, but not enough. Mostly, he simply advised soldiers to run faster.)

The army recognized that soldiers seldom were in actual battle. It was important that they learn techniques that could be applied to camp life—for example, *guard duty*. A guard might be mounted at the regimental "jail," a tent set aside for soldiers who had committed some infraction—drunkenness, sassing an officer, fighting. At night, guards marched along the edges of camps, trying to stay awake—or, if the night was cold or rainy, reasonably comfortable. They called out the hours, announced, "All's well"; they challenged people wanting to come in or go out sturdily, "Halt, who goes there?"

"Friend," was the usual reply, and the guard was supposed to respond, "Advance, friend, and give the countersign."

A volunteer from Minnesota admitted to his diary, "On guard—but I don't know 'beans' about a sentinel's duty." According to the army's official "Articles of War," read aloud to all troops when they were mustered in, a sentinel who fell asleep could be executed. This punishment was probably never carried out by either side in Virginia during 1861, since executing volunteers in those early months for such a common act would have been considered too harsh.

"Guard duty" seemed a bit silly when regiments were first formed and still near home, but as the two armies began to pat at each other along their edges, its cousin, *picket duty*, became more serious. With both sides having growing forces in Virginia, such an assignment, often miles from one's regiment, could be an almost surreal experience. At night, sitting all alone, the patter of shy critters rustling across the leaves detonated inside a picket's ears. A young man from Virginia wrote his brother about his first night's duty: "I was very busy listening to the Bullfroggs, crickets, &c. making a noise. Some of the Bullfroggs sounded like the old drakes at Home with a bad cold. About daybreak I heard a big owl hoot." Another Confederate later recalled, "No one but a soldier can form any proper conception of the feelings and imaginations of a green boy performing his first night's picket duty." He described his own first two hours. "The silence was oppressive. I stood peering through the darkness, away a half a mile or more from any human being, so far as I knew, imagining that every noise or bush shaken by the passing breeze was a veritable foe." A Union soldier from Maine wrote his mother: "I and two comrades are on our post as picket guard 2 miles in advance of the northern troops." It was the Fourth of July. "I have just raised the little flag you made me on a miniature flag staff twelve feet high, it looks like a little harbinger of peace. Only think, that little emblem of a mothers love is now floating farther into the enemys country than any other American flag in the Union." He told her he had to stop writing now because "I have got to keep a good lookout, for both of my comrads have drop'd to sleep." His brother, in the same regiment, also wrote their mother: "When we are out on picket guard, we can see the enemy pickets Guard pretty plain." Often, soldiers performing picket duty felt it best to maintain a kind of peace along the ragged edges where the two armies came together. In Leesburg, one Virginian wrote his father: "Our picket guards and their sentinels talk to each other constantly. They are continually asking us for some whiskie. Sometimes some of our sentinels let them have it. There was an agreement between each other."[24]

Marching, shooting, and guard duty formed only a small part of military discipline. Throughout history soldiers have usually died of disease, not battle. It was vitally important to teach volunteers — or at least their commanding officers — to concentrate on hygiene. The recent Crimean War (1854–56) had proved that necessity. Of the first 25,000 British soldiers sent to fight it, 18,000 had died within the first year, almost entirely from disease, and such information had appeared in all major American newspapers. But the need for cleanliness is not entirely natural, and, as one volunteer later admitted, "Men are only children of an older growth." Unless instructed — firmly — soldiers tended to remain quite casual about such matters. They bitterly complained about the rations they were given and the poor quality of their meals, but they seldom washed their utensils or cooking pots. They grumbled about the flies, then casually threw their kitchen refuse into piles within their camps. They objected to the revolting fact of army "sinks" (latrines) and the odors rising from them, but they whined when ordered to cover these sinks with dirt — a daily practice required in the regular army but commonly ignored in volunteer regiments. A Federal medical inspector, after wandering through a dozen camps around Washington, reported that, even after a week, some regiments had not yet bothered to dig a single latrine and that soldiers relieved themselves just outside their tent flaps.

A few days after the war began, the Sanitary Commission was born, a civilian agency that reviewed the camps in Washington and elsewhere and reported its findings to the army — and to the press. The Commission's "Report No. 17," released on July 8, 1861, was scathing. The Commission had examined more than forty regiments. While it complimented a few — especially two from Rhode Island — it found many that failed on most counts. Their sinks, for example, were often so foul that soldiers using them vomited. As to personal hygiene, the Report said, "In but few cases are the soldiers obliged to regard any rules of personal cleanliness. Their clothing is shamefully dirty, and they are often lousy... The clothing of the men, from top to toe, is almost daily saturated with sweat and packed with dust, and to all appearance, no attempt is generally made to remove this, even superficially."

In general the fault lay with the commanders. Colonels who had received their commands through an election often found it difficult to be firm. Some refused to take their jobs seriously. Many were observed reviewing their men while wearing bathrobes and slippers; others did not even bother with such military activities, leaving their charges in the hands of lower officers and booking rooms in hotels like Willard's, where they could eat and drink to their satisfaction, and occasionally enjoy female companionship. As to the regimental *surgeons* (medical officers), some had ability, others were incompetent. (The medical experience of one surgeon, a barber before the war, had primarily involved cupping blood.)

According to military regulations, every recruit who wanted to *muster in* (officially join) was to be physically inspected beforehand by the recruiter, and also by a surgeon. These two observers were supposed to detect if the applicant suffered a debilitating ailment—tuberculosis or syphilis, for example—or some other condition that ought to prevent his inclusion: obvious insanity, mental impairment, and so on. During the war's first year, however, apparently several dozen women successfully mustered in. Sarah Emma Edmonds, for instance, joined the Second Michigan Infantry Regiment as "Frank Thompson"; she served at Bull Run and other battles before being discovered. It is estimated that during the war 400 women successfully practiced this charade— which speaks volumes about muster examinations.[25]

Medicine and discipline and soldiering were also involved in the physical demands of marching. The typical soldier was a young man—five feet and seven inches or so in height, weighing between 140 and 150 pounds. Although he often came from a civilian life that demanded muscles (farming or the building trades), he generally wearied quickly when required to walk more than a couple of miles. Back home, even farm boys had ridden in wagons whenever they could, and few school children had to travel far to their classrooms. When the Fourth Maine arrived in Washington and was directed to an encampment only two miles away, several of its men dropped of sunstroke or exhaustion on the march there. Even their colonel, who rode a horse and did not have to carry a knapsack like his men, admitted he was glad to reach the campsite. After the troops of the First Massachusetts marched a few miles, they felt oppressed by the heat and the exertion. One of them wrote home: "Some of the boys fell out and could not stand it." Another wrote, "The way was long and tedious. Many of the men were worn out with fatigue." He admitted, "I hailed a negro on the route, and got him to carry my knapsack. Though nothing but a boy, he was tough notwithstanding, and did not think it very tiresome work." New Englanders were not the only ones to find marching a hardship; boys from the Midwest and the South bellyached just as loudly.[26] John Wesley Culpeper, a young teacher from Georgia, wrote in his diary about the first time his regiment maneuvered: "We marched a mile and a half, when we were ordered to rest; and I assure you every chap was glad to hear that, for it was very hot." A few days later, he described another march: "The dust with the excessive heat of the sun was almost insufferable. Not being accustomed to the heat of the sun, walking, &c., I took the headache and commenced bleeding at the nose." He shortly had to pull out and sit under a tree by the side of the road. A young soldier from Virginia felt little better: "The day was hot and the road dusty, and marching went quite hard with us, especially myself, who had never marched a day in my life." The causes for such complaints varied. Some troops — North and South — were unused to laboring much on sweltering days. Soldiers, like slugs, can melt in the sun. A number of volunteers were simply physically unfit for this strenuous life.

During the war's first months, women on both sides, desperately wanting to contribute, sewed *havelocks* for their boys — each made of a whitish cloth that fitted over the cap and fell behind the head. (Magazines like *Harper's* had made this headgear famous — named after a British general — during the Sepoy Rebellion of 1857.) In theory, the havelocks were to aid against sunstroke. In fact, they stored heat. They also flapped annoyingly against the sides of the face, and they deadened sounds, including crucial orders. By July most soldiers had thanked the ladies for these gifts and begun using them as rags.[27]

The weight the soldiers carried did not usually cause them to collapse, nor did the heat; the root problem was often their diet. The American army described in detail a soldier's normal ration: salted or maybe fresh beef, salted pork, beans, rice, split peas, dried vegetables or peaches or apples, soft bread, and, of course, the notorious *hardtack* — hardened crackers that came in wooden boxes, often dated "1848," that tasted suspiciously like wood chips. If followed to the letter, a day's ration provided 2,300 calories—just barely adequate for someone performing heavy labor for several hours. Sometimes the volunteers had enough provisions; at other times, a day or two might pass when they ate nothing. Sufficient provisions depended upon the availability of wagons (a quartermaster's job) and the efficiency—or honesty—of commissaries. Many factors—weather, for instance—could interrupt supplies.

Even when an army unit received proper provisions, the quality of the soldier's diet was often, at the very least, dubious. The problem tended to rest in the food's preparation. A regiment's commissary officer had fulfilled his assignment when he distributed whatever provisions he had received. His responsibility did not include ensuring that the food was properly cooked. That was the job of the soldiers. A company's captain, if efficient and motivated, might find a cook from outside. Southern units often had slaves perform this function. The *Charleston Courier* noted, "Every negro is instinctively a cook, and is never more at home than when groping in the smoke around a camp fire." A Virginia soldier, stationed at Manassas, wrote his wife that he and his comrades depended on "John," a "yellow-man-cook who renders perfect satisfaction." Two days later he wrote her again: "Our boy John proves to be a first-rate cook. He makes good tea, good coffee, and the veal of today & the broiled chickens were admirably prepared." Northern soldiers also found outside remedies. The Rhode Island regiments hired professional chefs. A Connecticut company utilized the services of a runaway slave.

But normal practice was for a group of friends in a company to form a mess (usually eight men). They shared a few pots and pans and often took turns cooking. Since volunteers had seldom done anything like this at home, the results tended to be unfortunate: half-cooked, half-burned meals, and much wasted food. Many men, whenever they had any cash, bought extras from *sutlers* (semi-independent civilians) who contracted to serve a regiment and who generally set up their tents near a regiment's camp. Sutlers usually had sweets for sale—honey and pies and cookies. And some sutlers, although the practice was not strictly legal, sold spirits. Several German regiments in the Union army were quite open about drinking beer, which they considered both necessary and medicinal. Given the quality of Washington's water, they were probably right.

There was also *foraging*. Some of this practice simply involved stealing a farmer's chickens or corn, a passing pig, some apples in a tree. A soldier from Maine wrote his brother: "Last night one of my mess mates & I went out on an exploring expedition. We went out about three miles to a house & spying a good-looking potato field we thought we would try a few of them . . . We had got our haversacks most full when came an old woman with a broom & hollered like the devil sure enough. Sais she, if you don't get out of them potatoes I'll blow your brains out. Sais I, you dry up, you old pispot . . . We laughed at her & plagued her as long as we wanted." Sometimes foraging was more honest; it involved going up to a house and asking for food. A Massachusetts volunteer and two comrades knocked on a door and asked the young lady who answered if they could buy a meal. They ate hot corn cakes and pork and washed them down with milk, then paid their hostess twenty-five cents each for this breakfast. As they were sitting there, one of the daughters asked, "What yer come here for — to take our lands, steal our niggers?" The three soldiers said no. The girl was surprised, and said, "The folks all said so; and if it be as you say, why don't Lincoln write the Southern people a letter and tell them all about it. That would save some of yer from being shot."

Some foraging involved neither theft nor purchase. Northern Virginia was covered with wild fruit, and soldiers on both sides took advantage of the nectar. "Cherries we have in abundance," a Louisiana soldier wrote home, "and dewberries millions." A young man from Wisconsin wrote to friends, "This is a glorious country for blackberries, whortle berries, in fact all kinds of fruit." Another wrote, "Blackberries are ripe here now and they are about as plenty as the damned flies, and if you knew how plenty they was, you would think the blackberries was thick." A Massachusetts soldier jotted this note in his journal: "Very warm. After breakfast went out berrying, found as many blackberries and thimbleberries as I could eat: made me think of home." A

New Yorker told his sisters, "Blackberries are plenty here and whenever we can pass a sentinel and go a-skirmishing, we feast on the delicious wild fruit." Another admitted to his diary, "I have contrived to evade the guards & got out after berries. I clawed the black berries off in double handfuls. I never saw larger or finer berries."[28]

Tentative Warriors

Eventually soldiering would involve more than berrying, more even than drill. All the preparations that the volunteers went through were supposed to lead to one place: a battlefield. Years later, in 1863, the Joint Committee on the Conduct of the Present War, created by the Federal Congress, issued a report about the events leading up to Bull Run. After interviewing scores of individuals, the committee stated flatly that Lincoln's government had made a costly mistake two months *before* that battle. In the committee's opinion, when the Union army crossed the Potomac on the night of the referendum, May 23–24, 1861, it ought to have pushed ahead immediately toward Manassas. That obscure railroad station was a strategic position, the committee said, and could have been taken easily. Having failed to take that initiative, the Federal army was put in the position of having to push itself two months later against a much stronger foe.

As to the actual Battle of Bull Run, the report stated: "The principal cause of the defeat of that day was the failure of General Patterson to hold the forces of Johnston in the valley of the

Shenandoah." In other words, the members of the Joint Committee were quite clear. The disaster at Bull Run was the fault of
Robert Patterson, the general in command of the army of Governor Curtin of Pennsylvania. It was as simple as that. Was the
Committee correct?[29]

Most history writing is a kind of decoupage. The historian
snips off a bit of this, tears a bit of that. He or she glues pieces together—to form a coherent picture. The writing of history is an art
form, often revealing much about the artist. Most Civil War historians have agreed with the Joint Committee, and many have pos-
tulated the reason for General Patterson's "failure": He was too
old. Bruce Catton, a superb writer, was sixty-two when he charac-
terized Patterson as "sixty-nine, a veteran of the War of 1812 . . .
handicapped . . . by old age." Shelby Foote, in his masterpiece on
the war, calls Patterson "a sixty-nine-year-old veteran of the War
of 1812"—which, though true, is all Foote really says about that officer. This label has become a handy cliché. James McPherson also
uses it in his magnificent *Battle Cry of Freedom,* where he describes
Patterson as "a sixty-nine-year-old veteran of the War of 1812."
The great historian Allan Nevins was himself sixty-nine when he
wrote: "And who faced Johnston? A soldier near seventy." A recent book on Bull Run, by Ethan S. Rafuse, simply calls Patterson
"a tired and indecisive old man." (There is no evidence Patterson
was "tired"; he lived twenty more years after his Valley campaign
and would spend much of those years energetically attempting to
controvert slanderous things said about him.) Each of the historians quoted here has suggested that Robert Patterson—gerontolog-
ically challenged, as it were—was too old to act aggressively. One
must consider, however, the following: Stalin was sixty-six at the
beginning of the Cold War and Mao Zedong was in his middle six-
ties at its height. Andrew Jackson was sixty-six when he threatened to crush South Carolina if it refused to collect American
tariffs. Ho Chi Minh was in his middle seventies when Lyndon
Baines Johnson sent ground troops to Vietnam, and Winfield
Scott was sixty-two when he won the Mexican War. It is true that
active campaigns are physically draining; they take stamina. But
aggressiveness—an animal toughness—can have an extended life.
The Civil War is an obvious field study of young generals who

became frozen by the weight of responsibility. Patterson ought to be judged not by his age but by what he did, or failed to do, when he was sent to the Valley to challenge Joe Johnston.[30]

Robert Patterson had fought in the War of 1812, rising to the rank of colonel. Although he then returned to civilian life, becoming a successful businessman and prominent Democrat, he kept his hand in the Pennsylvania militia and in time was granted the state title of major general. During the Mexican War he served as Scott's second-in-command. Patterson was handsome and quite distinguished-looking, with his bald dome and white, winged hair swept past his ears. He was intelligent, indefatigable, an excellent organizer, and he understood paperwork. He was a friend of Simon Cameron, Secretary of War, as well as of Winfield Scott. He was known to have sympathy for his many Southern friends and to be disinclined to press a brutal war on the Confederacy, but since Lincoln was being careful to keep this war bipartisan, Patterson's Democratic connections were important. Although Patterson had never led large numbers of men into battle, neither, of course, had Joe Johnston.

In early June Patterson went to Chambersburg, Pennsylvania, near the state's southern border, to take command of Curtin's army of volunteers. He was ordered to move with it against Johnston at Harpers Ferry, about forty miles away. Seizing Harpers Ferry would offer the Union several important benefits. It would reopen the Baltimore and Ohio Railroad, as well as give encouragement to folks in the western counties of Virginia who had voted against secession in the recent referendum.

Patterson had been in Chambersburg only two days when Scott ordered him to wait until some regular infantrymen and several batteries of artillery reached him to give spine to his volunteers. Ironically, in light of the Joint Committee's later accusations, at that time Winfield Scott was nervous that Patterson might be too aggressive. On June 6 he sent Patterson a message saying he thought Patterson's movement across the Potomac would likely succeed, "but there must be no reverse." And just so there could be no mistaking his meaning, Scott emphasized: "I have said that we must sustain no reverse; but that is not enough:

a check or a drawn battle would be a victory to the enemy, filling his heart with joy, his ranks with men, and his magazines with voluntary contributions. Take your measures, therefore, circumspectly; make a good use of your engineers and other experienced staff officers and generals, and attempt nothing without a clear prospect of success, as you will find the enemy strongly posted and not inferior to you in numbers."

Patterson had a practice of conferring frequently with his military staff. He also often asked the advice of his regimental commanders (one of whom was his son). During the next six weeks, the movements of his army were determined virtually by consensus. It seems unfair, therefore, to place all the blame on Patterson for feeble or craven maneuvering. It should be mentioned that several of his advisers would later gain fame for their military successes — for example, George H. ("Pap") Thomas, the "Rock of Chickamauga," and Abner Doubleday.

Winfield Scott knew Patterson well. Scott's later "discovery" in July that the Pennsylvanian lacked dash, and blaming him for that weakness, was like a woman marrying a man far shorter than she, then abusing him over his failure to rise to her expectations.

With Scott's orders and advices in hand, Patterson was uncertain how to proceed, but he wanted desperately to do the right thing. He wrote his fellow Pennsylvanian, Simon Cameron, Secretary of War, that he was beginning to obsess about Harpers Ferry. "I cannot sleep for thinking about it ... My reputation, and the reputation of our dear old State, is at stake on this issue. I beseech you, therefore, by our ancient friendship, give me the means of success. You have the means; place them at my disposal, and shoot me if I do not use them to advantage." His old friend Cameron apparently made no reply.[31]

Once his reinforcements arrived, General Patterson's army began to move. Just as it got under way, Scott sent him another cautionary note. The army had intelligence, the message said, that Joe Johnston intended to make a "desperate stand" for Harpers Ferry. (The source of Scott's information was never clarified.)[32]

Patterson did not exactly rush recklessly ahead, but it ought to be recalled that Scott had already emphasized that "*there must be no reverse,"* that Patterson must take all of his measures *"circum-spectly"* and *"attempt nothing without a clear prospect of success."* Patterson's army lacked sufficient cavalry. Once he crossed the Potomac, he would be uncertain about the strength or position of the enemy and would inevitably move like someone crossing a pitch black room crammed with tables and chairs.

Joe Johnston's Headquarters in the Valley

Meanwhile, at Harpers Ferry, Johnston was growing edgy. His army, he knew, was unprepared to fight a determined foe — and he assumed that that was what Patterson was leading toward him. Among other things, Johnston was aware his troops lacked enough caps and cartridges for a real fight. In mid-June he admitted to Richmond, "The want of ammunition has rendered me very timid." (Two weeks later he wrote to Jefferson Davis that this deficiency put him "almost in a panic.") One of Johnston's soldiers later recalled that his regiment (the Thirty-third Virginia) at that time had only "old, altered muskets and old flintlock rifles." They had no tents or other camp equipment, and each man carried only a handful of cartridges in his coat pocket. The Eighth Georgia, just arrived, had only nine rounds per man, enough to fight for but a few minutes. Johnston's artillery also lacked proper equipment. He had hardly any vehicles to transport artillery shells and other essentials. Johnston tried to make do, buying and expropriating local farm wagons, and nailing makeshift boxes to them. He also had problems with the health and stamina of his soldiers. Although he now had, in theory, over 7,000 men, many were weakened by disease — especially measles — or by the fact that most of them were unused to either walking any distances or even doing much physical labor. A Virginian one day noticed a disconcerting fact about his company: "There were only 34 men in ranks this morning. The balance are sick or complaining." Another Virginian, Michael Reid Hanger, one day told his diary that of the 103 men in his company, only fifteen had shown up that morning for drill.[33]

General Johnston had to consider another ominous fact. Not only was Patterson marching against him with an army, which

Johnston understood to be twice as large as his and presumably much better-equipped and far healthier, but a second Union army, perhaps a large one, seemed to be approaching from the west. This unexpected threat came from George B. McClellan, in command of a growing force of volunteers in southern Ohio. Before the war Johnston and McClellan had maintained a long and warm correspondence, and Johnston considered his friend smart and energetic. On June 13 a distinguished local citizen, James M. Mason, said he had learned that at least 2,000 of McClellan's troops had just arrived at Romney, Virginia, about thirty miles to the west. Johnston decided they were McClellan's advance guard and assumed that Scott was using two armies — Patterson's and McClellan's — to take Harpers Ferry. He believed he was about to be caught in a pincers.

Johnston could not know that the probe into Romney had nothing to do with him. Colonel Lewis Wallace — later the author of *Ben Hur* — had heard that a rebel force was there. Since that town was only thirty-three miles from Wallace's camp in Maryland, he put 500 of his Eleventh Indiana soldiers onto a train, with no authorization from any of his superiors. His battalion traveled twenty miles to the end of the line, got off, and marched the rest of the way to Romney. The rebels who had been there were gone. He burned some things and departed. But by that time, Johnston, concluding Wallace was the tip of McClellan's spear, acted quickly. He sent three regiments toward Romney to act as a shield and made preparations to move out of Harpers Ferry. On June 12 he ordered the sickest of his soldiers sent south to Winchester. He partially destroyed the bridges that crossed the Potomac near Harpers Ferry and burned as much of the Baltimore and Ohio Railroad equipment as he could. On the morning of June 15, his army started south.

(Johnston had not actually received permission from Richmond to abandon Harpers Ferry. But, although he did not realize it, official authorization had already been written in Richmond on June 13. When he read it, after already under way, he saw this snippy statement: "As you seem to desire ... that the responsibility of your retirement should be assumed here ... you will consider yourself authorized, whenever the position of the enemy shall convince you that he is about to turn your position." The tone of this "permission" hardly made him feel warm about headquarters in Richmond.)

His army moved unhurriedly, halting frequently, units bumping grumpily against each other. Each regiment carried far too much extra baggage, and heavily laden wagons waddled down the rocky pike like hippos seeking a water hole. Hundreds upon hundreds of slaves, personal servants, accompanied this army, many carrying the accoutrements of their masters who found the march too taxing. Johnston's army traveled only eight miles that day and arrived at their first encampment footsore. Then, late that night Johnston heard that Patterson was approaching. The next morning he turned his army around and advanced to a spot called Bunker Hill, and waited. (He probably did not recall that this day, June 17, was the eighty-fifth anniversary of that famous Revolutionary battle with the same name.) In taking this action, Johnston proved it had not been battle he had hoped to avoid, but being trapped at Harpers Ferry. He waited in vain; Patterson did not show up.

Patterson's Headquarters

The situation on the Union side of the Potomac had become frazzled. Patterson's army had started crossing the Potomac on June 15, the very day Johnston was withdrawing from Harpers Ferry. The river was not easily fordable, and Patterson's staff thought it would probably take two days to get their large force, with all the equipment, across. Most of Patterson's volunteers still felt enthusiasm. Few had ever laid eyes on any army as vast and impressive as they were that sunny day. The sight of their own apparent military brawn filled them with confidence. Certainly victory *must* soon be theirs. This war would be over soon — once they got their hands on the rebels. They laughed and sang. As they stepped upon Virginia's "sacred soil," they cheered, and their voices seemed to rattle the quiet leaves around them.

Then Patterson received another dispatch from Scott, telling him that Johnston's army had just left Harpers Ferry. Was Patterson, the message asked, determined to pursue it? If not — and the note indicated that Scott was opposed to any such action — Washington wanted Patterson to send, *immediately*, his best troops to the capital, especially the battalion of regulars he had with him. Patterson, of course, had no capability of pursuing Johnston. If nothing else, he lacked sufficient cavalry. Nor did he have a well-guarded supply line, and he would soon run out of provisions. He wired Scott back, asking to keep the professional troops for a while, just until he solidified his base at Harpers Ferry. Within minutes, Scott's headquarters wired back: The general in chief wanted those reinforcements *at once*. The next day, even after Patterson — always the efficient paper shuffler — had already started forwarding the designated troops to Washington, he received a third telegram: "We are pressed here. Send the troops I have twice called for, without delay." (These three notes, arriving closely one after the other, ought to be compared to the complete absence of any advice or information from Scott during several crucial days a month later, when Washington kept Patterson in the dark about significant changes occurring near him that he would be blamed for not reacting to.)

The tone of Scott's three messages of June 16–17 was shrill. What was the old general afraid of? The second note had stated somewhat mysteriously, "The enemy is concentrating about Arlington and Alexandria, and this is the line to be looked to." A diarist, George Templeton Strong, who maintained friendly sources in high places, jotted into his journal on June 13: "Washington reported in great agitation about a threatened advance of Beauregard with 60,000 men." The Federal army's intelligence failure, implied by these telegrams, boggles the mind. Beauregard had few troops in all of Fairfax County, the region that divided his Confederate base at Manassas Junction from the Arlington-Alexandria line. Nor had Beauregard sent any troops forward during that week. In fact, Scott's own army was slowly expanding outward from its position in Arlington-Alexandria. Whatever it was that spooked Scott remains unknown.

Having sent Washington the men that Scott had demanded, Patterson was left completely without artillery and had but a single troop of cavalry (who had only been in uniform a month and could hardly be expected to stand up to Jeb Stuart's regiment). Patterson still had his three-month volunteers, but he wisely chose not to hazard them in a battle without proper support. Besides, he was under direct orders from Scott to avoid any battle he might lose. So he ordered those soldiers who had already crossed the Potomac to come back. They were stunned by their turnabout and cursed him. Their mood blackened. Later, Patterson admitted that he was "mortified and humiliated" at what he was forced to do that day.

Patterson recognized that his men's morale was declining. To revivify it, on June 20 he proposed to Scott that he be permitted to recross the Potomac and set up his base at Leesburg, next to the river, about halfway between Arlington and Harpers Ferry. From there he could move in either direction, as needed. Absolutely not, replied Scott; Patterson's assignment was to remain in front of Johnston in a defensive posture. (This is startling, because it suggests that Scott believed Joe Johnston might advance into Maryland.) Scott did propose that Patterson could go ahead and cross the river again, but simply to attack Johnston, not to set up a base. Also, he must attack only if convinced his force was at least equal in strength to Johnston's, preferably superior. At that moment, as Scott had to have been aware from information Patterson had been sending him, Patterson's own local intelligence had determined that the rebels in the Valley had a far larger army. And that Joe Johnston had four batteries of artillery while Patterson had only one (whose guns could not even be moved because its horses had no harnesses). Even after receiving proper harnesses, it would take time to accustom the skittish horses to the unnerving sounds and confusion of artillery in motion. Despite knowing all this, Scott wired Patterson two days later, in obvious disappointment: "I had expected your crossing the river today."

Patterson became frantic to move — to satisfy his old friend in Washington who was obviously in a snit, and to give his own soldiers some encouraging motion. Their unhappiness was becoming obvious.

At last the harnesses arrived. Although he still felt at a distinct disadvantage, Patterson started.[34] The vanguard of his army reached the Potomac early on July 2. The river was shallow enough here that the men could strip off their pants and wade across. For the second time in a little over two weeks, they arrived in Virginia. They were not as lighthearted on this occasion, but most felt buoyed by the sheer fact of movement.

Patterson's army had 14,000 men, and it stretched out like a fat snake along miles of road. At the front marched men of the Eleventh Pennsylvania. Some Confederates, left near the river as scouts, saw them coming, took a few scattered shots, and quickly departed. The Pennsylvanians kept moving. Just behind them tramped the First Wisconsin.

Jackson's Position

Johnston, of course, was well aware that Patterson was on his way but was not sure from which direction, or when. He divided his army a bit, so as to cover various routes. He assigned Jackson to watch one of them.

Jackson had four regiments, a battery of guns, and Stuart's cavalry to act as pickets. Jackson's assignment was to avoid a full-fledged battle with any sizeable Union force that approached him but to observe it and feel the enemy out, at least well enough to determine whether this was really the front of Patterson's army or a feint. At 7:30 that morning one of Stuart's troopers rode to Jackson's headquarters; Yankees were approaching, exactly how many was still uncertain. Jackson led part of one of his regiments ahead, along with Stuart's cavalrymen and a single cannon. In all, Jackson had with him that morning only about 400 men. They arrived at a farm, its lush wheat fields stretching out from the main house. Beyond it, in a valley, was a small church, called by local people Falling Waters. Jackson's gunners placed their single smoothbore to cover the road. His infantrymen sat and waited.

Then, after all their weeks of tiresome drilling, all their campfire talk about battles and heroism and the like, the Confederates saw their foes emerging from some trees about a mile away. Almost none of Jackson's men had ever been in a battle, and actually catching sight of Yankee soldiers seemed a treat, as exciting as a county fair. One recalled: "So little did our men realize that we were going into battle, that they broke ranks and climbed upon fences, that they might obtain a better view. On they came in battle array, the first army we had ever beheld; and a grand sight it was—infantry, artillery, and mounted men; their arms and accoutrements glittering in the sunlight, their colors unfurled to the breeze, their bands playing and drums beating, the officers shouting the commands." But reality was less entrancing. "When the first shell exploded over us," he continued, "one of our company threw away his gun and fled down the pike at breakneck speed." Another fell down, apparently wounded, but helped to his feet, had enough strength left that he, too, was able to race off "with lightning-like rapidity."

Officially, this action—"Falling Waters"—was one of the first battles of the Civil War. The firing on this July morning was vigorous, and quite inaccurate. Jackson's cannon fired only eight shots, mostly high. But men on both sides were killed and wounded, and some prisoners taken. After an hour or two, Jackson had seen enough and withdrew. In light of what was going to come, the most telling incident during the skirmish involved Jackson himself. He had stopped beneath a tree and was calmly watching the action. A Federal cannonball, shot in his direction, smashed into the branches above him, one of which crashed to the ground. Some of his men, seeing this, noted that Jackson did not jump at all. He seemed serenely calm.[35]

Once the rebels had departed, the Union soldiers, entering the spot where Jackson's men had stood, felt they had won a fine victory. They celebrated briefly, then moved ahead a bit, and halted. The day was hot; they had not yet eaten; they were hungry and tired, and rather exultant. Their good cheer spread backward to the rest of Patterson's army, far behind. This was going to be a lark, after all.

By itself, the Battle of Falling Waters was of no military importance, but it did signify that, at last, Patterson and his army were ensconced inside Virginia. The question for them now was: What to do next?

The answer would obviously depend on directives they received from Washington. And in the capital, things had been heating up.

TO CARRY THE WAR INTO AFRICA

Public opinion in this country is everything.
—A. LINCOLN

The public, when aroused and excited by passions and prejudices, is little better than a wild beast.
—SENATOR WILLIAM PITT FESSENDEN

The *New York Tribune* did not have the nation's highest circulation, an honor held by the *New York Herald*. The *Tribune*, however, was America's most influential newspaper. Its readership not only included many Northern leaders, but Southern newspapers enjoyed reprinting its articles to demonstrate the outrageous attitudes of Yankees. "The *Tribune*," one historian has said, "was scarcely a newspaper in 1861; it was an article of faith." Horace Greeley was its publisher and most recognizable name, but lately he had retreated to his garden, allowing his managing editor, Charles A. Dana, to run things, a man whom Walt Whitman once described as a person of "excellent intentions." Dana loathed slavery and considered Southern leadership as, at the very least, culpable. In the spring of 1861, he hired Fitz Henry Warren to act as the *Tribune*'s Washington bureau chief. Warren, a horse-faced Republican from Iowa felt an even greater hatred of slavery. As for the war just beginning, he considered Lincoln's pace too cautious. Warren had a capacity for rage and a conviction that the enthusiasm of the volunteers was far more valuable than the vaunted "professionalism" of the Army's regulars. He considered Scott's planning — which looked toward action in the autumn — timid, and perhaps even treasonous.

When the Federal army crossed the Potomac on May 23–24, then stopped to dig entrenchments, Warren could not contain himself. He wrote an article asserting that "the people" wanted the army to keep moving; they wanted the soldiers to celebrate Fourth of July in Richmond. He wrote a headline for this piece, and Dana, in New York, mounted it in large bold type: TO RICHMOND! TO RICHMOND ONWARD!

Neither Lincoln not Scott heeded Warren's fevered words, and each passing day saw Warren become more outraged. On June 22 he wrote that the administration clearly had "no intention to press the suppression of the rebellion." The president, he said, secretly hoped for some sort of compromise. A few days later Warren penned an even stronger statement. Dana highlighted it, printed it — and reprinted it near the masthead each day for the following week. It looked like this:

THE NATION'S WAR-CRY.

Forward to Richmond! Forward to Richmond!

The Rebel Congress must not be allowed to meet

There on the 20th of July! BY THAT DATE THE

PLACE MUST BE HELD BY THE NATIONAL ARMY!

Some other Northern newspapers picked up the drumbeat and shouted this same yawp to their readers. (Southern papers also printed it, while hammering at its Yankee rudeness with fine wrath.)

Lincoln's government tried to butter up Warren, with little effect. The newsman remained aloof. (Warren was a trifle unstable. Dana finally recognized this unfortunate attribute and quietly replaced him before the summer was over.)

After the Battle of Bull Run, when angry Northerners looked for scapegoats, they had many candidates. Curiously, few — either at that time, or since — blamed Lincoln for being overly aggressive. Poor General Patterson, as we have seen, was a favorite whipping boy, but Greeley and his *Tribune* ran a close second. For example, one history of this era blames "those who cried 'Forward to Richmond!'—an entreaty to which even Lincoln and Scott succumbed and which led to the sobering defeat at Bull Run." Some historians have suggested that the culprit was "the popular mood." According to this theory, President Lincoln was merely a small chip, pressed forward by the vast swell of national hysteria. Curiously, none of these analysts has ever bothered to prove any direct connection between the *Tribune*'s raucous headlines and Lincoln's decisions. Many years after the war, his secretaries, John G. Nicolay and John Hay, wrote a ten-volume biography of the martyred president. Their theory about his insistence that his armies move forward toward Manassas makes some sense: "Congress would soon meet in extraordinary session [July 4], and of that body the Administration would be compelled to ask men, money, confidence, and authority." Even this argument, however, is weakened since the authors offer no proof that such a political motive had motivated Lincoln.

Abraham Lincoln had shown himself as being quite willing to clear his own path, to calculate the best way to preserve the American Dream, which was, in his view, mankind's "last best hope" of democracy. He had enormous willpower—and he would prove this repeatedly over the next four years, when lesser men waffled. To blame the emotionally unstable Fitz Henry Warren or "public opinion" or even "the pressure of politicians" is to belittle the greatness of Lincoln, to save him the embarrassment of having made a common civilian's mistake. Furthermore, it can be argued that the Battle of Bull Run might have gone a different way had a bullet eliminated some crucial individual like Jackson or Beauregard. In that case Lincoln could have properly claimed credit for his courageous stance. The fact is it was he who demanded an aggressive military policy, and his will prevailed. He justified it to his generals on the grounds: "You are green, it is true; but they are green, also; you are all green alike." The line was classic Lincoln: pithy, homespun, seemingly incontrovertible. Unfortunately, it was also banal nonsense, and fatal for many soldiers. He was making a *military* judgment about the comparative quality of troops and of their officers, a subject about which he himself was far too "green." He failed to understand the different qualities required of an attacking army and an army that was defending itself. Also, though his "greenness" theory held a nugget of truth, he was overlooking a subtle psychological factor that derived from the length of service that soldiers had signed up for. For example, one of Joe Johnston's regiments, the Eighth Georgia, only arrived at Harpers Ferry on June 9 and therefore was far "greener" than Patterson's Pennsylvania volunteers who had been serving since mid-April. But the Georgia boys had volunteered for long terms of service to protect their "homes and hearths," while the Pennsylvanians were surly short timers.[36]

Inside Washington, the decision-making process leading to Bull Run actually evolved slowly. Throughout May and June, Winfield Scott was quite candid about his own so-called Anaconda Plan. In his mind the three-month volunteers, whose terms would expire in July, had only been useful to protect places like Washington during the early weeks of the war when the Confederates might have attacked. But to defeat the Confederacy, he believed, the Union would have to put together and train a huge and well-disciplined army. This would take time — many months. Sometime during the autumn, he thought, a large portion of this force could begin to move southward, using the Mississippi River to assist in the transfer of supplies. One advantage of going through that section of the South was that it was far less populated, permitting both sides, if all went well, to keep down the number of casualties — and therefore lessen the long-range hostility of Southerners when they were defeated. He often described his notions to reporters, using a pointer to indicate key spots on large maps.

Perhaps the old general was not merely enjoying the limelight and attention but was hoping, by this public relations activity, to head off a more aggressive approach by the administration. On one rainy night in late May, he tried this technique on three cabinet members: Secretary of War Simon Cameron, Secretary of State William Seward, and, especially, Secretary of the Treasury Salmon Chase of Ohio, who had been virtually panting for weeks to have the Union army move on Manassas Junction, and perhaps beyond. Salmon Chase was a firm believer in the benefits of Action.

On this particular night General Scott asked other military experts to attend the session. Like an army tag team, the soldiers in the room tried to explain to the three politicians how difficult it was to move large armies, weighted down with heavy ordnance, across complicated terrain with bad roads and dubious bridges. Scott and the other officers also expressed their concerns about the three-month volunteers. These short timers, the soldiers believed, were too ill disciplined. Soldiers needed to be drilled and drilled, needed far more drilling than the three-month volunteers had had.

Scott's efforts to teach civilians—reporters, cabinet members, the President himself—about "sound military principles" were unavailing. Editors and politicians across the North, clerks and farmers, average folk of all sort, were desperate for the satisfaction of action. The Anaconda Plan required patience and smacked almost of a wistful fondness for the enemy. Lincoln and the more energetic members of his cabinet, like Salmon Chase, pressed Scott to develop another scheme, one that would utilize the regiments gathering in Washington—and soon. Chase's opinion was important because Lincoln—perhaps feeling that Secretary of War Simon Cameron was either overwhelmed by the demands of this wartime job or was simply out of his depth—began to lean heavily on Chase's judgments about military matters. (It was no accident that four men promoted to generalships that summer—George B. McClellan, William Tecumseh Sherman, Irvin McDowell, and Robert C. Schenck—all had close Ohio connections.) Secretary of State William Seward had previously worked closely with General Scott, but Seward now found this connection embarrassing and sought to distance himself. The President remained respectful toward his general in chief, but privately was wary of Scott, considering him too "political"—that is, Lincoln thought Scott overly sensitive to issues that did not fall strictly within his narrow purview of offering the administration military options.

On May 16, Secretary Chase received a sketchy written plan for an advance into Virginia, much more energetic than Scott's cautious suggestions. The author of the plan was a fairly young Ohio officer, stationed in Washington, with whom Chase had been conferring: Irvin McDowell.[37]

McDowell, forty-three, was a many-layered person. Physically he was rather unattractive. He looked ungainly, almost a cartoon of a huge Prussian artillery shell, with his short, stumpy legs, a great barrel body topped by a thick neck and a bullet-shaped head, his receding, close-clipped hair combed flat against his scalp. His cheeks were naturally florid, and jutting below his chin was a stub of a beard, flecked with gray. In manner, he tended to be modest, open-minded, and frank, but he lacked any sparkle of charisma. In conversation, he was never gruff or openly rude, but he had no gift for conviviality. Though quite bright, well-read, and occasionally capable of fluent conversation, he tended to be reserved. He had trouble remembering names or faces and often seemed absentminded, even vague, thinking about something else entirely. He was not a graceful fellow (and was known to fall asleep while riding and tumble to the ground), but he was filled with vitality and good health. Robust, he had virtually no vices. He did not drink intoxicants, coffee, or tea. He did not indulge in any form of tobacco and was not a spitter like so many of his generation. He did not swear, nor did he gamble or play cards. His only noticeable weakness was for food. He was a devout trencherman who took great pleasure in eating long and well. As a young man he had studied in France, and he could talk intelligently and passionately about continental cuisine. In fact, one officer who served under McDowell described him as "highly skilled in the preparation of recherché dishes as a Delmonico chef." (This trait may have helped make him acceptable to Scott, another noted gourmet, who was so entranced with the topic of food he could devote ten minutes to a lecture on why the practice of letting one's fork touch lettuce was culinarily gauche.) He loved music and fishing, and, despite his clumsy appearance, he was a superb dancer, "with sylph-like grace." He had a highly structured mind, so it is not surprising that among his interests were architecture and landscape gardening.

McDowell had graduated from West Point in 1838, where he had been a classmate of Beauregard. He had served creditably as a staff officer during the Mexican War and by chance was at the War Department early in 1861. During the crisis of that period, while many of his fellow officers there resigned and departed south, he served Scott energetically and capably. He was often the first professional soldier incoming volunteers met when they arrived in the capital. He would show them their assigned places and officially muster them into Federal service. Because he was at this critical spot, because of his relative youth and obvious intelligence and energy, he was inevitably a prime candidate for an important military slot. The only question remained, Which one? He was related by marriage to the governor of Ohio, William Dennison, who had considered asking him to take charge of that state's volunteers before eventually offering the position to the more magnetic George B. McClellan.

In early May Lincoln announced that, henceforth, volunteers would have to commit themselves to three-year hitches. He also said that the regular army would be expanded by over 22,000 men. This latter decision meant that a number of officers would be raised in rank. For example, using the usual military-manpower formula, Lincoln would soon be promoting three men to the rank of major general, just below Winfield Scott. Under the circumstances, the choice of these three individuals was almost certainly going to be more political than military. Chase wanted McDowell to be one of them, and Chase was in a position to guarantee it. Chase had discussed military strategy with McDowell several times and was impressed by McDowell's relatively aggressive attitudes that contrasted with Scott's more cautious approach. On May 14 the cabinet met to consider whom to designate as major generals. As soon as Salmon Chase learned this was on the agenda, he sent a message to McDowell. The meeting was under way by the time McDowell arrived, and he sent in his card to Chase, who came rushing downstairs to offer him the prestigious rank. McDowell modestly demurred and suggested three other names. He did, however, accept the lower rank of brigadier general.

After Scott's incursion of May 23–24 and the creation of the Department of Northern Virginia, Lincoln, his cabinet, and Scott discussed what the Federal army in that sector might do. Salmon Chase assumed that the movement across the river was simply the first step, to be shortly followed by more aggressive actions. McDowell would later say that the mid-May proposal he gave to

Secretary Chase, describing how the army in Washington could strike toward Manassas as part of a larger, more ambitious, plan to take Richmond, was quashed by Scott, whose thinking was that the army in the Washington area lacked enough wagons and artillery for a major offensive. The matter of Maryland's loyalty to the Union was still not entirely settled, and the old general's focus during the first half of June remained Harpers Ferry. He impatiently awaited Patterson's move toward that key spot and considered the army in Alexandria-Arlington only an *auxiliary to Patterson's attack*. It is also plausible that Scott was dragging his feet, hoping to satisfy politicians like Chase and Lincoln by focusing on rather small goals like Harpers Ferry, to stall any strong advance into Virginia as long as possible, keeping his Anaconda/Mississippi River Plan viable.

Whatever Scott intended to do with the army just across the Potomac, he still had to choose an acceptable commander to head the Department. He might have tapped one officer he had close at hand, Joseph K. F. Mansfield, who, like McDowell, had just been promoted to the rank of brigadier general and was in Washington and quite available. Although Mansfield had long white hair and the thin weathered face of a Yankee whaling captain, he was only fifty-seven — neither young nor old for antebellum high-ranking officers, and he was tough and independent and fierce. (He would be killed in battle a year later at Antietam.) Mansfield was less intelligent than McDowell but more self-confident. In fact, he would probably not have been a bad choice to lead the first great field army in this war. (Chase later said that Mansfield thought he ought to have been chosen over McDowell — and blamed Scott for not picking him.)

After a certain amount of ruminating, Winfield Scott named McDowell to take charge of the growing military force in Northern Virginia. Oddly, there is some evidence he was not happy with his own choice. In McDowell's later testimony to the Joint Committee, he would say, "General Scott was exceedingly displeased that I should go over there" — that is, to take command of the Department of Northern Virginia. McDowell claimed that someone — but who is unclear — had told Scott the old general *must* choose either Mansfield or McDowell for the position, and

Scott, for some reason, wanting Mansfield to remain in charge of the army in the District, was therefore *forced* to pick McDowell. As McDowell recalled that period, Scott remained curiously disgruntled, even sending an aide to urge McDowell to ask to be relieved of the assignment. McDowell told the aide he could not do as the general wished. As far as McDowell was concerned, his situation was delicate. He had been only a major a few weeks earlier. He had just been named a brigadier general and could not suddenly make demands of the cabinet or the president. Since the administration wanted him to take command of the army in Northern Virginia, he felt an obligation to do so. The aide took this reply back to the general in chief. Afterwards, as McDowell recalled: "The general was cool for a great while." This small incident is confusing. Since Scott had apparently been the one to pick McDowell, why would he then have been angry about it? Perhaps he felt that he had not really been given full latitude to make a real choice, that he had been squeezed into this position by someone in high position—Chase, most likely. And that the appointment of McDowell inevitably would lead to more aggressive movements in Northern Virginia, something he opposed.

Whatever the truth, Irvin McDowell was now stationed in Arlington, Virginia, in command of an inchoate "army." And back across the river in the District was a grouchy general in chief whose support McDowell desperately needed.[38]

In 1861 Arlington, Virginia, was not so much a town as a region dominated by several large, though decaying, plantations—one of which was the Custis place, where Robert E. and Mary Custis Lee had resided. Lee had departed in late April for Richmond; his wife had left a few weeks later, after a Washington informant told her about the planned military movement across the Potomac— that would be aimed directly at her house. The mansion now sat empty, except for a few slaves. A visitor at that time was unimpressed. "It's a queer place," he thought, "an odd mixture of magnificence and meanness, like the castle of some illustrious, shabby, half-insolvent old Irish family; for example, a grand costly portico with half-rotten wooden steps."

Out of a sense of propriety, McDowell never used the house as his residence. He wrote Mrs. Lee about his decision. "I assure you," he said, "it has been and will be my earnest endeavor to have all things so ordered that on your return you will find things as little disturbed as possible." He closed this note: "I trust, madam, you will not consider it an intrusion if I say I have the most sincere sympathy for your distress."[39]

To save Mrs. Lee "distress," he placed his official "headquarters" — four small, unimposing tents — in the yard, not far from the house's pillars. The tent he slept in contained a slender cot with a trunk at its foot. He had a tiny table for writing out his orders. Near it sat his little camp stool. That was all. This austerity reflected his modesty, and it also indicated that Scott intended to keep him on a tight leash.

Theoretically, McDowell might command a dozen infantry regiments, and eventually many more, but he found it hard to do much with them. He had almost no staff and had to spend hours each day painfully scrawling orders in longhand. In 1861 an infantry regiment was expected to come equipped with its own surgeons, its own commissary and quartermaster, and so on, but many volunteer regiments had arrived without such personnel or with individuals with insufficient training. McDowell also had no chief of artillery, no expert on military law, no signal specialist, no chief of intelligence. McDowell did have a few engineers, but their presence was due to Scott's desire to build fortifications that would protect Washington.

McDowell also had hardly any aides to carry orders to the regiments. The problem, however, was not how many aides he had but how knowledgeable they were about military matters. He later told the Joint Committee: Suppose he sent an aide to General Tyler, one of his divisional leaders, with orders to do something, and Tyler was uncertain what the message meant. "Does he want me to do this," Tyler might say, "or do that?" A proper aide would understand the nuances of the original order and be able to refine it on the spot, according to local conditions. McDowell's most critical deficiency was that he had no chief of staff, or even a second-in-command. He had to do far too much himself. One observer, after visiting him, noted, "I saw him do

things of details which in any, even half-way organized army, belong to the specialty of a chief of staff." When asked why that
was, McDowell informed him, "that General Scott allowed him
not to form a complete staff."

Under the weight of such handicaps, McDowell was often
discouraged. The newsman Henry Villard talked to him and
thought he "appeared to be full of misgivings from the start." His
army, McDowell told Villard, was not ready; it was "not sufficiently drilled and disciplined for an offensive campaign." An old
friend of McDowell's, after riding out one day for a visit, said:
"He walked with us through the camp. He said to me, 'This is not
an army. It will take a long time to make it an army.' He seemed
greatly depressed during our entire visit."[40]

McDowell's problems were about to become more complicated than just his skeleton staff. On June 3, Scott asked him
what he might require for a thrust toward Manassas. The next
day McDowell sent the general in chief a fairly detailed analysis.
At first, nothing came of this document, mainly because Scott
was only contemplating the move to assist Patterson's attack on
Harpers Ferry, and after Joe Johnston abandoned that town on
June 15, a move toward Manassas seemed unnecessary to Scott.
The administration, however, began pressuring for more action,
and Scott wrote notes to both McDowell and Patterson, asking
what they thought of a combined operation to push the small
rebel force out of Leesburg, halfway between their positions.
Both raised reasonable objections, and Scott dropped that idea.

Then, suddenly, Scott asked McDowell to consider a strong
assault—not a mere probe—against Beauregard at Manassas.
Three weeks had passed since Scott had first asked about the
possibility. In that period, as McDowell was well aware, his old
classmate Beauregard had received many reinforcements and had
used the time to dig extensive entrenchments and to place barriers
across some of the roads leading toward Manassas. McDowell
knew he would need a far larger force than the 13,000 men his
original proposal had suggested. He more than doubled his first
estimate of his needs. Given the nature of the heavily forested terrain, he proposed to advance in three separate columns, each
large enough to defend itself if attacked. He suggested that an

additional ten thousand men be stationed behind him, as a reserve. He suspected, he said, that the enemy might meet him in battle well before he arrived at Manassas but that if it did not, he hoped, when he arrived in the vicinity of Manassas, to swing to his left, to get along Beauregard's flank, rather than try a frontal assault against the Confederate batteries entrenched near the railroad station. Speed would be important, he knew, because Beauregard would certainly be fully aware he was coming. McDowell's plan specified the roads he would use and the villages his army would move through. He knew, he said, that when the battle came, its consequences would be "of the greatest importance to the country," with a major impact on morale — for both winners and losers — "the more so as the two sections will be fairly represented by regiments from almost every State." His new written plan concluded with the statement that he thought his army could move forcefully ahead "with every chance of success," but this phrasing did not resound with much confidence.

McDowell was concerned about the size of Beauregard's army, not just at this moment, as he was planning things, but on the day of the coming battle. He knew that most of his own regiments were "exceedingly raw, and the best of them, with few exceptions, not over-steady in line." He assumed the Confederate troops would be about the same, so the sizes of the two forces that met on the battlefield might make the difference. Beauregard, at Manassas, would enjoy the advantage of having two railroads that could carry troops to his position. One rail line came from farther south, and McDowell could do nothing about that one, and he assumed Beauregard would be receiving reinforcements from that direction almost daily. What most worried McDowell was Joe Johnston's army in the Valley. As he later told the Joint Committee, "I felt tender on the subject." But in June and July, Scott continued to reassure him, "If Johnston joins Beauregard he shall have Patterson on his heels." (Scott did not clarify why he thought Patterson — lacking wagons and far inside enemy territory, with an increasingly long supply line — could remain hard against Johnston's "heels.")

In late June Scott told the administration about McDowell's formal plan, and a meeting was arranged for June 29. Lincoln was there; so was his cabinet; so were Generals Scott, McDowell, and several other high-ranking officers. Scott opened the meeting by reiterating that he much preferred putting off a major attack till autumn (the Anaconda Plan). Having said that, he turned the floor over to McDowell, who explained his own scheme. Despite the importance of its implications, there was little discussion of the plan, no real attempt to parse it out, to analyze its strengths and weaknesses. After some desultory discussion about how McDowell's movement would relate to Patterson's actions in the Valley, the group agreed on McDowell's proposal. And General Scott graciously indicated he would do all he could to ensure its success.[41]

Several weeks later, in the hours just after the Battle of Bull Run, Winfield Scott, in the presence of several others, including three congressmen, began to wail to Lincoln that as general in chief, the disaster had all been *his* fault, that he ought to have remained firm against the clamor for action. He had been, he announced, the "greatest coward in America," and Lincoln ought to fire him immediately. "As God is my judge," he said, "after my superiors had determined to fight it, I did all in my power to make the army efficient. I deserve removal because I did not stand up, when my army was not in a condition for fighting, and resist it to the last." Lincoln chose to pass on Scott's overwrought suggestion that he ought to be fired, realizing that to dismiss the old general under these circumstances would be admitting his own culpability. But Lincoln did not like the general's implication. "Your conversation," he snapped, "seems to imply that I forced you to fight this battle"—which of course Lincoln had. Scott quickly backed off. "I have never," he said, "served a President who has been kinder to me." But it should be noted that Scott did not deny the inferences that the president's sharp lawyer's ears had caught.

Some days before the battle, Scott had spoken to a reporter who had told him, "The people are impatient for results." The general had replied, "Yes, sir, I know it, but they expect successful results." Then he had added, "War, sir, requires money, men, time, and *patience*."

Unfortunately, with the terms of the three-month volunteers due to end soon, with Congress set to reconvene on July 4, with pressure from important newspapers like the *Tribune*, with the glaring facts that the Confederate capital was now only 123 miles away and that the Confederacy was about to convene its own congress there on July 20, with Lincoln's notion about the equality of *greenness*, Scott could not stop the tide of impatience.[42]

Sonar

Manassas on the brain.
— Mary Chesnut

Both sides were edgy about spies. Mobs in the South had been lynching or terrorizing suspected Yankee sympathizers for months. Once the war began, people kept their eyes peeled for subversives — especially in northern Virginia. The *Richmond Dispatch* reported on May 25 that a man named Earnest Noke was jailed for being "a suspicious person," having been heard saying that Abraham Lincoln was "president of all the United States." Ira Richardson was jailed in Richmond because he was deemed "suspicious in looks and hailing from Washington, D.C., here without ostensible business." More often, such matters remained hidden from the public eye. At Manassas a young soldier on May 28 jotted in his journal: "A spy of the enemy shot; two more taken prisoners." Two days later he wrote: "A spy shot by the S. C. Regiment 7 or 8 miles below here, having platts of the encampment."

The Federals were almost as firm. In July a Union force of two dozen men — sailors and marines — accompanied by a small howitzer, steamed down the Potomac, searching for an ex-clerk of the Treasury Department, James Taliaferro, who had absconded with important documents. About midnight they stopped at Port Tobacco, on the Virginia side, went to a local inn, saw his name on the register, and arrested him. In his trunk were papers implicating him and others in Washington. While on this expedition they also noticed two houses, one on each side of the river, that aroused their suspicions. It turned out their owners, using lanterns at night and large shawls during the day, were signaling each other. When the coast seemed clear to the inhabitants of the two homes, the man on the Maryland side, a Mr. Watson, would use his boat to carry over messages and packets of Northern newspapers to a Mr. Grimes on the opposite bank. These two were nabbed, but many others in the region remained anxious to assist the Confederate cause. A number of them, as it turned out, became part of an intricate intelligence web run by a gentleman named Thomas Jordan.[43]

Beauregard's Headquarters, Manassas Junction

Many of Tom Jordan's contemporaries considered this Confederate officer unsettling. During the war he rose to the rank of brigadier general, serving almost entirely as a staff man. But something about him seemed *arachnid*. He was often described as a brilliant but bitter man with drinking problems. He was secretive and mysterious. A short biographical sketch of him, published in 1899, said he once married a woman named Kate Kearny but could provide no further personal data. It is known that after the war he was a major figure in a Cuban insurrection and that he coauthored a study of Confederate cavalryman Nathan Bedford Forrest. Beyond such meager details, the facts of his life remain murky. During and after the war it was whispered—probably inaccurately—that he was in some way connected to the New York City draft riots of 1863 and perhaps to a picaresque Confederate raid on northern Vermont.

In 1861 Tom Jordan was a dark and relatively handsome man of forty-one, born in Luray, Virginia, in the heart of the Valley. He had graduated from West Point in 1840 and served with minor distinction in the Mexican War. He was still in the army in early 1861, serving in Washington. He resigned his commission on May 21, but before leaving town he quietly contacted various individuals — housewives, physicians, government clerks, lawyers — all linked by a common thread, a strong emotional attachment to the South. He enlisted them in a complex web, connected to himself, designed to provide information for the Confederacy.

After the war Beauregard recalled the exploits of a pretty young brunette named Bettie Duvall. In 1861 Ms. Duvall was a courier for a spy network in Washington run by the redoubtable Washington hostess, Rose Greenhow. Mrs. Greenhow, an attractive dark-haired woman, was one of those individuals whom Jordan contacted before leaving town. He provided her with a cipher and a code name for himself, "Thomas J. Rayford." Mrs. Greenhow had many prominent acquaintances who dropped by her home on Sixteenth Street, including Senator Henry Wilson of Massachusetts, a prominent Republican and a man in a position to know things. When she heard something important, she forwarded it to Jordan, using couriers to carry the message past Union pickets.

Bettie Duvall was one of her couriers. In early July Mrs. Greenhow wrote this message in code: "McDowell has certainly been ordered to advance on the sixteenth. R.O.G." Mrs. Greenhow wrapped the note inside a scrap of black silk, and the younger woman placed the tiny package in the thick folds of her hair. Wearing a gray, inexpensive dress, of the style typically worn by farm women, she climbed aboard a rustic wagon and left Washington. She spent the night at the residence of a Confederate sympathizer, then changed into a riding habit and galloped to a Confederate encampment. When finally escorted into the headquarters of General Milledge Luke Bonham, a dozen miles from Manassas, she told him her purpose. Bonham recognized her from his days as a congressman in Washington. His account of the scene glows like a Harlequin romance: "She took out her tucking comb and let fall the longest and most beautiful roll of hair that I have ever seen on human head. Flushed with the morning's ride, with the glow of patriotic devotion beaming from her bright face, she looked to the Confederate general radiantly beautiful." She handed him Mrs. Greenhow's message, and Bonham forwarded it to Colonel Jordan at Manassas Junction.

The tale about Miss Bettie spread like wildflowers, entrancing listeners who embellished it. For example, on July 7 Mary

Chesnut wrote in her diary: "Women from Washington came riding into their camp—beautiful women. Where will they not go? They bring letters done up in their back hair—in their tournures &c&c." A soldier from South Carolina wrote his brother that a young lady, dressed as a milkmaid, had brought them intelligence that 37,000 Yankee soldiers were about to attack them. "She walked all the way & carried a milk bucket."

But the message Bettie Duvall brought was far too vague. All it said, after all, was that McDowell intended moving on July 16. Jordan needed more specificity. Five days after he received Duvall's note, an ex-clerk at the Treasury Department, George Donellan, handed him another message from Mrs. Greenhow: "McDowell, with 55,000 men, will advance this day from Arlington Heights and Alexandria on to Manassas via Fairfax Court House and on to Centreville." (A month after the battle, Rose Greenhow and other spies in Washington were arrested by Alan Pinkerton. Pinkerton's men found her cipher and a revealing diary—and sent her to jail.)

Years later, Beauregard would insist that Mrs. Greenhow's last message, the one that mistakenly claimed McDowell was coming with 55,000 troops—arriving at a time when other information could not get through—revealed McDowell's intentions. But was this the case? Or did Beauregard highlight the stories about Bettie Duvall and Rose Greenhow because they added a romantic touch to an otherwise drab military account, spicing up his dry prose with feminine derring-do?

Beauregard did wire Jefferson Davis at this time, "I have every reason to believe that the enemy will begin his advance from his present position, at or about Fall's Church, tomorrow or on the following day, with a force not short of 35,000 men, supported by a reserve of not less than 15,000 Infantry," but this information was noticeably different from Mrs. Greenhow's messages. General Pierre Gustave Toutant Beauregard knew, of course, that Irvin McDowell was coming. But when? With what force? From which direction? Rose Greenhow's notes did not provide the answers.

In fact both sides were receiving a torrent of stories from a wide range of sources, some accurate, most dubious. Sometimes the information—for example, the details about the exact size of an opposing force — was intentionally false, either invented by the information carrier or some other person farther back in the chain. The sources of information varied. Food peddlers, often women, wandered through military camps, selling fruit pies and such to hungry soldiers. Going from regiment to regiment, they observed much. Some seem to have used such opportunities to gather intelligence, then relay it to whichever side they felt a sense of loyalty, or to whoever paid them. Also, there was the wife of a Federal Post Office clerk who followed her husband to Richmond, carrying, sewn inside the folds of her dress, dispatches and maps. Reports surfaced that Winfield Scott chatted with "an Alabama negro," no doubt a runaway slave, who provided him with details about the Confederate force near Fairfax Court House — the number of men and cannon there — and that this information would turn out to be quite accurate. Prisoners captured by each side contributed to the pool of "intelligence" — like the Union private who claimed to have been attached to McDowell's adjutant general's office. Could any of such informants be trusted? How honest were they? How perceptive? Decisions about their reliability were made by men like Tom Jordan.

A different source of "intelligence" came through normal military reconnaissance missions, often performed by cavalry units. Jeb Stuart's men in the Valley provided outstanding service of this type. But not all cavalry troopers were good at that task. A Southern officer wrote his mother on July 6, "If you were to think a week you could hardly imagine anything more harmless and inefficient than a company of Virginia Cavalry acting as scouts." Any commander, preparing for battle, is inundated with a cacophony of rumors and advice. The ability "to hear" — that is, to detect and isolate — a single true *ping* while being washed with waves of noise is the essence of good military intelligence.[44]

It is impossible to know what Tom Jordan considered his most reliable source, but it seems unlikely he depended much on pie peddlers or Rose Greenhow. Coded messages in hair buns make for delicious melodrama, but he likely found Northern newspapers far better.

Shortly after Lincoln's June 29 meeting where McDowell's plan was discussed, someone in Washington — presumably the enterprising Fitz Henry Warren—sent the *New York Tribune* the details of it. On July 2, even the *Providence* (Rhode Island) *Daily Journal,* using a *Tribune* account, could analyze Washington's military intentions. The administration, the Providence newspaper said, would prefer initiating an attack immediately, but McDowell's army lacked enough wagons. Contractors, it added, were busy building these vehicles, so it could be expected that McDowell would launch his attack by July 15 or soon thereafter. (McDowell actually began moving his army on the sixteenth.) To be fair, the *Providence Daily Journal* also quoted other New York sources that did not agree with this conclusion, like the *New York Journal,* which thought the forward movement would begin immediately, and the *New York Times,* which specified the attack date would be July 4, and the *Journal of Commerce,* which was confident there would be *no* major military movements until the fall. Then, on July 5, one day after Congress opened its session, every major New York paper published quite accurate details about McDowell's plan, including who would lead each of his army's divisions, by what route that division would move, and how large the total army would be.

Such Northern journals found their way across the Potomac—often ending up on the desks of Southern editors. On July 3 the *Richmond Dispatch,* drawing from the *Tribune,* published the same news that the Providence paper had—that, because of the need of wagons, McDowell could not be expected to start before the fifteenth. Two days later, the *Dispatch* got more specific: Contractors were providing the Federal army with "eight hundred baggage wagons and three thousand horses. These teams will move forty regiments, or 35,000 men." Such remarkably accurate news snippets reached as far south as Charleston. There, the *Mercury* printed scads of military gossip from the North—much of it quite correct. The *Mercury* was positive that a battle was approaching, though it was not yet certain whether the main Federal thrust would be made by McDowell or Patterson, but it thought, presciently, by "perhaps both, simultaneously."

These newspapers did not depend solely on professional journalists. Before a volunteer regiment departed from its home area, literate members of it often agreed to write local editors newsworthy items. Also, families receiving messages from loved ones in uniform often turned them over to newspapers for inclusion. On July 10, for instance, the *Hartford Courant* printed a letter from Captain Joseph R. Hawley, who said his regiment, the First Connecticut, would lead the brigade when McDowell's army began to move. "We shall, I suppose, move in a northwesterly direction and a round-about to Vienna, and thence southerly toward Fairfax Court House. Whether we go directly thither, or avoid it and strike for Centreville, a few miles beyond, will depend upon circumstances." A few such letters would be far more valuable to Tom Jordan than Mrs. Greenhow's vague and overheated messages.

Winfield Scott recognized the dangers of a free press. He felt he had no power to order newsmen not to publish information, but he had an alternative. He could control what the telegraph office in Washington sent north. On July 8 he directed that, henceforth, no military data could be transmitted by wire without his prior approval. Unfortunately, he had left a loophole. The newspapers of the District itself could still print whatever they wanted, and their stories could be picked up by other papers — or by Tom Jordan. Correspondents representing powerful journals were outraged by the restriction, and their anger put enormous pressure on Scott. He met with them and explained his position, and asked them, on the grounds of patriotism, to restrict what they wrote. Most accepted his suggestion, if a bit grudgingly. After this, vital military information was still published, just slightly less reliably.[45]

Meanwhile, at Manassas Junction, General Beauregard, listening to the reports about Union planning, contemplated his own situation.

A generation later, a two-volume work was published, *The Military Operations of General Beauregard*. It listed its author as Alfred Roman. In fact, Roman did contribute to the work, but primarily as Beauregard's amanuensis, writing down what the general told him. Alfred Roman's name on the cover was simply a convenient gimmick, a disguise, that allowed Beauregard to say many complimentary, even gushy, things about himself. Given its real source, *Military Operations* offers us a fascinating window into Beauregard's thinking—especially when combined with a treatise he wrote a few years later, "Art of War."

As a boy, Beauregard had been fascinated with the battles of Napoleon and read about them avidly. In part, it was this reading that had led him to West Point. In that era the best-known synthesizer of Napoleonic tactics was Antoine Henri Jomini. Anyone reading Jomini learned that the great secret of battlefield success was *mass*—the commander's ability to focus more manpower and firepower at a single point than the enemy. Beauregard opened his "Art of War" with this Jomini-like statement:

> The whole science of war may be briefly defined as the art of placing in the right position, at the right time, a mass of troops greater than your enemy can there oppose to you.

Further down, Beauregard's "Maxim 23" emphatically stated: *"Never attack with a fraction of your force when a short delay will enable you to attack with masses."* There would be times, he said, when a commander would be tempted to disregard this advice, but he must *never* yield to the temptation. A commander, Beauregard said, should utilize what military men called *interior lines*—the shorter distances a defender often has, enabling him to move his men back and forth quickly within a compact area, while an attacker often finds himself stretched wide around a defender's position. Using interior lines could enable a smaller force to control the action, concentrating more power than his foe at the spot where actual fighting took place. (In a sense the concept of interior lines was valid for the entire Confederacy. Although the Union had a far greater population, and, inevitably, a far larger army, it had to spread its military power around the vast perimeter of the South. In turn, Confederate armies could swing here and there, massing together before a battle, doubling or tripling their local strength by moving quickly. This was why the Southern railroad system was critically important—and Beauregard knew it; in April he had found South Carolina's railroads useful for beefing up his attack on Fort Sumter.)[46]

From the time of Beauregard's arrival at Manassas, his troops liked him, appreciating his professional approach. His predecessor, General Bonham, had been rather casual about matters of discipline, but, as one young Virginian noted, when Beauregard took charge, "a decided change took place." The soldiers there now drilled often, and long.

During the day, their new general rode about, examining the terrain, checking out its defensibility. Bonham had already started building fortifications near the railroad depot, and Beauregard extended and improved them, using the labor of his troops and, eventually, thousands of slaves. The fortifications would prove useful, he thought, if a rather small Union force tried to take control of the station itself. But, Beauregard worried, if Winfield Scott launched a large army, one big enough to swing past the entrenchments and cut the rail lines behind them, the position might collapse all at once. The key to holding this place, as he correctly saw it, was the stream three miles from the station: Bull Run. He talked to locals about it. He learned that, although the Run was neither deep nor wide, its banks were precipitous along much of its length. He examined the fording places. He also looked at roads in the area. Most of the region's roads and paths eventually merged, like spokes on a wheel, at the hamlet of Centreville, several miles beyond Bull Run, six or seven miles from Manassas Junction. An army approaching from Washington would arrive first at Centreville. Inevitably, it would scout the surrounding area, looking for the best way to Manassas Junction. It would then cross Bull Run at one or more of the fords. But which?

Beauregard did not feel he had enough men to cover all the fording places simultaneously. He pleaded with Richmond for reinforcements, but until a sufficient number arrived, he concentrated most of his men behind two crossings, less than a mile apart, Mitchell's Ford and Blackburn's Ford. If a person coming from Centreville wanted to travel the shortest distance to Manassas Junction, depending on which path he took, he would cross Bull Run at one of those two fords.

The more Beauregard thought about it, the more his mind churned. He started contemplating an audacious offensive plan. On June 12 he wrote Jefferson Davis, offering "a diagram, with my views, relative to the operations of the present campaign in this State, which should be acted upon at once." This was his plan: In light of Robert Patterson's movement toward Harpers Ferry and the fact that Joe Johnston could not maintain his position there, Johnston ought to withdraw from the Valley entirely, leaving only a few men to plug up the passes eastward through the mountains. Johnston could "concentrate his forces with mine," and then, "by a bold and rapid movement forward, if the enemy be not too strongly posted [that is, entrenched], retake Arlington Heights and Alexandria." If Johnston could not reach Manassas in time, both Johnston and Beauregard could scuttle backward a bit, then, "acting on interior lines," they could destroy any advancing Union force, even one as large as 50,000 men. But, Beauregard's proposal asserted, the time had come to act quickly; otherwise he and Johnston, separated from each other, would be destroyed one at a time.

This scheme, based partly on his own realistic feelings about his insecure position, was wonderfully Napoleonic in scope, but it revealed some flaws in his thinking. Histories of great military captains like Napoleon, written on patient sheets of paper, speak glowingly about vast "sweeping" movements. They seldom mention mundane and boring details about the availability of wagons or about moving heavy siege weapons over rough roads—even assuming the armies had such heavy artillery, and Beauregard's did not. Not only did Beauregard ignore basic and significant details about logistics; he also completely ignored the enemy—the Union's intentions, its strengths, its weaknesses, and the possibility that Federal generals might refuse to follow Beauregard's assumptions about their behavior.

Davis replied immediately to Beauregard's proposal. He suggested, tactfully, that perhaps the general had better intelligence than Richmond about Johnston's situation in the Valley. "I can only reply that the present position and unknown purpose of the enemy require that our plan have many alterations." In other words, the Confederacy would have to keep its options open. Besides, Davis went on, "It can hardly be necessary to remind you that we have not at this time the transportation which would enable us to move upon those lines."

Beauregard, apparently, made no immediate response to this. He did, however, begin to reorganize his army into brigades, six of them. He sent several of these brigades forward into positions in Fairfax County, then contemplated what his next step ought to be. In *Military Operations,* he would later insist that he wanted his army to be in place where it could "strike a blow upon the enemy." Yet his instructions to his forward commanders — "Special Order No. 100" — told them: If the enemy advanced, they were to retreat. He even provided them with the precise routes he wanted them to take, saying these paths would draw the enemy into a trap: his strong position behind Mitchell's Ford. He sent a copy of this order to Davis, along with his promise to "act with extreme caution" — since his army was the main force standing between Irvin McDowell and Richmond. He told Davis he hoped to induce McDowell to attack him at Mitchell's Ford but admitted he was worried the Northern army might try to maneuver around his left flank. (This worry was interesting since Beauregard placed most of his strength on his *right* side — which, coincidentally, was precisely the side where McDowell's original plan meant to attack.) Beauregard begged Davis, again, for more reinforcements.

A day or two passed. Beauregard had time to think more deeply about his notion of combining his army with Johnston's in a one-two punch against McDowell. On July 13 he wrote Joe Johnston directly: "I write in haste. What a pity we cannot carry into effect the following plan of operations." He proposed that they join their two armies and use them to eradicate all the threats to their positions. He calculated that "this campaign could be completed brilliantly in from fifteen to twenty-five days." He then added: "Oh, that we had but one good head to conduct all our operations!" He did not specify who should be that "one good head," but he would later say in *Military Operations,* "Who can forget that, at the period of which we write, the Confederate commander at Manassas [Beauregard] was looked up to as the first and, unquestionably, the most promising of our generals?" Obviously, even though Joe Johnston outranked him, Beauregard considered himself the only proper candidate to be the "one good head." There is no record that Johnston replied to Beauregard's proposal.

But Beauregard's audacity did not stop there. He sent an aide-de-camp, James Chesnut, to Richmond to speak directly to Davis and Lee. Chesnut — now best known as the husband of diarist Mary Chesnut — had been a United States senator from South Carolina when Jefferson Davis was a senator. The two men were good friends. In March, as the crisis over Fort Sumter loomed, after Davis sent Beauregard to Charleston, James Chesnut had become the Creole's most important aide. It had been Chesnut who led the last delegation to Fort Sumter to ask for its surrender, and when that demand was spurned, it was he — representing Beauregard — who ordered the harbor guns to open fire. In June Mary Chesnut wrote in her diary: "My husband's gone to join Beauregard. Somewhere beyond Richmond. I feel black-blue with melancholy." A few lines down, after receiving a letter from James sent from Beauregard's headquarters, she wrote: "Tried to rise above the agonies of everyday life — read Emerson. Too restless — Manassas on the brain."

She also noted, after reading one of James's letters: "I discover that our generals have not a very high opinion of the efficiency of the administration — especially the War Department." Clearly, her husband's letter had revealed Beauregard's growing impatience with Davis — whom Beauregard was beginning to call a "stupid fool." Jefferson Davis, on his part, was becoming annoyed at Beauregard's hauteur. Soon after writing about her loneliness, Mrs. Chesnut rushed to Richmond, hoping to spend time with her husband. There, one night at the Spotswood, she heard Davis say, "Whoever is too fine, that is, so fine that we do not know what to do with him — we send him to Beauregard's staff." Relations between Davis and Beauregard were growing strained; their growing mutual antipathy was bubbling to the surface.

Early on the morning of July 14, James Chesnut, carrying Beauregard's latest plan, boarded the train at Manassas Junction. He arrived that afternoon in Richmond and called on the president. Davis was feeling quite unwell, but saw him briefly, listened a few moments, then told him the matter was important enough that it should be considered also by Lee, as well as Samuel Cooper, the Confederate army's adjutant general. Davis proposed that the four of them meet later that evening.

When they convened that night, Chesnut explained Beauregard's idea. McDowell, Beauregard thought, would use most of his army to swing wide, bypassing the Confederate fortifications. But the threat could be met, Beauregard proposed, by having Johnston rush most of his "25,000-man" army to Beauregard's support. The two armies would attack McDowell from both sides. McDowell would be caught in the pincers, and crushed. Then Johnston could go back and destroy Patterson. After that, Johnston, further reinforced, could cross into Maryland and swoop down on Washington, while Beauregard hit the capital from the south. The whole concept sounded quite grand — rather like a sophomore course on military tactics. Davis, Lee, and Cooper heard Chesnut out, then Lee politely explained that the idea — although "brilliant and comprehensive" — had several problems. The biggest difficulty, Lee said, was that Johnston did not have 25,000 men — far from it. Also, McDowell's army was already too close to Beauregard's position; the Union commander would not permit all this sweeping about, from left to right and bottom to top. Lee mildly suggested that, if Beauregard felt too strongly pressed, he ought to pull back behind the Rappahannock River, which would serve as a far better defense line than Bull Run (a point that Lee himself would later convincingly prove). James Chesnut was quite impressed with the objections, particularly General Lee's thinking. Chesnut wired Tom Jordan, urging Jordan to tell Beauregard what Lee had said. For some inexplicable reason, Jordan did not do so.

Years after the Civil War, Beauregard was still angry about the rejection of the ambitious plan that Chesnut had taken to Richmond. In *Military Operations* Beauregard wrote: "How Mr. Davis, with all this before his mind, could have assumed the responsibility of declining so far-sighted and far-reaching a campaign as was proposed to him, is more than we can well explain," especially since it *guaranteed* "the taking of Washington." By failing to follow Beauregard's advice, Jefferson Davis had, and Beauregard italicized the phrase: *"lost the South her independence."*

(By the time these words were written, Robert E. Lee was dead and had reached the status of Southern sainthood, and it is amusing to note that Beauregard chose to ignore the serious reservations that Lee had had about the plan.)

Other than Beauregard's absurd notion that several Confederate armies could spin about like a team of synchronized swimmers, precisely coordinating their attacks, the chief problem with his plan was his complete misunderstanding of Joe Johnston's situation out in the Valley.[47]

SCAPEGOAT

General Patterson's Headquarters

Robert Patterson was at Martinsburg, Virginia, up the Potomac from Harpers Ferry and about ten miles in from the river. Johnston's army, about twenty miles south, near Winchester, had been receiving provisions from the generosity of local farmers, while the Union army had to procure all its food—and also its grain for horses—from across the Potomac. This meant that Patterson had a long, thin supply line, which had to be guarded, forcing him to string a significant portion of his force behind him. And every additional mile he moved meant his already tenuous supply line would have to be stretched farther. He did receive reinforcements, but this meant more mouths to feed, more men who needed ammunition. On July 17 his army, on paper, numbered 18,200. But numbers on paper do not fight. If one discounted the sick and those guarding the supply lines, he had only about 13,000. Far more serious, the status of his eighteen three-month Pennsylvania regiments—the vast majority of his men—was unraveling.

Their uniforms, previously sorry in appearance, had grown embarrassing. The men looked like depictions of George Washington's pathetic Valley Forge crew. Thousands were barefoot. Many had gaping holes at their knees, and the backs of their pants had worn through, revealing their bare buttocks or filthy underdrawers. Some of the Pennsylvania volunteers had arrived filled with pep, but each succeeding day of waiting eroded their morale. Patterson wrote Scott that almost none of his Pennsylvanians intended to stay past their expiration dates, which were rapidly approaching. Their terms would start ending on July 18, and he expected that almost all of them would choose to go home immediately. Also, he noted, the discipline of these short timers was declining. It would be risky to count on them. Putting them into a real battle seemed madness. On July 12 he flatly warned Washington that the three-month volunteers "cannot be employed for active service." Four days later, he repeated his concern. "I am confident that many will be inclined to lay down their arms the day their term expires. With such a feeling existing, any active operations towards Winchester cannot be thought of until they are replaced by three-years men."

Johnston's army was reportedly getting stronger every day. So far as Patterson could learn from his sources, Johnston commanded at least 15,000 to 18,000 infantrymen, a regiment or two of cavalry, and perhaps twenty-two cannon. If this information was accurate, Johnston's army was twice as strong as Patterson's. And the Confederates' strength, according to what Patterson heard, was growing every day. Since Scott had ordered him to avoid serious losses, how should he proceed?[48]

Six months later, Patterson testified to the Joint Committee. On the question of the enemy's numbers, he said, "Reliable information was received by me that General Johnston was so largely reinforced with men and guns as to render an assault upon his entrenchments utterly hopeless." He learned this, he said, from Union loyalists living in the region, from prisoners, from deserters, and from assorted others (including a runaway slave). All these sources, he said, agreed that Johnston had about 40,000 men and over sixty guns. These figures, Patterson admitted in his autobiography, were "doubtless exaggerated." But, although he and his staff understood the likelihood of this exaggeration, they also felt it unwise to discount all the estimates they were receiving simply because they were probably inflated. His chief aide, Colonel R. Butler Price, told the Committee the same thing. When asked where these reinforcements might have come from, Price answered, "Somewhere between Winchester and Manassas; it was not known where." Another witness, Colonel Charles P. Stone, testified that the estimates varied widely — from 15,000 to 30,000.

We know that, if one discounted the sick, Joe Johnston's army numbered hardly more than 10,000. How could this figure have become so inflated? Part of the answer was that, although Patterson and his staff did not realize it, many of Johnston's "reinforcements" — thousands of them — were local citizens who had just been rounded up and impressed into temporary duty. Most were, at best, reluctant soldiers.

During the past three months, many of Virginia's white males had not volunteered for military duty. Some did consent to join local *home guard* companies, most of which consisted of thirty or forty elderly fellows and young boys, generally armed only with "their own fowling pieces." In theory, if Union soldiers approached one of the rural counties in southern or central Virginia, these home guard units would act as guerrillas. Out in the Valley, where enthusiasm for secession remained fairly weak, Confederate supporters kept their eyes on locals who had not yet volunteered. It was true that some healthy males who had not joined the volunteer regiments secretly supported the Union, but many had a variety of personal reasons to resist enlisting in The Cause. Some were married men with many mouths at home to feed; others were farmers with crops that demanded watchful care. By June men of military age who had no intention of volunteering were slipping north, out of Virginia, secretly moving to avoid dragnets. In July, as a great battle obviously neared, it became harder to escape. On July 13 Governor Letcher issued a proclamation, demanding "compulsory service":

> Every man that can bear arms, must in turn give his willing assistance ... and will provide himself with any arms to be obtained, without regard to the description.

At first, this policy only involved men in the northeastern portion of Virginia, but three days later it was applied to most of the state. The proclamation did not specify how long these men would have to serve.

Posters, bearing Letcher's decree, were nailed up throughout northern Virginia. July 13 was a Saturday. Men in Greene County, a poor rural area not far from Charlottesville, were herded together and drilled a few hours; on the following day, just after church services, they were sent to Manassas. In Loudon County, all local white men, aged eighteen to forty-five, were told that they would have until Monday to get their affairs in order; then they, too, would be sent to Manassas.

In the Valley, thousands of such men were impressed into army units and sent to Winchester. Joe Johnston actually used few of these conscripts in any military capacity—if for no other reason than he lacked weapons to arm them. He put most to work, digging earthworks, chopping trees, and the like.

Not surprisingly, resistance to the dragnets was common. Men fled the state. But objections to Letcher's proclamation also came from surprising sources: business leaders and planters. On July 17 the *Richmond Dispatch*—a shrill secessionist newspaper representing the backbone of Richmond's elite—published an editorial. "The call for the body of the militia," it warned, "would strip the business of the city." As a result: "Nearly every storehouse would have to be closed. Every workshop would be locked up. Every mill would cease to grind. Every working machinist and every effective mechanic would be called away from his useful and necessary occupation." To make matters worse: "The Banks would be closed. The notes of the people due them would go unpaid and protested, and universal bankruptcy ensue." Civil disobedience might also ensue. "The hotels and restaurants would lose their supervisory [that is, their Caucasian] force, and strangers would starve, or have to rob or steal food." Even more ominously: "Almost every overseer would be taken from the custody of his charge; and negroes would run riot, and plantations would go to ruin." White women would almost certainly be raped by rampaging blacks. And: "The newspapers would lose all their operating force, and the people of the interior be left in total ignorance of what is going on, and become prey to every idle rumor that sweeps over the land."

Eventually, the *Dispatch* calmed down when it learned that only 10 percent of each county's white males would be required for military service.[49]

The addition of such impressed men into Confederate service made Joe Johnston's army seem to explode in size. General Patterson and his staff were also concerned about Johnston's access to the rail line stretching from Manassas Junction to the Valley. If Patterson's Union troops moved aggressively against the rebels at Winchester, Johnston could call on Beauregard for assistance, and perhaps receive 12,000 additional men within twenty-four hours. Patterson and his advisers even suspected that Johnston *hoped* to lure them into an attack. According to this scenario, as soon as Patterson's army advanced far enough, Johnston would embrace and hold them with his greater numbers. Stuart's cavalry would cut their supply line. Patterson would then be destroyed, and, using Beauregard's reinforcements, Johnston could rush through the open back door to Washington. (Interestingly, of course, this possibility fascinated Beauregard.)

Yet, amazingly, despite all these concerns, Patterson still wanted to be aggressive. On July 8, after the arrival of two regiments of reinforcements, he ordered an advance on Winchester, to begin the next day. But even as these orders were being disseminated, he learned that his new reinforcements were too exhausted from their recent trek to start immediately. So the move was postponed—at least temporarily. In Patterson's testimony to the Joint Committee, he said that the next morning—the ninth—he became aware that some of his most important officers felt a "strong and decided" opposition to his "plan of advancing upon Winchester." He told the Committee, "I was induced, before renewing the order, to call a council of all the division and brigade commanders, the engineer officers, and chiefs of the departments of supply." He described to this "council of war" the facts of their situation, so far as they were known, and asked their reaction. With the recent reinforcements, he said, plus two more regiments that were due to arrive in a few days, would not these additions permit their army to be more aggressive? Moreover, should they continue to use Martinsburg as their base, or ought they move to a place where they could feel more confident about their access to supplies from across the Potomac? Their assignment in this region, he reminded the members of the council, was complicated. Part of their duty was defensive—to protect Harpers Ferry, along with both the nearby Baltimore and Ohio Railroad and the canal that stretched toward Washington.

The council of war also had to parse the meaning of two messages Patterson had recently received from Washington. On July 4 he had written Scott that he intended to attack Johnston's position at Winchester as soon as he had enough provisions on hand. Once the rebels were pushed out of Winchester, he proposed to move twenty miles east of his present position, to Charlestown. This would tighten his supply line. It would also allow him to continue to engage Johnston directly or swing farther east if Washington wanted him to assist McDowell's move.

The following day General Scott sent Patterson a curious dispatch. It said that reinforcements were being sent him and suggested vaguely, based on no evidence, that some of the three-month soldiers might agree to stay on; then he added: "Having defeated the enemy, if you continue the pursuit without too much hazard, [you might] advance via Leesburg (or Strasburg) towards Alexandria." But Scott then emphasized: "Move with great caution." Two days after this odd note, Scott's office sent an advisory about the status of McDowell's move forward. Since McDowell was "waiting for horses, we cannot say on what day we shall be able to attack the enemy in the direction of [*sic*] Manassas Junction. We hope, however, to be ready before the end of this week." Since this message was sent on July 7, Patterson could assume that McDowell would begin his move sometime within a week—that is, by perhaps Friday, the twelfth, or as late as Monday, the fifteenth.

Given the somewhat uncertain timetable of McDowell's movement and Scott's contradictory advices of a week earlier, Patterson's council of war contemplated their role. To assist McDowell, they ought to jostle against Johnston, to pin him inside the Valley, thus preventing him from reinforcing Beauregard.

To use a military term, they could *demonstrate*. But how? They lacked enough cavalry to try a probe. They might use their artillery, but their intelligence (rather accurately) advised them Johnston's army possessed four times as many cannon. This seemed to leave only an infantry move of some sort. Such a move would be chancy, and they were under Scott's strict orders not to take chances, not to allow themselves to be drawn into a major battle. Their only choice seemed to involve prodding Johnston, then backing away. Such a demonstration would have to be made with pinpoint timing. It should be done *just* before McDowell reached Beauregard's position. This matter of timing was complicated because Patterson had no direct access to a telegraph line to Washington. The nearest telegraph facility was at Hagerstown, Maryland, forty-two miles north, across the Potomac — almost half a day's ride away. Every message he received or sent had to be hand-carried. As soon as McDowell started forward, his army would also drift out of direct contact with Washington, and its movements would therefore be even more difficult for Patterson to follow.

Another matter — one that Scott gave no apparent heed to — was that Patterson's position was north of Winchester. If Johnston started to retire backwards (that is, south), Patterson might follow him, but Johnston would have a head start. And Stuart's cavalry could blur any Confederate movements, giving Johnston even more time. Furthermore, there was that pesky Manassas Gap Railroad. If Johnston's men boarded a train and took it with them, there would be no way Patterson could catch up, moving on foot — at least for several days. Besides, every mile Patterson moved ahead from his present position was another mile down which overburdened wagons and tired horses would have to travel with supplies. If Joe Johnston left Winchester entirely and went to Manassas, traveling through gaps in the mountains, how could Patterson possibly carry enough provisions to chase him, following the same route?

Eleven officers, including four generals, attended the war council. These men had accrued years of military experience; ten had served in the Mexican War. Patterson opened the meeting by reviewing how their purposes had evolved — from protecting

Maryland, to taking Harpers Ferry, to demonstrating against Johnston in order to assist McDowell's move forward. He reminded them that it remained uncertain when McDowell would start to move.

The first two members of the council to address their situation were the quartermaster and the commissary officer. Their force, they pointed out, was short on wagons, but they could probably make do. But they lacked enough forage for the horses, and if they moved too far from their base, this would cause a problem. The provisions for the men were adequate, yet if they moved against Johnston at Winchester, they would have to rely on the dubious policy of "living off the land." Next, the council heard the engineers. Their army's present position at Martinsburg, they said, was weak, while Johnston's at Winchester was strong. They ought to move east to Charlestown, at the minimum, with a view eventually of going back toward Washington, where they could be of greater assistance to McDowell. The colonels and the generals listened to this recital and then responded, one by one. They unanimously agreed that an immediate advance against Johnston—which Patterson had proposed the day before—was a bad idea; instead, they ought to go to Charlestown.

Following the meeting, Patterson wrote Scott. He reiterated his supply problems that restricted his ability to maneuver his army. He asked Scott to allow him to take his force to Charlestown. From that place, he said, he could attack Johnston at Winchester just as easily, and could also—if necessary—move even farther east to Leesburg. He told Scott he knew that General Sandford was about to arrive with reinforcements—and, he said with relief, he had heard that Sandford would come with a message from Scott about *when* McDowell was going to move. As soon as he knew the date: "*I expect to advance and offer battle* [emphasis added]." But, Patterson added, he was concerned that Johnston was hoping to lure him into a trap. So: "If the enemy retires, [I] shall not pursue." He then pleaded, "I am very desirous to know when the General-in-Chief wishes me to approach Leesburg."

Patterson had just laid out his thinking. He would prefer to be thirty miles east of his position, at Leesburg, which would have placed him directly alongside McDowell's right flank when McDowell started. From that position he could still pull back to defend Harpers Ferry, if necessary, but he could also support an attack on Beauregard. In closing, Patterson offered a simple code that Scott could use to tell him precisely when McDowell was going to start: "Let me hear from you on ___."

Three days later Scott replied. "Go where you propose in your letter of the 9th [Charlestown]." Scott also said that, if Johnston moved toward Manassas, it would seem foolish to trail after him; a better plan would be to come straight east toward Alexandria. (This was a remarkable suggestion — vastly different from Patterson "following on Johnston's heels.") Scott added: "Let me hear from you on Tuesday" — thus indicating in Patterson's code that McDowell would start toward Manassas on Tuesday, July 16.

The next day Scott sent Patterson some clarification. If Patterson thought his force was not strong enough to defeat Johnston, it was important, Scott said, to try to keep Johnston within the Valley by making some "demonstrations." If these failed to work and Johnston started toward Manassas, Patterson might start east himself, going by way of "Leesburg, &c." (It ought to be remembered that Winfield Scott had promised McDowell at the June 29 meeting with Lincoln and the cabinet that Patterson would hold onto Johnston's belt. But it is obvious from these two messages that General Scott had come to recognize the possibility — perhaps the likelihood — that Patterson would be unable to keep the rebel army in the Valley and away from Manassas.)

Patterson immediately wired Scott back. He said that neither he nor his officers considered his army capable of performing a successful frontal assault, but they would make the "demonstration" Scott wanted — an action he specified he planned to take on the day that Scott had proposed: Tuesday, the sixteenth.

The following day Patterson sent Scott another dispatch, promising to move forward the very next day — the fifteenth — in preparation for the "demonstration." It remained possible, he said, that he would try an all-out attack on Johnston but was concerned he might have only enough strength to push Johnston backward — right toward Manassas Junction. So he would not attempt a real attack unless he was confident he could "rout" the Confederates in front of him. He also told Scott he intended to transfer his army to Charlestown right after the "demonstration." (Unlike Scott's muddled messages from this period, Patterson's were quite clear about his intentions.)

On July 15, and again the following day, Patterson's army—or at least a few hundred members of it—clashed briefly with small sections of Johnston's force (primarily, several squadrons of Jeb Stuart's troopers). These movements were not very dashing, but they could certainly be considered "demonstrations." Numerous men on both sides were killed and wounded. The movements might have been seen by the enemy as the precursors of a major assault. In fact, as Patterson's army remained nearly within sight of some of Johnston's barricades for two days, he asked Washington for advice. Since he had received no information about the progress of McDowell's movement, he wanted a suggestion about his next step. While awaiting a response, he contemplated a more aggressive assault on the Confederate lines and wrote out orders to do so. Then he spoke to several of his officers, including the tough "Pap" Thomas. They persuaded him *not* to attempt such a move.

On the other hand, Patterson expected Johnston—with his supposedly superior force—to unleash an all-out attack upon *him*. Meanwhile, Patterson was aware his army was running out of provisions. Time passed. He heard nothing from Washington. On July 17 he moved his troops to Charlestown, as he had told Washington he would do, an action which Scott had approved. He sent another telegram to Scott. What should he do now? Should he stay here at Charlestown, go back to Harpers Ferry to protect that crucial position, or move to Leesburg? He reminded Scott once again that he lacked confidence in his three-month men. He indicated he had not heard from the general in chief for several days—critical days, obviously—and wanted to know what his orders were.

Then, after several days of silence, on the evening of July 17, Scott wired him again. This message was strange, but no doubt Scott's headquarters had begun to collapse under a deluge of demands and enquiries. Observers who knew Winfield Scott described him at this time as "sickly" and "aged." The pains in the old general's lower legs were causing him discomfort, and he had to spend increasing hours lying on his couch. This same week Jefferson Davis was also semibedridden, with excruciating, throbbing headaches—and Davis was more than twenty years younger than Scott. It seems plausible that General Scott was exhausted, having put in sixteen- or eighteen-hour days, seven days a week, since the previous autumn. The message he sent this day to Patterson was querulous. Scott said he had not heard from the Pennsylvanian for *days*—which, if true, meant that Patterson's recent messages may have been mislaid amid the clutter of so many others. Scott snidely said he had only learned, "through Philadelphia papers," that Patterson had "advanced." (Scott had obviously not heard that Patterson had transferred his base to Charlestown.) Scott then wrote a sentence that would be quoted countless times, usually to lambaste Patterson for his "failure" to prevent Johnston's army from going to Manassas: *Do not let the enemy amuse and delay you with a small force in front whilst he reinforces the Junction with his main body* [emphasis added]." Many Civil War historians have misunderstood Scott's use of the term *amuse*. It sounds sardonic, as though Patterson were a small child. In fact, the word was a fairly common military term that meant "to deceive" or "to confuse." All armies attempt to "to amuse" their opponents about their strengths or intentions. Scott's advice was sound, but far too late. As almost an aside, Scott added that McDowell had only just now encountered the enemy, but he, Scott, expected Beauregard's position at Manassas "will probably be carried tomorrow." (Assuming this last piece of information turned out to be the case, Johnston would certainly have been unable to move his army in time to be of any assistance to Beauregard, so Patterson had apparently done his job. As we will see, Scott was wrong.)

Patterson received this telegram from Scott after midnight. He recognized the nastiness in its tone and responded immediately. Because the terms of the three-month men were ending, he said, his army was on the verge of falling apart. It would be "most hazardous" to try to assault Johnston's position, but he was willing to try. *"Shall I attack?"* (Interestingly, Scott never replied to this last question.) The next morning, early, Patterson told his officers he intended to order an assault on Joe Johnston, immediately. This time he would not be dissuaded. Scott's most recent dispatch had indicated that such an attack was no longer necessary to keep Johnston from reinforcing Beauregard. A battle was expected this very day at Manassas Junction, which was too far from Winchester for Johnston to get there quickly enough to affect the result. But apparently Patterson was feeling whipped into greater activity by the mere tone of Scott's message. When Patterson was advised that the three-month soldiers (representing eighteen of his twenty-six regiments) would not fight, he spent the entire day, standing before each of them, entreating them to stay the course. They refused. Some men shouted at him, "Shoes! Shoes! Pants! Pants!"

It was no use; they would not move. Robert Patterson eventually grew discouraged.

That day — July 18 — Scott sent another, even more scathing, dispatch. "I have certainly been expecting you to beat the enemy." This was a remarkable phrase: *Beat the enemy.* (A few days earlier he had merely asked for a "demonstration," a far different thing. If Patterson had in fact attacked Johnston's position at Winchester during the previous day or so, what would have been the likely result? Probably a disaster. The sullen Pennsylvanians who made up the heart of Patterson's army would have been thrust against a somewhat entrenched foe — and not just any foe, but one that would soon prove itself to possess the soul of a great army.) Scott's dispatch continued: Assuming Patterson had not DEFEATED Johnston, he, Scott, expected to discover that Patterson had at least "felt him strongly, or, at least, had occupied him by threats and demonstrations." Scott added: "You have been at least his equal, and, I suppose, superior, in numbers." Why Scott thought this is curious. Patterson was on the scene, and his intelligence — wrong, as it turned out — told him that Johnston's army was, at this moment, significantly larger than his, maybe even double its size, or greater. More important, Robert Patterson — correctly — believed that the *quality* of Joe Johnston's army was vastly superior to his, especially when one took into account the abysmal morale of the Pennsylvania regiments. Scott's next question must have been based on some intelligence his office had just received (which has never since come to light): "Has he [Johnston] not stolen a march and sent reinforcements toward Manassas Junction?" Scott then closed with a flurry of contradictory thoughts. "A week is enough to win victories" (whatever that was supposed to mean). "The time of volunteers counts from the day of muster into the service of the United States [not from when they left home, and therefore perhaps their terms are not quite over]. You must not retreat across the Potomac," an action Patterson had not suggested. "If necessary, when abandoned by the short-term volunteers, entrench somewhere and wait for reinforcements."

Patterson, receiving this snippy message from his old friend, felt pain. "The enemy has stolen no march on me," he immediately wrote back on July 18. (Depending on the exact time Patterson wrote this sentence, he was probably correct. The bulk of Johnston's army did not get under way until that afternoon. Without a strong cavalry arm, Patterson could not know of their departure, especially with Stuart's men acting as a wall.) Patterson told Scott that he had in fact made demonstrations and that these had been so significant that Johnston had just been reinforced (a statement which indicated that the recent movements inside Johnston's camps had probably confused Union reconnoiterers). "I have accomplished in this respect more than the General-in-Chief asked or could well have expected."

Had he?

After Scott's testy July 18 dispatch, the old general did not again contact the Pennsylvanian, even though he might have simply responded to Patterson's question, "*Shall I attack?*" with the reply, "*Yes! And immediately!*" (Amazingly, Patterson learned about McDowell's great battle at Bull Run only from newspaper accounts. Secretary of War Cameron actually wrote official orders relieving Patterson of his command on July 19, two days before the battle, though Patterson did not learn of this change for a while. By itself, Cameron's order was not precisely an insult. Patterson's command had been based on his leadership of the Pennsylvania regiments, and these were now disbanding.)

Patterson's military career now came to an end. Like his Pennsylvania volunteers, he had only accepted this assignment for three months. His command was given to someone else, and he returned to Philadelphia. Glancing through newspapers and speaking to friends, he immediately recognized he was being made a scapegoat for the events at Bull Run. He asked that a court-martial or other military tribunal review the evidence. His request was ignored. Late that year he was offered an opportunity to speak to Lincoln. At the White House Patterson read aloud to the president the relevant dispatches that have been laid out above, then asked Lincoln's opinion. The president said that he had never really blamed Patterson, adding a bit frostily, "I am satisfied with your conduct."

Several months later, General Scott, now himself retired from the service, was asked of his reaction to Patterson's recent lengthy testimony to the Joint Committee. By this time Scott no longer had any personal aides who might look through his old correspondence. His response, therefore, was brief. Its main point was this: "Although General Patterson was never specifically ordered to attack the enemy, he was certainly told, and expected, even if with inferior numbers, to hold the rebel army in his front and on the alert, and to prevent it from reinforcing Manassas Junction." This sentence sounds clear enough. Orders, Scott was suggesting, are not merely precise, legalistic terms; they can be nuanced things, thick with implications — and everyone with much military experience knows it. Here is the essence of Patterson's own defense: "Every dispatch I ever received impressed upon me, not the necessity of striking a blow, or making a bold dash upon the enemy, but the exercise of the greatest caution; to risk nothing, and never to give battle without a well-ascertained superiority. All [that is, Patterson's superiors in Washington] felt that the first blow should be a decisive one, and that any success by the rebels would prove, as it did, an encouragement to years of resistance."

During the next few years Patterson contacted many of the participants of the July 9 council of war at Martinsburg. In 1864 "Pap" Thomas, recognized as one of the Union army's best generals, agreed with Patterson that the three-month troops had become exceedingly troublesome. Had he been their commander in July 1861, he admitted, "I should not have been willing to risk them in a heavy battle." Furthermore: "I have always believed, and have frequently so expressed myself, that your management of the three months' campaign was able and judicious."

Major General W. H. Keim had also been at the Martinsburg meeting. He later told Patterson that he still agreed with the decisions made at their council of war: "I know that you had the advice and support of the regular army officers, as well as those of the volunteer service." Other officers wrote him supportive letters. For example, General George H. Gordon described Patterson's Valley troops thus: "Some regiments appeared more like mobs than soldiers." And, he added, about the council's joint decision to go to Charlestown, he clearly remembered that by July 17 they had *all* been convinced that McDowell had already fought and defeated the rebels near Manassas. When they discovered on July 18 (from Winfield Scott's angry telegram) that a major battle down there had not yet been fought, as Gordon clearly recalled the events of that moment, Patterson had tried desperately to persuade the Pennsylvania regiments to remain just a few days and fight, but those efforts had gone in vain.

One of the most fascinating analyses of the Valley campaign was Beauregard's. Patterson sent him a copy of his recollections. Beauregard wrote him back (in 1872), saying, "You have exculpated yourself from the unjust charges . . . You certainly kept Johnston's forces at Winchester long enough to have insured my defeat at Manassas, if I had been properly attacked on the 18th of July."

It would seem that the Joint Committee's harsh judgment of Patterson was unfair. The elderly Pennsylvanian had indeed acted cautiously, as he was under orders to do (and not because he was sixty-nine). It is true he might have been more aggressive. In hindsight, had he been so, Johnston would almost certainly have been unable to reach Manassas Junction in time to assist Beauregard. It is also likely that McDowell would therefore have defeated the Confederates at Bull Run, or at least have forced Beauregard to retreat south of the Rappahannock River. But it is not clear what would have happened to Patterson's disgruntled troops had they charged Johnston's force. The Federals might, of course, have become inspirited by a forward thrust and might have crushed Johnston's army that was, despite Patterson's faulty intelligence, somewhat weaker, at least on paper. On the other hand, a Union attack against Johnston's reasonably entrenched Confederates might have led to a terrible slaughter of Lincoln's volunteers, followed — as an unlikely prospect — by Johnston's victorious army crossing into Maryland, as Beauregard had suggested, and picking up steam and Maryland supporters as it moved toward Washington. Of course, such a series of alternative events would have been very implausible. Hindsight is not always as insightful as it seems.

The Joint Committee, dominated by grim-jawed Republicans, had a convenient scapegoat in Robert Patterson. He was out of the army by the time they began their hearings, and he was a Democrat. It appears as though the members of the Committee had their minds made up when they began their investigation. The real reasons for the Union failure, and the Confederate success, near Manassas Junction on July 21, 1861, as we shall see, are more complicated than the virtually nonexistent "timidity" of Robert Patterson.

BOOK TWO

BUMPING HEADS

We were all novices in the art of killing each other.
—JOHN N. OPIE[50]

JOSTLING TO THE STARTING LINE

While Irvin McDowell was briskly making final preparations for his move on Manassas Junction, some of his soldiers grew bored. As the heat of Virginia's summer rose and hours oozed by, as ennui replaced enthusiasm, as military routine ceased being new, volunteers grumbled. "Life is becoming flat, stale, and unprofitable," a young soldier from Rhode Island wrote home. "The heat of the weather and the languid spirits of the men have conspired to render our existence as monotonous, and devoid of true vitality, as though it were passing away upon the sands of the great Sahara." A member of the First Massachusetts thought his existence "much like a dog's life." Another volunteer wrote in his diary: "Our work is hard or else we have none at all. It is like being in a state prison, for we cannot leave the ground and have to do as the officers say and when they please." A young man from Connecticut told his sister, "I dont like soldiering very well, but I guess that I can stand it a little longer." As it was, he said, jobs in Connecticut would be hard to find just now. Besides: "I am a-going to stand by the flag like a man, and fight for it . . . I am as tuff as any ox and can eat anything that is placed before me." Then he admitted, "I have seen some very hard times since I left home. I am up about two nights in a week on guard and out cuz of Spies. I have not had my clothes of[f] a night since I left home."

At this stage of the war there seemed little genuine hatred — at least among the soldiers — on either side. Mostly, the volunteers saw their opponents as lambs led astray by politicians, not as evil foes. A Minnesota chaplain reminded his flock that, while their own government was a good one, they were going "to war with misguided brethren." A fellow in a New York regiment told a friend, "I confess the truth when I think calmly of the matter, it seems impossible for me to kill, or even wound anyone, even in self-defense. It seems to me I would rather die than do it. And this feeling is increased when I recollect that the men we are to slaughter are as innocent of any crime against us as men can be."[51]

McDowell's task was to turn men like these into an army that he would soon push westward. (Though this fact seems counterintuitive, Manassas Junction is almost directly west of Alexandria, not south. Before McDowell's regiments started, they were sprinkled over a large region. Once they finally set out toward the enemy, having come from their assorted camps, some would be marching southwest, some straight west, but for the sake of convenience, this narrative will use *west* to indicate Beauregard's relative position to Washington.)

Although, at the June 29 meeting, Winfield Scott had inexplicably assured Lincoln and his cabinet that McDowell would be ready to start in little more than a week, that day came and passed. Lincoln's young secretary, John Nicolay, would later claim that Scott embraced McDowell's plan "with hearty goodwill." McDowell was not so sure. He later told the Joint Committee, "I got everything with great difficulty." He suspected that General Mansfield, out of spite at not having been chosen to lead the expedition, was dragging his heels. McDowell officially complained about not being provided enough wagons — to which Mansfield replied, "I have no transportation." When McDowell turned to the army's quartermasters, they claimed they needed all their wagons at the moment but would be willing to loan him some, once he was ready to move, but not before. He did not receive most of his ambulances until July 13, and then not nearly enough.

His supply problems were really the predictable result of turning a small peacetime army into a huge battle force. But his chief problem was that his "army" was far from becoming an organic unit. He later admitted to the Committee that he grew exasperated because much of his force — which should have been working together to iron out rough spots — was still stationed inside the District and out of his control until just before he departed. In fact, some of its elements did not join him until he was already under way. "I had no opportunity to test my machinery," he told the Committee, "to move it around and see whether it would work smoothly or not." When he did put eight regiments through their paces — simply marching them together and reviewing them — General Scott, he said, criticized him for it, as if he were "trying to make some show." McDowell was painfully conscious that he had never led a large body of men. He was being ordered forward with raw troops — and, far worse, with raw officers. He should have had an opportunity to shake his army up by some mechanism, to find and eliminate the deadwood. Scott ought to have been encouraging him to do this, not rebuking him. Perhaps on that occasion McDowell either misunderstood the old general or Scott was feeling momentarily testy.[52]

Traditionally, an army's *infantry* divided its officers into several broad categories. There were *general officers*, who commanded groups at least as large as a *brigade* (a unit consisting of two or more *regiments*). *Field grade officers* were colonels and majors who led regiments, each consisting, in theory, of ten companies and auxiliaries like medical staff. (In 1861 many regiments did not have ten companies. Some were still only semiformed when they entered battle; others had purposely left behind one or more of their companies to perform alternate duties like guarding the regimental camp. One Confederate regiment at Bull Run, for instance, consisted of only three companies. The manuals would have called such an organization a *battalion* — which traditionally meant any fighting unit larger than a single company but smaller than a regiment — yet the after-battle reports almost always re-

ferred to these units as regiments, probably out of respect for
their commanders or the states that they represented.) Field
grade officers were permitted to ride horses so that they could
move quickly from one company to another and so that infantrymen could see them and their signals from some distance away.
Company grade officers were captains and lieutenants, men who
commanded a *company* of infantrymen — the captain, on foot, literally leading the company, assisted by his lieutenants, each lieutenant often heading a *platoon.* These officers remained on foot
because, during a battle, they were expected to move individual
soldiers from one spot to the other, often by physically tapping
them or shoving them into position. Officers did not carry rifles;
their weapons were supposed to consist only of sabers or hand-
guns. Rifles would encumber their critical role — which was to
lead and direct. In theory an infantry company consisted of over
ninety men — three officers, four sergeants, eight corporals, and
the rest privates.

In practice a military unit was almost always smaller than its
theoretical size. On any day some men were sick or missing or in
jail or on leave back home. A few would have other responsibilities: taking care of horses, performing sentry or picket duty, carrying messages. When in camp, a company in formation would
typically number no more than fifty or sixty men. Once a company started from camp, even this figure dropped — often precip-
itously. Stragglers dropped out — some for valid physical reasons
(blisters or cramps, for example), others because they were lazy
or became frightened. If they marched any distance, a unit's numbers inevitably and steadily declined. A company of eighty men
heading toward battle often arrived with half that many. Then, as
soon as shooting began, and men were hurt, their companions,
often relatives or good friends, would help them seek medical attention, several men often carrying a wounded soldier back to a
field hospital, reducing the size of the company by many more
than the actual casualties. Military manuals usually suggested
that band members could perform this service, but many regiments did not have bands.

It is impossible to know how many members of McDowell's
army reached the "battlefield" on the day of the battle of Bull

Run. On paper, McDowell that day had more than 30,000 men, but most estimates say that only 18,000 of these actually saw action. Perhaps 18,000 Union soldiers reached one or another of the various battle zones where bullets were flying, but not all of these soldiers were fighting men; some, for example, were medical specialists. And it is highly likely that only a fraction of those carrying guns actually fired them. Many men arrived on the battlefield, but, because of circumstances, acted essentially as bystanders; others, it is clear, may have fired their weapon once, generally wildly into the air, then avoided further participation. Some, of course, were on the scene but avoided doing anything that might be dangerous. It seems probable that only about 10,000 Union soldiers, perhaps as few as 7,000, participated *energetically* in the fighting. Realistically, on the Confederate side the actual participants numbered about the same.

As to the organization of his army, McDowell had been at his Arlington headquarters only a few days when he began *brigading* it — that is, he divided the regiments on his side of the Potomac into three brigades. According to military custom, the regiments in each brigade ought to have camped fairly close to each other, and the brigade commander ought to have been allotted a staff of aides-de-camp so he could communicate easily with his regimental leaders. (By tradition, brigade commanders held the rank of brigadier general, but McDowell was not permitted to make such promotions, and, on the day of the battle, ten of his eleven brigade commanders remained colonels.) Long before entering battle, a brigade leader ought to have maneuvered his command around, testing its organization. Among other benefits, his troops would come to recognize him physically. In turn, he would learn lessons about them — which officers, for example, were lazy or stupid, which could be counted on when times got tough. That was the theory, and it was valid, but in 1861 the practice was different.

Many of McDowell's regiments, like Patterson's, had volunteered for only three months, and the end of their terms was drawing close. Of the forty-three regiments that would eventually make up McDowell's army, almost a third were short timers. In general their mood was not as sullen as that of Patterson's flock, perhaps because they had been camped in the Washington area, under the watchful eyes of members of Congress who saw to the care of their military constituents. Despite their relatively upbeat mood, McDowell had to wonder whether soldiers whose terms were nearing a conclusion would be willing to fight or choose, like Patterson's Pennsylvanians, to go home. The term of the Fifth Massachusetts, for instance, would expire shortly. He visited their camp and asked them to stay on a bit longer; by doing so, he said, they could win everlasting glory. They agreed to remain.

He also had units that had just arrived in Washington and could hardly be expected to become, overnight, cogs of a well-organized machine. This was, for example, the case of the Twenty-seventh New York Infantry Regiment, formed in the Elmira region. The War Department had decided it would be better for them to remain at home, drilling, until called upon. During their first six weeks of training, the Twenty-seventh had neither uniforms nor guns. On July 10 they received orders to start for Washington. By that date, some new members of the regiment had yet to fire a gun or participate in even a single drill. But the Twenty-seventh was commanded by an efficient West Point graduate, Henry Warner Slocum, and he had them ready to move immediately. They arrived in Washington so quickly, in fact, the army was unprepared for them. All they found awaiting them at their campsite were two barrels of salt pork. Slocum, knowing they were due to leave for battle in a few days, then put them through some drills and had them do some minimal target practicing in a nearby lot. Yet, on the day they departed for Bull Run, it is likely some of his newest recruits were still unsure how to manipulate a ramrod.[53]

As McDowell was preparing to leave, he did some last-minute organizing. One of his divisions was led by Brigadier General Theodore Runyon, an ex-lawyer with a keen mind but little military experience. The core of Runyon's force consisted of four three-month regiments from New Jersey and assorted New York units, almost six thousand men. McDowell assigned the New Jersey man two tasks. Runyon was to keep his division in reserve, prepared to rush forward if called upon. Also, he should guard the railroads in his sector and improve the rail line from Alexandria toward Manassas Junction — so it could be used to transport supplies if McDowell was able to get his army past that station.

The rest of McDowell's plan was a refinement of his June 29 proposal to Lincoln and the cabinet. Since then, he had learned more about the confusing terrain between the Potomac and Manassas, and this knowledge reinforced his original idea about splitting his force into separate pieces, moving them toward Manassas Junction along relatively parallel roads. At the last moment — the day he departed, July 16 — he officially divided his army into four divisions (each a unit consisting of at least two brigades). His largest division — four brigades strong, almost 13,000 men on paper — would act as his right wing. It was comprised of fifteen infantry regiments, a squadron of cavalry, and a number of cannon. This single division was larger than the army Scott had used to take Mexico City and was at least as large as Joe Johnston's force in the Valley. Its commander was Daniel Tyler, sixty-two. McDowell's orders to Tyler were to try to sweep *around* the Confederate base at Fairfax Court House. If things went well, the division might capture some or all of the several thousand Confederates camped near that town. If this could be accomplished, Beauregard's remaining army would be much weaker, and the Confederates might simply withdraw from Manassas. If nothing else, Tyler's division would protect the right flank of the army as it moved, in case Johnston rushed down from the Valley to attack it.

Daniel Tyler, born in Connecticut, had attended West Point not long after that school was created. Following his graduation in 1819, he was recognized as one of the army's leading experts on artillery. He traveled to France to further his knowledge and spent a year there, studying French military techniques. His book on field artillery — really a translation of a French text — remained the army's manual for years. But his energy and ambitions made him find military routine frustrating and promotions glacially slow. He resigned in 1834 and became a highly successful businessman back home in Connecticut. When the war began, Governor William A. Buckingham persuaded him to take charge of the state's first regiment. He led it to Washington. When Connecticut sent additional regiments to the capital, he was put in charge of all of them.

Tyler was a striking individual, tall and erect, with strong, handsome features, receding gray hair, and a thick beard. His manner was clipped. He had been successful in everything he had put his hand to; he had strong opinions and felt no need to keep them to himself. He believed—firmly—in discipline. As a businessman, he had insisted on it from his employees; he now demanded it of his troops. From the beginning, he made sure they were well-equipped but drilled them hard. He had no patience with men who complained. At first, many of his troops were disgruntled, and some officers considered his manner too brusque, and they resigned. Then, after a month or so, opinion about Tyler began to change. A Hartford newspaper admitted he had been unpopular, but now claimed: "There was not a man in the 1st regiment who did not hold him in the highest estimation as a soldier and a leader, while many, both of officers and men, loved him as a father and friend." This article might have been a journalistic puff piece, but one enlisted man wrote home about Tyler at that time: "[He] is a blunt man, but what he says once, you never hear again. He takes great pride in us, and the men will follow him anywhere."

Tyler's brigade, one of McDowell's original three, moved its headquarters to Falls Church, deeper into the Virginia countryside than any other Union force, and there his troops, often brushing against Confederate pickets, were involved in a number of skirmishes. When Tyler was chosen to command McDowell's First Division, it was unclear who tapped him. Was it Lincoln, who may have wanted to show appreciation for Governor Buckingham's energetic support of the war effort? Was it Winfield Scott, who, though not a close friend of Tyler's, had known him for decades and recognized him as an intelligent and hard-working leader? Maybe McDowell picked him simply because he considered him the best man for the job—even though Tyler felt a barely concealed disdain for his far younger commander, whom he later called a mere courtier. The relationship between

Tyler and McDowell would remain strained, and this was potentially significant since Tyler commanded the army's largest division by far and was essentially second in command.[54]

Forming the opposite wing of McDowell's army and expected to move toward Manassas Junction along southern roads, was a division consisting of three brigades (a dozen regiments), led by Brigadier General Samuel Heintzelman. This division's position, marching along the southern roads, was important since McDowell planned to sweep eventually in that direction, skimming past Beauregard's southern flank and avoiding the entrenchments at Manassas Junction. Unlike Tyler, Heintzelman had remained a career soldier. He had graduated from West Point in 1826 and was now fifty-six years old. He appeared unprepossessingly scrawny and more than a bit scraggly and disheveled. But he was as tough as boot leather, grizzled, scowling, beady-eyed, with a vocabulary that could be, when he chose, remarkably colorful. When angry or contemptuous — and this was often — he expressed himself bluntly. "Grim old Heintzelman," as he had been called for years, tended to intimidate many of the young volunteers under his command. He did not care. He was a professional soldier and was suspicious of their amateurishness. He had fought bravely in Mexico, and he intended that his soldiers do their duty. His diary of this period is terse and military, but it shows him to have possessed a clear strategic sense of what the war would entail; he understood its likely nature far better than many others. His specific assignment from McDowell was to push his division south, along the Orange and Alexandria Railroad, heading toward Sangster's Station, the last small depot before the track crossed Bull Run, the next stop Manassas Junction.

McDowell's two other divisions, following each other more or less in a single line, would bring up the middle. One was commanded by Colonel David Hunter, fifty-eight. Although he had graduated from West Point and served on the frontier, he had never actually fought in a battle. Of average height, Hunter was thick-chested and sturdy. He was mildly vain about his appearance and had dyed his beard as well as the thinning hair on his scalp that he brushed forward. The main reason for his present position was support from the president. In 1860 Hunter, holding at the time the rank of major, had been one of the few relatively high-ranking army officers to openly favor Lincoln's election, and he did not hide this fact from the president-elect after November 1860. Early in 1861 he left his post at Leavenworth and traveled to Springfield, then accompanied Lincoln on the president-elect's extended trip toward Washington, using the proximity to lobby for promotion. After Fort Sumter and the crisis atmosphere in Washington, when it seemed like the capital might be invaded by rebel forces, Hunter was among those who protected the White House from possible attack, sleeping in the East Room for some days. How much all this led to his command of McDowell's Second Division is murky — but probably a lot. (It may also have helped Hunter's rapid rise that he frankly opposed slavery and was a teetotaler, two factors that would have appealed to Salmon Chase.)

The last division was commanded by a warhorse named Colonel Dixon S. Miles, fifty-seven. He was a bit boneheaded and he sometimes drank to excess, but he was a fighter. He had seen action in Mexico, in Florida, and on the frontier. McDowell placed him in charge of two brigades whose purpose was to serve as a mobile reserve. Once the army reached the battle zone, its role was to be determined by circumstances.[55]

It was not until the day his army actually started that McDowell gave his division leaders their assigned roles. He added some cautionary words to their orders. "The three following things," he said, "will not be pardonable in a commander: 1st. To come upon a battery or breastwork without knowledge of its position. 2d. To be surprised. 3d. To fall back." He explained that proper reconnaissance would eliminate the first two concerns. As to the third matter — retreating — he pointed out that each column had been made intentionally strong. If it was attacked, he expected a division — even a brigade — to stop and defend itself. He emphasized that he wanted his army to move as quickly as possible. He stressed the importance of keeping the men moving, not allowing them to straggle. The army would not be bringing tents — and the men would have to bivouac (which, in general, meant sleeping out in the open). Nor would the army waste wagon space on unnecessary extras, like personal trunks. Each division, he indicated, must include a sufficient corps of men assigned to be *pioneers* (men with tools, mostly axmen). He knew the Confederates had dropped trees here and there to create what were called *abatis* (wooded road blocks), and he expected the pioneers to work quickly to eliminate these barriers. He suspected that some soldiers, forced to march longer distances than they were used to, might try to climb onto the wagons or the ambulances, and he specifically said this must not be allowed unless a surgeon or high-ranking officer gave written permission. But having emphasized the importance of marching expeditiously, he also ordered his division commanders not "to be surprised"—especially by what the newspapers were repeatedly calling, in dread terms, *masked batteries.*

One of the standard manuals for army officers, the *Military Dictionary*, written before the war, defined a *masked battery* as two or more cannon that were "artificially concealed" until they opened fire on the enemy. Hiding artillery was no more treacherous than infantrymen firing from behind trees or walls. But in mid-June two incidents brought the phrase to public attention. Ben Butler, the Union general at Fort Monroe, ordered part of his force there to sweep away a Confederate post near a local church sometimes called Big Bethel. But his troops, following a series of blunders and uncoordinated attacks, were forced to retreat. Southern papers exulted; Northern papers expressed shock and outrage. A Southern woman wrote in her diary how gloriously happy she was, praising the "consummate skill" the Confederates had used with their "blind battery" (certainly a phrase she had just read). A Polish immigrant named Adam Gurowski, who had fought in Europe and was now living in the North, noted in his diary: "There is a new bugbear to frighten the soldiers; this bugbear is the masked batteries." He was sure the fault at Big Bethel had been the "inexperience of commanders," but, he said, the "stupid press resounds the absurdity" about hidden guns. "Now everybody begins to believe the whole of Virginia is covered with masked batteries."

Then, a week later, near the small town of Vienna in Virginia, a Confederate battalion of infantrymen, accompanied by two cannon, learned that some Union troops were approaching them by rail. The Confederates hid near the track, their two guns pointing down the line. When the train appeared, most of the Union soldiers were sitting or standing on flatcars. The two Confederate guns opened fire, killing and wounding a number of Federals.

More headlines, more hysteria, more talk of "masked batteries." Clearly, McDowell was referring to these in his advisory to his division commanders. By emphasizing this concern, he may have encouraged them to be too cautious—to move more slowly than they might otherwise have done—but there is concrete evidence that only one brigade commander, William B. Franklin, probably took McDowell's cautionary advice to heart. Franklin did admit to his wife that on the march he took "every precaution to guard against surprise, and went very slow all day."[56]

On the one hand, McDowell commanded by far the largest army in the history of the Western Hemisphere (assuming that the numbers mentioned in Aztec, Incan, and Mayan chronicles were absurdly inflated). But any reasonable assessment of McDowell's huge force would have seen potential problems. The British correspondent, William Howard Russell, after riding through the camps just before the army left, was caustic. He found the artillery "deficient...badly horsed, miserably equipped, and provided with the worst set of gunners which I ever beheld. They have no cavalry, only a few scarecrow-men, who would dissolve partnership with their steeds at the first serious combined movement." He considered most of the officers "unsoldierly-looking men." Furthermore, his inspection revealed a number of ominous signs. The camps were "dirty to excess"; many wagon drivers were civilians (which might cause trouble, he thought, since civilian teamsters were notorious for becoming easily unnerved); the soldiers' clothing was hardly "uniform" since the troops wore dozens of different outfits, and, en masse, they looked like a kaleidoscope. He felt that the mood of the three-month men was uncertain. "Perhaps worst of all, I doubt if any of these regiments have ever performed a brigade evolution together, or if any of the officers know what it is to deploy a brigade from column into line." Russell was correct on all counts — these were elements that might lead to disaster — but had he had a chance to observe Beauregard's army at that time, he would have seen the same problems.

In fact, the leaders of McDowell's army seemed solid enough, though their capacity to deal with the madness of a battlefield was yet unproven. Most of the soldiers appeared healthy and motivated. Few had ever been in battle, of course, but that was true of their enemies. The weapons they carried were a mixed bag — some modern, some not — but, generally, considering the flurry that had thrown them into this place, they were well-armed. And McDowell's men were not all amateur volunteers. In addition to the volunteer regiments, his army included almost two thousand professionals. These consisted of eight companies of infantrymen, several companies of cavalry, assorted batteries of artillery, and an unfortunate battalion of 350 marines (professionals in name only, almost all of whom had only been in service a few days).

A week before their departure, it became obvious to McDowell's soldiers that they would be leaving soon. On July 10, Private Philo Gallup, of the Second Michigan, wrote his sister: "We are a-gowing to verjinia to hav a little fight." On July 13 orders were read to the regiments at their evening parade to prepare their baggage for a march. They should carry a bedroll but would leave their knapsacks behind. All the cooks were told to prepare three days rations for each man. That evening, W. B. Reed, a member of the Second Wisconsin, wrote some friends. Although the rebels might run, he supposed they would fight. "If they make a determined stand at Manassas, where it is said they have extensive fortifications and a force of about eighty thousand men, the battle will necessarily be a bloody one. The result of this can hardly be questioned as we have a much superior force."

That same night, in a different brigade, a dark-eyed, handsome soldier from Smithfield, Rhode Island, wrote his wife. A graduate of Brown University and a lawyer in civilian life, Major Sullivan Ballou of the Second Rhode Island was thirty-two. Back home, he was highly respected. After having been elected to his state house, he had been chosen its speaker. What he now penned certainly ranks as one of history's most remarkable love letters.

"My very dear Sarah," he began:

The indications are very strong that we shall move in a few days—perhaps tomorrow. And, lest I should not be able to write you again, I feel impelled to write lines that may fall under your eye when I shall be no more.

Our movement may be one of a few days duration and full of pleasure—and it may be one of severe conflict and death to me. Not my will, but thine, O God, be done. If it is necessary that I should fall on the battlefield for my country, I am ready. I have no misgivings about, or lack of confidence in, the cause in which I am engaged, and my courage does not halt or falter. I know how strongly American Civilization now leans upon the triumph of the Government, and how great a debt we owe to those who went before us through the blood and suffering of the Revolution. And I am willing— perfectly willing—to lay down all my joys in this life, to help maintain this Government, and to pay that debt...

I cannot describe to you my feelings on this calm summer night, when two thousand men are sleeping around me, many of them enjoying the last, perhaps, before that of death—and I, suspicious that Death is creeping behind me with his fatal dart, am communing with God, my country, and thee...

Sarah, my love for you is deathless, it seems to bind me to you with mighty cables that nothing but Omnipotence could break; and yet my love of Country comes over me like a strong wind and bears me irresistibly on with all these chains to the battlefield.

The memories of the blissful moments I have spent with you come creeping over me, and I feel most gratified to God and to you that I have enjoyed them so long. And hard it is for me to give them up and burn to ashes the hopes of future years, when, God willing, we might still have lived and loved together and seen our sons grow up to honorable manhood around us. I have, I know, but few and small claims upon Divine Providence, but something whispers to me—perhaps it is the wafted prayer of my little Edgar — that I shall return to my loved ones unharmed. If I do not, my dear Sarah, never forget how much I love you, and when my last breath escapes me on the battlefield, it will whisper your name.

Forgive my many faults, and the many pains I have caused you. How thoughtless and foolish I have oftentimes been! How gladly would I wash out with my tears every little spot upon your happiness, and struggle with all the misfortune of this world, to shield you and my children from harm. But I cannot. I must watch you from the spirit land and hover near you, while you buffet the storms with your precious little freight, and wait with sad patience till we meet to part no more.

But, O Sarah! If the dead can come back to this earth and flit unseen around those they loved, I shall always be near you, in the garish day and in the darkest night — amidst your happiest scenes and gloomiest hours — always, always; and if there be a soft breeze upon your cheek, it shall be my breath; or the cool air fans your throbbing temple, it shall be my spirit passing by.

Sarah, do not mourn me dead; think I am gone and wait for thee, for we shall meet again . . .

Sullivan

A few days later, Major Ballou, a man obviously capable of writing magnificent and moving passages, would be killed, leading his men at Bull Run. The world — never knowing him — would be diminished by his loss.[57]

Each Journey Begins
with a Single Step

*I shall never forget the march ... 'Twas one hundred and sixty-seven
Saint Patrick's day picnics, minus the lemonade, all rolled into one.*
—Second Lieutenant Horatio Staples, Second Maine

*The march demonstrated little save the general laxity of discipline;
for all my personal efforts I could not prevent the men from straggling
for water, blackberries, or anything on the way they fancied.*
—William Tecumseh Sherman, brigade commander[58]

On July 15, when McDowell's regiments held their evening parades, they were told that Union forces had just won great victories not too far away, in the mountains of western Virginia. (On July 11 and July 13, George B. McClellan's soldiers had indeed won two rather significant battles.) The news seemed a good omen. After this announcement the troops were advised they themselves would be leaving the next afternoon.

At the camp of a Connecticut regiment, one man wrote home. "I hear the loud hurrahs of the various regiments around us, as they receive their orders. All," he said, "are eager for the fray." He admitted, however, that he had an odd feeling—"this weighing in the mind of the chances of life and death on the morrow." A New Hampshire officer, assigned to read aloud the official orders to his regiment, noticed the words included a reminder to the regimental surgeons to bring their amputating equipment. "I don't think I ever read any other sentence which made me feel so uncomfortable." The men of the Sixty-ninth New York were mostly Irish. After parade, many of them went to confession. Others drank whiskey that they had stashed. A soldier from Michigan wrote in his journal, as his regiment bustled all about him, that he could hear the hoofbeats of horses and the squeal of wagons. "This looks like war," he thought.[59]

McDowell's orders were to start moving in midafternoon, rather than earlier in the day. While this might seem curious, his plan was carefully crafted. He wanted his divisions to go only a few miles, to positions where his outer pickets had been stationed. The rebels might not notice their motion. His immediate goal was Fairfax Court House, where Bonham was camped with his five thousand troops. While part of McDowell's army could have reached that town easily in a day's march, a general attack on the rebel position could not have been properly coordinated. The elements making up McDowell's army were spread over almost fifty camps throughout northern Virginia and the District. Some regiments were already deep within Fairfax County; others were beginning their march twenty miles away.

By the morning of July 16, departure day, McDowell felt edgy. His army still did not have everything he felt it needed. Many of his eleven brigades were only units on paper, their assorted regiments having never even laid eyes on each other. So much still needed to be done that he himself did not intend to start off with his personal staff until after his army was well on the road.

About five o'clock that afternoon, several hours *after* the army was on the march, William Howard Russell, the British correspondent, was at the Washington train depot. He saw McDowell, pacing about the station. The general was vainly searching for two batteries of artillery he had thought were shortly to arrive. He admitted to Russell he was uneasy. He had received reports that Beauregard had moved his whole army to Fairfax Court House. Conceivably, there might be a great battle there the next morning—twelve hours from this moment. McDowell modestly—and, Russell assumed, jokingly—said he was not sure how good a general he would be.[60]

Yet, all things considered, the army's leadership performed well this first day. At some point that evening, each brigade reached its assigned position.

To newspaper readers the next day, the most notable brigade was probably the one commanded by Ambrose E. Burnside, because, when the march began, it was still encamped in different parts of the District, and dozens of reporters, staying in Washington, used its movement to represent the actions of the whole army. When Burnside's four regiments met together and formed a line on Pennsylvania Avenue in midafternoon, it was the first time his brigade had ever actually assembled. Onlookers thought Brigadier General Burnside looked splendid on his horse. An 1847 graduate of West Point, he had just turned thirty-seven. He was tall and handsome, sturdy and genial; men liked him. A decade earlier he had designed a new and excellent carbine rifle and had then resigned from the army to try his hand at manufacturing it. When that venture did not work out, he tried railroading. Because of his connections with Rhode Island, as soon as the war began, he was asked to command that state's first regiment leaving for Washington. During the following three months, he had performed with distinction every duty handed to him. Now, on this July day, as his brigade departed Washington for Virginia, the sun shone down on them; the sky was blue; the regimental bands played; citizens along both sides of the avenue clapped and cheered. Women and girls handed flowers to the fine-looking general as he passed, astride his dancing steed — and his arms grew so full he seemed a vast bouquet in motion. What a grand Army! What handsome warriors! What wonderful weapons! Of course we will be victorious! Hallelujah! Jubilation!

That night, when Burnside's brigade settled down near Annandale, the men lit fires to brew their coffee, and hundreds of small blazes lit the night. After a while, drums and fifes in one of the regiments tapped out tattoo, followed by others in echoing choruses. One volunteer would later recall his feelings on listening to those notes: "Now near, now distant, now full, and now subdued, we almost forgot we were soldiers, in our admiration of the music." Another wrote in his diary: "We lay for a long time gazing at the starry heavens before we slept."[61]

Not all members of McDowell's army, of course, found this day so romantic. Problems had developed. Although most sickly or obese soldiers had been left behind to watch the campsites, in-evitably some marchers faded quickly under the sun's rays. Their sweat, picking up red Virginia dust, formed ocher masks upon their cheeks and caked their necks. Their sodden, sweaty uni-forms chafed their armpits. The bedrolls, canteens, and assorted accoutrements weighed heavily on the weaker men. A few regi-ments had received new shoes just before their departure. Within an hour, soldiers were limping with blistered and inflamed feet. Marching is never easy for new recruits. At least one soldier — a private in the Second Connecticut — died.

The southern wing, led by Heintzelman, found the going par-ticularly hard. The region they marched through, southwest of Alexandria, was poor and mean, spotted with clumps of scrubby trees and fields overrun with sassafras and briars. The roads were bad — little wider than farm wagons, rutted and rocky. Few of these soldiers could really be termed "warriors." They were but travelers, tiredly staggering through a drab countryside, stumbling up steep hills, then stuttering back down into sharp ravines. The roads hereabout were crisscrossed by streams with-out bridges, and deep boggy patches that sucked at soldiers' legs. Most of the male population had disappeared, and gaunt women, surrounded by dirty and ashen children, stared vacantly at Heintzelman's infantrymen as they passed. A soldier from Min-nesota wrote home: "This is miserable country, thinly settled, the buildings poor and old, without paint, but some are whitewashed. The water is poor, the people poor and ignorant."

The rebels had burned many of the area's narrow bridges. The pioneers, with their axes and spades, led the way, repairing what they could. The going was slow and tedious. As the pioneers labored in the heat, volunteers, who had started out strong, grew tired and cranky, wondering aloud why they had to endure such endless standing around. It got worse after dark, as soldiers tripped on the stones and trod the heels of men in front of them. After a while most of the marchers stopped talking, lost in their own weariness and agony. By midnight, even the officers found it hard to shout, "Close it up!" to their men. The jingle of canteens and the creak of wagons were almost the only sounds. Some of

Heintzelman's regiments did not stop until after 3:30 in the morning. Years later, as men recalled this grim march, they often mentioned one particular moment. Following an inexplicably long delay, caused by some mysterious jam-up in the front, each marcher found himself arriving at a ravine about twenty feet across with a narrow stream running through it. A single hewn log crossed it. The delay had come because the troops had started crossing this log, one by one, each man following the path of the fellow in front. This had caused a ripple effect, a slowdown that had reached miles back to the very end. The image of thousands of marching men brought to a crawl by a single log is riveting, but while there must have been some truth to the yarn — since so many told of it — there remains a question that throws doubt on the tale: How did Heintzelman's cannon and his hundreds of wagons get across? Whatever the truth about that single log, it is certain that Heintzelman's division was passing through rough terrain. This was ominous because McDowell's plan depended on his whole army eventually moving into this region. It was beginning to seem that the landscape might not permit it.

Tyler's troops bivouacked on that first night near Vienna, bedded down only six miles from Bonham's headquarters. McDowell's two middle divisions — Hunter's and Miles's — were bivouacked near Annandale, about eight miles from Fairfax Court House. Miles's division had not had to go too far from their camps, and they settled down a mile in front of Hunter's, whose men had marched a greater distance. McDowell's plan was that in the morning Miles would move first and turn onto a left fork, which paralleled the turnpike that Hunter's division would use. With Miles moving from the south, Hunter in the middle, and Tyler coming from the north, they all could reach Fairfax Court House about the same time — almost 20,000 men against Bonham's 5,000. The plan was excellent. It might even work.

Before starting off this day, William Tecumseh Sherman, one of McDowell's brigade commanders, wrote his wife Ellen. They might have to fight tomorrow, he told her, somewhere near Fairfax Court House, but he thought it improbable. Most likely, he said, the battle would occur near Manassas Junction. If that happened: "We will have our hands full." As to the prospects: "I still regard this as but the beginning of a long war."[62]

The Confederate Position, near Fairfax Court House

The Confederates in Fairfax County had known for weeks that something was brewing. When the wind was right, they could easily hear the drums and bugles from the Union camps. Almost daily, the Confederates sent men to probe their enemy's intentions. Private Dick Simpson, a twenty-year-old from South Carolina, wrote his aunt that his regiment was camped only six miles from the Union lines, and almost every day he and his comrades were sent ahead two or three miles to scout out the roads. They would break into small groups that would separate, creep forward, and hide in the bushes. Union pickets, of course, would simultaneously be moving in their direction to spy, so staying extremely quiet was prudent. Simpson described how his company had recently gone out. They had stopped at their usual post; then, about two in the morning, they were ordered to sidle ahead another two miles. "We marched in perfect silence, and expecting to be fired into at every step." They reached a likely spot and halted. After daybreak a Confederate rider galloped up and told them some Yankees were nearby and persuaded Simpson and his comrades to join him in checking them out. They inched ahead. "I felt very funny creeping through the woods with my rifle ready to shoot — to shoot what? Why, my fellow men. But I believe I could do it with as much grace as I could eat an apple pie. All I wish is that the wars were over." They did catch sight of a group of enemy troops, then turned and ran, "laughing and talking all the way."

Probes like this — far more than reports from spies like Rose Greenhow — indicated that the game was almost afoot. On July 10 a New Orleans battalion that had brought along some *vivandières* (women camp followers who dressed in semimilitary outfits) sent them away. Two days later, the Sixth Alabama, camped at Fairfax Station, began hurriedly digging earthworks and sent their sick to a medical facility in Culpeper, about sixty miles west. On July 15, at dawn, the men of the Nineteenth Virginia were suddenly shunted about in great haste. Their officers lined them up and marched them out; then, for some reason, they marched them back to their camp, where they ordered them to take down their tents and pack. Teamsters prepared the wagons to scoot away. Then—nothing. After a while the men put their tents back up.

The following day—July 16—a Virginia soldier jotted into his diary: "Nothing new in camp today." But that evening, several miles away at Fairfax Court House, the high-ranking officers of Bonham's South Carolina brigade held a meeting. They reviewed the local topography—the hills, the ravines—to make sure there would be no mistakes. The brigade was to bring their baggage wagons inside the perimeter—ready, if need be, to haul away the tents. Late that night the wagons rattled into place, waking men who asked what all this meant. Told that these activities were just cautionary, most of them went back to sleep.[63]

Precautions were understandable—but, amazingly, the Confederates in Fairfax County still did not realize that McDowell and his 30,000-man army were already moving toward them. Pickets knew something was going on, but had not yet deduced that the entire Union army that they had been watching for weeks had finally risen to its feet and was approaching.

The two armies would begin to fight the next day.

There is a board game, *kriegspiel,* similar to the movements of Wednesday, July 17. In this game two players sit back-to-back, each with a chessboard. Each player has his own chessmen, and only his own, in front of him; he cannot see his opponent's pieces. When he makes any move, therefore, he is uncertain where danger lies. A third individual—the Judge—sits above the two players with his own chessboard, watching and duplicating the moves both sides take. Only the Judge sees the entire pattern. He announces when a move is "impossible" (that is, when an opponent's piece barricades the pathway of some proposed sweep by, say, a bishop or rook), but the Judge does not indicate whether the obstruction is relatively unimportant (a pawn) or critical (the king). The Judge also announces when a piece has been taken ("a man has been taken on queen's rook five"), but not the importance of the piece. The two players, hearing these words, try to interpret their meaning. They know there has been some sort of contact. Is their opponent organizing an all-out attack or a minor probe? The players, shuffling their men about, remain uncertain whether to become aggressive or act defensively. Players often grow nervous and overreact, moving their men into position to defend a space the other side has no intention of attacking.

McDowell and Beauregard seemed to be playing this game. Everyone knew a fight was coming, but where? McDowell's ultimate goal was to cut the rail lines coming into Manassas Junction, but to reach that spot he first had to move a sizeable portion of his army through Fairfax Court House. Would Bonham fight? Would Beauregard move more men up to assist him? Had Beauregard done so already? Would Joe Johnston escape from Patterson and come in this direction? McDowell felt he must move cautiously.

On his part, Beauregard had no intention of fighting at Fairfax Court House—though he did have regiments, other than Bonham's, in relatively nearby positions. He had ordered his brigade leaders to pull back as soon as they were *positive* McDowell was advancing on them in force. Beauregard's most northern troops, a small demibrigade commanded by Colonel Nathan George Evans, sensed the movement of the Union army early. Evans, isolated from the rest of Beauregard's army, immediately marched his men toward Manassas. (On the night of the seventeenth, he crossed Bull Run and placed his force near a stone bridge—the main bridge over the stream and a local landmark.) Colonel Philip St. George Cocke had two regiments camped not far from Fairfax Court House. These started packing very early Wednesday morning, between two and three o'clock. By daybreak they were taking down their tents and were ready to move. As soon as they heard some gunfire in the distance, they started back—quickly. Bonham did not act so expeditiously; he was almost trapped.

Months later, when McDowell testified to the Joint Committee, he spoke about that morning. He said that Bonham would have been captured had Tyler moved faster or sooner, though McDowell had to admit, "None of us got forward in time." Part of the fault, he said, derived from undue cautiousness (what, today, might be termed "masked battery syndrome"). But, he added, the problem involved more than that:

> The men were not used to marching; they stopped every moment to pick blackberries or to get water. They would not keep in the ranks, order as much as you pleased. When they came where water was fresh they would pour the old water out of their canteens and fill them with fresh water; they were not used to denying themselves much. They were not used to journeys on foot.

His chief medical officer, William Shakespeare King, was less critical. "The day was unusually hot," said his report, "and the troops plucked with avidity the blackberries growing abundantly by the roadside as a means of relieving both thirst and hunger."

By midmorning, Wednesday, July 17, the temperature was in the nineties and the air was humid. In this part of Virginia, these conditions meant that the atmosphere was palpable, almost soupy. With the air so sultry, men began falling out of line from exhaustion. Some troops had to be sent back to their original camps. Since the region was impoverished and houses were few, the area offered few wells. The wells the army did pass quickly attracted swarms of soldiers, standing in long, impatient lines to get a drink. One soldier paid a week's wages for a canteen of muddy water. This is why some soldiers slaked their thirst by devouring the moist fruit they passed. "I never saw blackberries more plenty," wrote Elisha Hunt Rhodes of the Second Rhode Island. "We stopped and ate what we wanted and then moved on." (Since Rhodes's regiment led Hunter's division that morning and since McDowell was up with them, no doubt he was thinking about men like Elisha Hunt Rhodes when he later complained to the Joint Committee about the indiscipline of his army on this march.)

Another reason for the slow pace of that morning was the need for *skirmishing*. When entering enemy territory, an army did not travel at the speed of a marching infantryman. It went at the pace of a clambering *skirmisher*. Armies had been expanding the role of such specialists. Essentially, skirmishers were infantrymen who did not stay inside the main body. Once their unit—generally a regiment—started moving, they swarmed in front or unfurled on either side, to probe for danger. Unlike the advice of "Hardee" to keep one's elbows touching one's neighbor, a skirmisher was supposed to remain several paces apart from every comrade. A skirmisher's primary job was to prevent an army from falling into an ambush. They were to swarm ahead, or on the sides, their guns held at *trail arms* as they peered around, looking for masked batteries, or, more likely, enemy pickets. A regiment's *skirmish line,* made up of a whole company, was often half a mile long, with its far end out of sight. Since they were so on their own, often out of view, the army had taught skirmishers special techniques. In addition to learning the basic fifteen drumbeat signals for normal infantrymen, a skirmisher had to learn twenty others: including "move to the left," "rally in groups of four," "fix bayonets," "lie down." If the terrain was exceptionally jumbled and distant skirmishers were beyond hearing even drumbeats, twenty-three different bugle calls could be used, and had to be memorized. (Artillery units and cavalrymen had their own bugle calls, so a skirmisher was supposed to be able to distinguish a message intended for him from one designed for an entirely different service.) A skirmish line was supposed to maintain its *dress* (that is, its linear straightness and its constant pace) as best it could. On flat, cleared fields this was easy. Fairfax County, however, was not conducive to rapid skirmishing. Although farms had once been sprinkled plentifully here, many of them had been abandoned, leaving behind decayed buildings, ditches, and fences. Here and there, McDowell's skirmishers did go through an occasional working farm, treading past outhouses and gardens and silent families, who watched them in surprise and fear. But usually the skirmishers stomped across wasteland: stony ground and ravines; marshland and pools of water; thick, thorny brambles everywhere. As one soldier wrote, "The pretty white stripes on our broadcloth pants were in shreds and our hands and faces scratched with the blackberry bushes we had pushed through." Back on the main road, colonels and generals watched their progress. The rest of the army could only march as fast as the sweating skirmishers.[64]

There was also the problem of the obstructions—the *abatis*—dropped by the rebels. These had to be cut through. Infantrymen could walk around them, but vehicles needed better surfaces—and McDowell's army included about a thousand vehicles. Tyler's division, for example, had around four hundred ambulances, wagons, caissons, and such. (Among the complications of moving a vast host like McDowell's army was feeding and watering the horses and mules, perhaps 8,000 of these beasts.)

The three divisions that were designated to move toward Fairfax Court House on July 17 began heading toward it at dawn. Tyler's skirmishers were slipping through fields before five o'clock. Numerous civilians—mostly reporters and politicians—were sprinkled among the divisions, hoping to see the battle, if such occurred. One of these observers was Elihu Washburne. In Washington that morning, he and three other civilians had hired a carriage. They arrived at Hunter's division just as it was beginning to start out. There, they found McDowell with his staff, up near the front. "The column," Washburne later wrote his wife, "extended three or four miles, and it was the most exciting scene I ever witnessed—a great army on its march to the battlefield. There were the two Rhode Island Regiments, with their white forelocks and red blankets on their backs—their bright bayonets gleaming in the hot sun. Then followed the long trains of heavy artillery, some immense guns requiring eight horses to haul one of them . . . There were also other regiments, and then such a host of baggage wagons, carriages, ambulances, etc., as you can hardly conceive of."[65]

When two armies approach each other, men on the perimeters—generally pickets or skirmishers—will spot their foes and take potshots. A spattering might not, at first, mean all that much. It was normal to hear the sound of gunfire near an army encampment. Pickets shot at shadows or passing hogs. And soldiers with loaded guns made mistakes with them. So the Confederates did not immediately react when they first heard a smatter of gunfire. Even after reports filtered back to Bonham's headquarters that Union soldiers could be seen in the distance, Bonham remained uncertain whether these Yankees represented McDowell's whole army or a mere reconnaissance party. He did not want his large brigade to flee from an enemy's probe.

Since his regiments were spread out in an arc across almost two miles and since McDowell's army was coming at him in three directions, the timing of the first encounter is unclear. At their most fundamental, military actions are experienced by individuals who afterward can describe only what they *personally* saw and felt. Anyone who later tries to portray the events often makes the mistake of drawing upon the testimony of one or two participants whose isolated experiences did not represent the whole. And, of course, eyewitnesses often disagree. McDowell would tell the Joint Committee he had expected Tyler's division to arrive at Fairfax Court House at eight o'clock that morning and that it did not arrive there until three. He indicated he found this inexplicable, even outrageous. But he was flatly wrong in his testimony. A Connecticut soldier at the front of Tyler's division, whose commander had been yelling all morning, "Keep your intervals, damn you!" recalled they came in sight of Fairfax Court House "about noon," when they arrived at an intersection called Flint Hill, two miles from the county seat but within sight of that village. Tyler stopped here to consider what to do next. Should he proceed straight into the town, or take a right fork that might permit him to get behind Bonham and trap him, as McDowell's orders had proposed?

While Tyler was contemplating his next step, Hunter's division, coming from a different angle, also came in sight of Fairfax Court House.

The Confederate Position, Fairfax Court House

Several Confederates, writing letters just afterward, thought the first encounter occurred much sooner. One said the "enemy" was seen about seven o'clock that morning, though he did not say by whom or how many enemies came in sight. Another thought the time of the first encounter was before breakfast, "soon after we had taken our morning wash." A third thought it was "about daylight" when they first heard gunfire from their pickets. One official Confederate report said that Tyler's men were glimpsed — at least by somebody — at eight o'clock; another said the time was "soon after sunrise."

The appearance of a large number of Yankees — "an immense army," one Confederate called them — was a bit unnerving. "The glistening of the bayonets as they approached appeared like a sea of silver," one Southerner wrote home. A South Carolinian wrote his wife: "The enemy were fast approaching upon us and we could see from the bristling bayonets that there were thousands of them." Another — Thomas J. Goree, a tough officer from Texas — saw the Yankees coming and a few days later admitted to his uncle: "When I saw them it almost seemed as if there were 500,000 of them." (It is normal to perceive an enemy army as a "horde" — though it is also true that one never thinks of one's own force that way.) At midmorning Bonham changed his mind about the danger. He ordered everyone to get out, fast. He told the Second South Carolina to bring up the rear.[66]

There then followed a rather manic scramble. Goree concluded that Bonham was *"totally* unfit for a military leader." Bonham's regiments only began loading heavy items *after* the Union army appeared — in Goree's view, hours after Bonham had received sufficient warning of its approach. Since the South Carolinian commander had waited so long, thousands of his troops were forced to rush in all directions, striking their tents and loading wagons served by nervous teamsters. According to Goree, Bonham appeared frazzled — brave, but a bit high-strung and obviously placed in a command above his abilities.

The Confederate officer at Fairfax Court House who handled the pressure best that day was Colonel Joseph B. Kershaw, leader of the Second South Carolina. When he received his orders to start retreating, he was aware almost a hundred of his men were still out on picket duty, and he refused to abandon them. One after the other, he sent three different couriers to call his pickets in. Meanwhile, he decided to try a ruse to slow the Yankee advance. He ordered his second in command, Lieutenant

Colonel J. W. Jones, to take two or three companies and string them out in some nearby entrenchments as though they were more numerous and were ready for a fight. Given this assignment, Jones turned to a captain and asked for some of his whiskey. He took a long pull from the container, then gave what he probably assumed was a pep talk to his tiny battalion (less than 150 men) which was being ordered to stall as many as ten thousand of the enemy. "Men," he said, "you must do your duty." He added unhelpfully, "We will all be cut to pieces in five minutes."

Jones's men stood in a ditch, behind sandbags, a bunch of flags waving above them, each banner supposedly representing a separate regiment. They silently watched an entire Union division, with all its gleaming bayonets, only a few hundred yards away, and moving ever closer. It seemed as though Jones's pessimistic prediction was about to come true.[67]

McDowell's Approaching Soldiers

The skirmishers of the Second Rhode Island noticed the earthworks and an unknown number of rebels hiding within them, and stopped. Because of the various gaps in the enemy's sandbags, it looked to the Rhode Islanders as though the rebels had eight cannon there — and a large number of troops. Burnside quickly rode up and spoke calmly to his men, steadying them. He sent orders to bring forward his battery of six guns. It rushed up, unlimbered, and began throwing shells at the sandbags. In a few minutes it was obvious the rebels in the entrenchments were now retreating, apparently in fear of the Union artillery. (In fact, Kershaw's missing pickets had just appeared. His trick had succeeded and Kershaw ordered his regiment to pull back, to follow their Confederate compatriots who had already departed.)

The Confederate Withdrawal from Fairfax Court House

With the exception of Kershaw's handiwork, Bonham's retreat from Fairfax Court House was a disorganized nightmare. Since he had waited too long and the enemy was in sight, his men were frightened. It is a fearful thing for a soldier to turn his back on an armed foe moving remorselessly toward him. Bonham ordered his regiments to *double-quick.* Officers screamed at the men to speed up, but the advice was unnecessary. In the oppressive heat of that July afternoon, thousands of Confederate troops, laden with knapsacks and guns, canteens and haversacks, tramped clumsily along, trying to speed away from the Yankee bayonets. The brigade lost its cohesion. Crowds of frightened slaves raced ahead. Frantic teamsters drove their wagons as fast as they could make their horses gallop. Many men fell to the ground, too exhausted to move. A number died, and were buried in Centreville.

One man, pulled along in this tide, was the venerable civilian, Edmund Ruffin, a fiery hater of the Union. Late in 1860 he had traveled from his home in Virginia to Charleston to urge the South Carolinians to secede. While there, he was adopted by one of South Carolina's most elite militia companies. Its young men grew fond of the white-haired Virginian and appreciated his ardor. After Fort Sumter fell, Ruffin returned home, but when the Yankees sent their army into northern Virginia, he could not resist the challenge. He came to the danger area and discovered his old friends, the troops from South Carolina. Again, he joined them. He was now with them, withdrawing from Fairfax Court House. But the pace of Bonham's panicky retreat exhausted him, and he hitched a ride on a passing caisson. He found even this seat problematic. In his diary he described the trip from Fairfax Court House as "very tedious & disagreeable, with the jolting over the rough road, & my back aching for want of any support to lean against."

The only positive thing that can be said about Bonham's retreat is that its frenzied pace saved the brigade. (Bonham's official report claimed that his brigade moved back to Centreville "in perfect order," a military phrase meaning they had marched in a well-disciplined way.)[68]

Fairfax Court House

The time was about 11:30 when the first Union soldiers actually entered the little town, three skirmishers from Rhode Island. They walked the length of its main street. They found the place mostly deserted; the only inhabitants they observed were some slaves and a few white women standing nervously in doorways. The streets were littered with knapsacks and other belongings of the departed rebels. This trio of Lincoln's volunteers nodded to folks as they strolled by. A few minutes later the rest of the Second Rhode Island arrived. One of them noticed an abandoned secession flag atop the small brick county court house that had given the town its name. This flag was pulled down and handed to a civilian accompanying the expedition, the daughter of Thurlow Weed, the mayor of New York. A United States flag was raised to replace it, while the regimental band of the Second Rhode Island played "The Star-Spangled Banner." Other Union troops appeared. A member of the Seventy-first New York was unimpressed by the town; he considered it "a wretchedly dirty, straggling little village." As to the white women: "I never saw so many poor, ill-fed, dirty-looking creatures."

The Federal soldiers stacked their arms and began exploring their surroundings. They found a mail pouch, stuffed with undelivered letters for rebel troops. One was from a South Carolina woman who asked the recipient to "tell John to shoot a Yankee for me." Another said that the people of South Carolina had just learned Yankees had burned Alexandria to the ground after ravishing its women. One item uncovered was disconcerting: a map of Fairfax County recently completed by the War Department in Washington. It had been stolen and sent here, a sign that many traitors still worked in the capital.

A few soldiers grew destructive. They broke into empty houses and plundered them. They stole some objects as mementoes. They flung books into the yards, and a piano, which they half-destroyed. They cut pictures from frames and smashed furniture. They ransacked a printing office. At least two enlisted men found women's gowns and bonnets and put them on and swished about the streets. McDowell and most of his officers were outraged. The "Articles of War," which had been read to the men of each regiment at least once, were clear: "Whoever shall commit any waste or spoil, either in walks, parks, warrens, fishponds, houses, or gardens, corn-fields, enclosures of meadows, or shall maliciously destroy any property whatsoever belonging to the inhabitants of the United States" would be severely punished.

The whole point of this war up to this moment was that secession was legally unacceptable, that in fact the citizens of Fairfax Court House were *still* Americans, no matter whether their political leaders had pushed Virginia into secession. Destructive actions against such people were counterproductive. Another thing wrong with such depredations was that soldiers who committed such acts had already put aside part of the veneer of civilization, and this loss of discipline could spill over to the battlefield when the army arrived there. McDowell immediately sent orders to every regiment: Such activities would not be condoned, period. "Any persons," he stated, "found committing the slightest depredation, killing pigs or poultry or trespassing on the property of the inhabitants, will be reported to the then headquarters, and the least that will be done to them will be to send them to the Alexandria jail." He went further than mere words. He had his provost marshals search out miscreants. By late that afternoon, at least eight soldiers had been arrested and sent back to Alexandria, under guard. What happened to them is uncertain.[69]

Meanwhile, Tyler's division, at the Flint Hill intersection, was confused by the activity they could observe at and near Fairfax Court House. They noticed a stream of soldiers in the distance moving westward from the town. Since the uniforms of both armies were so similar, the federal soldiers could not be positive which side those troops represented. Orders, apparently from Tyler, announced that the passing soldiers must be left undisturbed. Just before noon, Tyler ordered his division to bypass Fairfax Court House entirely. They should now move quickly down the right fork, which would take them well west of the town and enable them to intersect the turnpike between Fairfax Court House and Centreville — at a bump called Germantown. If the division jumped fast enough, they might intercept and capture Bonham.

His men now marched as quickly as they could, but Bonham's brigade had placed two timber barricades across this side road, as well as an earthwork, six or eight hundred feet long. These slowed Tyler's men down. After hacking through the abatis, the earthwork appeared like it might be a greater concern. Tyler's advance scouts could see rebel heads above it. Artillery was called for. Guns rushed up and flung some shells at the rebels, who disappeared, and the division inched forward. The first Federal soldiers arrived in Germantown only minutes after the tail end of Kershaw's regiment had slipped through. Bonham's brigade had escaped, just.

Germantown was poor, by any definition. One Connecticut soldier called it "two houses, one pigsty, three barns, and a pump." That was a slight exaggeration, but not by much; its eight or ten houses were little more than huts. And these were almost deserted. (Two unfortunate Confederate soldiers were in one of the buildings. They had contracted smallpox and had been abandoned by their comrades, as too sick to move. One of the two men was asked why he had joined the rebel cause, asked if it didn't seem wrong to try to destroy the Union. To which he replied: "Don't know. Think it right to fight against invasion.")

Burnside's brigade marched through Germantown first, raised an American flag, drank some water, and moved on. Then came Sherman's brigade, three New York regiments, and one from Wisconsin. A few soldiers of the so-called Irish Regiment, the Sixty-ninth New York, placed flags on the rebel breastworks on either side of the road — the American flag on one side and their own green banner on the other. As the Sixty-ninth passed between the two flags, many of the men held their hats aloft on their bayonets and cheered and cheered.

The discipline of Sherman's troops then began to dissolve. Germantown seemed to offer little worth stealing, but it did have a few farm animals, and these were quickly slaughtered for food, or fun. Sherman sent his aides to order the men to stop. Both the aides and his orders were met with catcalls and taunts. "The bearers of these orders were treated rather cavalierly," a member of the Seventy-ninth New York later recalled. Someone shouted, "Tell Colonel Sherman we will get all the water, pigs, and chickens we want!" His soldiers scrambled through the hovels, looking for anything that might be worth grabbing. One stole a feather bed, another took a sledgehammer, a third a quilt, a fourth a mirror. And so it went. They ignored their officers—who seemed only slightly less larcenous. Then somebody lit one of the buildings on fire, and a second and another—and smoke drifted into the sky. "No Goths or Vandals," Sherman wrote his wife, "ever had less respect for the lives and property of friends and foes."[70]

Many of Lincoln's soldiers, writing home in the next few days, said the acts of vandalism of that afternoon, especially the burning of Germantown, made them ashamed. Civilians often speak of the "horrors of war." Battlefields, strewn with mangled bodies, are nightmarish scenes, and seldom are new soldiers unaffected by the sight. But war also involves other "horrors," far from the battlefield. In northern Virginia, during the war's first weeks, an uncountable number of people were murdered for their opinions, by one side or the other. As to property—something that had been acquired through hours or months of effort, and was perhaps cherished (a quilt), or at least appreciated (a cow, a rail fence)—a lifetime's accumulation could disappear in a moment. Although the depredations in Fairfax Court House and Germantown apparently did not involve any physical attacks on civilians (though the emotional trauma of seeing thousands of armed strangers pass through one's land must have been severe) and therefore were not precisely "atrocities," they represented an ugly reality that would grow worse the longer this war lasted.

In midafternoon, Irvin McDowell sent messages to two of his divisional commanders to halt: Miles (who had reached Fairfax Station, several miles south of Fairfax Court House) and Heintzelman (the front of whose division had reached Sangster's Station). McDowell himself rode to Germantown to see what progress Tyler was making. He found the front of Tyler's division well beyond the unfortunate smoking hamlet, and seemingly settled down for the night. He returned to Fairfax Court House, where, obviously disappointed that Bonham had escaped, he sent a message to Washington. He said he had captured Fairfax Court House and would have liked to have gone on to Centreville, "but the men were too much exhausted to do so." This message seems disingenuous. His goal for this day had been to take Fairfax

Court House, and his army had done so. Had he been leading hardened veterans, accustomed to long marches — say, Stonewall Jackson's men of 1862 or Sherman's of 1864 — he could have continued on that afternoon, but, even then, doing so might have proved unwise. His troops had been marching in the July heat for many hours; even veterans would have been somewhat affected. McDowell could not be positive what he would find if he advanced immediately into Centreville. Given that uncertainty, it seemed best to stop, and start again tomorrow.[71]

First Blood

Thursday

Early in the morning, July 18, Irvin McDowell, at his headquarters at Fairfax Court House, considered his situation. Before leaving Washington he had assumed he might launch his assault against Beauregard's position at Manassas Junction on the third day of the expedition—this very day—and Winfield Scott was quite confident the attack on Beauregard would begin at almost any moment. In fact, McDowell had already realized he needed to postpone any such assault for at least another day. Unexpected problems had arisen.

One glitch involved provisions. Frederick the Great of Prussia, or maybe Napoleon, supposedly declared, "An army, like a serpent, travels on its belly." An army with insufficient food can fall apart, and much of McDowell's force was clearly almost out of their provisions. Each regiment had been told before leaving Washington that every man should carry with him three days' rations. On the morning of their departure, the soldiers were handed coffee, salted pork, hardtack, all of which they promptly jammed, in a lump, into their greasy haversacks that they then slung over their shoulders. Since then, two days had passed. In theory McDowell's troops ought still to have enough food for another day. But to assume such a likelihood was to imagine these 30,000 men as prudent dieters, mathematically dividing their rations into three parts, then further splitting them into separate meals. Believing such a thing would be nonsensical, even if one were dealing with veterans. Most hungry men were likely to eat until they were satisfied—especially when they realized that a haversack filled with three days' rations was heavy, and the more one ate from it (or threw the contents away), the easier marching would be. Officers, particularly company captains, ought to have supervised the meals, but in many cases they were as improvident as their men. Inevitably, therefore, by Thursday morning, although a few soldiers in some units had enough food to last another day or so, others had nothing. A private from Maine wrote in his diary: "Got up in the morning hungry as a bear. Nothing to eat however. Started off and got plenty of blackberries."

The commanders within the army were growing concerned. The original plan had involved the Army forwarding provisions immediately after McDowell's force began their march. Herds of cattle were supposed to be waddling along behind the divisions; and, in theory, so were three separate wagon trains, carrying rations. The cattle and the wagon trains were to have been assembled the day McDowell's army departed—Tuesday, the sixteenth, and were to have started out the following morning. (It is unclear why the quartermasters and the commissary department did not start organizing on Monday, when McDowell's decision to depart was announced, but the failure to do so probably involved the availability of wagons. Still, it is hard to understand why twenty-four hours made such a difference—that is, why 168 wagons could be found on July 16, but not the day before.)

The wagon trains and the cattle were to have joined the army on the evening of the second day's march. They did not. The first train, along with its herd of beeves, did arrive on the morning of the third day; the other two did not reach the army until the fourth day — the nineteenth. Several factors caused this delay. The commissary officers, responsible for the deliveries, learned, to their dismay, that many of the wagons they had been handed were inadequate with a decided tendency to break down. The horses to pull them, moreover, were untrained at performing this task or were physically too frail or sickly to do so. Some horses arrived unshod; others had had no training in being part of a team. Further, the commissary officers realized that the teamsters, as a group, were dubious. All the teamsters were civilians, hired for this occasion. Many, including even the wagon masters, had had absolutely no experience in such difficult work. Too often, as the commissaries later reported, the teamsters were "refractory" and "utterly unfit for their business" — a critical weakness because, with so many horses being sick or balky, none of the wagons could be fully loaded. A more remarkable fact was that no one had informed the commissary officers which routes they were supposed to use. Two of the three wagon trains wandered about aimlessly throughout their first day on the road, searching for the army. Eventually, the teamsters, the horses, and the cattle became too exhausted to continue.

By the time the wagons and cattle did arrive, McDowell's soldiers were so ravenous, the commissary officers, breaking army rules, simply distributed the provisions quickly, without normal paperwork, then turned their wagon trains around and went back for more. (As it turned out, the battle was over before they arrived again with their second loads.)

The coming of a wagon train did not immediately result in soldiers eating. After all, it required the efforts of many people to distribute 225 cattle and 166 wagonloads of various supplies, including about 160,000 rations. Parceling everything out took time. Once a division received its supplies, the food had to be divided among the brigades, then further separated and sent to the regiments and artillery batteries and cavalry units. Then it had to be allotted to the companies. Then to the various messes. All of this assumed far more organizational skills than the army had thus far shown. Men on picket duty, away from their regiments, often did not receive any food for at least a day after it appeared at divisional headquarters.

To put it simply, the provisions — including forage for the cavalry and artillery horses — were not fully distributed until the fourth evening of the march, Friday, so McDowell could not have considered an assault until at least the next day, Saturday, July 20.[72]

Meanwhile, that Thursday morning, as he waited for provisions to arrive, McDowell faced other problems. He wanted to examine Centreville personally, but he had grown uneasy about his left flank. Heintzelman had not contacted him in more than a day. (In fact the men of Heintzelman's division had done the only real fighting the day before, in a firefight with part of the Fifth Alabama, before that Confederate regiment had retreated.) Heintzelman's silence troubled McDowell, who ruefully wrote a note to Washington about the division: "I think they are at Sangster's Station." Overcome with anxiety, he jotted a hurried note to Heintzelman, asking him rather plaintively where he was and urging him to check in more often. Yet McDowell still received no word. Finally, losing patience, he changed his mind about riding to Centreville and decided he had personally better track down Heintzelman.

About eleven o'clock that morning, he found his divisional commander at Sangster's Station. Heintzelman expressed his own impatience at not yet receiving the promised provisions. McDowell, calmer now, was aware that, here at Heintzelman's headquarters, he was only about two miles from where the railroad bridge crossed Bull Run, where he had contemplated moving his army over Bull Run. He decided to examine that area for himself. As he rode around, he did not like what he saw. The roads in this region were little more than cow paths, crookedly jerking through thick woods, up sharp hills and down steep slopes. A huge force like his army, with so many vehicles, would get tangled up. Immediately he altered his basic plan. He decided not even to attempt to bring his army this way, but to find another route around Manassas. He would order his engineers to explore the whole area carefully and come up with an alternative.

McDowell began to write out orders for his divisional commanders. He verbally told Heintzelman to start moving toward

Centreville and to bivouac his men somewhere south of that village, far enough away from the other troops that he would have his own water supply. (This order reveals another matter McDowell had been growing concerned about. On the one hand, his army was too spread out; he wanted to concentrate it near Centreville, a convenient gathering place because so many roads crossed there. On the other hand, this notion had an inherent weakness: The region lacked sufficient water for the whole army, with its 30,000 men and thousands of horses and mules. The town had some wells and springs, but certainly not enough; the area did have a few small creeks, meandering toward Bull Run, but these were low since it was already past mid-July.) Given McDowell's sudden uncertainty about which direction his army was going to move and his recognition of the inherent water problems of Centreville, he was forced to keep his orders vague. He directed Tyler to place his division *somewhere* to the west of Centreville, near the turnpike that crossed Bull Run at the stone bridge three miles away — McDowell could be no more specific than that. He told Miles, commanding the smallest division, to situate himself almost in the center of town, and Hunter to come forward until he was "as near Centreville as he can get water." In other words, McDowell's four divisions were to wait for food, which, he mistakenly thought, would be arriving shortly, and then they were to place themselves in four encampments, separated by enough distance that each had a sufficient water supply, but close enough together that they could act in concert. But his army would have to stretch itself out across six miles, front to back, and almost three miles, side to side. This formation would be more than a bit clumsy and uncoordinated, but the situation required it.

Having sent out these intentionally vague directions, McDowell became aware of another, and unexpected, disturbing matter. He was riding near Sangster's Station when he clearly heard cannon fire not far away. This boded ill. He sped up his pace, hurrying ahead to investigate.

General Tyler had awakened his division early that morning and began getting it ready to move toward Centreville. About nine o'clock he received a dispatch, sent by McDowell before leaving Fairfax Court House. The note told him he was unlikely to encounter any rebels in Centreville. After arriving there, it said, he should investigate the various roads stretching westward out of the village. The message also contained a sentence that had unfortunate results: "Do not bring on an engagement, but keep up the impression that we are moving on Manassas." These words would seem to mean: Look *assertive*, but not *aggressive* — a subtle distinction, open to various interpretations. This hand-scrawled dispatch was hand-delivered by one of McDowell's aides, James Wadsworth, who verbally emphasized the part that cautioned against doing something that might initiate "an engagement." [73]

Tyler listened to Wadsworth's advice and rode into Centreville. He ordered his forward brigade, led by Colonel Israel B. Richardson, to continue through town and scout out a likely spot to bivouac, somewhere with available water. Richardson started his brigade in motion. They had no problem finding such a camp-site, because less than a mile beyond town was an abandoned rebel camp, complete with handy springwater and earthworks. They settled down. Tyler, meanwhile, went to Centreville, where he spoke to half a dozen citizens, brought to him by his cavalry-men. These locals told him that thousands of rebels had indeed stopped in town the night before but had begun departing about midnight, the last of them drifting out only a few hours ago. Some, they said, had headed straight west out the Warrenton turnpike toward the stone bridge (Evans's men), but most, the largest group (Bonham's brigade), had taken the southwesterly road that led straight to the railroad depot at Manassas Junction, six miles or so away. This information piqued Tyler's curiosity. He pressed these citizens about the latter route and whether any rebel forces remained on this side of Centreville. The citizens de-scribed the road as rather good, it being the path that locals used whenever they wanted to catch a train. It crossed Bull Run, they said, at a shallow spot called Mitchell's Ford. They were rather sure Bonham was camped just beyond the stream.

Tyler decided to order a reconnaissance. If nothing else, this might fulfill that part of McDowell's orders that told him to "keep up the impression that we are moving on Manassas." He rode to Richardson's brigade and said he wanted to scout down in that direction. The time was about eleven o'clock.

The Confederate Position

A few miles away, General Beauregard waited. He, too, had a plan in mind. Unlike his grandiose dreams about Johnston's joining him in a series of sweeping movements, ending in the taking of Washington, this scheme had at least some potential. Beauregard knew, of course, that McDowell's army was coming toward him, but he did not know where McDowell planned to cross Bull Run. It seemed likely that the Yankees would use either the stone bridge, where the Warrenton pike crossed Bull Run, or one of the few good fords, where the water was shallow enough and the stream bed firm enough to permit the passage of heavy artillery equipment. Beauregard was still convinced that the Yankee army would take the most direct route from Centreville to Manassas Junction, not the Warrenton pike, several miles to the north, nor any of the other nearby fords, none of which had as sturdy a bottom. He assumed McDowell's goal would be the railroad station, and the road from Centreville across Mitchell's Ford was the shortest way there.

By this time Beauregard had seven brigades, positioned behind Bull Run, using the stream as a barrier. On his far right flank was Brigadier General Richard S. Ewell's brigade, keeping its eye on Union Mills—the place where the railroad crossed. (Two days earlier Ewell had been up at Fairfax Station, but he had withdrawn, under Beauregard's orders, when Heintzelman approached.) It seemed unlikely a Yankee force of any size would try to cross there, but Beauregard wanted to play it safe. He felt the same about the stone bridge, and he placed his leftmost brigade there, the small one commanded by Colonel Evans that had also just pulled back from its forward position. Between these two extremities he positioned his other five brigades. To the right of Evans, Beauregard placed Cocke, stretched out to cover two fords, eight hundred yards apart. Far downstream, next to Ewell,

Beauregard put Brigadier General David Rumph Jones, whose assignment was to stand behind McLean's Ford. In Beauregard's mind, his two flanks were adequately covered.

Beauregard considered the middle sector the most critical spot, because here was Mitchell's Ford. He ordered Bonham, commanding the largest brigade, to place his men there. But Bonham's men were exhausted from their hasty retreat from Fairfax Court House the day before. They had rested at Centreville a few scant hours during the evening; then, about midnight, they had staggered through the darkness the three miles to their assigned position—a series of trenches and earthworks they themselves had occupied a few weeks earlier. Immediately to their right, Bull Run flowed in a horseshoe shape, straight north for half a mile, then back south again. At the place it turned south was another crossing called Blackburn's Ford. Although the main road tying Centreville to Manassas Junction did cross Bull Run at Mitchell's Ford, as Centreville's citizens had explained to Tyler, another, narrower path wended away from it, passed over Blackburn's Ford, then rejoined the Centreville-Manassas Junction road. Near Blackburn's Ford, Beauregard put his sixth brigade, commanded by Brigadier General James Longstreet. (The seventh brigade, led by Colonel Jubal Early, was to act as a reserve behind Beauregard's right wing, ready to move forward to support any of the brigades on that side.)

Beauregard intended a simultaneous assault on the Yankee army just as it arrived. According to his after-action report, he had worked everything out carefully in advance. He declared that he suspected McDowell would follow closely behind Bonham, as the South Carolinian pulled his brigade from Fairfax Court House. McDowell's troops would still be tailing along as Bonham crossed Bull Run. When the Yankees started to follow and were about to cross Mitchell's Ford, Bonham, from his entrenched position there, supported by artillery, would stop the Yankee advance, thereby fixing it in place. This would allow Longstreet, Jones, Early, and Ewell, coming from the right, and Cocke from the left, to fling their brigades across their respective fords—moving, according to Beauregard's orders, "with celerity." McDowell, caught between these pincers, might be crushed—and would almost certainly be defeated. If the Yankee army was not instantly destroyed, it was Beauregard's plan to follow vigorously after their retreat until they were "beyond the Potomac."

Beauregard knew his army of about 20,000 men would probably be outnumbered, but he thought a properly coordinated attack might work for him — as it had for Hannibal at Cannae two thousand years earlier. On the other hand, if McDowell arrived with a force that was simply too "overwhelming," Beauregard's plan designated that he would retire southward thirty miles to Fredericksburg and line up behind the Rappahannock, a wider river than Bull Run, as Robert E. Lee had suggested. Beauregard hoped it would not come to this.

As soon as he was positive McDowell had started from the Washington camps, he wired Richmond, asking for as many reinforcements as they could send immediately. He specifically mentioned the brigade of Theophilus H. Holmes, which he knew was camped at Acquia Creek, not far from Fredericksburg, and — once again — he pleaded for Joe Johnston's army, still sitting behind the breastworks at Winchester, facing Patterson. Richmond did order Holmes to move up to support Beauregard and did order assorted other units to hurry toward Manassas. These additions would increase Beauregard's army by several thousand men — if all of them arrived in time. But Lee and Jefferson Davis knew that moving Johnston from the Valley would be tricky, because of Patterson. Besides, even if Joe Johnston successfully eluded Patterson's grasp and started toward Manassas, he could not possibly arrive for several days. By that time, it would almost certainly be too late.

Beauregard, who did not know of McDowell's problems with provisions — and in fact during this whole war would never quite appreciate logistical matters — was sure the confrontation between his army and McDowell's was going to take place immediately, on Thursday, the eighteenth. By that morning, he had received only one additional regiment and part of another as reinforcements. He assigned them to assist Bonham. (The Eighth Virginia, actually coming from Leesburg, somehow slipped past Tyler that afternoon and joined Cocke. Holmes's brigade did not reach Manassas Junction until the following day. As to the dubious prospect that

Johnston's army, even if it started in his direction, would reach him in time, Beauregard had wired Richmond rather grumpily the day before: "I believe this proposed movement of General Johnston is too late. Enemy will attack me in force tomorrow morning"—that is, Thursday, July 18.

Now that time had arrived, and Beauregard was aware that the front of McDowell's army was passing through Centreville. He knew he could count only on the force he had on hand. For his plan to succeed, since it involved an intricate combined assault by unconnected units, it would have to go like clockwork. He chose to ignore the exhaustion of so many of his soldiers, thousands of whom were still trickling into their positions at dawn. And, inanely, he chose to overlook the difficulties involved in having five separate brigades converge, coming by five different routes—and in having them arrive at the same place, more or less simultaneously.

Another question remained: Suppose McDowell decided not to use that one road from Centreville and the Yankees did not cross Mitchell's Ford? Beauregard had no real backup plan— other than a mad scramble backward to the Rappahannock, thirty miles away, with the Yankees closely following.[74]

In midmorning Beauregard and his staff left his headquarters near the railroad station and rode two miles to the place owned by Wilmer McLean, an ample and prosperous farm overlooking Bull Run. Mr. McLean, forty-seven, was a short, stubby, hard-working man; he had owned this farm for the past nine years and took much pride in it. From his handsome home atop a knoll, he could look out on his pastures and on his orchard and on his corn-fields, now green with thick stalks. His corn crop was especially important to him. He owned a corncrib and, not far away, a corn grinder that sat by itself in his front yard. He also owned slaves, who lived in nearby huts, and a large barn, a stable, outhouses, and a log building he used as his kitchen (so that if it caught fire, as kitchens were wont to do, his house, separated by some distance, would remain safe). The farm, set in the heel of the Bull Run "horseshoe," was perfectly situated for Beauregard's purpose, because it gave him easy access to three of the fords, the nearest one, to the right, named after Mr. McLean. (It is uncertain where

McLean's family were that day. Presumably, they had retreated to a safe haven, but, if so, they returned in a few days. But not long after these events, he sent his family farther south to Appomattox, Virginia, where things, he was confident, were bound to be quieter. In 1862, after the Second Battle of Bull Run, he joined them there. Ironically, it would be his parlor in Appomattox where Lee and Grant signed peace terms in 1865.)

After Beauregard transferred his headquarters to McLean's farm that morning, surgeons arrived, looked the situation over, and chose the barn and stable to serve as a hospital. They set up operating tables to perform amputations and laid out their instruments. They hung a yellow flag just outside, the traditional indication of a military hospital. Throughout the morning couriers galloped in with messages for Beauregard; others rushed off.

James Longstreet's brigade was a mile from the farmhouse. Longstreet was destined to become one of the major military leaders of this war. Born in South Carolina forty years earlier, he had attended West Point without noticeable academic enthusiasm, graduated third from the bottom of his class, and followed that with a rather lackluster army career. Recently he had served as a paymaster for troops in New Mexico. When secession came, he started east, arriving in Richmond at the end of June. He modestly requested an assignment in the payroll department of the Confederate army. For some reason Lee, or someone else in authority, saw something in Longstreet — perhaps a calmness, a strength of character, an honesty. He was told he had been given the rank of brigadier general and he should report to Beauregard. He had arrived at Manassas on July 2. Beauregard had assigned him a brigade that was camping near the station and told him that his assignment was to use his new brigade to cover Blackburn's Ford — if McDowell, as Beauregard had suspected, moved at Manassas Junction. (By Thursday, July 18, Longstreet was still getting acquainted with the men of his brigade; he still had not met all his officers.)

On Wednesday afternoon, when word arrived confirming McDowell's approach, Longstreet ordered his three Virginia regiments — the First, the Eleventh, and the Seventeenth, approximately two thousand men — to march the few miles to Blackburn's

Ford. He directed about a hundred of them to wade across the stream and set themselves up as pickets in the woods on the other side. He placed part of his brigade near the stream; the rest he stationed back a few hundred yards, as a reserve. The bank of Bull Run opposite his right wing was, in places, forty feet above the stream, and his men there had to crane their necks to see its top. The ancient road that crossed the ford here ran through a narrow notch in that bluff. If rifle-bearing Yankees broke through the trees on the highest point, they would be looking straight down on the Confederate position, as though standing on the roof of a four-story building and peering at the sidewalk across the street. Longstreet's men hurriedly grabbed logs to form makeshift breastworks and used their bayonets to dig trenches in the soft, yellow soil. (Why Beauregard had not ordered sturdy entrenchments built here, and at the other fords, is baffling. It is also puzzling that he had not built roads to tie together the positions he had laid out weeks earlier. Beauregard was recognized as an excellent engineer, but he had focused on improving the fortification near the station. These lapses were not only odd; they almost proved fatal.)

One of Longstreet's soldiers, Private Alexander Hunter, a member of the First Virginia, vividly remembered that Thursday morning. He and his comrades had heard rumors that a huge Yankee army was on its way. With the exception of Longstreet, who had had some experience in the Mexican War, perhaps none of them, he thought, had ever heard a gun fired in anger. Now, as his regiment waited, he noticed some of his comrades reading their Bibles, others fiddling with the hammers of their muskets. Except for the drone of beetles and bluebottle flies and the cawing of crows in the distance, the air was still. He described the reactions of one, probably fairly typical, soldier:

> He repeated the Lord's prayer over and over about seventy-five times, having in his head the idea that the oftener he said the prayer the better he would become, and the less there would be of the Devil getting him in case a Yankee bullet should knock him cold. He would begin slowly, he said, and with much fervor, but always ended rapidly; then, commencing over again, would rattle through at a tremen-

dous rate and dove-tail 'Our Father' with 'Amen.' He threw
away a pack of cards and made an oath never again to utter
a profane word so long as he might be allowed to live;
vowed that if by chance he should come out of the battle
safe and sound he would be a moral, as well as a model, warrior; determined to crush down his hasty temper, and carry
all the canteens to the spring; to give the first sop of the skil-
let to his surviving comrades; to do his share thereafter of
police duty without so much as a grumble; to black the captain's boots if he should order it, in a meek and lowly spirit;
resolved to imitate the noble Christian soldier of the Crimea
war—the brave Havelock—and follow faithfully in his footsteps; forgave all the enemies—o! when he came to think of
it, all except that scoundrel who stole his canteen the fight
[night?] before, and about whom he made a mental reserva-
tion; thought he would go to church and give up his pipe,
and if he got through safely would become a minister and
preach the gospel. I know all this too well, for I was that
guileless, innocent youth.

As the morning wore on and the sun rose in the sky, the Virginians grew listless and began to relax. Maybe the Yankees
weren't coming after all. Someone near Hunter pulled out a pack
of cards and proposed a game. Hands were dealt. Hunter, forgetting his vows of Christian asceticism, joined in. He heard comrades laughing at jokes. Some of them talked of taking a dip in the
stream. Men crawled into the shadows under the trees and began
to snooze.[75]

Across Bull Run were several scattered farms, cut from the thick
forests of the region. About a mile above the stream, where the
two roads that crossed Bull Run at Mitchell's and Blackburn's
Fords joined together, was one owned by Pierce Butler (who
had moved from Pennsylvania three years earlier). About dawn,
Kershaw's Second South Carolina, the rear guard of Bonham's
brigade, passed by Butler's farm on their way to Mitchell's Ford.
Colonel Kershaw assigned one of his companies to remain there,
not far from the farm, as pickets. Once Kershaw had gotten his
regiment settled in their entrenchments, he pushed forward two

more companies, along with two cannon. They settled themselves about halfway between the stream and the Butler place. Sometime during the morning a solitary rider approached them, wearing blue, like many Confederate officers. The rider asked the pickets where "the general" was. Which one, they asked, Bonham or Beauregard? No, he said, uneasily, McDowell. Kershaw's pickets started to stir, and the rider, realizing his error, turned and started galloping back toward Centreville. The pickets fired at his retreating form, and killed him. It is not certain, but he seems to have been a Captain McNeil, who, before the war, had helped survey the laying of the Orange and Alexandria Railroad, and had been acting as a guide for McDowell's army. He was the first to die in the Battle of Blackburn's Ford.[76]

The Union Army

Before Colonel Israel Richardson had left his bivouac that morning, he ordered an officer from one of his two Michigan regiments, Captain Robert Brethschneider, to create a battalion of skirmishers, forty men from each of the four regiments. Now, several hours later, when General Tyler rode up to Richardson's position outside of Centreville and said he wanted to explore the roads to Bull Run, Brethschneider's makeshift battalion rose. Along with a squadron of cavalrymen, Brethschneider's infantrymen accompanied Tyler and Colonel Richardson, the group heading cautiously toward Bull Run.

There are several kinds of *reconnaissances*, though all are designed to gather information. One involves fairly small detachments like Brethschneider's. Their usual purpose is simply to scout; normally, they avoid any serious engagements with the enemy. Tyler was under orders from McDowell to examine the roads. Using Brethschneider's battalion, he was doing so. But Tyler also had been ordered by McDowell "to keep up the impression that we are moving on Manassas," and this small body of soldiers would find it hard to accomplish that mission alone. There were just too few of them. To fulfill that part of McDowell's orders would require a *reconnaissance in force*. Traditionally, this is made by a sizeable unit. It seeks out the enemy and punches forcefully into its lines to discover its strength. Once this information is determined, it backs away.

Brethschneider's infantrymen, acting as skirmishers, slunk carefully past the heavy woods on either side. The contour of the road, undulating up hills and down, prevented the party from seeing very far to the front. They had been moving almost an hour, and Tyler, growing uneasy, was about to turn his little group around when one of his mounted scouts rushed back and announced they had seen something. Tyler rode forward, and, at a rise in the road, he found himself at the juncture of two roads. The main one, angling to his right, dropped gradually downhill toward what was probably Bull Run, though trees blocked any sight of the stream. Peering in that direction through a glass, he thought he detected some rebels about half a mile away. Because of the gradation of the land, he assumed the stream was probably behind them. Beyond what he, correctly, believed was Bull Run, he was rather sure he saw many more rebels. When he swung his glass to his left and peered down the other, less-maintained, road, he was struck by how empty it appeared, as though the rebels had not fortified it in any important way. This sight intrigued him, and he turned to Richardson and ordered him to send back for a battery of cannon and the rest of his brigade.

Tyler had just decided to try a reconnaissance in force. (Since that day, some people have speculated, without any evidence, that Tyler really intended to burst all the way through to Manassas Junction, that he was seeking the fame that would adhere to that success, that he was hoping to grab for himself immortal glory. This hypothesis is dubious, since Tyler did not immediately order up his entire division but only Richardson's single brigade.)

A few minutes later, the artillery arrived. Two of the guns were immediately aimed down the main road on the right and opened fire. (Their target was Kershaw's advanced companies of South Carolinians. Kershaw's two cannon returned fire with half a dozen shots, then turned around and crossed the stream, along with their infantry support.) The route to Mitchell's Ford now seemed clear, but beyond it—where Bonham's large brigade lay quietly waiting—was obviously a large body of rebels. Tyler was uncertain about the size of that force but decided to be cautious.

He turned his attention to the — apparently empty — left road. He may not have known its name at this moment, but he was looking toward Blackburn's Ford. He could make out, in a clearing on the other side, a couple of cannon. When his artillery opened fire on them, they moved out of the way (as Longstreet, suspecting the range of his guns was too limited to reach the Yankee artillery, had ordered them to do).[77]

Tyler, apparently frustrated by his inability to get the rebels to reveal their positions and their number, decided to press a bit forward. Colonel Richardson was ready. Israel Richardson, an academically undistinguished 1841 graduate of West Point, had acquired the nickname "Fighting Dick" years earlier, during the Mexican War. He was a large, irascible, muscular man, generally slovenly and without detectable social skills — at least until a few weeks earlier when he had married an attractive woman who was so strong-willed she had accompanied him on this venture and was at this very moment waiting for him two miles away near Centreville. Since his marriage, people had noticed a mellowing of his usual abrasiveness. But though his loins may have become more relaxed, his fighting instinct remained. Right now he was anxious to throw his troops against the rebel positions. It was he, not Tyler, who was convinced a strong thrust here could achieve a breakthrough.

By this time, more of Tyler's artillery had rumbled up, making eight guns now unlimbered near the Butler house. Richardson ordered Brethschneider and his skirmishers ahead, to scout out things and clear away any rebels. Tyler — or someone — ordered two cannon, commanded by Captain Romeyn B. Ayres, to press forward and take a position in a farm field, not far from the stream. Brethschneider's skirmishers were to move ahead of the two guns, into a fringe of woods separating the field from the stream. (Across the way, still unseen, were Longstreet's 1,200–1,400 men.) Shortly after Brethschneider's skirmishers disappeared into the trees, Tyler heard a sudden smatter of musketry, and with it the deeper crash of Ayres's artillery.

Observers drifted in from Centreville. One was Major John Gross Barnard, McDowell's chief of engineers. His primary responsibilities were mapping terrain and erecting bridges and such. He was also expected to examine any possible battlefield and offer suggestions. His job was important, and such assignments were given only to the brightest army officers. Early that morning, he had spoken to McDowell before the general left to seek out Heintzelman. At that time McDowell had indicated he still wanted to move his army to the left, that is, toward Heintzelman's position. Barnard was confident General McDowell would not want Tyler to suck the whole army into a major battle just now, so when Barnard, back at Centreville, learned that Tyler had called up all of Richardson's brigade, he was concerned. He rode ahead to see what was going on. He joined Tyler and Richardson as they were staring across Bull Run. He cautioned Tyler about becoming too aggressive, though he did agree that a "demonstration" seemed appropriate. McDowell's adjutant general, Captain James B. Fry, also rode up. Fry was an important member of McDowell's personal staff, and he concurred with Barnard's expressed opinion. The two staff officers watched, uncomfortably, as Richardson advanced his brigade.

Tyler's artillery fire could be heard at Centreville. Correspondents, representing prominent newspapers in New York and Boston and Philadelphia, rushed to see "history in the making." Henry Villard of the *New York Herald* had beaten his rivals to the scene since he had been accompanying Tyler that morning and was therefore already there. Now, two other newsmen arrived: Edward H. House of the *Tribune* and Edmund Clarence Stedman of the *World*. They were young men, in their twenties; and, like most of the soldiers, this was their first battle. The three correspondents wanted to get closer to the action and inched forward until they were a hundred yards from the tree line. They had not had time to eat lunch, and as they passed a cherry tree, Villard offered to climb up and drop some down. "I had just got on a branch when a terrific roar burst out from the woods," he later wrote, "seemingly within a few steps of us, followed by a mighty whizzing and clattering." Bullets from the woods pelted around them, followed by an artillery shell, and Villard tumbled to the ground and scuttled to safety. Other reporters, arriving, observed "the battle" but could make little sense of it—beyond its frightful, chaotic nature. "I tell you," one wrote home, "the first

experience of a round shot, whirring over one's head, is a sensation." But, he had to admit, "It was the most exciting experience of
my life, yesterday, and I could hardly sleep, tired as I was." Another reporter became so unnerved when a bullet just missed his
head that he leaped on a horse and rode all the way back to Washington, where he submitted an absurdly exaggerated report.

The correspondents who remained at the scene began to pick
out certain details. Just now, most of the Union troops were
quiet, but the rebels could be clearly heard across the stream,
cheering and yelling and screaming in an odd, high-shrieked way.
The reporters noticed that some Union soldiers were hiding behind trees, crouching down one behind the other, six or more in
queues. The correspondents noted that some officers were cool
and brave, as if at a picnic; others were cowardly. Several reporters were shocked by the gore — a soldier's face being ripped
apart by gunfire, a leg being snapped like a twig by a cannonball,
the shrieking of the men in the ambulances, the doctors at work.
One later recalled that he burst out, "If this is war, let it stop right
here. Let the Southern States go. Let them set up their Confederacy. Anything rather than this." Other civilians also arrived, including several politicians who pitched in and helped with the
wounded. Later that evening, the politicians were seen moving
about, still covered in blood.[78]

The official after-action reports of Richardson and Tyler are
murky and contradictory. The recollections of individual soldiers
are little better, since each man could describe only what he himself experienced or saw, and if he entered the darkness of the
woods, his situation grew almost dreamlike. Since the uniforms
of the Union troops differed from each other, much confusion
was inevitable. One group, moving through a deep ravine, saw
some human forms near them and almost opened fire; they
turned out to be those of federal troops. On the other hand, one
Union lieutenant spied other soldiers and ran toward them, asking who they were. "Who are you?" came the reply. "Massachusetts men," he answered, and the rebels shot him dead.

This much seems fairly clear. After Brethschneider's skirmishers were fired on and retreated, Richardson ordered three
companies of the First Massachusetts to skirmish in the trees on

the road's right side; then, a few minutes later, he told the Twelfth New York to plunge into the woods on the left. Richardson himself rode with the New Yorkers toward the tree line, yelling at them to "sweep the woods," then galloping back to organize the rest of his brigade. His purpose in advancing these two units of infantrymen was to protect Ayres's most advanced guns, which were coming under a great deal of fire.

The troops of the Twelfth New York crossed an open field, climbed a rail fence, and disappeared into the woods. Within moments, recalled one, "We received a terrible volley of musketry from concealed foes." A portion of these New Yorkers kept going, but most of the regiment skedaddled. Across the road, the three Massachusetts companies performed a bit better, probably because their officers showed more spunk. The Massachusetts men continued moving, shooting at rebels. Under heavy fire, they pulled back a bit, then went forward and tried again. In the murky ambiance of the woods, however, there was little organization. Some of the soldiers reached the far side of the tree line, saw some rebels, and fired down at them. Others bumped around among the trees.

Although the firefights lasted only a few minutes, they were fierce. One Union soldier miraculously survived, after one bullet went through his rolled-up blanket, which was slung across his body, and banged into his belt buckle, while another bullet clipped the cap box completely off his belt. Then, a wounded comrade fell heavily against him. He decided to flee. As he was moving back, a cannon ball landed in the ground behind him and smacked against the back of his knee. Yet, though he had been twice knocked to the ground, not a single one of these enemy's shots actually drew blood, and he was able to hobble away. Before departing, he saw a rebel officer, an artillery lieutenant on the other side of Bull Run. The man was waving his sword in the air and shouting across the stream, "Come on, you sons of bitches."

The canister fire of Ayres's two guns did significant damage to the rebels, but one cannon soon ran out of ammunition and had to pull back, and the other had most of its horses killed. (Hours later, this gun would be recovered by Union soldiers.) The remnants of the Twelfth New York and the First Massachusetts were recalled from the woods by bugle blasts. They joined their comrades who had been waiting on the hill well behind them—including members of the Second Michigan, who had used the opportunity to glom handfuls of blackberries from handy bushes near their position. (Even though far behind the firefight, some of these reserves were killed or wounded, mostly by cannon fire.) With the infantry fight over, the two armies became engaged in an artillery duel with seven guns on each side, while the Union infantrymen sat on the ground and watched. This action lasted two hours or more.[79]

As all this was going on, back in Centreville Tyler's other brigades could hear the distant rumble. "We strained our eyes," a soldier from Connecticut wrote home, "and wearied our arms holding field glasses to get glimpses of the contest." He stood on a fence rail to see if he could catch a glimpse of the battle, but the "impertinent woods" prevented any clear vision.

A messenger from Tyler rode up to Colonel Sherman and told him to bring forward his whole brigade, posthaste. Sherman ordered his men into formation and rode before them toward the sound of the guns. He had never been in a battle. His troops had more than two miles to march in the heat, and their officers shouted at them to double-quick. Hurry, hurry! At first, driven by excitement, the soldiers spontaneously began to yell. But soon the pace wore them down, and they found themselves marching rapidly along in a kind of gasping silence, often staring uncomfortably as bloody ambulances passed them, heading toward Centreville. They also noticed stragglers from Richardson's brigade on both sides of the road. Some of these men were sitting, perhaps weakened by the sun's fierce heat; others were wandering vacantly away from the fighting. When they were asked what was occurring down below, their responses made little sense, though a few muttered, "We are all cut to pieces."

As Sherman's brigade arrived near Butler's farm, the artillery duel was still going on, the two sides blasting away at each other's smoke. Sherman ordered his men off the road and into the trees that bordered both sides. Under his instructions, most lay down. Shells, hitting the braches overhead, caused some of them to wince. To calm them, he rode slowly through their position, speaking quietly. He said they needn't bother to duck, because when they heard a cannonball hit, it was already too late, so they should stop worrying. "Hardly had the words left his lips," one of them recalled, when a cannonball crashed against some branches just above him. Sherman instinctively crouched his head down almost to his horse's neck, then sat upright again. He looked around at the grinning countenances of his soldiers, smiled wryly, and said, "Well, boys, you may dodge the big ones."[80]

The Confederate Side of the Stream

Late that morning, at McLean's farm, before the appearance of the Yankees, one of Beauregard's staff officers had gone into the main house and brought out a chair that he plunked onto the yard. He used it to steady his spyglass and stared with it off toward Centreville. He finally saw, a mile or so away, some Union horsemen appear, followed by two cannon and some infantry (Tyler and his scouting party). He watched the two artillery pieces unlimber, then saw one gun aim and fire a round in his direction. He recalled it later as "the first hostile shot I ever heard." The ball went far over his head and landed in one of Wilmer McLean's corn fields. Another shot hit the corn grinder and broke it into pieces; a third smashed through the log walls of the kitchen and ruined the meal McLean's slaves were fixing for General Beauregard.

At Blackburn's Ford, as soon as the Yankee guns started firing, Longstreet's sleeping infantrymen came alive. Officers shouted directions. Some faces turned ashen. In the distance the men could hear the shrill sounds of Yankee bugles. Then began Ayres's terrible canister fire, some of it coming in their direction. A few minutes later, Longstreet's troops could see, through the trees and thick undergrowth bordering the stream's far side, uniformed men edging toward them. The two sides opened fire on each other, at first sporadically, then in a continuous roar. Great puffs of thick smoke belched from their muskets and grew so thick soldiers found it hard to see their foe, firing instead at the smoke. The noise was terrible — and terrifying.

"It was useless to attempt any order now," Alexander Hunter would remember, "for every man imagined he was about to be killed. The volley from the muskets had frightened us, but the bursting of those infernal shells was demoralizing. Every man acted for himself." Hearing the Yankees cheering loudly was also disconcerting. Hunter noticed that on his side of Bull Run, behind one large tree, almost forty of his comrades had thrown aside their weapons and were hiding in a long, wavering line. He saw them swaying from side to side of the thick tree trunk, depending on which way they thought the shells might be coming. He himself, with no hate in his heart for his enemies, found it hard to fire at the Yankees, even after he and about a hundred others were ordered to charge across the stream. This probe of the Union side of Bull Run lasted only a few minutes, but during it two young volunteers from Boston did stumble up to Hunter and admit they were lost; he escorted them back as prisoners. They seemed relieved. "I am free to confess," he later admitted, "that had they ordered me to follow them when in the woods, I certainly would have obeyed."

Another incident involved a fat middle-aged Virginian. As he started off toward the stream, he saw his son down the line and waved to him, then splashed across the water. In the woods on the other side, he got into a wrestling match with a Yankee, almost as large as himself. The two men pummeled each other with their fists and rolled around in the dirt. Their fight brought them to the edge of the embankment, and they tumbled over it, into the muck at the bottom. Finally, covered in mud, the obese Confederate turned his prisoner over to Longstreet, who congratulated him and suggested he go back for another.

When the infantry firefight began, both sides had about 1,200 men in action, but most of the Twelfth New York had quickly scattered away, leaving less than 200 New Yorkers to continue the fight, with another 200 men from the First Massachusetts to their right. Within a few minutes, therefore, the Union infantry fighters had become outnumbered about three to one. It would seem that the reason more Virginians than Federals stayed at their task was the presence of James Longstreet. As the bullets flew, the ex-paymaster rode calmly back and forth among his soldiers, a cigar stuck in his mouth, muttering to them constant encouragement. On three occasions, bunches of his troops, unable to bear another moment, broke for the rear, and each time, using his horse and the flat of his sword, he squeezed them back toward their lines.

The result of the firefight — lasting between ten and thirty minutes — was that Longstreet's men won. When bugles recalled the last Union remnants, his troops still held their positions. During its first moments, Longstreet had requested support, and Beauregard had ordered Jubal Early to bring his brigade forward to reinforce or relieve Longstreet. (Longstreet seeing Early's troops approaching his lines, suddenly realized that they, in excitement, might start firing indiscriminately, hitting his own men before they could move out of the way. He planted himself between the newcomers and his men, to indicate that the reinforcements ought to wait. But Early's men could not contain their excitement and started shooting wildly. To save himself, Longstreet leaped from his saddle and lay for a while flat on the ground, his imported French opera glasses now broken. His bay horse, riderless, raced off, and it took him a while to track it down and pull himself, now covered with dirt, back in the saddle.) [81]

The Union Position

About four o'clock all firing ceased. Richardson, still pugnacious, wanted his brigade and Sherman's to make an all-out assault on the Confederate position. He pleaded his case, but General Tyler turned him down, firmly. The purpose of the "demonstration" had been accomplished. Perhaps Barnard's and Fry's remonstrations to Tyler had sunk in, or maybe he came to this reasoned conclusion by himself.

(If Richardson's arguments had succeeded in persuading Tyler, the two Union brigades of Richardson and Sherman would have banged into both Longstreet and Early, who were backed up by others. Yet, months later, Richardson told the Joint Committee that he was *still* convinced a Union attack could have been successful — if nothing else, at least capturing the seven rebel guns. He said he thought the enemy in front of them numbered eight to ten thousand. His estimate was not far off. But his proposal was absurd. He had no reason to think that his broken brigade and Sherman's, exhausted from its double-quick three-mile march, could have successfully charged another mile and a half against an entrenched foe almost twice as numerous. The result would have been a bloodbath. This may partly explain why McDowell removed Richardson's brigade from Tyler's division, and why "Fighting Dick" Richardson found himself acting in a reserve capacity during the much more important battle three days later. But at least his young wife was pleased to see him when he got back from Blackburn's Ford; in front of his men she gave his meaty red face a big kiss.)

A few minutes after Tyler ordered a withdrawal, McDowell arrived on the scene, having ridden fast all the way from Heintzelman's position. It had taken him several hours, and during the whole ride he could hear the crash of battle. He was now quite displeased, and his expression showed it. But he controlled himself, merely telling Tyler to write up a full report. "The attack at Blackburn's Ford," he later said, "had a bad effect on our men. They were all in high spirits before that, but had not succeeded in their first attack." Two days later, when the terms of some units ended and they chose to depart, he was convinced their decision resulted from a gloomy mood, which, he sensed, had permeated his whole army after the Blackburn's Ford affair.

Was this conclusion accurate? Perhaps it was McDowell's unconscious attempt to blame Tyler for the whole Bull Run disaster, but was he correct? Could the events at Blackburn's Ford have so depressed the rest of his army that it was unable to function for days? Certainly, the command of the Twelfth New York ought to have been changed, though making any such alteration would have been of dubious legality since the officers of a volunteer regiment were generally elected. But most of Richardson's troops had not actually fought, nor had Sherman's. The men who participated in or witnessed the battle—what little they could see of it—no doubt felt strong emotions, but few of even these men seemed discouraged. It is true that the childish insouciance that some had previously felt now dissolved, but that was a benefit. As one of Sherman's men recalled: "The sight of the dead and dying made us feel rather sober." The men of other brigades and other divisions would have been even less affected. When the sounds of

battle died that afternoon, the troops of Burnside's brigade, several miles from the action, merely marched into a field, stacked their arms, kindled fires, brewed some coffee, and chatted to each other, as usual. It would appear as though McDowell's later recollections, at the very least, exaggerated the repercussions of the affair at Blackburn's Ford.

The official casualty reports came in. The Union side had lost 83 men (26 of whom were listed as "missing"); the Confederate report claimed a loss of 68. Later in this war, such figures would have been considered so paltry that the incident, if mentioned at all in the press, would have been termed "an insignificant skirmish." But official casualty reports always overlook the human element. During the next few days, there would be weeping in Alexandria, Virginia, and Chelsea, Massachusetts, among other American towns. In these first weeks of war, a military company often represented an entire community, sometimes little more than a handful of extended families. When the names of the dead and wounded and missing arrived back at home, families and friends pored over the lists with intense concern. A woman with children who had lost her husband, the family's sole source of income, perhaps had just been made destitute. The death or maiming of a man was never "unimportant" to people like her.

The mayor of Chelsea, Massachusetts — Frank B. Fay — understood the worries of the people of his small town. One of the three Massachusetts companies in the battle had been from there. When he learned of the events at Blackburn's Ford, he went immediately to find out how "his boys" had fared. Before returning home, he sent a preliminary report to his hometown paper, the *Chelsea Telegraph and Pioneer.* When the "Chelsea Volunteers," as the company called itself, had entered the trees that day, they numbered perhaps eighty men. Most were between their midtwenties and midthirties; many were fathers with broods of children at home. Six of these men were killed in the firefight; many others were wounded, some severely. Mayor Fay's letter to the citizens of Chelsea described the fate of each of these "casualties," by name. To him, and to the readers of the *Telegraph and Pioneer,* these men were not statistics but individuals. He spoke of their words, of how one wounded man, whom he named, had shaken a comrade's hand, then died. His letter is remarkable because it was decent and humane and sensitive, yet it made no effort to romanticize or glorify. It was a statement of facts, reporting matters that, he knew, families at home wanted to learn.[82]

How important was the skirmish at Blackburn's Ford to the Confederates? Longstreet's aide wrote home two weeks later that it "went a long way towards winning the victory of the 21st, for it gave our troops confidence in themselves." Jubal Early agreed; he would later claim that the skirmish had "a very inspiring effect upon our troops generally." But it is as hard to accept this conclusion as it is to swallow McDowell's theory. Most of the Confederates who fought this day contributed little to the events three days later. Much of the fiercest fighting that would take place on the greater battlefield of Bull Run was in fact going to be done by men who, at this moment, were still out in the Valley— Joe Johnston's men.[83]

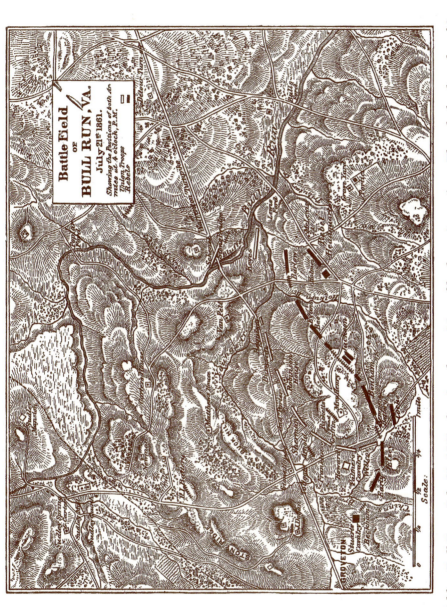

The battlefield at Bull Run, July 21, 1861, showing the position of both armies at 4 P.M. Though the date that this map was drawn is unknown, it was probably done by a Union artist, as the Confederates are referred to as "Rebels." *Library of Congress*

This scene is typical of both Union and Confederate attitudes at the beginning of the war—here, happy-go-lucky, naive Confederate volunteers depart for battle. *Library of Congress*

This is a wood engraving of Confederate troops at Bull Run, created by Thulstrup Evans, that gives a good sense of the topography and foliage at Bull Run as well as of the general frenzy of the battle. *Library of Congress*

Manassas Junction, looking toward Bull Run and Centreville from the fortifications southwest of the railway depot. Frank Leslie's illustrated newspaper
ran this sketch by Edwin Forbes on April 12, 1862. *Library of Congress*

The nightmarish, twisted, jumbled, muddy nature of Bull Run.
This photograph was taken between 1861 and 1865. *Library of Congress*

The tired Virginia hamlet of Centreville served as the Union headquarters before the battle. Here, in March 1862, Union soldiers keep watch. *Library of Congress*

Union surgeons perform an amputation in a hospital tent. This photo was clearly taken after Bull Run for two reasons. First, it seems no photographs were taken on the battlefield of First Bull Run. Second, unlike the surgery depicted here, the medical work at Bull Run involved only on-the-spot treatment on the field or in nearby buildings. Later in the war, armies traveled with fairly elaborate hospital tents. *Massachusetts Commandery Military Order of the Loyal Legion and the U.S. Army Military History Institute*

The men and horses of a typical Union artillery battery, lined up and waiting with their guns and vehicles. This photo was taken in June of 1862 at Fair Oaks, Virginia. *Library of Congress*

Union General-in-Chief
Winfield Scott was reluctant
to push troops forward too
soon but was overruled by
President Lincoln. Photographers of the time often
hounded important men to
have their pictures taken;
the photographers then sold
copies of the photo and used
them to lure in common soldiers for sittings. Photographs of men in uniform
were prevalent at this time,
as men sought to establish
their newfound importance
as well as their patriotism.
U.S. Army
Military History Institute

Brigadier General Irvin
McDowell, the Union com-
mander at Bull Run, had a
good brain, but he lacked
charisma, confidence, and,
as it turned out, luck.
Library of Congress

Brigadier General Joseph E. Johnston, in overall command of the Confederate forces at Bull Run, was personally courageous, but not inclined to fling troops willy-nilly into mortal danger.
Library of Congress

Brigadier General P. G. T. Beauregard, second-in-command of the Confederate forces at Bull Run, was touted as the "Hero of Sumter." Much was expected of him; he concurred with that notion. This photograph of him was likely taken during the winter of 1860–1861 as he is still wearing the uniform of a major in the U.S. army.
Bill Schultz Collection, U.S. Army Military History Institute

Colonel Ambrose Burnside and officers of the 1st Rhode Island regiment taken at their campground in Washington, D.C., during the first days of the war. By July 1861, Burnside was a brigadier general, and his Rhode Islanders were the first major Union troops to engage the enemy in the battle of Bull Run. *Library of Congress*

Confederate Brigadier General Thomas J. "Stonewall" Jackson would win immense fame as a result of the battle of Bull Run—more than he deserved at that time. This etching was drawn from a photograph that was taken just before he died in 1863.

Massachusetts Commandery Military Order of the Loyal Legion and the U.S. Army Military History Institute

VALLEY BOYS

The Confederates: Joe Johnston's Valley Army

In Winchester, Virginia, twenty-three miles south of Patterson's growing discomfort, Johnston was considering his own next move. Although he had been receiving reinforcements, these were trickling in, generally ill equipped. When he pleaded with Richmond to send more men so he could be more aggressive, Jefferson Davis told him it was impossible. The Confederate president said he was desperate to "drive the invaders from Virginia and teach our insolent foe some lessons," but, he sighed, because of "delay and mismanagement," the Confederate armies must act cautiously. As an example, he noted that 20,000 men in his home state of Mississippi were impatient to join the fight, but the Confederacy lacked arms or supplies to enlist them. General Johnston must sit tight in Winchester—at least for now.

Beauregard, frantic since he had learned that McDowell was finally under way, was importuning Davis for every available soldier. He was told by Richmond that he himself could contact Joe Johnston and ask for assistance. On July 17 Beauregard wired Johnston a self-serving and inaccurate message: "War Department has ordered you to join me; do so immediately, if possible, and we will crush the enemy." Johnston did not know how to react to this. He had heard nothing from Richmond about joining Beauregard and had become well acquainted with Beauregard's tendency to propose grand gestures. Also, here in Winchester, he was trying to decipher Patterson's intentions. He knew that moving his entire army from Winchester to Manassas would likely require three days — assuming Patterson did nothing to interfere with such a move. Johnston wired Beauregard back, asking for more details. Among other things, he wanted to know if the Yankees were *already* assaulting Beauregard's army. If Beauregard was in the act of tussling with McDowell, or expected to do so within the next day or so, going there — arriving after the battle — would be either unnecessary (if Beauregard's army had been victorious) or regrettable (if McDowell had won and taken control of the region).

A few hours afterward, late on the evening of the seventeenth, the War Department in Richmond wired Johnston that Beauregard's army had come under attack (at Fairfax Court House), adding: "To strike the enemy a decisive blow a junction of all your effective force will be needed." The word *effective* meant that Johnston should leave behind his sick and the "militiamen" who had just been swept up by impressment gangs and would certainly not be dependable fighters. Since the Confederate military decision makers understood the precarious nature of Johnston's situation, with Patterson's army nearby, they left the move to his discretion.

Military dispatches are often byzantine in their lack of directness. Instead of a crisp directive saying, "Go there," orders tend to be far airier. One reason is obvious: Fuzziness permits the recipient to use his own judgment about his situation. War zones are usually fluid, and the local commander is in the best position to decide which actions are feasible, which are not. But there are often other, more subtle motives hidden within the seemingly genteel language: If things go sour, the sender of the order has given himself room to avoid full responsibility. In this case, the

Confederate War Department (almost certainly at Davis's behest) was declaring that it desperately wanted Johnston to go to Manassas Junction, but he should do so only if, in *his* judgment, the move was "practicable"—that is, if Patterson did not press him too closely. The message, therefore, was not exactly *peremptory* (which means, in military or legal usage, something not open to challenge); it was merely a strong "suggestion."

Johnston received this telegram after midnight (ironically, at almost the precise moment that Patterson was wiring Scott the question: "Should I attack?"). Johnston read it and understood he had better make every effort to get to Manassas Junction or he could be blamed if Beauregard lost the battle. Although the hour was late, he sent orders to his highest officers to come to headquarters immediately. After conferring for a while, all agreed they must go to assist Beauregard—if Patterson permitted them, by his inactivity if nothing else. Johnston told them he would cut orders to make the move but would not issue them until Patterson's camps had been carefully watched during the morning (of the eighteenth) for any activity. If nothing seemed to be going on, Johnston would officially issue those orders. Speed would then be essential. Wagons would have to be hurriedly readied, horses hitched. Rations for three days would need to be cooked and stuffed into haversacks. Those men too sick to travel would be culled out—1,700 of them, as it turned out (that is, 15 to 20 percent of Johnston's army). Johnston chose to ignore the War Department's advice that he send the sickly to Culpeper. Doing so, he knew, would be foolish. It would consume space in too many of his wagons, and his move to Manassas Junction would then be slowed. He opted to leave the sick behind in Winchester.

Given the situation, Johnston's commanders were in something of a bind. They could not do anything too blatant, but they must secretly get their particular units prepared to move quickly. Whatever they did must not reveal their purposes to Patterson. Most of such activities could be performed furtively, or at the last moment. The troops themselves could not be told where they were heading. Many of them were from communities in the Valley and might not take kindly to deserting their homes and families to the dubious charity of the Yankees. The army as a whole would feel especially guilty about abandoning the people of Winchester, folks who had treated their Confederate guests with generosity and who would now be left to their fate, which, if rumors were true, would mean looting and rapine by Yankee hordes. Johnston understood that his troops might feel anger and shame — unless they thought they were heading *north* to assault Patterson. Johnston decided, if his army did move, that was what he wanted his men to believe.

On the other hand, he could not leave until he was totally convinced Patterson was not about to assault his lines. He ordered Jeb Stuart to ride quietly toward the Yankees. If the enemy was preparing to move, Johnston assumed they would be heading in his direction. But if their camps seemed quiet, he would issue his orders to leave, turning his back on his foe, and, like a triumphant, if slightly uneasy, matador, march away.

Stuart's cavalrymen performed their assignment superbly. Without unduly agitating Yankee pickets, they scouted Patterson's camps till midmorning and observed no apparent movement there. (Actually, it was during these hours at the Federal camps that Robert Patterson was unsuccessfully pleading with his Pennsylvania regiments to fight.) Stuart told Johnston about his observations. The orders to start for Manassas Junction were now given. Immediately, his army sprang into action. The militiamen and the sickly, staying behind, would serve as scarecrows to fool the Yankee scouts.[84]

This moment held great drama. The situation was like a western movie: A wagon train (Beauregard) was being besieged by whooping and hollering hostiles (McDowell's army), and valiant troopers (Johnston) were on their way. Would the heroes arrive in time to save the settlers? Chances seemed slim. Winchester was miles from any rail line. Several tiny railroad stations were on the other side of the Blue Ridge, many miles away, but it would take time to march to them. Besides, a typical train — especially in this part of Virginia — was limited in what it could haul. Johnston was starting off with about 9,000 men and his equipment, which included twenty artillery pieces and all those things that accompanied such batteries (horses, ammunition, forges, and at least sixty wagons). No railroad in all of Virginia was equipped to transfer his army in *under a week,* and each passing hour might mean the difference between success at Manassas and the destruction of the Confederacy.

Johnston told Jeb Stuart to divert Patterson's soldiers. They should "demonstrate"—riding up toward Patterson's lines actively and aggressively, as though contemplating an attack. They must perform a kind of hocus-pocus, an act of military prestidigitation. Using Stuart's actions as a magic curtain, Johnston intended to slink away, almost in plain view, while the audience was distracted. His plan, to say the least, required aplomb. He planned a *forced march* to Manassas, hoping to arrive there in time to make a difference. But the distance was almost sixty miles. Even later in the war, remarkable marchers like Stonewall Jackson's "foot cavalry" and Union General John Sedgwick's Sixth Corps would have been hard-pressed to reach Manassas in much under three days, and, likely, by the effort, they would have become too exhausted to fight effectively. Johnston was aware his men were already physically ill equipped to endure day after day of hard marching. Some of his soldiers had only recently arrived. (One day before they started, a diarist noted that a new company had just been added to his regiment, and although these men were proudly calling themselves the "Shenandoah Sharpshooters," they had arrived with no weapons and had been handed ancient flintlock muskets.) But Johnston felt he had no choice; he would play the cards he had been dealt.

During the late morning couriers with orders from headquarters galloped about. At the camps, soldiers began striking their tents, stowing them onto wagons. They cooked rations, most believing they were attacking Patterson.[85]

About noon, the army started moving out of Winchester, Jackson's brigade in the lead. When soldiers asked their officers where they were heading, they received shrugs. Before departing, an Alabamian jotted a quick note to his wife that they were leaving soon: "We are totally ignorant of the movement, whether in advance or retreat."

The troops of the Eighth Georgia were representative. A drumbeat had called them together, and their regimental commander, Lieutenant Colonel William M. Gardner, forty-four, rode to their front and gave them a little speech. Gardner was a wealthy Georgia lawyer and planter, and though not possessing a warm personality, he was a decent sort and strived to be a good leader. He usually joked with his troops when he could and during marches sometimes alighted from his horse and walked with them, chatting democratically with this man or that. Now, he told his regiment they were about to embark on an arduous march. He could not yet tell them, he said, where they were heading, but he wanted them to act like real men, to accept the situation with fortitude. They started off. It quickly grew obvious they were not going north toward Patterson but were moving southeast, through the city of Winchester, then beyond. The town's citizens warily watched them pass, contemplating the implications. As it dawned on them that Johnston was abandoning them, families began loading their belongings onto wagons, and merchants hid their valuables. Johnston's marching soldiers watched these activities and murmured to each other their embarrassment.

Then, one by one, out on the road several miles south of Winchester, each regiment was halted. Under the baking sun, commanders like Gardner told the regiments that General Beauregard, the Hero of Fort Sumter, was under attack at Manassas Junction and they were on their way to assist him — to defend The Cause. The Confederacy was in the balance. The men listened closely. This meant, they realized with relief, that they were not "retreating," they were not "cowards," they had a chance to make a difference, to be heroes. Each regiment in turn cheered and yelped its enthusiasm. On to Manassas Junction! On to save Beauregard! To save the Confederacy!

The regiments started marching again. The afternoon hours dragged. Legs grew tired. Occasionally, regiments would halt for a rest, and men would seek shady spots by the roadside. One soldier, an ex-schoolteacher, was drowsing under a tree when he heard shouting. He looked up and saw General Johnston riding by, his hand lifted slightly in a kind of generic greeting. The men yelled their pleasure at him. He was leading them to glory.

It was almost totally dark by the time Jackson's men, at the front of the whole army, reached the Shenandoah. They stared at the water. This spot was reputedly a fording place where the river's depth only reached the hips of an average soldier. A couple of flat-bottomed ferryboats transported the heavier gear and some of the soldiers who had sickened during the day's march. Wagons, moving slowly, could rumble across the ford, but most troops had to wade to the other bank. A few of the men modestly tiptoed through the water fully dressed, but most stripped off their shoes and pants, tied them into bundles that they draped from their guns, tucked their shirts into their armpits, and stepped off. The river bottom here was not soft with silt, but rocky, and the sharp edges made them wince, and the stones were slippery, and many a poor, half-clad wretch stumbled and fell, greatly entertaining his laughing, still-dry comrades. One drummer boy found that the water level reached his neck, and another diminutive fellow was carried across by a taller comrade. On the far side Jackson's men stopped, dressed, rested a bit, and moved on.

Johnston's army moved like a snake with a badly broken spine. Each regiment marched by itself. Some units became so separated from the others they took wrong turns and got lost. Crossing the river took a long time. The wait on both banks seemed endless, as each man stopped to undress, then redress, while their unit's equipment was being slowly boated over. One of Jackson's men, keeping a diary, declared that it took his brigade six hours to cross the Shenandoah. Another soldier thought they made it in four.

On the far side of the river came another trial. Now the army had a mountain to cross, which meant much uphill marching. A man's leg muscles burned painfully and his feet grew sore and blistered. Some fell out, others fainted. For hours, almost the only sound Jackson's men heard was the shuffle of their own boots.

Behind them, other brigades found the going even harder, particularly after dark. Bartow's men, coming next, reached the Shenandoah about eleven o'clock that night and had to light the fording place with huge fires on each side. In the flickering light the footing was even more treacherous. The men of General Bee's brigade, near the rear of Johnston's army, did not even leave Winchester until almost sundown, and did not arrive at the riverbank until near dawn the next day. A private in the Eleventh Mississippi wrote his wife afterward that Bee's troops marched with hardly a break, not resting at all throughout the night, stopping only once to eat, though they did pause for several hours at the river.[86]

General Johnston was not happy. "The discouragement of that day's march," he recalled, "to one accustomed, like myself, to the steady gait of regular soldiers, is indescribable." (It is interesting that Johnston's sentiments so closely mirrored the ones McDowell had felt the day before during the march through Fairfax Court House.) Volunteers, Southern as well as Northern, were not automatons. Many men broke down and could not continue. Some deserted—like the ten members of the Second Virginia, part of Jackson's later famous "Stonewall Brigade," who simply slipped away when the regiment left Winchester.[87]

Johnston's plan had been to march his infantry the entire way, using a fairly direct route, but it soon became obvious the pace was ponderous. In fact his army was slowing down. He considered utilizing the Manassas Gap Railroad, although its nearest depot, an infinitesimal dot on the map called Piedmont, was well south of the path he had wanted to take.

Years later, both Johnston and Beauregard separately asserted that using the train was their own brainchild. Each had some evidence to support his claim. The remarkable thing, however, is that, up to this moment, no high-ranking Confederate had seriously suggested using this short, almost obsolescent railroad for serious military purposes. During the war's first three months, the Confederacy's official records seldom mentioned it. The War Department focused far more on the Virginia Central line, which trailed off from the Valley into the western mountains. It seems that, only in retrospect, was using the Manassas Gap Railroad so obvious. The decision to do so was distinctly slapdash.

In his memoirs Beauregard claimed he made advance arrangements with the Manassas Gap Railroad's president to keep the trains available to bring "reinforcements" from the Valley to Manassas Junction (though which reinforcements are unclear, and Johnston's men were not the only Confederate soldiers in the long Valley). On the eighteenth Beauregard did send an aide, Alexander R. Chisolm, to ride and find Johnston, wherever that general happened to be, and give him a message that trains were ready to carry him east. But the real point of the note that Chisolm carried was Beauregard's proposal that Johnston ought to split his force in two, moving a portion of it directly to Manassas Junction by train and marching the rest—presumably the great majority of it—by a northerly route against McDowell's right flank. If Johnston, the message said, would take this more aggressive step, Beauregard would launch his own assault against the Yankee front as soon as he heard the sounds of battle coming from McDowell's flank.

After an exhausting thirty-five-mile ride, Chisolm did find Joe Johnston, but by this time the general was already at the Piedmont railroad station, so any advice about using the railway was superfluous. Johnston later recalled reading Beauregard's dispatch and immediately dismissing the absurd proposal of a simultaneous assault. Even if his army consisted of regular troops, it would be extraordinarily difficult to coordinate two unconnected attacks. In his recollections Johnston said: "It would have been impossible, in my opinion, to calculate when our undisciplined volunteers would reach any distant point." (Beauregard's memoirs suggest another reason for Johnston's reaction: The Virginian, the Creole thought, was timid, his entire career filled with hesitation and cautiousness.)

Despite Beauregard's later attempt to grab credit for the idea of using the railroad, it really was Johnston's decision. On the first day of the march from Winchester, even before nightfall, Johnston told his aide, William Henry Chase Whiting, to ride to Piedmont and see if he could scrape together some trains there, then report back. Chase Whiting was extremely bright. He had not only been the top student in his West Point class but was, from that time, the cadet with the school's highest academic record. He immediately galloped toward Piedmont. When he reached the station, he found no trains there and telegraphed officials of the railroad and asked for their assistance. They wired back they could piece together two trains and send them but he should not expect their arrival until the next morning. Although the railroad was a single-track, antiquated line, they thought it might be able to carry the entire army—or at least the infantry—to Manassas Junction within twenty-four hours, though it would obviously take a number of trips. Whiting considered this answer sufficiently promising, remounted his horse, and sped back toward Johnston. He had no way of knowing where on the road the general might be by this point but intended to track him down. The general turned out to be at Paris, Virginia, a small town at a Y in the road where a person could continue straight east (the route Johnston had originally intended to take all the way to Manassas Junction) or south to the railroad depot at Piedmont.

After listening to Whiting's optimistic report, Johnston made a decision. He sent orders back that his artillery and cavalry must continue to travel to Manassas Junction by road, while he and the infantry would board cars and entrain to that destination. Despite Beauregard's derision about Johnston's "cautiousness," this decision was audacious.[88]

Back in the Valley, Jeb Stuart had been watching Patterson's army and screening Johnston's departure. After twenty-four hours of this, he ordered a portion of his men to remain and continue what they had been doing, while he started toward Manassas with the rest. He and his cavalrymen rode all day and through the night. When blocked by Johnston's infantrymen jamming the road, they abandoned their food wagons and rode through the fields. Luckily, local citizens, as one private wrote his mother, supplied them with "plenty of good things, such as chicken, Biscuit, Butter, Eggs, Ham, Mutton, Honey & I don't know what-all." After two days in the saddle, they arrived at Manassas, well before most of the infantry. To their weary eyes, one of them recalled, the place seemed a madhouse, with trains arriving and leaving, wagons filled with supplies bumping along from one encampment to another. "Great crowds of men stood around everywhere, who seemed to have nothing to do, and among them, pushing their way regardless of imprecations showered upon their heads, rode orderlies, quartermasters and commissaries with the pompous gravity of those who believed the cares of the nation rested upon their sleek, well-greased heads."

Johnston's chief of artillery, William Nelson Pendleton, had orders to bring his five batteries to Manassas as a single unit. Three did arrive at the Piedmont station and paused to await the other two. Johnston, finally growing impatient, told Pendleton to move ahead without the two missing batteries. Pendleton left Piedmont after dark. The road was rutted and rocky and hilly, and in the darkness his gun carriages and caissons banged from side to side, jostling the exhausted artillerymen, who held on as best they could. It started to rain. The road turned muddy and sucked at the horses' hooves. The artillerymen stopped to rest the animals, and the soldiers threw themselves down and slept for an hour, pelted by the rain, then began moving again. Couriers from Beauregard found them and urged them to hurry, since Beauregard thought McDowell might attack in a few hours. About daybreak the artillerists stopped once more, this time to feed their horses, then continued on. The weather cleared, and road dust soon swirled into their nostrils and throats, making them painfully thirsty. They arrived at Manassas late that afternoon, July 20. McDowell had not yet attacked. One young artilleryman remembered: "I lay on the ground & slept as I never had slept before." The other two batteries, wherever they had been, finally stumbled in late that night, the last one arriving after one o'clock.[89]

Jackson's infantrymen started arriving at the Piedmont depot at six in the morning on the nineteenth, their second day on the road (the day after the Battle of Blackburn's Ford). No train awaited them. When the first one did chug into the station about eight, it proved to be old and rickety, designed to move freight and cattle. Jackson ordered his troops on board, but the train was too small to carry the entire brigade, so he jammed in those he could and departed. Some men rode in boxcars; others squashed themselves into open cattle cars, the rain falling on their heads and shoulders. Dragged down with too much weight, the train moved slowly, and stopped often. It took about seven hours to reach Manassas Junction, thirty-four miles away.

Jackson went immediately to Beauregard's temporary headquarters at McLean's farm to report. Beauregard was in the process of explaining to his brigade commanders that he expected Johnston to be assaulting McDowell's flank tomorrow, probably quite early in the morning. McDowell, Beauregard was explaining, would certainly turn to face that attack. He was saying that he wanted his commanders prepared to spring into immediate action, to fling themselves upon McDowell's back. Just then, Jackson appeared. When he told Beauregard that General Johnston was sending *all* of his army's infantry by train directly to Manassas Junction, Beauregard expressed astonishment, since this meant Johnston was ignoring his suggestion about attacking McDowell's flank. (That Beauregard seemed surprised by Jackson's announcement is curious. Beauregard's aide Chisolm had returned hours earlier, after meeting with Johnston at Piedmont Station and certainly would have formed an opinion of Johnston's reaction. Either Chisolm misunderstood Johnston's intentions or miscommunicated them to Beauregard.) Beauregard expostulated: Jackson's information had to be inaccurate! Jackson, standing there, facing Beauregard, was a close-mouthed man, and he had said his piece, he had nothing to add; he merely turned and left to see to the placement of his brigade. After his departure, Beauregard told the others in the room that he was quite confidant Jackson was incorrect, that Joe Johnston *would* in fact be attacking McDowell in the morning on the flank. And, insisted Beauregard, at least as Jubal Early recalled the words, as soon as Beauregard's army sprang his trap on McDowell, the result would be "a perfect Waterloo." The Yankee army would collapse; Beauregard's men would chase after them, cross the Potomac, and all of Maryland would rise up. The other officers at this meeting agreed that Jackson was oddly stolid, and no doubt something of a simpleton.

About sundown a second train left Piedmont with the rest of Jackson's troops, along with two Georgia regiments that were part of Bartow's brigade. One young Georgian decided the day was too hot to be cramped inside a stuffy freight car and climbed on top. Although the roof seemed a bit warm from the sun, he thought this a capital place to sit—until the train started off and the smoke billowing back choked him and bright hot embers flew against his face. As soon as the train stopped to take on more fuel, he swung himself into the boxcar below. There, the heat almost overpowered him. A few years back he had read about the poor souls who had suffocated in the Black Hole of Calcutta. He wondered whether he would survive this trip. He was greatly relieved to detrain at Manassas Junction the next morning.

Back at Piedmont, Johnston attempted to remain calm. Between the disjointed, desultory movements of his army and the empty hours dawdling at the depot, awaiting trains that seemed never to appear — with the fate of the Confederacy possibly hanging in the balance and Patterson almost certainly heading now in this direction — Johnston found tarrying difficult.

Little by little, pieces of his army stumbled in from the Valley, flooding into and around the station, spreading in all directions, thousands of bored men, lazing about, trading rumors. One train rumbled in from Manassas Junction about midnight, but before any soldiers could board it, its conductors and engineers vanished. The railroad men were exhausted after a day or two of unrelieved labor — since running a train in that era was physically taxing — and they apparently went off to rest. They did not reappear until the next morning, Saturday, the twentieth. (For some inexplicable reason, the remainder of Bartow's brigade did not then get on the cars; instead, about 1,400 of General Bee's brigade, who had arrived after Bartow, did so.)

Johnston finally concluded he could no longer remain here, acting as some sort of usher, and he boarded this train after ordering one of his brigade commanders, Kirby Smith, to take charge of organizing the rest of the army onto arriving trains. (Exactly what then happened at Piedmont and along the tracks is murky. Another portion of Johnston's army departed the depot several hours after the general left with Bee's brigade, but this train had a problem — a collision or a mechanical breakdown of some sort. Someone on board seems to have decided the conductor must have been secretly pro-Union, so the poor man was summarily "tried" and shot. The commander of the Sixth North Carolina, Charles Frederick Fisher, who was aboard, announced he was a railroad man, as were many of his North Carolinians. They repaired the engine or lifted it back on the tracks, and the train continued to Manassas Junction, where they arrived just as the battle was starting. Another trainload, carrying four regiments, left Piedmont in the middle of the night. Whether they would get there in time to fight seemed doubtful.)

Only about half, perhaps less, of Johnston's Valley army arrived at Manassas in time to participate in the main phase of the battle. But it was they, after their anabasis from the Valley, who would do much of the coming battle's hardest fighting.[90]

When Johnston arrived at Manassas, he felt drained. Although healthy and fit, he had hardly slept in three days. He also was concerned about the matter of seniority: Who was now in command here at Manassas Junction? He assumed it should be he, by the complex formulas of military tradition, but just to be sure, before leaving Winchester, he had wired Jefferson Davis a query. Davis telegraphed him that he indeed did outrank Beauregard and was in charge — which settled that question. But realistically, Johnston knew that Beauregard's knowledge of the terrain of Manassas gave the Creole an advantage, so, as Beauregard now rapidly sketched for him his proposals, Johnston listened. To his groggy mind, they sounded too grandiose, too Napoleonic, involving a series of coordinated assaults, but, under the circumstances, perhaps not unreasonable. He was fairly sure Patterson's army was already rushing after him from the Valley, and it would be prudent to try to defeat McDowell quickly, before Patterson reinforced the Union force. Johnston was dubious about some of the specifics of Beauregard's proposal but nodded vague approval. He asked Beauregard to have the necessary orders written for each brigade commander and said he would sign them (as the official commander of the combined forces). He turned away, found a quiet grove of trees, lay down, and fell asleep.[91]

INITIAL INERTIA

Centreville had once been a fairly prosperous little town, a crossroads where travelers stopped at its tavern to eat, drink, or rest. The village center sat atop a small ridge. From it, one could see in the west a stretch of beautiful, low mountains that appeared almost violet beneath the summer sky. On Sunday mornings Centreville's parishioners, along with families from dozens of outlying farms, attended services at the slate Episcopal church. It, like the town, had seen better days. Townsfolk had built a dozen or so homes that clustered where the roads intersected. Inside the backyards were assorted outbuildings and a frail tree or two. The dwellings looked dingy; many had fallen into disrepair. Some log houses showed wide gaps in the walls from which the mud used as filler had disappeared. A Virginian, passing through a few weeks earlier, called Centreville "a very old worn out vilige." Some houses, he noticed, were "without wroofs and some of them about to tumble down." A Union soldier nicely defined her: "It looks, for all the world, as though it had done its business, whatever it was, if it ever had any, full eighty years ago, and since then had bolted its doors, put out its fires, and gone to sleep." Confederate impressment gangs had swept up many of the white males. White women who could afford to leave had taken their children and essential belongings and fled, to stay with relatives. The town's blacks and its few remaining whites stared at the Union troops with trepidation.[92]

The tavern and the church stood vacant—until one of McDowell's surgeons appropriated them, along with a fairly large house, to serve as hospitals after the Battle of Blackburn's Ford. Late on that afternoon, ambulances started carrying the wounded (and several soldiers who had collapsed from hyperthermia or exhaustion) to the hospitals. (Two ambulances, arriving last, were forced to wait along the roadside while regiments in Tyler's division, marching in close order, passed by. The ambulance drivers tried a few times to break through, but their passage was denied, so the wounded men had to lie in the sun two extra hours, mere yards from proper care.) The church became the primary hospital, and the scene there that day was chaotic. As surgeons hurriedly put dressings on wounds and performed amputations, curious soldiers meandered in and looked about. Some wanted to check on the status of comrades; others came in search of food or water. The town's wells had quickly been sucked dry by Tyler's thirsty men, and the medical staff went to some lengths to find water to wash the wounded, but after setting some basins aside, when they came back to them, they found them emptied by stragglers. On Saturday, two days later, wounded soldiers who could be moved were transported back to a hospital in Alexandria.[93]

By that evening, most of Tyler's division had camped between the village and Bull Run, and much of the rest of the army had settled down two or three miles behind the town. The majority of the troops bivouacked in open fields, wrapping themselves in their blankets. Many assumed they would start moving the next morning. But the following day, after realizing they were staying a while, some of the more energetic soldiers built themselves better quarters to protect themselves from the sun's rays or raindrops. The practical Rhode Islanders, for example, created little huts by bracing boughs against fence railings and trees, actually lining them into neat rows like those of their prim Camp Sprague in Washington. They named this spot "Bush Camp." By Saturday, when it was beastly hot and the army still had not moved, more troops raised shelters of brush or blankets to block out the July sun. During these two days, troops scoured the countryside for food, and when they espied farm animals or even beehives, they often concluded these critters had "sesech" (secessionist) sentiments and could quite legitimately be expropriated. The hours dragged. On Friday an officer wrote in his diary: "Lounging, chatting & taking in the theory of initial inertia."[94]

Not everything during this hiatus was placid. Where the two armies abutted each other, the crackle of musket fire was often heard. Sometimes it involved pickets of one side shooting at those of their enemy, or it was merely a sign of nervous trigger fingers, pickets spooked by shadows or animals. On Saturday, after nightfall General Jackson was nearly killed by uneasy Confederates (presaging his death two years later) when he and a guide were riding near some of their breastworks. "I could hear the click of the musket locks being cocked all along the line," the guide would recall, "and I was mortally afraid they would fire on us." (A day earlier General Heintzelman had jotted into his journal: "This morning there was firing for hours, so that it was really dangerous to be about. With these long-range muskets & raw vols. it is really dangerous to be near them.") The pickets were made edgy by the noisy hum of enemy activities: laughter, bugle calls, drums. On Friday Tyler ordered Richardson to take his brigade back down the road toward Mitchell's Ford and position himself near Pierce Butler's farm. Confederates a few hundred yards away uneasily listened to the shouted orders from Richardson's officers, the ringing of axe blades, the crashing of timber, as the Yankees constructed a breastwork.

Colonel Cocke had never withdrawn one regiment, the Eighteenth Virginia, from the Centreville side of Bull Run, and, the day after the Battle of Blackburn's Ford, he sent a second, the Twenty-eighth Virginia, to join it. These two regiments, about 1,200 men, were within a long stone's throw of a Federal position. The men of the Sixty-ninth New York, part of Sherman's brigade, decided on a whim to bathe in a creek near their campsite. When they were fired on by Virginia pickets, they scuttled, naked, back to their own lines. Sherman apparently still did not realize how close the enemy was, because that night he led forty men on a scouting mission down the turnpike toward Bull Run, wanting to see if he could discover the presence of one of the famed rebel "masked batteries." With rain on its way, the night sky was inky. He split his team into two platoons, one on each side of the turnpike. He told them to creep quietly through the trees that bordered the road's edges, and, as they moved, he signaled his orders in pantomime. "We reached the Run after midnight," one of the men later recollected, "and failing to find any batteries, retraced our steps. A bunch of reb cavalry, on their own scouting mission, rode quietly by in the other direction."[95]

A few incidents during the days near Centreville were less bloodless. Friday morning Union scouts captured seven rebels and escorted them to the town while Union troops hooted at them and threatened to hang them. Someone noticed that one of the prisoners had been captured once before and had taken an oath of loyalty. Unlike his comrades who were sent to Washington, this captive was executed in Centreville Saturday morning.

To most Union soldiers, the grimmest moment during their sojourn in Centreville involved the punishment of two of their own comrades. By Federal law, soldiers could still be whipped, but only for one infraction: desertion during peacetime. The two men in question were members of the regular infantry. Some weeks earlier, apparently before the attack on Fort Sumter, they had absconded. This was not unusual, for the army normally lost almost 20 percent of its manpower each year through desertion. But these two unfortunates had recently been caught. On Friday the battalion of regulars drew themselves into formation. As curious volunteers watched, the two culprits were brought to the center of the square formed by the regulars. Their heads were shaved. Each was branded with an inch-and-a-half letter *D* (indicating "deserter"). They then were given thirty lashes. Every time the whip landed, blood squirted from their backs. One of their own officers, watching in horror, fainted. The gaping volunteers were shocked. A volunteer asked if this would be his punishment if he deserted. "No," he was told, "you would be shot" (such being the prescribed punishment for desertion in wartime).[96]

On Thursday evening General McDowell had conferred with some of his officers. He announced he was changing his original plan. He had decided, he said, that the roads to the south could not handle any meaningful military maneuvering. He intended, therefore, to sweep by some path to the north and pass around Beauregard's left wing. He was uncertain, he admitted, what the roads were like in that direction or where the best fording places were, but since the army must stay here until all the provisions arrived—presumably sometime the next morning—and would then need about twelve hours to distribute the food and cook it, they had at least a full day to check out the terrain. He told his chief engineer, Major Barnard, to coordinate the reconnaissance. McDowell said he wanted a report as soon as possible because he wanted to surprise Beauregard. (If too much time passed, a surprise attack would be impossible. As it was, a *New York Times* reporter wired his newspaper that very evening the news about McDowell's decision to order the army around the Confederates' left side.)

Performing this kind of reconnaissance is tricky. One does not wish to reveal one's intentions, so it is generally best not to probe forcefully. But, simultaneously, one has to find the best pathways for the army. Which roads can handle the passage of heavy artillery? Where are the fords? Which fords are shallow enough for infantrymen? Which for artillery? Are there bridges the army might or must cross? Are these strong enough to handle the stresses caused by an army in motion? What distances are involved? What is the nature of the soil (since soft dirt can bog down vehicles or, on dry days, be flung into the air as dust clouds, revealing the army's presence)? And, of course, what is the enemy's strength in this or that direction, and has he placed obstacles in the army's way? The best method of answering such questions is personal inspection. Sometimes this is possible, sometimes not. If one cannot examine each step along the army's proposed path, one may be forced to depend on local citizens or prisoners rather than one's own eyesight, but doing so is risky.

Are these people reliable? Are they honest? Normally, it is best to assume not, but circumstances may give one no alternative than to lean a bit on what they say.

Major Barnard's role was now critical. He performed it abysmally. Many factors are involved in combat, and luck always plays a prominent role. When analyzing a battle, one must recall that two sides are involved — and, in the case of Bull Run, it can be argued the outcome derived mostly from the abilities of certain Confederate generals rather than failures on the Union side. Yet, if any single Union officer bore responsibility for the disasters on Sunday, July 21, it was not Robert Patterson near the Valley or Winfield Scott in Washington, or Tyler or McDowell at Bull Run — although each of those men would later receive much criticism — it was John G. Barnard. This officer was forty-six years old, had a keen mind, and was a well-respected engineer in the prewar army. He had been responsible for several important military building projects and had served as superintendent at West Point. Shortly after Bull Run he was promoted and would eventually rise to the rank of major general, becoming the Army of the Potomac's chief engineer. But on this Friday and Saturday, July 19 and 20, 1861, his performance was overly cautious and sloppy.

His official report, written several days later, is revealing. It stated that, when he began carrying out McDowell's assignment, he was aware of the existence of the stone bridge, where the Warrenton turnpike passed over Bull Run, but he did not want McDowell's army to use it. Why? Because: "Such a point could scarcely be neglected by the enemy." In other words, logic, not personal observation, persuaded him that the stone bridge offered such a perfect crossing place the rebels *had* to have recognized this fact and placed there a strong defense.

"Information from *various quarters*," he hastened to add, "gave good cause for believing that it was guarded by several thousand men." What were these "various quarters"? He was probably not including Sherman's reconnaissance probe of Friday night, because he had rejected the stone bridge from the start. Most likely the "various quarters" were local citizens and prisoners. If so, the information they gave him was inaccurate; Beauregard had fewer than 1,000 men near the bridge at the time.

Barnard also had other concerns about the bridge. He believed that "at least four cannon were stationed to lay upon it and the ford not far below." This assumption was only partly correct. The Confederates had two small smoothbores at the bridge, though Cocke, whose brigade guarded the two fords half a mile downstream, had several cannon available to him. Barnard had also heard that the rebels had cut down trees and laid an "extensive abatis" on their side of the bridge. This was true, because Evans had had his men do just that after marching across the bridge the day before. But McDowell's army had already shoved aside dozens of such obstructions in the past few days, generally taking only a matter of minutes. One more abatis should not have been so intimidating. Barnard's last concern about the bridge was that it was mined. Again, he—or someone at headquarters—must have heard this tale from the "various quarters." While it is indeed surprising that Beauregard did not do so, the bridge was not mined.

(It is interesting to contemplate what might have happened had McDowell ordered a powerful direct assault on the bridge. His army might have either pushed through easily or gotten hung up there, like a soldier snagged on barbed wire. It seems most likely that a powerful thrust would have succeeded. A Union breakthrough there would have meant McDowell's soldiers would have had to go only a relatively short distance before they encountered their enemy and would have been far fresher when they battled the Confederates on the other side.)

With the stone bridge eliminated from Barnard's thinking, he had to consider alternatives upstream. So far as he knew, there were no bridges up there, but certainly there would be fording places. Since McDowell's plan involved having his army "sweep around Beauregard's flank," it would have to march north a distance, cross the stream, then march back south again. The fewer miles they marched the better. It was important to find adequate fords as near the stone bridge as possible. Barnard had a map of the region that indicated a ford called Sudley Spring two or three miles upstream. "Reliable information," his after-action report would say, "justified the belief that the ford was good; and that it was unfortified; that it was watched by only one or two companies." (This "reliable information" again came from interviews, not observation, but in this case his "various quarters" were correct—sort of. Sudley Ford *was* a good fording place and it was not well guarded, but the distance to it turned out to be far greater than two or three miles, and that discrepancy partly accounted for the ensuing disaster.)

Barnard understood there was another good ford somewhere between the stone bridge and Sudley Ford. Unfortunately, his map showed no roads leading directly from Centreville either to Sudley Ford or the intermediate, unnamed one. If such a path existed, he would have to find it.

He was aware that between Centreville and Bull Run was a stream called Cub Run. He understood that it meandered across the turnpike about a mile or so below the village. Reportedly, a cow path branched north from the pike just beyond Cub Run. Perhaps it was the "road" he sought, leading to one or both fords. But Major Barnard was troubled. Until he personally examined this path, he could not recommend it. He needed to determine if it could sustain the pounding of thousands of marching feet, to say nothing of heavy artillery vehicles. He also was concerned about the nature of the fords themselves. These must not only be relatively shallow, but their banks could not be too steep since that would hinder the advance of vehicles. In addition, the nature of the river bottom at the two fords was important. Small gravel would be best, but mud could be a disaster.

Thursday evening, after receiving McDowell's orders, Barnard made plans to search out the path in the morning. If he found it, he could follow it all the way to the ford, or fords, and inspect them. Since the army could not move until the provisions had been properly distributed, he had the entire day. If all went well, he hoped to report his findings to McDowell early enough—say, late afternoon or early evening—to permit the attack at dawn the following day, Saturday.

On Friday Barnard was accompanied by a company of cavalry. Governor William Sprague of Rhode Island also joined him. Sprague was in Centreville with two of his state's regiments and apparently went with Barnard simply for excitement. Another man with the party was Daniel P. Woodbury. Captain Woodbury, forty-nine, like Barnard, was a bright professional army engineer.

His specialty was topography, and he had had a distinguished record in the exploration of the West. (Later in this war he would rise to the rank of brigadier general.) Woodbury and Barnard, two of the best engineers in either army, formed what should have been a superb reconnaissance team. Why they failed is puzzling.

Barnard's party struck out from Centreville until they reached Cub Run, then swung to the right, following "the valley of Cub Run." But where did they first encounter the stream? Did they ride straight down the turnpike, the most direct route? If so, it is astonishing that neither Barnard nor Woodbury noticed that the bridge over Cub Run was old and narrow—too narrow, as it turned out. McDowell's army had brought materials to build bridges. An engineering team could easily have built one or two of them alongside the inadequate bridge over Cub Run. Their failure to do so would lead to irredeemable problems and, at the end, a military disaster. Proposing such constructions was Barnard's responsibility. One must assume he never examined the Cub Run bridge during his reconnaissance, an execrable error, fatal for many Union soldiers. It is probable he and his party rode northwest out of Centreville, moving at an angle, crossing fields until they came to Cub Run well north of the turnpike, too far away from the bridge to observe it for themselves. It seems likely that after splashing their horses across that stream and continuing on, they stumbled across the "road"—though, as Barnard would later admit, it was "a mere country path." He suspected this was the trail that led to the fords, and he and his party started following it.

But they soon glimpsed some rebels and stopped. "As we were most anxious to avoid attracting the enemy's attention to our designs in this quarter," he said in his report, "we did not care to pursue the reconnaissance farther." (His report did not say, but it is possible he was under orders from McDowell to avoid any contact. If so, this would soften somewhat his failure to check the fords himself.) The short distance Barnard's party traveled this road, perhaps a mile or so, did convince him "of the perfect practicability of this route."

Barnard was satisfied. Captain Woodbury, however, still wanted to scrutinize the two fords—to see whether they would, in fact, support the passage of artillery. He asked Barnard for permission to sneak to them after dark, along with "a few Michigan woodsmen from Colonel Sherman's brigade, to endeavor to find them." He did so but again ran into rebel pickets and chose to slip quietly away. (It seems possible that Sherman's reconnaissance party that night included Woodbury among its members.)[97]

Irvin McDowell was unsatisfied with the information gathered by these reconnaissance missions. He did not blame Barnard or Woodbury or Sherman; they all had faced the same obstacle: rebels on the Centreville side of Bull Run. But vexatious questions lingered about the nature of the path and the positions of the fords. The success of his army might depend on getting answers. On Saturday morning he sent the War Department a report about his progress so far. He said he had wanted to throw a "reconnaissance in force" at the rebels, but men, in his words, of "better judgment" had talked him out of it, proposing, instead, the use of "stealth." His men had, he said, tried five probes but had been unable to discover much. Because stealth had failed, he said, he was going to try greater force: "I propose to drive in the enemy [on the Centreville side of Bull Run] and get the information required." Pushing the rebels back across Bull Run would allow him to "examine it more closely than we have been able to do." It was probably an excellent idea.

The record now becomes murky. After writing this dispatch, McDowell changed his mind again. Why he did so is puzzling. We do not know who influenced him or what arguments they used. Five months later, when he testified to the Joint Committee, he only said that Barnard reported to him about noon on Saturday "they had found a place." What "place" this was, McDowell did not say. Nor did he clarify why it took Barnard until noon to make his report. Two things are clear. Barnard did not realize he had seriously underestimated the distance to Sudley Ford, and he totally failed to find the intermediate ford. McDowell's instinct that he needed more information had been correct.[98]

Sometime on Saturday, during the early afternoon, McDowell announced his plans. He told his division and brigade commanders to get ready to move at six o'clock. This would give them several hours to organize matters and have their men cook provisions. His plan was fairly simple.

Miles's division would be kept as a reserve near Centreville, with Richardson's brigade, still in its encampment not far from the Butler farm, temporarily attached to it. Richardson's assignment was to create a diversion, using his artillery as though he were about to thrust across Blackburn's Ford.

Tyler's division, now without Richardson's brigade, but still large and strong, would position itself near the stone bridge and open an artillery barrage as another feint, pretending it was about to cross. If all worked well, these two artillery bombardments would distract Beauregard.

The real attack would be made by McDowell's other two divisions, which would furtively slide north, using the path Barnard had found, hoping to remain unnoticed. Hunter's division, presently camped a couple of miles behind Centreville, would march through the village, down the turnpike until they passed over the Cub Run bridge, then turn off to the right onto Barnard's path. Following it, presumably two or three miles, they would reach Sudley Ford. Heintzelman's division, also camped two miles back of Centreville, would follow directly behind Hunter's, so close the two would be like railroad cars. But halfway up the path, a mile or so, Heintzelman would turn to the left and cross the intermediate ford that Barnard felt sure was in the vicinity (though he had failed to designate where, since he did not know). Heintzelman's division would cross the stream about a mile below Hunter's crossing at Sudley Ford. Hunter, having passed over Bull Run, would now hurtle down from the north, sweeping aside any rebels attempting to interfere with Heintzelman. Then, together, they would roll up Beauregard's left flank — which, McDowell correctly assumed, was probably laid out for eight miles against the stream. As the two divisions drove southward, they would scatter any rebels guarding the stone bridge. By this time engineers, with Tyler's division, would have built a wooden bridge next to the "mined" stone bridge, and the whole division would cross. Beauregard, caught by surprise, might be crushed, his back against the railroad station.

This plan, obviously, depended greatly on a certain amount of deception and rather precise timing. McDowell wished to mislead the Confederates about his intentions, but he knew he could not bamboozle them indefinitely. Inevitably, rebel pickets would inform their superiors that something was going on. But would Beauregard (and McDowell still assumed Beauregard was in command at Manassas Junction) correctly interpret the meaning of the reports he would be getting? McDowell thought, by advancing his army in different directions, Beauregard might become mesmerized by Richardson's and Tyler's activities, or at least misunderstand their significance — like a boxer confused by an opponent's left-handed jabs. On the other hand the feints of the artillery barrages could not be maintained indefinitely; the guns would run out of ammunition. More importantly, this sort of feigned "assault" could only fool an enemy, if in fact it did, for a limited time. Eventually, Beauregard would realize no attack was intended by either Richardson or Tyler. He would then be free to turn and face the real assault. McDowell worried about how steadfast his volunteers would be when facing cannon fire. The flight of the Twelfth New York at the Battle of Blackburn's Ford was disquieting. Yet, if his army got into position as they were supposed to and then moved ahead with even reasonable, not extraordinary, coordination, the plan could succeed.[99]

As he was finalizing its details, McDowell was quite aware that Beauregard was at this very moment receiving reinforcements. Richardson's men, in their forward position, could easily hear railroad cars arriving at the station. Trains had been coming in all day Friday, throughout the following night, then again on Saturday. Richardson's troops could easily hear cheering from rebels happily greeting the reinforcements. (The *New York Times* reported on Saturday that Richardson's men responded "derisively" to the cheers.)

Did McDowell think that the arriving rebel reinforcements were Johnston's men, or did he assume they only represented support being sent up from Richmond? A *New York Herald* correspondent told his newspaper he thought the arriving trains might be bringing in Johnston's army from the Valley, adding that

McDowell thought this was "probable." Someone on McDowell's staff, looking west with field glasses toward Manassas Gap, did detect a large wagon train coming toward them. A scouting party sent toward it on Saturday afternoon returned, convinced the vehicles were a segment of Joe Johnston's army (it was almost certainly Pendleton and his artillery). When the Joint Committee asked McDowell in December about when he learned of Johnston's arrival, he disingenuously replied that he only *really* knew it during Sunday's battle, after rebel prisoners were questioned. The Committee was puzzled, and a member asked: "Did no one tell you before?" McDowell's response was emotional, and muddled: "A man came to me before. But, great God! I heard every rumor in the world, and I put them all aside unless a man spoke of his own personal knowledge." It was true, he admitted, that he could recall someone saying, "We heard the cars coming in last night." But: "I expected that. I expected they would bring into Manassas every available man they could find." In short, McDowell knew on Saturday that Beauregard had received rather significant reinforcements — including at least some of Johnston's men. The Committee might have asked McDowell why he did not begin his attack earlier, before Beauregard received even more reinforcements. They might also have queried why he did not call up reinforcements from his own army — the division led by General Runyon, camped in reserve only a few miles back — and ask for additional manpower from the dozens of regiments still in the District.

One thing is certain: McDowell felt he could wait no longer. As Barnard told the Committee: McDowell and his advisers were in agreement that "the moral effect of a delay would have been bad, and that action at Blackburn's Ford had a bad effect upon the army." When the Committee asked Winfield Scott about the matter, the general admitted that there were discussions in Washington on Saturday about delaying the attack and that he had been urged to do so "by one or more members of the Cabinet." But, Scott told the Committee, it was "too late to call off the troops from the attack and, besides, though opposed to the movement at first, we had all become animated and sanguine of success."[100]

———

On the other hand, an observer who saw McDowell late Saturday afternoon thought he "appeared to be a good deal discouraged and in low spirits," at least in part because he "supposed the enemy to be in very large force." Another vexation for him was the prospect that his army was on the verge of coming apart. The terms of several regiments ended this very day. That evening the troops of the First Connecticut took a vote on whether or not to stay. Their initial reaction was to go home, but when their colonel told them a battle was coming tomorrow, only one man, a private, opted to leave. The men of the Seventy-first New York were offered a similar choice. Anyone who did not want to fight tomorrow should step forward three paces. Eyes peered from side to side. Finally a corporal stepped ahead—and stood there as the regimental adjutant ripped off his stripes and buttons, then departed. Similar scenes were repeated in other regiments. Unlike Patterson's men, most of the regiments that legally could have departed elected to stay, to see this campaign to its conclusion. But one regiment—the Fourth Pennsylvania—did not. McDowell pleaded with them to stick with him. Almost unanimously, they refused. (Their colonel, John Frederick Hartranft, was mortified. A thirty-year-old lawyer, he had raised this regiment himself. When it left Centreville to return to Washington, he refused to accompany it and volunteered to serve McDowell's army in any capacity. He was assigned to be an aide, and during the battle he performed admirably, then returned to Pennsylvania and raised another regiment. By the war's end he had become a major general, and eventually went on to be elected governor of Pennsylvania.) The Eighth New York Militia Regiment also agreed to stay—though an artillery battery, connected to it, voted to depart. McDowell told the artillerists they had to leave behind their guns—in a sense, their badge of honor.

The retirement of these two units and the simultaneous disinclination of most of Patterson's men to fight stand in stark contrast to the avidity of most Confederate troops. The differences were complicated but in general would seem to have derived from one fact: Although Union troops often thought of themselves as defending "America," the Confederates saw themselves as defending their "homes." One could make too much of the following analogies, but it is interesting that when two crickets fight, the one closer to his own niche almost always fights harder, and wins. The same pattern of behavior has been observed in monkeys, in birds, in fish. Robert Ardrey has called this trait "The Territorial Imperative."

Secretary of War Cameron arrived in Centreville Saturday morning. To do him honor, McDowell had Hunter's division pass in review. Cameron planned to spend the night, no doubt to observe the battle the following day, but changed his mind and rushed back to Washington in early afternoon—apparently to scare up reinforcements for a worried McDowell.[101]

After Cameron departed, McDowell spoke to Ambrose Burnside. The only other officer in attendance was the adjutant, Captain Fry. Burnside objected to the idea of starting at six o'clock. He told McDowell he thought his volunteers would be more drained by moving a few miles this evening, then more in the morning, than they would by swallowing the entire march in one gulp. Since Major Barnard's map indicated the distance from Burnside's present camp to Sudley Springs was six miles, his brigade would only have to march about seven miles before actual fighting. His men could march that far in less than three hours during the early morning. McDowell thought the objection reasonable. Besides, his plan was based partly on surprising Beauregard about his intentions, and the movements of Hunter's and Heintzelman's divisions this evening might reveal too much. Without giving the matter sufficient thought, McDowell accepted Burnside's objections. Had he realized that the distance to Sudley Springs was four miles farther than Barnard's map showed and that, as a result, some of his troops would be marching twelve or thirteen miles before even beginning to fight, he might not have been so quick to change his mind. As it was, he sent out couriers immediately, informing his commanders they would not be leaving this evening after all but, instead, tomorrow. He also told them to come to headquarters at eight o'clock that night for further clarification.[102]

At twilight his four divisional commanders and most of the brigade leaders arrived at McDowell's tent. They had to wait for a period as McDowell and his staff fine-tuned a few details. Sherman used the opportunity to jot a quick note to his wife. "We were under orders to march at 6 P.M.," he told her, "but it was properly countermanded as night marches with raw troops are always dangerous." He was feeling uneasy about the quality of Lincoln's "green" volunteers. He had heard disconcerting grumbling from many three-month men, including some of his own. He suspected that the volunteers might run—*stampede* was the word he used in his note to her.

McDowell finally opened the meeting by laying down Barnard's (inaccurate) map and, under the flickering light of candles and lanterns, sketching out the roles for each major unit. He read the orders aloud and did not hand them copies. He did not seek their advice. Unlike Patterson, he considered the give-and-take of war councils unproductive. Heintzelman asked for some clarification about the timing of his own march. Tyler later told the Joint Committee that he pressed McDowell about whether Johnston's army had joined Beauregard and that McDowell made no reply, but no one else recalled Tyler saying that. After an hour or so the meeting broke up, and the commanders went out into the night. It was almost eleven o'clock. The essence of McDowell's orders was that the units should begin to move in about three hours or so, around two o'clock in the morning.[103]

In Richmond the Confederate congress had reconvened that afternoon. President Davis had been hoping to be at Manassas Junction when the battle began but had felt the need to remain in the capital for this important political occasion. With the full government now in place and functioning fairly well, the Confederacy was much stronger. Even a rout at Manassas was unlikely to induce a Confederate collapse, no matter what the politicians and editors assumed in the North. This is essentially what Davis now told his congress: "To speak of subjugating such a people, so united and determined, is to speak a language incomprehensible to them." That evening, he made arrangements to leave first thing in the morning. He wanted to reach the battlefield before too late.

———

In Washington on Friday, John B. Crittenden had proposed that
Congress pass a resolution: "That this war is not waged, upon
our part, in any spirit of oppression, nor any purpose of conquest
or subjugation." And that Union troops would not interfere with
slavery. His resolution stated that, as soon as the Confederates
again agreed to accept the Constitution, "the war ought to
cease."

On Saturday the British journalist, William Howard Russell,
who was in Washington, decided to wander over and observe
Congress. He was unimpressed. A senator was orating endlessly
about some uninteresting topic, but none of his colleagues paid
any attention. They wandered about chatting with each other or
sat at their desks, reading newspapers or writing letters. This, he
sniffed, hardly constituted parliamentary "debate." He also heard
from some source that Joe Johnston had left the Valley with his
army.[104]

Near Sudley Ford was a church that local folks attended on Sundays. Most of the nearby population expected to be at service in
the morning. Normally, John F. Thornberry would have joined
them. He and his wife and five children lived across the road
from the church, and he fully intended to take the children to
Sunday school. But about seven o'clock Saturday night, Mrs.
Thornberry's brother appeared at their door and insisted that it
seemed too dangerous here; she and her children ought to come
stay at his place. She resisted but then reluctantly agreed. The
family left.[105]

At the camp of the Sixty-ninth New York, Father O'Reilly that
evening heard the confessions of many an Irish lad. He sat at the
base of a tree, and troops stood in a queue before him. One by
one, each man shuffled up, sank down to a kneeling position,
lowered his head, and asked for forgiveness.

On the other side of Bull Run, a Virginian wrote a prayer into
his diary: "Oh, Lord, give us the victory. Oh, Lord, help us in
this, our time of need. Oh, Lord, scatter our enimies before us, as
chaff before the wind. Oh, Lord, hear and answer my prear. I beg
for thy son, Jesus Christ sake. Amen."

A Union soldier wrote in his diary: "I pray that I may have the strength & courage to carry me safely through or to die decently & in a manner becoming an American soldier." Another federal soldier, feeling a different fervor, slipped inside the Episcopal church in Centreville and scrawled on one wall: "Death to all Sessessionists, Senterville, Vergenia, July 20th, 1861—By God." Someone else wrote nearby: "Death to Traitors—thus saith the Lord!" A third person, less biblical, simply scribbled: "J.D. [Jefferson Davis], the son of a bitch."

Men on both sides of the stream wrote letters home. Many spoke of the possibility they might soon die. "Give my love to everybody," a Georgian wrote. "Tell them that if I never see them again to try and forgive me if I ever have done them any harm." A Maine soldier wrote his brother: "Should I be slain ... forget my faults & forgive." Not everyone was so somber. "We are very sure of routing the enemy," a soldier from Wisconsin wrote his sister, "and we shall be in Richmond in one month from this time." But, he added, less confidently: "I do not think they will make much of a stand here; but I do not know."

At twilight, those glancing westward toward the Valley saw the blue shimmer of mid-July licking the graceful mountains. The evening air was warm, almost sultry. At the Union camps men sat quietly, smoking their pipes, thinking their own private thoughts, oblivious to the sounds of the katydids and the whippoorwills and barking dogs. Some talked to each other, musing aloud how they hoped they would behave in battle.

Across Bull Run a Virginian was so frightened he put his gun against his foot and tried to shoot off a toe, but his aim was bad, and he blew so much of his foot off that surgeons had to amputate it. Members of the Nineteenth Virginia, posted uncomfortably close to the stream, grew nervous and started digging a deep trench. The next day one wrote in his diary: "We concluded last night that our rail breastwork were not serficient for cannonballs & we comenced about dark to dig an entrenchment which would protect us better." They lacked shovels so used their knives and tin cups. "We worked on it untill 1 o'clock at night and then went to sleep."

A private in the Third Connecticut read a letter he had just received from his brother. "If you have a chance to send me one of them dam Rebel coats, with one or two bullets in it, I wish you would, as I want one . . . Don't forget to send me a Rebel coat without fail, SURE. Anything you can get which comes from the Rebel army, I wish you would send to me, as I want them for keepsakes. Now don't forget — anything you can get that a Rebel has or had, send to me by express."

About six o'clock the Union soldiers ate their evening meal: mostly hardtack and coffee. They were also provided with another three days' rations, but, as one admitted to his uncle, many threw the food away immediately because it was heavy and "bothered us in loading and firing." After eating, the men loitered around the campfires. They listened to nearby bands. Sometimes they sang aloud the lyrics. A few tunes were patriotic, others, like "Dixie," were simply fun. Many songs involved home: "Lorena," "The Girl I Left Behind Me," "Annie Laurie," and, of course, "Home, Sweet Home." When the Marine band closed its evening's recital with that number, hundreds of nearby soldiers, hearing it, wordlessly and intently listened, thinking.

Along the Union army's perimeter, almost two thousand pickets tried to stay awake. These men, in a few hours, would join their more rested comrades, marching toward the foe.

Stars scuttled across the sky — advising those who cared about such things that these marked the last hours of Cancer the Crab.

Cool air tenderly caressed them all, animals and men, offering no hint of the terrible, killing heat to descend on them in a few hours.

At eleven o'clock Henry J. Raymond of the *New York Times* submitted his latest report to his newspaper. It was lyrical. "This is one of the most beautiful nights that the imagination can conceive. The sky is perfectly clear, the moon is full and bright." He said he had just come back from McDowell's headquarters, where he had gone to see if anything new was happening. "As I rode over the crest of the hill, and caught a view of the scene in front, it seemed a picture of enchantment. The bright moon cast the woods which bound the field into deep shadows, through which the campfires shed a clear and brilliant glow . . . Everything is quiet, save the sounds of the music and the occasional shout of a soldier, or the lowing of the cattle, whose dark forms spot the broad meadow in the rear." He reminded his readers, "We are on the eve of a great battle."[106]

STUMBLING

No battle plan ever survives contact with the enemy.
—FIELD MARSHAL HELMUTH VON MOLTKE

Irvin McDowell spent the last hours of Saturday night and the following morning vomiting. He had eaten something that disagreed with him — perhaps some tainted canned peaches. The queasiness apparently began shortly after his conference broke up. Sometime after midnight he gave orders that a carriage be placed near his tent, since he might be too weak, too sick, to ride a horse. A few hours later, in the early morning darkness, as his army rose to its feet and began to shuffle forward, he remained in his quarters, trying to rest, hoping the nausea would subside. He was unaware that things already were starting to fray.[107]

The Union army, spread out around Centreville, came gradually awake after midnight. Drumbeats roused the men from their blankets The *tap-tap-tap* leaked from one regiment to the next. Thousands of campfires burst into flame to heat countless cups of coffee. The air had cooled, with a strong northwest breeze, and men shivered. Some soldiers gobbled down food, most did not. Silhouettes passed between the fires and the shrouded darkness,

as men checked their weapons and their accoutrements, performing the ancient rituals of warriors preparing for battle. Horses
whickered. There was the jangle of harnesses and bridles and the
creak of vehicles wheeling into position: the open-topped artillery
caissons, the white-covered supply wagons, and the black-
cloaked ambulances. The bright moon still lingered, but lower
now on the horizon. In its fading light, infantrymen lined up in
columns of four, their guns held against their torsos, their shiny
bayonets twinkling in the moonlight. At that moment the army,
seen from above, would have appeared like phosphorescent
plankton, swirling in some primeval formula.

Then, things bogged down. During the next five hours,
McDowell's 30,000 men functioned less like an army, more like a
traffic jam, their convolutions almost as random as thousands of
sports fans departing a venue at the same time. Did the problem
lie in the plan or its execution? According to Major Barnard's
after-action report, Tyler's division was supposed to have used
the turnpike to get into position near the stone bridge by about
four o'clock, permitting General Hunter, following immediately
behind and using the moon's last glimmerings, to turn right onto
the cow path well before dawn—that is, before five o'clock. All
the commanders were to be in motion by 2:30 A.M. Since two
of Tyler's brigades—Schenck's and Sherman's—were already
camped well in front of Centreville and the third—Keyes's—was
near town, according to McDowell's plan they should have had no
difficulty staying out of the way of Hunter's and Heintzelman's,
several miles behind them.

It boggles the mind that McDowell and Barnard thought
Hunter's and Heintzelman's divisions, equidistant from Centreville and starting at the same time, would not bump into each
other as they arrived at the bottleneck of the village. But that was
only part of the muddle. A worse snarl came on the turnpike west
of town, a mess created by bad planning.

Military men of that era applied certain formulas to determine how fast an army ought to move. A country road used
by wagons and pelted by a thousand storms normally has a natural crown running down its middle and ditches along its sides.
Columns of four men, marching side by side, should encounter no

trouble on it, even at night. With normal intervals between units, 3,000 infantrymen (the marching portion of a typical brigade) would take up a mile of road. But an army involves far more than infantry. Tyler had several batteries of guns, each of which usually took up a quarter of a mile of road. Ambulances and other necessary wagons absorbed more space. Putting these figures together, a fully-equipped brigade would likely cover about two miles, perhaps a bit less. And Tyler had three brigades. Of course, they would not be on the turnpike at the same time, because the men at the front would have pulled off the road and be in position while the tail of the division straggled along far behind. A normal pace, with breaks, usually averaged two miles an hour, but Tyler's division would inevitably be slower, since it had no cavalry to ride in front and scout for the enemy and would therefore have to depend on skirmishers. The distance from Tyler's camps to their destination near the stone bridge was less than three miles, with Cub Run as a potential stumbling block somewhere in the middle. The turnoff to the right that Hunter was to take lay a few hundred yards beyond the Cub Run bridge. Assuming Tyler's forward brigade crossed the bridge at three o'clock, which seemed not unreasonable given their starting time, the tail of that single brigade was unlikely to have cleared the cutoff before four o'clock — assuming no Confederates chose to interfere with the movement. And Tyler had two other brigades that were supposed to precede Hunter. It was unrealistic to assume all of Tyler's men could get past the turnoff when Barnard predicted. McDowell's timetable had built-in flaws. Worse, it left no room for snafus. These should have been expected — and of course they arose.

Vexations began almost immediately. Just as automobiles, driving through a thick nighttime fog, depend on the front driver's efficiency, the progress of McDowell's whole army relied on Tyler's forward brigade, under the command of Brigadier General Robert Cumming Schenck. The decision that Schenck should lead the way is curious. Of Tyler's brigade commanders, Schenck, fifty-one, was the only one without military experience, whose most noteworthy skill seems to have been poker, a subject he later wrote a book on. Although physically fit, his main qualification for his rank derived from politics. He was a Republican with more than two decades in politics, and he had campaigned hard for Lincoln the previous autumn. When the war began, he quickly rose to his present command. A month earlier he had been accompanying the Ohio companies that had fallen into the "masked battery" trap at Vienna. It was known that many of his men did not respect him. On Saturday, at his Centreville camp, there had even been an ugly incident. According to the *New York Times*, many members of his brigade had "publicly protested against being led by Gen. Schenck." This quasi mutiny was only resolved when the well-respected commander of the First Ohio, Colonel Alexander M. McCook, and a few other officers stepped forward and calmed matters. This makes Tyler's choice of Schenck to lead the entire army that morning almost daft.

Night marching, by its nature, is difficult. The macadamized turnpike had decayed. Here and there it was pitted and cratered. Men stumbled in the holes, cursed, and fell against comrades in front, who cursed them back. It was worse for the five companies of skirmishers fanned out on both sides. The pace of McDowell's entire army depended on these few hundred men, and they found the going slow. The fading moon hung low in the sky now, and the skirmishers often tumbled into ditches. Branches and thorns tore at their cheeks and their clothes. When they came to groves of trees, they literally had to feel their way. One would later recall: "We never knew where a fence or tree was located in front of us, until we ran slap against it. Many of the skirmishers had bloody noses and bruised limbs from such collisions." They communicated with each other in whispers and found it impossible to maintain lines perpendicular to the pike. The distance from their camp to Cub Run was less than a mile. Since their brigade had been responsible for maintaining pickets, at first they could move rather rapidly, confident they were unlikely to encounter many rebels. They arrived at Cub Run a little before four o'clock, and halted. They peered down at the stream suspiciously. The ditch it made was too wide to jump. Its banks were steep and fairly high, and the dark water below seemed deep. Even if the water proved fordable, the skirmishers would have to clamber up the opposite side. In the murk of predawn, the task of crossing this stream seemed formidable, perhaps dangerous. An officer ordered them to return to the pike and walk across the narrow wooden bridge, then spread out again. This particular operation probably took ten, maybe fifteen, minutes. Back along the road, thousands of soldiers stopped. Many sat down. A ripple effect occurred — halting and starting, halting and starting. Moving like this is annoying, and a person grows quickly exhausted and his legs and back stiffen up. Barnard's failure to prepare bridges for Cub Run was coming back to haunt the army before it had moved a mile, before it had yet laid eyes on the enemy.

Luckily, one potential difficulty did not arise. Attached to Schenck's brigade were several cannon. One was a gigantic, three-ton Parrott rifle, which fired a four-inch projectile, weighing almost thirty-three pounds. Maneuvering it on fairly flat roads required ten panting horses. Getting it up hills demanded the assistance of more than two hundred men, straining at long ropes hooked to the axles of its carriage. Since it was McDowell's biggest cannon, its roar could be heard at great distances, and it had been chosen to fire the signal that Tyler's entire division was in position near the stone bridge. But first it had to get there. When it approached the rickety Cub Run bridge, there was some concern its weight might be too much for the structure, but it passed across with comparatively little trouble. (Oddly, only *then* did an engineering crew hammer some wooden supports under the bridge to strengthen it.)

Meanwhile, Schenck's skirmishers, now three-quarters of a mile past Cub Run, finally caught first sight of their foes. Two Confederate *videttes* (pickets on horseback), hiding near a log schoolhouse, appeared suddenly, fired a few shots at them, and galloped away. One skirmisher later remembered seeing dust kicked up by the two bullets, so one can assume the sky was beginning to lighten, which would have made the time a few minutes after 4:30. The skirmishers edged ahead again, more cautiously. Now and then, as they approached rebel pickets, the two sides took potshots at each other, the pickets scuttling away in the morning murk.

Meanwhile, McDowell had grown aware something was awry. He could see from his headquarters that the army outside his tent was standing stock-still. He went to find what the problem was. He passed Heintzelman's men, jammed up behind Centreville, and rode past Hunter's two brigades, whose front man had hardly moved a single step beyond the Centreville intersection. (Andrew Porter, one of Hunter's brigade commanders, was still angry several months later when he testified to the Joint Committee: "We kept pottering along, pottering along in the way," he groused. "The whole affair was very disagreeable to me. I was disgusted with the whole thing.") McDowell finally discovered the logjam at the Cub Run bridge. He acted quickly, ordering Tyler's rear brigade—commanded by Erasmus D. Keyes—to move off the road and sit in a field on the left side of the turnpike until the two divisions behind it passed by. With Keyes's brigade out of the way, Hunter's men picked up their pace. The sun was rising now. Keyes's troops, watching their comrades go by, cheered them on. "Bully for you!" they shouted. "Go, Rhode Island!" "Give it to them, New York!" And a lot of good-natured whooping about which anatomical parts of Jeff Davis the victors ought to bring back and share.

A few hundred yards beyond the Cub Run bridge, a small blacksmith's shop sat just off the right side of the pike. Directly beyond it was Barnard's almost invisible path, leading into the distance. The time was about 5:30 when the horsemen at the front of Hunter's division turned onto the trail. Stretching for miles behind them were the two divisions that would require many hours to reach this turnoff. McDowell and his staff set up a temporary headquarters near the blacksmith shop. They remained here several hours, holding a kind of impromptu military review.[108]

On the far left wing of the Union army, a mile and a half from the blacksmith shop, Israel Richardson waited with two batteries, backed by his four infantry regiments. A few hours earlier, using the moon's last dim rays, he had placed his guns in their assigned positions, then spread infantry around them to shield them from surprise attacks. He also sprinkled pickets along the outer edges to watch for enemy advances. He was making his final arrangements when another colonel rode up: Thomas Alfred Davies, fifty-one, an 1829 graduate of West Point, who had been sent by their divisional commander, Dixon Miles.

Miles had decided, perhaps independently, he could best perform his reserve duty by entrenching one brigade — commanded
by Colonel Louis Blenker — at Centreville and sending the other —
led by Davies — to join Richardson. Davies had been ready to
move at 2:30 but had been caught by the Centreville jam-up. After
an hour or two of frustrating delay, he and his men struck out
across open fields. After a mile of arduous maneuvering in the
gray light just preceding dawn, they swung back to the road and
soon appeared at Richardson's position. The two officers then
danced a fine military pas de deux. "About this time Colonel Davies
came up with his brigade," Richardson told the Joint Committee,
"and inquired the date of my commission of colonel, and told me
his, and found he ranked me by eleven days. He took command of
the two brigades." Since Richardson had already been at this position three days and therefore knew its terrain, he pointed out to
Davies a nearby hill, six hundred yards away. Davies's guns could
be placed there. It was almost six o'clock.[109]

The Warrenton turnpike seems flat enough, when one looks at a
map, but it actually heaved up and down a series of ridges after
leaving Centreville. Then, about three-quarters of a mile from the
stone bridge, it crested the last ridge and sloped gradually down
toward Bull Run. If a person stood on this ridge, he could see
across the stream, though his vision would be partly blocked by
the overhanging trees on either side of the road. The nearer the
person approached the bridge from here, the more he could see
on the other side, beyond it, and left and right. Schenck's men
began moving over this ridge just before six and started turning off into the fields on the left. Directly behind them marched
Sherman's four regiments. They took a position on the right of
the pike. Then came the artillery pieces, the horses straining,
their leather creaking. The great Parrott gun was unlimbered and
its tail dropped onto the dusty turnpike. The commander of this
monster was Peter Conover Hains. Four weeks earlier Hains,
twenty-one, son of an impoverished Philadelphia shoemaker, had
graduated from West Point, nineteenth in his class. (Many years
after this moment, Hains would be the only Civil War officer to
serve during the First World War.) While Schenck's and Sherman's

infantrymen settled down on either side of the turnpike and other guns unlimbered off to his right, the beardless Hains, a large meerschaum pipe clenched between his teeth, loaded his huge cannon with a percussion shell and carefully aimed it at a white house he could see across Bull Run. He calculated the range and opened fire. His orders were to fire three shots—the required signal. And off they flew: *one—two—three.*

The time was— And here lies a minor mystery. Hains later thought it was "a little after six o'clock." A fellow artillery officer wrote in his report that it was "5 a.m. exactly." Beauregard later said it was 5:30; though on another occasion he declared it was six. Tyler's report said 6:30, and McDowell, no doubt merely following Tyler, said the same, though Tyler later admitted he had been wrong in his report, that it was likely closer to six o'clock. The most plausible estimate was provided by Henry J. Raymond, the *New York Times* reporter. Not only had he accompanied this division and was in sight of the scene; he was always precise about such matters, recognizing his duty to act as History's herald. One can be rather confident Raymond looked at his watch when Hains fired his first shot and recorded the moment. His report to New York that afternoon stated that Schenck's brigade had reached its position at 5:50, and that Hains's first mighty blast had come at 6:10.[110]

Richardson heard the heavy explosions to his right and knew it was Hains's signal. He and Davies ordered their own artillerists to open fire on an area a mile or so away. There seemed few targets over there—patches of trees that might contain rebels, some buildings that might be hiding troops. For an hour their guns whanged away. A few men were seen scattering from the buildings, but unlike the previous Thursday, this time there was no other response. After about an hour of this odd silence, Richardson, using a glass to examine the far side of Bull Run, saw large bodies of men moving here and there with some clear purpose in mind. He thought they might number as many as two brigades, perhaps more. Maybe they were about to attack. At present they were too distant to reach with his artillery. He had an engineering crew begin digging more earthen breastworks and chopping down trees, to form an extensive abatis—just in case.

The Confederates

Yarns were later told about civilians who caught glimpses of the Yankee movements and, by rushing to tell the Confederate leaders, saved the Southern army. An Englishman named William Thornton owned a place just on the Centreville side of the stone bridge. According to one story, he was one of the first to espy the approaching Yankee soldiers, and he hurried across Bull Run to tell someone. He seems to have reported his sightings to Colonel Evans, whose demibrigade guarded the stone bridge. In the 1930s an interviewer heard from an elderly local citizen another tale: "When Cousin Welby Carter saw the Yankees he got on his black horse and rode nine miles to tell General Beauregard that McDowell had flanked him."

Whether or not such stories were true, men like Evans and Beauregard were too experienced to listen to the overheated observations of civilians. Besides, by dawn Beauregard was receiving other, more reputable reports—though he could not yet decipher their pattern.

During the hours of darkness, a Confederate colonel, William W. Kirkland, twenty-eight, was splashing back and forth across Bull Run. He was a conscientious officer, in command of the Eleventh North Carolina, one of Bonham's regiments, sitting behind Mitchell's Ford. He could not sleep and decided to check on his outer pickets on the other side of the stream. When he reached their position, about two o'clock, he could hear in the distance, coming from Centreville, what sounded like heavy vehicles in motion—possibly artillery, he thought to himself. He considered the matter important enough to wake up General Bonham, who ordered him to investigate further. Kirkland went back and listened some more. It was still dark when he returned to Bonham's headquarters and reported he was positive the enemy was in motion—a significant number of infantry, along with artillery and cavalry, but he was not positive which way they were

headed. Meanwhile, after Kirkland's first report, Bonham had
sent an aide, Samuel McGowan, to go check on what might be
happening over there. McGowan, forty-one, a respected South
Carolina lawyer and politician, had served with some distinction
in the Mexican War, after which he had held high rank in his
state's militia. He was a good observer and not inclined to hysteria. Bonham trusted him. When McGowan returned from
his reconnaissance, confirming what Colonel Kirkland had said,
Bonham ordered him to carry this news to Beauregard. It was
light by this time, probably almost six o'clock.

Bonham decided he had better look for himself, so he, too,
crossed the stream and rode almost as far as the Butler farm.
Bonham stared through field glasses to his left — totally missing
the presence of Richardson's brigade a few hundred yards away,
hidden by trees. The contour of the land provided him a clear line
of sight to the turnpike, more than a mile away. He could make
out columns of soldiers moving along the pike. He was certain
they were headed in the direction of the stone bridge or, perhaps,
just downstream from it: Cocke's position. He sent word to
Beauregard that an attack was about to begin. Then, according to
his after-action report, he "directed my whole command to prepare
for action, as I supposed the assault would be made early along our
entire line." About that same time the artillery of Richardson and
Davies opened up in his direction, confirming his suspicions.

Bonham had been, to put it simply, fooled. He had no inkling
about the northern sweep of the two Yankee divisions. Thus far,
McDowell's plan seemed to be working.[111]

Beauregard was also getting reports from his commanders
stationed near the stone bridge. Colonel Eppa Hunton of the
Eighth Virginia was actually a long-time resident of this area. He
knew about the many roads that fanned out from Centreville, including the one leading to Sudley Ford. Although his post this
morning was at Cocke's position, half a mile below the stone
bridge, he had posted pickets at key points across Bull Run. Five
of these men were in place somewhere on the road that Major
Barnard had designated would lead the army to Sudley Ford.
Early that morning, these pickets reported to Hunton that an un-

determined number of Yankees were using that path. He forwarded that information to Beauregard.

Other reports began arriving from Cocke's two regiments still
on the Centreville side of Bull Run: the Eighteenth and the
Twenty-eighth Virginia. During the night they had maintained
pickets who had positioned themselves near Cub Run. When
McDowell's army first started moving, the squeaking of the wagons and the voices of the men carried easily through the night
stillness. The pickets knew at once something was going on and
informed their commanders. Colonel Robert Enoch Withers, who
headed the Eighteenth, would later recall he was awakened early
by a messenger and immediately went out to the picket line,
where he "could plainly hear the rumbling of the artillery, and
ambulances, and even the words of command as the column
passed along the pike not more than a quarter of a mile away."
Colonel Robert Preston, of the Twenty-eighth Virginia, did not
even have to go that far. "The passing artillery," he said, "was
distinctly audible from my quarters." No doubt, both Colonel
Withers and Colonel Preston reported to Cocke what they were
hearing, and presumably Cocke forwarded this information to
headquarters, though no such record exists. Evans did send
Beauregard a message about increased small-arms fire coming
from somewhere to the right of the stone bridge (the little firefight between Schenck's oncoming skirmishers and Cocke's pickets beyond Bull Run).

All these shards of information made an impression on
Beauregard, but they were also confounding — especially since they
partly contradicted what he had anticipated. It seemed as though
McDowell was not flinging the whole weight of his army toward
Mitchell's Ford; apparently he was jabbing at least a probe against
either the stone bridge or Cocke's position next to it. Beauregard
impulsively concluded that those supposed "probes" were not significant enough to alter his plan. In his mind he had McDowell
right where he wanted him. All he needed do was to close the trap.
Beauregard's plans also were about to encounter some snags.[112]

Beauregard remained fixated on Mitchell's Ford. He was so
convinced McDowell would attack there he had, a day earlier,

moved Evans's brigade from the stone bridge to a reserve position behind Bonham—in the process leaving the bridge completely defenseless. He only sent Evans back to his original position at the bridge a few hours later, after another contingent from Johnston's army arrived. Beauregard obviously did not consider the bridge important.

On Saturday evening, as we have seen, Johnston and Beauregard had conferred, and Beauregard had explained his idea about launching an attack in the morning—taking the offensive rather than awaiting McDowell's pleasure, and Johnston, believing that Patterson's army was probably on his tail, hounds after a fox, had agreed. During this discussion both Confederate generals had been exhausted. It is likely they did not communicate well with each other. Since Johnston had no knowledge of the terrain, since neither he nor Beauregard could know how many of the Valley army would arrive by morning, some ambiguity in their conversation would have been inevitable. Although they agreed on a strategy, each had left their meeting with different assumptions about the plan. One can surmise, however, that the two generals concurred on this: On the left wing, Evans would be at the stone bridge, and when the fighting started, he would remain there. Downstream from him, Cocke and Bonham would splash across Bull Run, using the fords in front of them, and attack. This thrust would be backed up by Ewell, Jones, Longstreet, and Early, each of whom would cross the ford directly before his position. Johnston's men would act as a reserve, mostly stationed near McLean's farm, from which they could cross quickly, using any of the three fords near that spot. If other Valley troops arrived in time, they could be plugged in as needed. As a package, it was not unreasonable, but, as Beauregard himself later stated, proper orders ought to be, when and where possible, exceedingly precise about matters of time and routes to be taken. (Just a month earlier, near Big Bethel, Union regiments on the march had started shooting at each other. Such mistakes often occurred when unconnected military units, unable to communicate with each other, stumbled across an uncharted landscape.)

Years later, Beauregard jotted some words of wisdom for military men. One morsel was this: "Nothing should be left to accident." If a commander, he said, failed to focus on each detail of his planning, "a thousand accidents may disconcert it." A commander cannot "trust to the intelligence of subordinates." He must "anticipate and provide against every misconception or stupidity it is possible to foresee." It is wisest, he said, to consider one's subordinates — those who would execute one's orders — "to be the most stupid of mankind." When he wrote those words, perhaps he was recalling this particular Sunday morning.

After Johnston had left their conference Saturday evening to rest, Beauregard had the responsibility of writing out the specific orders. Normally, he would have depended on his chief of staff Colonel Jordan, but he discovered this was impossible. A few hours earlier, a physician, noticing Jordan's "nervous exhaustion," had prescribed a narcotic, and Beauregard found the staff man slumped over a stack of papers strewn across his desk. Beauregard kindly retreated from the room and ordered a guard to stand outside the door to prevent anyone from disturbing his sleeping aide. (After the war Jordan earned a living as a writer. On Saturday night, if he had been less fatigued, or drugged, the orders he would have penned would have been relatively crisp, especially since he was used to refining Beauregard's sometimes scrambled thinking.) With Jordan unavailable, however, Beauregard had to find an acceptable replacement. He chose Major Chase Whiting, Johnston's chief of staff, a man of extraordinary acuity, but himself no doubt also bone-weary after his trek from the Valley. During the next few hours, Beauregard and Whiting, working together, produced orders that, all in all, were startlingly foggy in their prose and fatuous in their implications. Presumably the fault was Beauregard's, for he later admitted he dictated the orders as Whiting merely transcribed them.

Beauregard's orders, as written, were scrambled. They referred to nonexistent "divisions," and they specified movements of a brigade that was not even at Manassas Junction. The orders repeatedly stated that the brigades should remain "more or less distant [from each other], according to the nature of the country and of the attack." While military orders ought to allow for a certain flexibility on the battlefield, this phrasing was extraordinarily vague. The central core of the plan was to have Bonham's and

Cocke's brigades, backed up by two of Johnston's, cross Bull Run and attack Centreville. Instead of attacking with six brigades, as Johnston thought they had agreed, Beauregard was now proposing to use only four. This meant that the assault on McDowell's large army was to be made by, at most, 8,000 men. Six other brigades were to cross the stream, but they were to hang around near their separate fording places, miles from each other, awaiting developments. And, to confuse matters further, the attack was not to be launched at a specific time. The plan repeated five times this sentence: "The order to advance will be given by the commander in chief." But the orders never named that person—General Johnston—and this was a significant lapse, since many in Beauregard's army remained unaware that Joe Johnston was now in overall command.

Johnston had gone to sleep in midevening, thinking he would be awakened in a few hours and handed the orders. This would allow him time on Saturday evening to review the plan and sign off on it, permitting the orders to be distributed before midnight. But it was morning when Johnston first got a chance to check them. He later remembered he read the orders by the light of day. (Since first light that morning was 4:29, presumably the time was near five o'clock.) He was not happy with them. The placement of the brigades felt wrong to him. The army's strength remained in its center and its right. As he saw it, the left was weak—and nonexistent above the stone bridge. Johnston thought he had, the night before, clearly indicated to Beauregard he wanted his own Valley men, mainly Jackson's, Bartow's, and Bee's brigades, moved over to the left—behind Cocke's position. This had not been done. In Beauregard's orders they were miles away, near McLean's farm. Nor did Johnston like the muddled movements the orders described. Since the original assault would be made by, at most, four brigades (in fact three, since the fourth had not yet even arrived), the other six hung in the air. In theory these six might reinforce the main assault—or, if McDowell's troops fell back, they could try to intercept the retreat. To Johnston, the orders were likely to result in a series of piecemeal attacks, allowing McDowell to crush the Confederates a section at a time.

On the other hand, Johnston thought it too late to change things. He assumed that he had merely been handed copies of the orders for his signature, that the brigades, being stretched for miles in all directions, had no doubt already received their own copies—and that the brigade commanders were at this moment in the process of obeying them. Actually, what was happening along Beauregard's right flank was a classic Keystone Kops routine, resulting from miscommunication.

When Beauregard started receiving reports about Yankee movements, it seemed obvious McDowell was directing at least part of his attack down the Warrenton turnpike. So, changing his orders, Beauregard told Evans (at the stone bridge) and Cocke (just below it) to maintain their positions "to the last extremity." According to Beauregard's revised thinking, Evans and Cocke would hold McDowell near the stream's edge, and the other four forward brigades (Bonham, Longstreet, Jones, and Ewell) would cross Bull Run. Using Mitchell's Ford as their pivot point, they would swing around and crash down against McDowell's flank, crushing him. Bonham and Longstreet only needed to push ahead a bit to get into position; Jones's men would have to march several miles. Ewell's brigade—off on the far right flank—would be moving the farthest. So, to coordinate this imaginary swinging line properly, Ewell must start first. (In a sense, Beauregard's mousetrap plan was similar to one the German general staff later devised to defeat the French, named after its creator Alfred von Schlieffen, whose dying words reportedly were, "Keep the right wing strong." But Schlieffen and his staff spent *years* analyzing with meticulous care the roads and bridges and waterways their army would have to use; Beauregard had only the vaguest picture of the region in his mind.)

Beauregard sped a courier to Ewell: "I intend to take the offensive throughout my front as soon as possible." And: *"You will hold yourself in readiness* [emphasis added] to take the offensive on Centreville at a moment's notice, to make a diversion against the enemy's intended attack on Mitchell's Ford and, probably, the Stone Bridge." (This last sentence is convincing proof Beauregard was still confident McDowell's main assault would be at Mitchell's Ford—though, years later, he recalled himself as much more prescient. He would later say that the first reports "caused me to apprehend that they would attempt my left flank at the Stone Bridge.") This dispatch did *not* order Ewell to start moving, so Ewell—quite properly—did not.

Beauregard's new orders of that early morning had to be distributed over a confusing area the size of a middling village, with insufficient roads and no markings to indicate where the brigade headquarters were. Couriers galloping about apparently got lost or were misdirected. Beauregard would later blame *them* for the confusion. "It is next to impossible to find out who was the bearer of the order," he told Ewell, who never received Beauregard's dispatch. A few days later Beauregard was still seething about the whole thing. "Our guides and couriers," he said, "were the worst set I ever employed, whether from ignorance or over anxiety to do well and quickly, I cannot say." Probably he was at least partly correct, but he was also overlooking his own later advice: *Nothing should be left to chance.* (Years after the battle a Union surgeon told a story that, although probably apocryphal, was not impossible. He said he heard that the horseman with the critical message for Ewell stopped at a farm house to get a sip of water and that the farmer there offered him some peach brandy instead. Once he started again, he was a trifle woozy and cracked his head on a tree limb, knocking himself out.)

In the stillness before dawn, the men of Longstreet's brigade, still positioned at Blackburn's Ford, heard the rumble of Yankee artillery moving—Richardson and Davies setting up their guns. Shortly afterward, Longstreet received Beauregard's preliminary orders to advance, and almost simultaneously the Yankee guns opened their fire, aiming in his direction and at Bonham upstream. Longstreet decided to split four of his five regiments into two wings (with the fifth regiment to act as a reserve), each wing consisting of one regiment, backed by another. Both wings were to get into position so they could launch assaults, each focusing on a single battery. With all four regiments acting simultaneously, the Yankee guns could not reinforce each other. As a preliminary step, Longstreet ordered each wing to throw out skirmishers in swarms to confuse the enemy. He would launch his attack as soon as he received the follow-up orders from his superiors. His men crossed Bull Run before seven o'clock and crept cautiously forward. (Remarkably, commanding some of Longstreet's skirmishers was a regimental chaplain, the Reverend James Sinclair, who had volunteered for the assignment because several officers in his regiment were too indisposed to proceed.)

As soon as Longstreet's skirmishers crossed, they encountered the swollen and partly decomposed bodies of Yankees killed there three days earlier. Men retched at the smell and the sights. Although ordered to bury the remains, they found themselves too revolted to do an adequate job. They threw some dirt over the bodies, just to reduce the stench, and moved on. The Yankee artillerists observed their advance, turned their guns, and opened fire with canister, shot, and shell. Following orders, Longstreet's men lay down. But the bombardment was terrifying and four companies stood up and ran. (In his later report their regimental commander admitted that the panic had involved the officers.)

While Longstreet's skirmishers were splashing across Bull Run, two of his aides rode to see if they could discover the enemy's intentions. One of the two was Benjamin Franklin Terry, forty, a large, well-to-do Texan who had volunteered his services to the Confederacy, which had assigned him to Longstreet up at Manassas. With him was Thomas (or Thompson) Saltus Lubbock, forty-three, also of Texas. They reached a hill on the Centreville side and Terry climbed a tree. He saw in the distance, off to the left, a long column of Yankees in motion, apparently heading in the direction of the stone bridge. He reported this to Longstreet, who sent this information back to Beauregard. Shortly afterward, Longstreet received orders to return to his original position behind Blackburn's Ford, and he abandoned his notion about charging the two batteries.

To Longstreet's right, Jones received his orders at 7:10, telling him that Ewell would be attacking and that Jones should *follow* him—that is, Jones should not move until Ewell did. But Jones, hearing nothing further and getting edgy, decided to cross the stream. Here he halted for hours, awaiting word from Ewell. Nothing. Finally, at 10:30, he was handed a dispatch from Beauregard that he must come back. Meanwhile, at least three other brigade commanders never received their morning's orders: Cocke, Holmes, and Early.[113]

By seven o'clock that morning, Beauregard's optimistic notions had vanished inside that cliché, "the fog of war." But he did not yet know it. Beauregard continued to believe he was about to hear the sounds of an epic battle taking place near Mitchell's Ford as the forces he and Johnston commanded threw themselves at the unprepared Yankees. Two days later one of the Creole's aides described the mood at Beauregard's command post. "We got up in the morning at daylight, took a cup of coffee and remained quietly laughing and talking at headquarters, while the scouts were passing in and out bringing news from the enemy." They heard the opening booming of artillery fire but were not noticeably concerned.

In fact by nine o'clock many troops in both armies were feeling quite lackadaisical. Mail was distributed to some regiments and was avidly read. Soldiers sat about, ate, and chatted with each other.

Charles A. Jackson, a young private from Chelsea, Massachusetts, was a member of Richardson's brigade. He and his comrades had moved forward during the night and lay on their bellies not far from the rebel pickets. They spoke to each other in whispers or remained silent. At dawn they pulled back a bit and were drawn up behind the guns that were firing across Bull Run. "I have just finished my breakfast," he wrote home that morning. He said he had drunk some coffee and eaten a chunk of fire-charred beef, slaughtered the night before. He complained that he had neither salt nor pepper to put on it and said he "could relish a good solid meal, I assure you!" Even at this moment he was not convinced there was about to be a fight. "We may have a battle again today, and we may not." As to his own role: "If I fall I shall be content that it was in my country's cause, and in performance of the duty I came here to fulfill." He closed his note:

"There go the big guns somewhere. I expect I will have to 'fall in' now."

At that same moment, on the far side of Bull Run, another man was jotting a note home. Willie H. Hardy was a member of the Second South Carolina, part of Bonham's brigade, which was presently being bombarded by the Yankee guns. "Upon this beautiful Sabbath morning," Private Hardy wrote his mother, "I am writing to you on the eve of a battle." Someone nearby, he said, had just offered "a most appropriate prayer." "Everyone," he told his mother, "seems to think that this Battle will decide this War on the part of the enemy. If they are defeated they will be very likely to give up the War." He added, "We are hourly expecting an attack."[114]

En Garde

At the front of McDowell's sweep toward Sudley Ford was Ambrose Burnside's brigade: two Rhode Island regiments, one from New Hampshire, and one from New York. With them were six cannon manned by Rhode Island militia artillerymen and two little naval guns the New Yorkers had borrowed. On Saturday night any of Burnside's men lucky enough to fall asleep had been awakened shortly after midnight. They were camped well behind Centreville. McDowell's orders were to be ready by two o'clock and the officers wanted to do things right. Ambrose Burnside, a conscientious man, soon had his brigade organized and in motion. They passed through the core of Centreville well before three o'clock, but a few hundred yards down the pike they were forced to halt behind Tyler's slowly moving division. They waited here a wearisome, interminable two hours. Finally, after the efforts of Tyler and McDowell cleared the way, they started up again.

The sun was rising slowly behind them as they crossed Cub Run bridge. A few minutes later they arrived at the blacksmith shop and made the turn. They found themselves crossing farms, through cornfields and pastureland, through fields of sedge and other low brush. Captain Daniel Woodbury, the engineer who had scouted this area at least twice, showed them the way. The path through the farmland was virtually invisible, and riders checked ahead to keep them on track. They finally entered a forest trail. Once beneath the leafy canopy, their pace slowed. The lead regiment was the Second Rhode Island. Accompanying them was a wagon filled with tools, and these came in handy. Here and there fallen trees and stumps and limbs, the impediments nature drops across narrow woodland trails, had to be cut away to allow the wagons free passage. Twenty-five pioneers from the Second New Hampshire wielded axes as fast as they could, but the work was hard and the pace, by necessity, sluggish. Even after cutting back foliage, the trail remained so narrow that wagon wheels scraped the bark from trees on both sides. For miles behind them, more than 10,000 men shuffled along.

Except for the tramp of their feet, the crack of axes, and the occasional cock crowing at an isolated rustic farmhouse, the march was quiet, almost serene. "I wish I could adequately describe the loveliness of this Sabbath morning," one of the men later wrote. "In the midst of war we were at peace. There was not a cloud in the sky; a gentle breeze rustled the foliage over our heads, mingling its murmurs with soft notes of the wood-birds; the thick carpet of leaves under our feet deadened the sound of the artillery wheels and the tramp of men. Everybody felt the influence of the scene, and the men, marching on their leafy path, spoke in subdued tones."

They passed a log hovel. Standing near it was a filthy woman. She shouted to them they were marching to their deaths, that a huge Confederate army—her husband with it—anxiously awaited them. Her derision, as well as the signal shots from Hains's big gun behind them, reminded them what they were heading toward.

Beyond the main forest, they might have cut straight toward Sudley Ford, but Captain Woodbury chose to take them on a far more roundabout route, to remain unnoticed as long as possible, apparently guided by a local citizen, Mathias C. Mitchell. So for a while their path actually drifted east, away from Bull Run, then northward, well past Sudley Ford, before curving back down toward the stream. From the blacksmith shop to Sudley Ford, their march quite resembled a question mark. When the first troops reached Bull Run, they were two hours behind the schedule that McDowell had anticipated. Later critics would blame Tyler or Schenck for having been laggards earlier in the morning, but most of those two hours derived from Captain Woodbury's decision to move furtively rather than quickly. Because the brigade followed his circuitous route, Sudley Ford was not two miles from the turnpike, as Barnard had thought, but was closer to seven. Not only did this mean McDowell's schedule was off; it also meant that troops who had had, at most, two or three hours of sleep, marched at least ten miles before they even reached the ford. And they would be expected to go more miles, then engage the enemy — which inevitably would involve much running about. Although they were not lugging knapsacks, the things they did have to carry — their guns and ammunition, their blankets and haversacks — weighed more than twenty pounds. A cool front was approaching, but it was still miles away and would not arrive till evening. The morning temperature was a trifle less stifling than it had been, but the difference felt hardly noticeable to heavily laden men marching for hours. Sweat coursed down their sides and faces. They carried canteens but had been urged by their officers not to drink too greedily since no one knew how much water they would find along the way. As it turned out, they passed a few creeks, but most of these, in mid-July, were bone-dry. Inside the forest, under the branches, the heat seemed not too bad at first. But whenever they left its leafy protection, the sun hammered upon their shoulders. Men began to drop by the side of the road — to examine the blisters on their feet or chew some hardtack or suck from their canteens. Some of these stragglers later rejoined their comrades; others chose not to or found themselves physically unable to continue.

McDowell's chief medical officer, William Shakespeare King, was with the general and his staff at the blacksmith shop. As the army marched by, he noticed that the regimental officers, "from an idea that great haste was necessary, constantly repeated the command to close up." Since the front of the army stopped occasionally to allow the axmen do their work and because the path was uneven and men often stumbled against rocks and broken chunks of wood, the pace of the march for those in the back of any unit was erratic. The orders to "close up" meant that men who had had insufficient sleep and were carrying many pounds were frequently running a few feet, then slowing, then stopping, then running again. Over and over. Surgeon King told McDowell he thought "the men would be exhausted before they reached the scene of the action." McDowell urged the men not to run, but only a few heard his admonitions. Elsewhere, his officers urged speed.

It is unwise to force men to run before a battle. In combat they will need energy and stamina. On a battlefield they may have to charge uphill carrying their weapons and accoutrements or fight hand to hand. Men who have double-quicked any distance have left on the path behind them much of their strength.

The front of the Second Rhode Island reached the end of the forest trail about 8:30. Sudley Ford was an hour away, but the road was better now and clearly marked. They found themselves walking through a collection of rather prosperous farms. This region, along with Sudley on the far side of Bull Run—where were clustered a mill, a post office, a cooperage, and a fair sprinkling of homes—was essentially a single settlement. When the Second Rhode Island appeared, local inhabitants—parents and children dressed in their Sunday garb—surprised by their emergence from the forest, were hitching up carriages to carry them to the church near Sudley Ford. Few words were exchanged between the soldiers and the civilians, other than some questions the curious locals asked and the pleas from soldiers for victuals, or water.[115]

Burnside's men were becoming desperately thirsty. Those who analyze war without taking account of the soldier as a human being cannot understand battle. In 1861 people commonly used the term *sunstroke* for what is now recognized as *hyperthermia*. Even a young person, in fit condition, can quickly fall apart when overheated, particularly if he has recently suffered some health problem like measles or diarrhea. The brain has a thermostat, the *anterior hypothalamus*, which determines when the body's temperature has risen too high, and reacts. At first, it causes blood vessels to expand; the heart beats faster and harder to increase blood flow, as blood pumps toward the skin. Sweat appears and evaporates, trying to cool the body. Perspiration contains *electrolytes*—substances that conduct critical electrical currents inside the body's system. If fluids are not replaced, *heat exhaustion* can result. Drinking water, by itself, cannot instantly provide energy; it takes time to restore the necessary sodium and chloride ions. A person suffering mild dehydration can feel light-headed and suffer nausea, might faint, become disoriented, tense, and argumentative. As the condition worsens, an individual will lose coordination or grow confused and lose the ability to make proper judgments, might even suffer hallucinations. The muscles grow less flexible; movement becomes more difficult. A person now might suffer *heat syncope*, and faint. The sufferer can develop *heat cramps* (muscle spasms, usually in the legs or abdomen, caused by the loss of electrolytes) which can grow so painful that the sufferer cries uncontrollably. The best way to deal with such spasms is to rest. By this stage, a person's skin is no longer flushed—it has become pale and often clammy. The pulse speeds up (reaching 160–180 beats per minute) but also grows weak. Breathing grows faster now and becomes shallow. The hypothalamus, to save the body's core, dilates the skin's blood vessels. Perspiration may now cease. Blood pressure falls. The body temperature rises. When it rises beyond 104 degrees Fahrenheit, *heat stroke* occurs, a condition that is life-threatening; an individual can die in less than thirty minutes unless his body temperature is rapidly lowered. Even horses suffer dangerous heat reactions. For example, while pulling army wagons in the sun, they might develop *anhidrosis*, the inability to sweat—and drop dead, in their traces.

A typical Civil War uniform weighed four to six pounds, not counting the shoes that usually added another three pounds. Around his waist a soldier normally wore a leather belt, from which hung a four-pound box containing forty cartridges. Strapped across his body, from right shoulder to left hip, was his haversack, where he kept his food and utensils—perhaps six more pounds. When his canteen was filled, it weighed about four pounds. His gun and bayonet totaled at least ten pounds. Burnside's men carried rolled-up blankets (four pounds) and a rubberized mat (another two pounds) slung together around their bodies. Altogether, therefore, each man was supporting almost forty pounds. (Today, soldiers often carry far more weight, but their burden tends to be much more artfully balanced.)

When Burnside's men reached Sudley Ford, the flowing water of Bull Run felt enticingly cool. For a few minutes the Second Rhode Island lost all organization. The horses stooped their heads into the stream to drink; men rushed forward to plunge in their canteens and burning feet. One of Burnside's aides, along with some cavalrymen, rode ahead to scout. Shortly, they galloped back with word that an unknown number of rebels were half a mile or so beyond the ford. Burnside reorganized the Second Rhode Island as best he could and ordered them forward. These men were about to open the Battle of Bull Run.

The troops of the Second Rhode Island, about 800 strong, respected their colonel, John Stanton Slocum, thirty-six (not related to Henry Warner Slocum, who commanded the Twenty-seventh New York). Although not a West Point graduate, he had been a lieutenant of Rhode Island troops in the Mexican War, where he distinguished himself by his courage. Scion of a wealthy Rhode Island manufacturing family, he had made himself a prominent munitions maker in his own right. He was fascinated with military matters and studied battlefield tactics as a hobby. In 1860 the War Department even appointed him a member of a West Point examining board. When the Civil War began, he was appointed major of the first regiment that left Rhode Island. Then, when the Second Rhode Island was formed, he was put in charge of it. Slocum was of average height and build and sported a giant mustache that jutted from both sides of his face like bull horns. He seemed a kind man, solid and sensible. He radiated simultaneously an avuncular concern for his men's welfare and a no-nonsense professionalism about their training.

His second in command, Lieutenant Colonel Frank Wheaton, was also from a well-to-do Rhode Island family. He had been a restless young man. At seventeen he had dropped out of Brown University and gone West, accepting a position as a surveyor for a team drawing the new United States-Mexican border. He stayed at this task five years, impressing someone in the Army enough that he was appointed a regular army lieutenant even though he had had no military training. He was assigned to the cavalry, and he served on the Indian frontier. An extremely attractive fellow, he married Maria Cooper, the daughter of the army's adjutant general, Samuel Cooper. (This family connection, just now, was something of a problem, for Wheaton's father-in-law had abandoned the Union army for the Confederacy and had become one of Jefferson Davis's right-hand men.) Wheaton, who had recently turned twenty-eight, had been asked to take a temporary assignment with the Second Rhode Island to guarantee that a professional soldier was part of its regimental leadership. He had accepted the position only a few days earlier and was still in the process of getting acquainted.

The Second's third field officer was the lawyer Sullivan Ballou, who had written his wife that remarkable love letter. Beneath these three officers were ten companies of infantrymen, wearing blue flannel shirts, gray pants, and the absurd *kepi*, the forage cap common on both sides of this war. They carried old-fashioned smoothbores, converted from flintlocks to percussion muskets. The effective range of these weapons was a few hundred yards when they were aimed with some skill. The .69 cartridge the guns fired was not a minié ball, which could only be used by rifles, but contained one large round ball and three smaller buckshot. At close range this weapon could do the trick, but a shooter had to get uncomfortably near his foe.

Almost all members of the regiment were native New Englanders; most in fact had been born in Rhode Island. One of these was Corporal Elisha Hunt Rhodes, nineteen, from Pawtuxet. Son of a sea captain who had drowned three years earlier, Rhodes was his mother's oldest child. After his father's death, he had dropped out of school and started clerking at a nearby textile mill. When the war began, he asked his mother for permission to join. She said no, certainly not, the family needed his income and the leadership he provided. He brooded. He later recalled she came by his bedside one evening and said, "My son, other mothers must make sacrifices and why shouldn't I? If you feel it is your duty to enlist, I will give my consent." Then she turned and left. He did not sleep well that night. In the morning he rose while it was still dark, took the six o'clock omnibus for Providence, and enlisted in a company. He had not the slightest clue about military matters, but he was proud to don his new uniform and rushed home to show himself off to his friends and family. His mother wept when she saw him.

In early June ten Rhode Island companies had been shuffled together to form the Second, and Colonel Slocum tried to transmogrify them into some semblance of "soldiers." Two weeks later they left their state, arriving in Washington on June 22 and plopping themselves down next to the First Rhode Island. Accompanying them that day was their governor, William Sprague. And therein hangs a tale.

In 1861 Governor Sprague was something of an enigma. He was an enormously wealthy young man, with money drawn from the family businesses started by his father and uncle, mostly textile mills. Young William was only thirteen and away at boarding school when his father was murdered. He left school for good and began working at one of the family's mills, first as a clerk, then in a counting room, then as a bookkeeper. His uncle died when he was twenty-six, making him a partner in the business, along with his brother and a cousin. These three, led mostly by William, made the company even more profitable. He had a well-organized mind and seemed, as people said, to have a "good head for business." In 1860, as a twenty-nine-year-old Democrat, he ran for Rhode Island's gubernatorial chair and won. Although a bit short and quite slender, although bespectacled and noticeably stoop-shouldered — perhaps from so many years poring over ledgers — he was nice-looking in a romantic-poet way. His brown hair was wavy, his eyes were gray, and he sported a wispy, uncertain mustache. By nature he was amiable and shy, rather in the manner of Bob Cratchit. Perhaps his awkwardness partly explains why he entered politics. Maybe the governorship offered him an aura of pizzazz that he felt he lacked and could not get from the business world. A decade earlier, at eighteen, he had joined Rhode Island's "Marine Artillery" as a private and in time became its colonel. He liked to lead it in parades, riding a spirited, prancing horse. He personally outfitted this artillery unit in rather exotic

Zouave uniforms. When heading its marching formation, he himself wore a blue jacket with huge gold epaulettes — perhaps, some have believed, to hide his narrow shoulders. Jutting from his hat rose a jaunty, operatic yellow plume. When the war opened, he escorted the First Rhode Island to Washington, then went back and brought down the Second. He dithered over these two regiments like a mother hen. Ensconced with them at Camp Sprague in Washington, he made sure they got nutritious food, received mail promptly, had entertainment and spiritual guidance, and were given the best medical attention. Everyone admitted their band was superb. All critical observers of the volunteer regiments recognized the two from Rhode Island as being the healthiest and as having the highest morale. President Lincoln and his cabinet often visited their camp, not far from the White House, to review their evening's evolutions.

People also began to notice that Governor Sprague seemed quite enchanted with the fetching, vivacious daughter of the secretary of the Treasury, Kate Chase. He was seen to squire her here and there about the city. She also seemed drawn to him — or perhaps to his money.

On this day of battle, Governor William Sprague, although a civilian, rode at the very front of McDowell's army, astride a beautiful white steed called Snowdrop (a sweet but unmartial moniker he did not much care for). Officially, he was a volunteer aide to Burnside. Unofficially, he was here to watch over his charges, the Rhode Islanders — and to participate in this Grand Moment. No one, not even he, knew how he would react to gunfire.[116]

It was not quite 9:30 when Governor Sprague and Colonel Slocum and General Hunter, the divisional commander, led the troops of the Second Rhode Island beyond the stream and up a slight hill beyond it, past the post office and the cooperage and the church. Of necessity, they moved at the pace of a walking man. They could see fields through gaps in the trees but little else. They saw no movement. Then they rounded a copse. To the left, several hundred yards away, was a small house with some outbuildings. To the right was a cornfield. Rail fences drew brown lines across the landscape. The Rhode Islanders had just stepped into History.

The Battle of Bull Run, about to open, would really be half a dozen "battles," maybe more, depending how one wishes to count, many occurring at the same time in widely separated parts of a battlefield that stretched for miles in all directions, with hills and woods that blocked visibility and inevitably separated units from each other and generals from their commands. The region was sprinkled with houses and farms. This meant that buildings and fences were about to become both impediments and guideposts. The homes of certain unfortunate families were about to become...landmarks.

The Confederate Position, near the Stone Bridge

Before the first glint of dawn, as the skirmishers of Schenck's brigade were inching past Cub Run, moving toward the stone bridge, pickets of the Fourth South Carolina heard them coming. The pickets could distinctly detect voices—especially the sharp orders of commanders—approaching from Centreville. They informed the officer of the guard. In turn he went to his commander, Colonel J. B. E. Sloan, and woke him. Sloan would later recall the time as three o'clock, though it was probably closer to 3:30. He sent word to his superior, his brigade commander, Colonel Evans.

When Nathan George Evans, thirty-seven, had been a student at West Point, his fellow cadets, searching for an appropriate nickname, looked at his scrawny legs and found their answer. From that time on, they called him "Shanks." He stood third from the bottom of his class. Born in South Carolina, Evans graduated a few months too late to participate in the Mexican War. He spent most of the next thirteen years in the West, exploring the land and contending with Comanche warriors, sometimes hand to hand. He developed a reputation in the small fraternity of America's army officers as being slightly feral—not very bright but contentious and tough, a fierce fighter. One of his classmates considered him "a rude brawler," and said he was "insubordinate, gruff, rough-hewn and intemperate."

Evans was of middling height and muscular. His hair was receding and he compensated with a bushy mustache and a long thick brown beard. His icy blue, porcine eyes were as pale as a South Carolina mountain stream. People whispered that he drank to excess, and folks liked to repeat the Paul Bunyanesque tale that he kept a Prussian orderly near him at all times, toting a gallon drum of whiskey so Colonel Evans could have a swig anytime he wanted.

During the previous few days, "Shanks" Evans had been using as his headquarters a house not far from the stone bridge. Its owners, Abraham and Jemima Van Pelt, had lived there with their daughter Elizabeth, thirty-six. Some locals considered the Van Pelts a trifle sympathetic to the Union. Their home was hardly majestic. It was a simple, white-sided structure, but, like their neighbors, the Van Pelts had given it a grand name, calling it "Avon." Evans was probably asleep when the officer of the guard came and informed him what the pickets had said. Soon afterward, he himself could hear the desultory chatter of occasional musket fire from beyond the bridge. Clearly, something was afoot. He sent a dispatch to Beauregard with this information, sketchy though it was. He had no way of knowing that he and his little demibrigade were across the stone bridge from an entire Yankee division, outnumbering him almost ten to one. Nor could he know that in a few hours two additional enemy divisions, crossing Sudley Ford, would be charging right at him. "Shanks" Evans and his little force — isolated at the far northern corner of the Confederate army — were between gigantic pincers that were closing on them.

In a sense, the actual attack began when young Lieutenant Hains yelled, *"Fire!"* to his gun crew, and the shell from the giant Parrott hurtled toward Avon — for that was the white building Hains had aimed at. If Hains's recollection was correct, that first projectile actually struck the house. Whether it did is not relevant; Evans was no longer there. He was already scurrying around outside, positioning his men as best he could. His meager force consisted of something over a thousand troops, plus two measly six-pounder smoothbores, manned by a score of artillerists. The heart of his force lay in the fortitude of its two disparate infantry units: the Fourth South Carolina Regiment, commanded by Colonel John B. E. Sloan, and a battalion from New Orleans, led by Major Chatham Roberdeau Wheat.

The Fourth South Carolina had arrived in Virginia a few weeks earlier. Most of its members had been residents of the hill country in the western corner of the state. Not much is known about this regiment, for its records were destroyed in Richmond's conflagration of 1865, but one can deduce a few things. There were no vast plantations in that section of South Carolina, and few families there were extremely wealthy. Towns in that region were small, villages mostly, with a wide sprinkling of isolated farms and clusters of families. Few folks in that mountainous area had extensive education, but neither was the region impoverished and backward, populated by sallow-skinned "clay eaters," as were some parts of the state. The best insights about the Fourth South Carolina come from letters written by Private Jesse Walton Reid to his wife back in Greenville. We know that Reid accepted the unpleasant necessity of this war, but he was neither enthusiastic about it nor naïve. "Big men," he told her, "seem willing to drink all the blood that will be spilled in this war. I do not feel quite drouthy enough to do so myself." "I mean to do what fighting I have to do as soon as possible," he wrote from Virginia, "and get back home to Dixie." (It is interesting that he seems not to have considered Virginia part of "Dixie," but perhaps he was merely being whimsical.)

The Fourth South Carolina arrived in Richmond and was forwarded up to Leesburg. The men liked this place fine, but they were here only a couple of weeks before meandering slowly southwest—toward Manassas Junction, halting along the way a few days at a time. At Frying Pan, a spot Private Reid did not care for, they joined another unit, this one from Louisiana. The union was not entirely blessed.

The men from New Orleans usually were called "Wheat's Battalion," or, in newspapers, the "Louisiana Tigers." Wearing colorful

Zouave uniforms and affecting a pugnacious swagger, they attracted notice—and quite liked the attention. They consisted of only five companies (less than 400 men). They would have become a full regiment had they been willing to wait at home a few more weeks, but they were anxious to get to Virginia before the war—the fun—was over. Inside their home state they had been incorrigible; on their train ride north they were obstreperous; and on their arrival in Richmond they were raucous. A Southern reporter described them as "the most picturesque, romantic, ugly, undescribable-looking set of daredevils who ever shouldered a musket... [I]n their harum scarum style of doings, the absence of all restraint and their unquestionably fierce aspect, they are calculated to produce a sensation, both morally and at the point of the bayonet, wherever they go." He added optimistically: "Small, wiry, active as squirrels, brown as Malays, and full of aqua fortis, they are certainly the most dangerous set of individuals who have yet been brought into the field." A Confederate clerk agreed, finding them "a splendid set of animals; medium-sized, sunburnt, muscular and wiry as Arabs; and a long, swingy gait told of drill and endurance." He did note, however, that their "faces were dull and brutish, generally." He believed their orders were given in French, "the native tongue of nearly all the officers and most of the men," but he was wrong. Though they fiercely enjoyed their reputation as a bunch of madcap French Algerians, most of the enlisted men, coming from New Orleans's levees (or, some said, its alleys and its jails), had either been born in Ireland or were the children of Irish immigrants. They shaved the tops of their heads, often leaving a long pigtail to fall against their napes. When marching, they belted out a Zouave song, whose chorus allowed them to shout, "*Zou-Zou.*" They drank themselves into stupors, or violence. They stole things; they broke into people's houses; they carried knives and brass knuckles. The good citizens of Richmond were happy to see them depart. They arrived at Frying Pan, Virginia, and were brigaded with the Fourth South Carolina. The mountain boys—not exactly angels themselves—found the New Orleans Zouaves repellent. Private Reid told his wife that, in less than a week camped together, three of the Tigers were dead or dying from accidents. One South Carolinian, whose own company happened to abut the camp of the Tigers, did not appreciate the close association. "I got enough of them in short order," he recalled. "A day or two after we got into camp two of his [Wheat's] captains, both named White, fought a duel with their rifles, but neither was killed." He thought that "no one but Bob Wheat could manage them. I have often seen him tie them hand and foot, gag them, and pour water down their throats to make them stop fighting among themselves."

Roberdeau Wheat was himself an interesting character. A sophisticated young girl from New Orleans who knew him slightly—in an unromantic sort of way—considered him a charming fellow. When he died, she remembered him as "a genial, warm-hearted friend, a jolly companion, generous, and affectionate son and universally beloved by all." In a way, this was a fairly good, if limited, description of Wheat's personality. He could be quite endearing. He had a puppy dog quality, was a sort of antebellum version of Peter Pan—boyish, undisciplined, perpetually immature, drawn more to "adventure" than settling down and practicing the law he had trained for. He was striking, with sparkling dark eyes and wavy brown hair. Extraordinarily tall, he was lean when he was young, but as he grew older, his love of food expanded his girth until he tipped the scales at 275 pounds—not grossly fat, exactly, because he had a kind of gargantuan quality, with hulking, brawny shoulders and a thick chest. A man's man, he never married, though he often spoke longingly of it. The son of a minister, he was an eloquent, Scripture-quoting public speaker, and had he applied himself to politics, he would have been a successful politician. When still a young man, he had moved to New Orleans. Here, among the Creoles and filibustering expansionists, he found his niche. He became an adventurer. He fought in the Mexican War as a volunteer cavalryman, then twice more in Mexico during the decade afterward, supporting several Mexican revolutionaries. He also led a band of freebooters in an unsuccessful "invasion" of Cuba. He even spent a few weeks in Italy, as a volunteer in Garibaldi's cause. A dreamer, he was habitually in debt. Men were drawn to him and his exploits. Though far too capricious to participate in any extended enterprise like a long war, he was transparently both courageous and decent. To him, the Civil War was just one more adventure. On the morning of July 21, he and his motley crew held the farthest post on the Confederate left wing. He had just turned thirty-five.[117]

By five o'clock that morning, "Shanks" Evans was totally convinced a major Yankee force (Tyler's division) was heading in his direction down the Warrenton turnpike. He assumed they would either press over the stone bridge and through the abatis his men had placed there or would cross just above or below the bridge. He wakened his troops. He split Sloan's Fourth South Carolina into pieces. He pushed four of its companies ahead — two to hide behind the trees lining the stream to act as skirmishers, the other two to serve as a reserve, downstream from the bridge. He told the rest of the regiment to go back and lie down behind a hillock where they could not be seen.

During the next hour the two sides along Bull Run sniped at each other. One of the South Carolinians was B. B. Beazeale, a member of one of the companies below the bridge. His captain ordered him to take a squad of four other enlisted men even farther downstream. The five of them sidled along until they found themselves all alone, the right wing of Evans's thin brigade. Beazeale decided to sneak his little band over Bull Run, crossing on a log to keep their feet dry. They were lying in some broomsedge brush when they saw two Yankee horsemen approaching, unaware of their presence. Beazeale and a comrade crept closer, using a rail fence to conceal their movements. Suddenly, his companion, standing a step behind him, unable to bear the tension any longer, fired at the riders. The Yankees dropped from their saddles and disappeared in the thick brush. Beazeale ran to the fence and peeped over to see if he could see them. He was astonished when a Yankee bullet flew by his ear, and flung himself to the ground. "This was," he would recall, "the first intimation I had that a Yankee would shoot you if he had the chance." The four foes, two on one side of the fence, two on the other, stayed low. Time passed. Birds began their morning chirping. Apparently the Yankee videttes, if that is what they were, withdrew.

Beazeale and his friend slipped back to the rest of his squad, and waited.

Meanwhile, "Shanks" Evans had ordered Rob Wheat to place a single company of his Louisianans near the bank of Bull Run, upstream from the men of the Fourth South Carolina. Evans also sent his little unit of cavalry to support Wheat's battalion. Wheat sent them to the stream to reconnoiter.

The Union Position, Just Across the Stream

Somewhere on the far side of Bull Run, hidden by the trees that lined the opposite bank, was a Yankee brigade, led by the ever-watchful, redheaded Colonel Sherman. A few days later "Cump" Sherman wrote his wife about this morning. Although his orders were simply to perform a demonstration, he, always edgy, positioned his men, then rode ahead. He peered at the stone bridge and the abatis but saw no evidence of the "strong fortifications we had been led to believe." Astonishingly, he even espied a local citizen, out quietly hunting with his dog this fine Sunday morning. Everything else seemed quiet: "About nine o'clock I was well down to the Run with some skirmishers, and observed two men on horseback ride along a hill, descend, cross the stream, and ride out towards us. He had a gun in his hand which he waved over his head, and called out to us, 'You d__d black abolitionists, come on,' etc. I permitted some of the men to fire on him, but no damage was done." The defiant Confederates were probably two of Evans's cavalrymen. Some historians have speculated that maybe one was even Major Wheat himself, but this seems implausible; even Rob Wheat was not that vapid. Whoever they were, they had altered the coming battle.

Between the stone bridge and Sudley Ford were actually two fords, not one—again, Major Barnard had been wrong. One, about a mile north of the bridge, was locally known as Poplar (sometimes Red House) Ford. It was a fine fording place, capable of supporting farm wagons and carriages. Many local people used it when they wanted a shortcut to or from Centreville. Almost certainly, this was the one Major Barnard had heard about two days earlier, which, he suggested to McDowell, Heintzelman's division could utilize, while Hunter crossed Sudley Ford, a mile farther up the stream. But Major Barnard's inept, or at least overly cautious, reconnaissances had failed to uncover the path to it. (Apparently, McDowell's army only found this ford late that afternoon, if at all. Had they discovered it earlier, this might have changed the battle's outcome by greatly shortening the distance the Federals had to travel.)

Another ford crossed Bull Run between the Poplar Ford and the stone bridge. When the two rebel horsemen pulled their bone-headed stunt, the thing that caught Sherman's eye was that they splashed across a shallow place in the stream. If their juvenile antics had not drawn attention to it, he would not have noticed it. This place was *not* a very good ford. It was so crude it even lacked a local nickname, simply being referred to as "the farm ford." Its banks were too steep for artillery vehicles, but it could sustain men on foot. Sherman made a mental note of its existence.[118]

The Confederate Position, near the Stone Bridge

"Shanks" Evans found the next two hours puzzling. Yankee artillery continued to pound around him, but since the artillerists could not see much, their barrage had relatively little effect (though one round happened to land among the hiding South Carolinians, killing a soldier). Evans could make out several large clumps of Yankees a mile or so across Bull Run, but they seemed disinclined to cross. He continued to move his two cannon about and shuffle his infantry. But, mostly, he waited. He wondered if what he was observing involved Yankee subterfuge. Then, about 8:45, he received word from a vidette, stationed near Sudley Ford, that a passel of Yankees were crossing up there and seemed to be heading his way. Almost at that same moment, he received a second message.

Nature had graced Edward Porter Alexander. Born into an extraordinarily sensitive and loving Georgia plantation family, he was bright and perceptive. In 1861, twenty-six years old, he was

Hollywood-handsome, muscular and athletic-looking, with deep-set, intense eyes, high cheekbones, and a firm jaw. Graduating third in his 1857 class from West Point, he chose the path of the academy's top students: engineering. He had unsuccessfully wooed Robert E. Lee's daughter, Mary, when Lee was superintendent of West Point, then fell in love with and wedded another Virginia beauty, Bettie Mason. The two of them had a rich, fine marriage. After the Civil War he would apply his many talents to engineering, railroading, making gobs of money, and writing — doing well at all these endeavors.

His contribution to the Battle of Bull Run involved a skill he had acquired in 1859 when he assisted a man named Alfred J. Myer. Dr. Myer, a native of New York and a one-time telegraph operator, was an army surgeon who had once studied how deaf-mutes communicated with each other. Then, during the 1850s, while stationed in New Mexico, he saw Comanche signaling each other over long distances, using lances. He wondered if he could devise a system by which American soldiers could communicate far more complex messages. Utilizing the binary concept of Samuel Morse's telegraph, he discovered that waggling cloth, attached to long poles, left or right, in certain patterns, was quite visible on sunny days. Waving a flag three times to the left meant one thing, twice to the right plus once to the left meant another. Once one learned the system's "alphabet," one could use torches at night. He met young Porter Alexander and the two men worked together, refining Myer's brainchild. For several months the two of them, standing as far away from each other as fifteen miles, sent messages back and forth. They grew so adept they could signal with mere hand gestures or handkerchiefs dangling from canes. The army officially adopted the system.

Then the war came. Porter Alexander resigned his commission and went to Richmond to offer his services. At Manassas Junction, Beauregard told him to choose a dozen enlisted men to act as signalers and teach them the system, then locate some high spots that could serve as "signal stations," and get ready. It sounded easy enough. He tapped ten or twelve privates. At first they seemed apt pupils, but he later concluded they were "so stupid that I have to knock them down & jump on them & stamp &

pound them before I can get an idea in their heads." He rode around the region, on both sides of the stream, and selected four knolls with good visibility. One was in Centreville, not far from the intersection. The other three were on the Manassas side of Bull Run. He situated one near the Van Pelt house, Avon, above the stone bridge, another six miles south, beyond the Orange and Alexandria Railroad track, and the third in the middle, not far from Wilmer McLean's place. Later in the war, signalmen on both sides often used wooden towers, some as tall as thirty feet or more, but Alexander did not. He simply had "stations" on his designated knolls, primarily tents with his equipment inside, his poles and flags and such.

On this Sunday morning, since he was part of Beauregard's staff, he found himself at command headquarters near the station, with Johnston, Beauregard, and their staffs. They all ate breakfast, while listening to the cannon fire coming from the areas near both Mitchell's Ford and the stone bridge. About eight o'clock, not in any great hurry, the two generals, with their staffs, rode toward Mitchell's Ford—going to what Beauregard was certain would be the central scene of the coming battle. On the way Beauregard called young Alexander over and ordered him to ride to the southernmost signal station atop Wilcoxen Hill. Porter Alexander felt disgruntled. He would now miss all the excitement. But he obeyed orders and took couriers with him so he could relay back anything of interest. (Wilcoxen Hill was just a few hundred yards from the railroad bridge across Bull Run, where McDowell had originally considered crossing. Why did Beauregard send Alexander there? Apparently, he did not realize the roads on the other side would not sustain a major movement—which seems to say a lot about Beauregard's claim to have well scouted the entire region.)

Alexander arrived here and signaled the other two stations (the fourth one in Centreville now being occupied by Yankees) that he was in position. He put most of his attention on the most northern station—probably assuming that, since Beauregard and Johnston were right next to his middle station, he himself should focus on the one near the Van Pelt house. As he stared in that direction, a few degrees to the right of his line of vision was a large band of thick woods. In mid-July the trees were green and lush and formed a dark background. The sun was rising over Alexander's right shoulder. He turned his powerful glass left and right, searching for — truth.

About 8:45 something odd caught his eye. A flash of something, a quick glitter. "I recognized it at once as the reflection of the morning sun from a brass field-piece." He stared intently at the foliage eight miles away. (He was in fact peering into the forest through which Hunter's division was slowly moving. He had just detected one of Burnside's cannon.) "Closer scrutiny soon revealed the glittering of bayonets and musket barrels" (Burnside's infantrymen crossing Bull Run and disappearing into the woods near the Sudley church). Captain Alexander, thinking quickly, signaled his men at the Van Pelt station: "Look out for your left, you are turned." He also jotted a note to Beauregard and handed it to a courier: "I see a column crossing Bull Run about two miles above Stone Bridge. Head of it is in woods on this side; tail of it in woods on other side. About a quarter mile length of column visible in the opening. Artillery forms part of it."

At the Van Pelt station Alexander's signalman deciphered the message and told a messenger to take the information to Colonel Evans. Evans received this dispatch just as the vidette from Sudley Ford dashed up and gave him the news about some approaching Yankees.

"Shanks" Evans had to make a decision, and quickly. The steps he took were remarkable in their audacity. He had already concluded that Tyler's relative inaction meant that the Yankees just across Bull Run were not intent on an immediate assault on this spot. (Captain Woodbury's decision to make a wide sweep before crossing at Sudley Ford had added an extra — and it turned out — critical hour. If the Second Rhode Island had crossed the stream at, say, eight o'clock, Evans would have been cautious about abandoning his position. But the extra hour of Tyler's inactivity convinced Evans he might safely leave the bridge virtually unguarded.) He notified Cocke, his nominal superior, that he was moving away from the stone bridge. To keep watch on the bridge, he left the four forward companies of the Fourth South Carolina and took the rest of his little army with him: two guns and about

800 men. It was an amazing gamble. On the far side of the stone bridge, Tyler had two brigades, almost 7,000 men, with Keyes's brigade due to join them soon. If Tyler suddenly decided to cross Bull Run, the only thing now standing between him and Beauregard's entrenchments at Manassas Junction were two hundred South Carolina infantrymen.

"Shanks" had no idea how many of the enemy were on their way from Sudley Ford, but he intended to try to stop them, or at least slow them down.[119]

In a few minutes "Shanks" Evans's small force and the Second Rhode Island would come face to face. The fate of the Confederacy might be in the balance.

BOOK THREE

AGLEY

The best laid schemes o' mice and men gang aft a-gley,
An' lea'e us nought but grief and pain, for promised joy.
—ROBERT BURNS

Everyone has a game plan until you get hit in the mouth.
—MIKE TYSON

First Glimpse
of the Elephant

*I was exceedingly anxious to see an engagement, not that
I should perform heroic deeds, but rather to satisfy the craving of
an indefinable feeling as to my ability to stand or run.*
—Frank Holsinger[120]

Sudley Ford was almost six miles from Manassas Junction. A wagon road, stretching north and south between the two, was relatively straight much of the way. The Warrenton turnpike, heading east to west, crossed this road about halfway to the station. A toll gate, where fees had been collected for the turnpike's upkeep, once stood at the intersection. Next to where the toll gate stood was a stone house, often used as a tavern, a convenient stopping place for drovers to rest and have a drink or two before moseying eastward with their herds of cattle. One could imagine the two roads as geometric X and Y axes, dividing the landscape into four quadrants. During the coming battle men would fight in all four of these quadrants. One could think of the Sudley-Manassas road as forming the western border of the northwest quadrant, with Bull Run, from Sudley Ford to the stone bridge, its eastern border. Most of the morning's clashes would occur in this sector. Its area, almost exactly a square mile, was thickly forested in its upper corner, just below the Sudley community. It also contained more than a dozen other copses and thickets of varying sizes. A long ridge slashed sideways across its middle, so a traveler strolling south from Sudley would initially be walking slightly uphill through the woods before arriving at the crest of the ridge, from which he could look down toward the pike, almost half a mile away, or toward the stream on his left. Halfway between this high spot and the stone house by the turnpike was a modest farm, owned by the Matthews brothers: Edgar, Carson, and Martin.

(Not surprisingly, most Civil War battles would swirl across farms. The reasons were simple. A farm has open land, and its fields permitted the movement and use of artillery. A farm is usually near at least one fairly good road and generally also contains several wagon paths; these permitted the easy movement of troops. Farms had fences that infantrymen could use as breastworks. And water, which was important to surgeons.)

The Matthews house, set back a bit from the Sudley road, was a small, one-story, white, wooden structure. Around it stood the usual farm outbuildings and rail fences. Fields of hay and corn stretched away from the main building. A couple of hundred yards to its east were large clumps of trees. Local citizens called the high ground north of the main house "Matthews Hill." Here is where the Battle of Bull Run began.

The Confederates

As soon as "Shanks" Evans made his decision to turn away from the stone bridge, he sent an order to Rob Wheat, off on his northern flank, to start moving northward. Wheat and his several hundred Louisiana Tigers began walking through fields. Behind them, and off to their left, came Evans's few cavalrymen, then J. B. E. Sloan's Fourth South Carolina. After a few hundred yards, Evans halted and looked around. The Yankees had not yet appeared, and he decided this position was unsatisfactory, so he moved his men forward a bit. As his two infantry units pushed ahead, they separated. Wheat's Tigers, exhilarated by the prospect of actual battle, ran excitedly, outdistancing the more disciplined South Carolinians. The Tigers stopped in front of an open field with a copse on their left. The Fourth South Carolina had to swing wide to get around the clump of trees. As they did so, their right flank skirmishers stumbled through the woods — and suddenly saw strangers off to their right. They opened fire, killing three and wounding several others. Unfortunately, they had just attacked the Louisianans, not the Yankees. Roberdeau Wheat immediately saw the problem and screamed at his troops not to return the fire, but, in the noise and confusion, not everyone could hear him, and his Tigers blazed away at the men lurking in the woods. Luckily, their fire missed completely — not entirely a good sign, considering the coming battle. Before a second fusillade from either side, strenuous efforts by both Wheat and the commander of the South Carolinian skirmishers prevented any more bloodshed.

The reasons for this bloody blunder at the tree line certainly involved the inexperience and edginess of the Confederates. But it also sprang from the fact that Evans's two infantry units wore different uniforms. During the next few hours, the muddle of uniforms was going to lead, as it had at Blackburn's Ford three days earlier, to tragedies. Such confusions had been anticipated. Weeks earlier, the *New York Times* had expressed concern about the "bewildering variety" of uniforms worn by Union army units, and, on the other side, the *Richmond Dispatch* had said the same thing about Confederate uniforms. Before the war, each militia company had had the right to choose its own uniform, and since these units wanted to look snazzy in parades, they had often festooned themselves like characters in an operetta. In 1861, when the first volunteer regiments were brought together from such militia companies, the results sometimes looked like patchwork quilts. The state governments that raised the regiments clothed their volunteers — when they could find sufficient cloth — but each state had its own notion of what colors would be proper. The result was that both sides had men dressed in shades of blue or gray, or combinations of the two, and both had colorful Zouaves. With the exception of Blenker's "German" regiments that McDowell had left back in Centreville and assorted "German" companies sprinkled throughout the two armies, both sides spoke the same language, they used the same drum signals, and their officers shouted the same orders and exhortations. Flags should have helped, but each regiment normally carried two: its own and their central government's. Since scores of regiments, from both sides, participated in this battle, regimental flags often confused men from different units in the same army. Worse, the United States flag and the Confederate Stars and Bars were not dramatically different. And with the air this morning so still, banners hung limply. The result was that soldiers had no quick way to differentiate friend from foe.

Beauregard had worried about this issue for weeks. He had urged Richmond to send him sashes his men could wear, but his pleas had been ignored. Then, in the days just preceding the battle, he had tried other methods to prevent confusion. He had proposed armbands, passwords (including "Sumter" and "Our Homes"), and special salutes. These might have worked adequately, but word about them never reached all Confederate units, so they were virtually worthless — or worse. Besides, in the noise and smoke of a battlefield, hand gestures and passwords would prove mostly irrelevant.

As we have seen, both armies had units with insufficient training. And both included individuals who had been civilians a few days earlier and men who had never fired a gun. Not surprisingly, most rookies would perform, at best, clumsily. As to entire units, some would do well, others not. In most cases the quality of their performance depended on their officers — especially their company captains and their regimental colonels. When a unit, of whatever size, fell apart, it was usually because its commander did not lead it properly. Sometimes this was not his fault; many officers were injured early or killed. But far too many leaders panicked and ran. More typical of disorganized units, however, was the officer whose capacity for leadership was weak. Sun Tzu once advised: "If the orders are clear and the soldiers disobey, the officers are to blame." It quickly became obvious that being a prominent lawyer or a wealthy planter was no guarantee a man would respond to battlefield chaos with the unruffled air that can keep subordinates calm. Units that had success this day stayed together and worked as one. Other than luck (which must never be overlooked), the commanders of most of them had one characteristic: They perceived patterns amid the jumble. The professionals, particularly those who had served in Mexico, had an edge. Since they had been in battle or at least had trained under those who did, many were able to ignore confusing sights and sounds and to focus on their goals. On the other hand, some professional officers functioned badly, and some volunteers rose to the occasion. It would take many months, even years, to sort through all this, to promote the wheat and send the chaff packing.

The first test of the two armies came when Evans's demibrigade confronted the men of the Second Rhode Island. After Evans's officers disentangled the Louisianans from the South Carolinians, his men turned to face the approaching Yankees. Evans placed his two cannon behind his infantrymen, one off to the left, the other far to the right. His little force was about as ready as it was going to be. All of a sudden they saw Yankees approaching. One South Carolinian thought the enemy advanced so calmly they seemed "as though they were going on dress parade."[121]

The Federals

As the Second Rhode Island marched along the Sudley road, many of its members felt almost jaunty. They saw no rebels in front of them, and it seemed a fine Sunday morning for a stroll. Some even stopped to grab berries along the side of the road; others traded jibes with each other, perhaps to break the tension. Men laughed, genuinely or nervously. Suddenly they were startled by the unexpected sound of musket fire not far away (Wheat's and Sloan's men exchanging shots at each other). This quieted them. The Rhode Island skirmishers moved more cautiously now. A few hundred yards away, on the left of the road, they could see a farm house sitting on the far side of a rail fence and a field. Then, Evans's skirmishers, hiding behind the fence, opened the battle. As Elisha Hunt Rhodes recalled, "We were saluted with a volley of musketry, which, however, was fired so high that all the bullets went over our heads. I remember that my first sensation was one of astonishment at the peculiar whir of the bullets, and that the Regiment laid down without waiting for orders." One of the Rhode Islanders looked at his watch and announced it was ten minutes after ten o'clock.

Though on paper the two sides confronting each other just now were equal in numbers, the men of the Second Rhode Island were in a pickle. Except for their skirmishers, they were strung out in a column on the road, while most of Evans's men were in position, relatively safe behind trees and fences. Evans also had his two cannon playing upon the Yankees.

During the next hour or so, as each side brought up reinforcements, first one, then the other, they often, for a few minutes, would outnumber their opponents. The soldiers on both sides had entered this battle feeling contempt for their foes. Southerners had been taught for years that Yankees were merely money-grubbing clerks and were far from manly. In turn, most Northern soldiers believed their cause was special, even holy, and for the past week, all they had learned about rebels was that they retreated. The soldiers of the two sides had only had an opportunity to observe their own armies, and, when comparing themselves to militia encampments back home, their own force seemed huge, disciplined, and impressively well armed. This day was about to provide them an education. As it would turn out, the volunteers in both armies performed rather well, with surprising grit and spirit for men who, a few weeks earlier, had been plowmen or saloon keepers or students. But, for the first hour or two of this battle, it was not heroism or even leadership that held the ground; it was whichever side directed the most firepower against the enemy. And that advantage waggled back and forth. It came not from the side that had the most men in the region or that had the most *potential* firepower, but from the side that had the most fighters right *here*. "Potential" troops do not fire guns. It did not matter that the Union force had two divisions on the way or that the Confederate leadership had forwarded four brigades toward the area.

People of that era often used the metaphor "to see the elephant" to define a memorable adventure. Soldiers who had fought in the Mexican War used the phrase. Those who had been in battle would say, "I have seen the elephant." Forty-niners, arriving at the California gold fields, used the expression to describe their feat of making it across the continent. During the earliest weeks of the Civil War, volunteers sat around campfires talking about what it would be like, how they would behave when they got to "see the elephant." Now, here on Matthews Hill the men of the Second Rhode Island discovered the beast.

A muzzle-loader was a complicated weapon to load. The process went something like this: Some men carried cartridges in their pockets, but this was not a good idea; moisture (sweat, for example) affected the powder's efficiency, and a cartridge box was designed to be rather waterproof. A soldier grabbed a single *cartridge* (that looked much like a thick cigarette) and stuffed its rolled-up end into his mouth and ripped its top with his teeth. (Toothless soldiers had problems.) In his hurry, some powder inevitably ended up on his lips and tongue. It tasted acidic and blackened his face from nose to chin. The effect left him feeling quite parched. He poured the powder from the cartridge into the muzzle of his gun. He squeezed the bullet — somehow — from the rest of the cartridge ("Hardee" vaguely suggested one should "disengage the ball from the paper"), then dropped the ball into the muzzle. Shoving a small round object into a narrow hole is an uncertain task. After marching any distance, one's fingers become swollen and dexterity declines. Perspiration makes the fingers slippery. Adrenaline causes them to tremble. Also, if one is firing a rifle rather than a smoothbore, it is critical to put the minié ball in with its flat end first. Once the bullet was inside the barrel, the soldier was supposed to ram it down, in order to compact the charge properly, using the *rammer* attached to his gun. He needed to slide that long prong up from its slot next to the barrel, twirl it like a baton, and press its cup-shaped end into the muzzle. Since the rammer was several feet long, maneuvering it was easiest if the soldier was standing erect. (Of course, when someone is being shot at, it is natural for that individual to want to lie down. But if he does so, he will find it difficult to reload. A coordinated — or highly motivated — individual can do it, but not always predictably.) The soldier then drew the rammer back out of the barrel and returned it carefully to its slot. He cocked his gun, pulled a *cap* out (usually from his cartridge box), and placed it carefully onto a small metal nipple that rose above the trigger mechanism. (This action was also problematic. Caps were tiny, and a man often dropped several before getting one into place.) The soldier then aimed, and pulled the trigger. And started the process again.

After the rebels opened fire on the Second Rhode Island's skirmishers, using both cannon and muskets, Union officers tried to bring order to the shaken regiment. At the moment Burnside was back a mile, trying to bring ahead the rest of his brigade. General Hunter, however, was absurdly near the front, almost among the skirmishers, where he was incapable of performing his role as divisional commander. Fortunately for the Union cause, Colonel Slocum of the Second kept his head. After Hunter gave the troops a short pep talk, Slocum ordered his men to cross the rail fence into the field that led toward the farm house. "By the left flank — *march!*" he shouted. His men were energized. A lieutenant with a badly blistered foot, who had hobbled this far with a cane, threw it down and stood erect. The Rhode Islanders flung aside their blankets and haversacks and, one of them remembered, giving out "a most hideous scream," they ran into the field. Adrenaline and norepinephrine pumped through them from their adrenal glands, driven by fear and ferocity. "One of our boys," Elisha Hunt Rhodes wrote in his diary, "by the name of Webb fell off of the fence and broke his bayonet. This caused some amusement, for even at this time we did not realize that we were about to engage in battle. As we crossed the fence, the rebels, after firing a few scattering shots, fled down a slope to the woods... On what followed I have very confused ideas." He remembered odd bits and pieces. Like the fact that his gun grew so befouled with gunpowder he had to smack its ramrod against a fence to push in a cartridge. And how a bunch of his comrades, becoming unnerved, hid behind a haystack until a rebel shell hit it, making them scurry back to their line. And how a Rhode Island private captured one of the Louisiana Tigers and escorted him to Slocum to be interviewed.

Rhodes also saw Colonel Slocum, on foot, leading his men toward the farm. He saw the colonel personally going ahead to make a reconnaissance, then returning to encourage his troops. The colonel was moving back toward them, climbing the fence, when he was simultaneously struck with three bullets and catapulted to the ground. It was Corporal Rhodes who washed the blood from his colonel's face and saw the deep furrow across his scalp. It was Rhodes, along with others, who carried his colonel to the regimental ambulance that transported him to a makeshift hospital in the rear. Other officers began to fall. A few minutes after Slocum was hit, a rebel cannonball smashed into Major Sullivan Ballou, along with his horse, mortally wounding Sarah Ballou's loving husband. Two company captains and two lieutenants were also killed. Others were wounded. A swath had just been cut through the regiment's leadership. That the Second Rhode Island did not turn and flee probably was the residue of the solid morale built up during its weeks in Washington — for which it could thank Slocum, Burnside, and Governor Sprague. Yet, during the next half hour, its organization did become, as Rhodes admitted, "much scattered." He lost track of his own company and fought alongside another. A comrade, Corporal Samuel J. English, wrote home three days later, convinced, he told his mother, that his regiment had faced "three or four thousand rebels."[122]

Casualties continued to mount. The soldiers' smoothbores seemed inaccurate at almost any distance. Their training had emphasized the importance of neat lines and crisply worded orders from superiors and loading and firing in the nine motions that "Hardee" insisted on. But all such regularity broke down. Men advanced or retreated spasmodically. They loaded their guns and pointed and fired them in however many motions it took. With their leadership decimated, the Rhode Islanders started to fall back.

Some actualities of battle surprised most soldiers. They had arrived at Matthews Hill with impressions about what war would be like. They assumed they would see men in lines or columns and horsemen galloping about, looking quite gallant. They knew there would be a bit of death but fancied it would be dignified and off to the side. Such images were the stuff of *Harper's Weekly* and *Frank Leslie's Illustrated Weekly* or had been drawn from dimly remembered pictures in schoolbooks or from fine Romantic paintings in museums. These images had a certain decorum. Above all else, they were orderly, and even stately. Reality was far different.

When the infantry action began, someone ordered the Second Rhode Island's battery, six fine brass James rifles, into action (named after Charles Tillinghast James of Rhode Island who had recently patented them). Who gave the order? General Hunter? Colonel Burnside? Perhaps Governor Sprague, who always felt a special closeness to his artillerists and who stayed with them throughout the day? Whoever it was, saved the Second from possible destruction. The battery galloped forward. In fact, for a while, it stood in advance of its own infantry. The rebels saw the gunners unlimbering and gave the battery their full attention. Bullets whizzed around the guns. An officer who served for the next four years would recall: "Above us and around us on every side, they seemed to be hissing, writhing and twisting. I have been under many a hot fire, but I don't think that, in nearly four years experience, I ever heard so many bullets in such a short time." He was frightened. "I remember the first thing that came into my mind was the wish that I was at home out of danger's way." But he stayed to do his duty. He and the other gunners fired at the woods in front of them where the rebels were hiding. When musket fire from there slackened, they turned their attention to Evans's two artillery pieces. Then to a four-gun Confederate battery that appeared on a hilltop across the turnpike, less than a mile away.

The Rhode Island battery's horses stood quietly, but one by one they began to drop. All too often the artillerists could hear a *thunk* when a ball struck a horse in the side, and a soft, wheezing equine gasp. Sometimes a cannonball, bounding across the turf, would rip off one of a horse's legs, and it would fall to the ground and twitch horribly as its lifeblood spurted across the grass. When the battle was over, many men remarked sadly about the poor horses lying about the field. They were such gentle animals, with no allegiance to secession or the Union, and their deaths seemed so poignant. The Rhode Island battery entered the day with 130 horses; it left with 65.

The experience of battle assaulted an individual's sensory system. The training of the volunteers had not prepared them for this. There were horrible sights. Uncharitable pieces of iron treated a man as a butcher handles meat. Matthews Hill was soon covered not only with corpses but with chunks of what had recently been warm flesh. Soldiers were killed or wounded by more than bullets or shells. Jagged splinters of exploded tree trunks did the job, or the sharp bones of a shattered comrade. Those who walked this battlefield the next day spoke in awe of what they saw: intestines hanging like confetti from low bushes, soldiers with no faces or with holes blasted completely through them, men whose dying agonies had made them tug spasmodically at the grass until their fingertips turned green.

Soldiers became acutely aware of the randomness of death. Courage or intelligence seemed to mean little. A cannonball could hurtle past one of them and smash into a comrade a few inches away —*splat!*— covering him with his friend's blood. "Why him? Why not me?" the survivor might ask. There seemed no logic to it. A young man from New Hampshire wrote home: "A cannonball passed between myself and the man next to me and struck a man just behind us and killed him instantly. Another man near me was facing the enemy and someone said something which made him laugh. Just then a ball struck him in the mouth and knocked his head off." Or a minié ball could whip off part of a soldier's belt or his collar, but leave him unscathed. Or a spent enemy bullet could slap into him and do no more than frighten him and leave a bruise.

Another surprising thing was how little infantrymen could actually see. When the Rhode Islanders lay down —and they often did —they found that all they could make out was the red Virginia soil beneath them, and tall sprigs of weeds or cornstalks and the blue sky above them, and perhaps the pant leg of a comrade. When they popped their heads up a bit, they sometimes observed an unknown number of the enemy moving in their general direction. But mostly their foe was invisible. The rebels, just like the Rhode Islanders, were keeping themselves hidden by whatever was available: trees, outbuildings, haystacks. And both sides made good use of the fences. By themselves, rail fences would not have concealed much, but over the years farmers, during harvesting, had purposely stayed a foot or so away from the fences so as not to damage their planking. The result was that every rail fence was half-hidden by an almost impenetrable barrier of weeds and brush that a soldier could kneel behind and shoot through. Another factor reducing visibility was the smoke billowing from all the muskets and cannon. The air that morning was magically still. Porter Alexander would later say he never again in his life saw such a phenomenon. No breezes wafted the smoke away from the battlefield, so it hung like a London fog between the two sides, before imperceptibly rising above the treetops. (The same was true of the road dust, stirred by marching feet, which slowly ascended higher and higher into towers, hundreds of feet high, giant mesas hovering above the troops—in the process, revealing their presence and their movements.)

Another unexpected experience was the unearthly cacophony. Men, awed by the din, unable to hear their comrades' words or their officers' orders, grew disoriented. Some sounds were familiar: the gasping, the panting, the grunting of men performing hard labor, the ripping open of cartridges, the rattle of ramrods plunging into musket barrels, the clink of canteens against metal, the squealing wheels of artillery vehicles, the drum signals, the shouting and swearing. Some sounds were unexpected. The otherworldly shriek of artillery shells. The clatter of musket balls into branches overhead, sounding amazingly like hailstones. The curious bumblebee humming or whizzing that a bullet made as it passed close by. The sudden crack of a tree or thick limb hit by a cannonball, followed by the rich smell of sap and soft flutter of leaves settling to the ground. And the screams, of course. When wounded, no matter how badly, some men screamed, often from simple fear more than pain—though others hardly made a sound beyond a single gasp.

A young Northerner struggled to describe all this to his sister, Libby. "Seance I left home," he told her, "the awfulist site I ever sawe was at the Battle ground. It is a site that nere can be forgoten.

To see the men slaterd, some of them ded, some of them with there legs off, one in partickler with a Canon Ball through his Boddy, there was a hole throught him Big enough to stick your head in. O, libby, it is awful! But I fear it not all through."

A South Carolina sergeant described how he felt when the Yankees opened fire: "It seemed as if the earth had burst up. They threw cannonballs, bomb shells, canister, grape, musket balls, minnie balls, and rifle balls which wrought havoc among us... The groaning of the wounded and dying chilled my very soul." He felt so vulnerable. His comrades seemed so few, the enemy so numerous: "four hundred against eighty thousand." Another South Carolinian tried to make sense of this experience in a letter to his wife. "The cannons," he wrote her, "although they make a great noise, were nothing more than pop guns compared to the tremendous thundering noise of the thousands of muskets. The sight of the dead, the cries of the wounded, the thundering noise of the battle, can never be put on paper. It must be seen and heard to be comprehended. The dead, the dying, and the wounded; friend and foe, all mixed up together; friend and foe embraced in death; some crying for water; some praying their last prayers; some trying to whisper to a friend their last farewell message to their loved ones at home. It is heartrending. I cannot go any further. Mine eyes are damp with tears."[123]

Some men felt a strange alienation wash over them. They were puzzled that total strangers actually wanted to do them bodily harm. Many have tried to put this feeling into words, but it was Leo Tolstoy who captured this reaction best in *War and Peace*, written only a few years after Bull Run. One of that novel's main characters, Count Ilyá Rostóv, was in his first battle. He suddenly realized he felt no special antagonism against the French, his presumptive enemies, whom he could see in the distance. On the other hand, he was quite patriotic, and as he and his companions, on horseback, charged toward the foe, he found himself happily yelling, "Hur-a-a-a-ah!" But all of a sudden his horse received a wound, and it stumbled and fell, and he tumbled to the ground. As he rose to his feet, he became acutely aware he was quite alone. His comrades had disappeared. He saw men running toward him and at first was pleased, assuming they were coming to assist him. But then he realized they were French. He wondered, "Can they be coming at me?" He could hardly believe it. "And why? To kill me? *Me* whom everybody is so fond of?" He turned and fled.

A few soldiers at Bull Run fell into a kind of combat narcosis, an intoxication, a joy of battle—a state of elation, really—the kind felt by warriors the ancient Vikings called *berserks*. Others found themselves immobilized by fear. And there were men who felt first one of these emotions, then another, separated by only a few minutes. David Hackworth, one of America's most decorated heroes, speaks of fear in his autobiography, *About Face*. "When you're fighting," he says, "you're scared. And it's such an all-pervasive sort of fear you can't even pinpoint what the feeling is." Bravery, he says, is not fearlessness; "it's the ability to get off your ass and charge even when your mouth is dry, your gut is tight, and your brain is screaming *Stay down!*" And he reminds us that courage has its limits. He says, "Even the bravest of men have a breaking point." The only question involves when. "I concluded," he said, "that a man is like a bottle. On the battlefield, fear is what fills him up and fuels him to perform. But some bottles are smaller than others. When a man becomes unglued during a firefight, it's just that his bottle has filled up." Even Hackworth, one of America's most stout-hearted men, during his long and distinguished military career, occasionally discovered his own "bottle" had become too full, and he found himself running.[124]

The first half hour of the battle for Matthews Hill was a struggle between Evans's men and the Second Rhode Island, each supported by cannon. It was touch and go. After the first few minutes, the Rhode Island skirmishers succeeded in pushing back the rebel skirmishers. But then the main force of rebels—especially Wheat's men—charged. And the Rhode Islanders reeled away. Back and forth the two sides fought, neither utilizing its entire force at any one time, so the fighting continued to involve only isolated groups, at most a few companies—maybe two hundred men—working together. And even then the fastest men would be in front, the rest coming up or leaving in clumps of six or eight. It is impossible, therefore, to describe this "battle" as much more than a melee. The artillery on both sides did some damage, but, all things considered, not as much as it might have. The Rhode Island battery was at first strangely ineffective. If the gunners had loaded their pieces with canister and aimed them accurately at the rebel infantry, the slaughter would have been frightful and the battle for this hilltop soon over. As it was, some Confederates, probably Wheat's charging Tigers, got within twenty yards of the guns before being forced to retreat.

Then, a few moments later, most of those same Tigers, overcome by terror, raced from the battlefield, abandoning their South Carolina comrades. The Tigers were the first unit on either side to dissolve. Swaggering, puffed-up bullyboys, deluded by their own reputation for toughness, they proved the adage that bullies do not always make good soldiers. Rob Wheat tried to reassemble them but was shot through the chest, the bullet going in one side and out the other. (At the field hospital, after surgeons told him he had no hope, he replied, "I don't feel like dying yet." And he did not. He survived to fight again.)[125]

On the Union side, David Hunter, the divisional commander, was attempting to get the Rhode Islanders to stop shooting for a moment and charge forward with their bayonets, when, suddenly, a rebel shell ripped open the side of his neck and left cheek. He pressed a cloth against the gashes and headed toward the rear. Today was his fifty-ninth birthday; the wounds turned out to be a nice present. He was the first of McDowell's high-ranking officers to arrive in Washington, his face all bandaged and bloody. For a long time, his wounds gave him a kind of military panache. Although he had never previously seen a battle and had only acquired his present rank by buttering up Lincoln, he would now rise even higher. Yet, ironically, his actions and orders at Bull Run had been ludicrous. It is hard to characterize his leadership this day without combining words like *courageous* and *incompetent*. For reasons Hunter never clarified, when the battle opened, he ordered Burnside not to bring up the other three regiments of his brigade, though their numbers would have quickly overwhelmed or outflanked Evans. When Hunter finally did conclude that the Second Rhode Island needed assistance, he ordered Andrew Porter to bring up his brigade, even though it was back some distance and Burnside's men were on hand. In fact the position of Burnside's troops actually blocked the road, preventing Porter's brigade from moving ahead expeditiously. The result of these appalling decisions was that Slocum's Rhode Islanders, theoretically backed up by almost 5,000 men, had to fight alone against a determined foe of equal number, well entrenched inside woods and behind fences. Luckily for the Second Rhode Island, Hunter's wounds came to their assistance. As he departed the scene, he passed Burnside and said, "I leave the matter in your hands." Burnside was far more competent. So was Porter, who, being senior to Burnside, would soon take official command of the whole division.[126]

The nature of the battle, its tempo and its size, was about to change.

CARNAGE

Fighting is the hardest work I ever did.
—ANTHONY B. SHELBY, FIFTEEN YEARS OLD, FOURTH ALABAMA

I done my duty.
—ANONYMOUS, FIRST RHODE ISLAND[127]

Confederate Headquarters

Unless a battle ends in a stalemate, one side has won, the other lost. Using that formula, it seems obvious that the Southerners could claim that they "won" the Battle of Bull Run—and so, in a sense, they did, or least the Union side lost. But how and why? Was it pure luck or Federal blundering? Or did it involve some canny maneuvers by one or more Southern generals? The sequence of the decisions made by Confederate leaders that morning remains cloudy. Some proposals worked out, others led to disasters—and, as the saying goes, many men claimed parenthood of the successes, while the failures remained orphans. Certain things are clear. The Confederates would have lost the battle had not several brigade commanders been at the right place at the right time. Was their presence at those critical spots accidental? Or did certain individuals deserve credit for making the right decisions? The answers are not easily arrived at. During the morning hours, as McDowell's army was maneuvering itself in unexpected ways, the Confederate leadership jumbled in confusion. For example, in a short period that morning General Jackson received five separate and contradictory orders. First he was told to send two of his regiments to reinforce Longstreet; then this was countermanded, and he was ordered to stand as a reserve behind Bonham at Mitchell's Ford; then, not much later, he was told to move again, this time to support Cocke. Still later, he was shuffled once more, to get into a position to reinforce either Cocke or Bonham, whichever might need his assistance most. Finally, Cocke told Jackson to keep his eye on the relatively unguarded stone bridge.

Both Confederate high commanders — Johnston and Beauregard — would later write extensively about the battle. At first, neither pretended to have controlled events. Beauregard, for example, said he did order Jackson to get somewhere behind Cocke and Bonham, and "the brigades of Bee and Bartow, under the command of the former, *were also sent* to the support of *the left* [emphasis added]." His use of "the left" is obviously vague, and there is the passive voice in his phrase "were also sent." One might ask: Sent by whom? Johnston's official report was also hazy about this: "General Bee, who *had been placed* near Colonel Cocke's position, Colonel Hampton with his Legion, and Colonel [*sic*] Jackson, from a point near Bonham's left, *were ordered* [emphasis added] to hasten to the left flank." Again, this use of the passive voice is a sign of the uncertainty about who ordered what.

But many years later, after Johnston had time to ruminate, he remembered being disturbed that morning when reading the orders Beauregard had written and recalled that he had told Beauregard the night before that he wanted Bee and Jackson (each commanding a brigade from the Valley) to be moved toward the left flank. He also recalled that, after looking at the orders in the morning, he "desired General Beauregard to transfer them."

When Beauregard read this new explanation of Johnston's, he, too, wrote a follow-up account about the battle, in which he snidely suggested that Johnston's recollections reeked of self-congratulation — though he did not deny their basic accuracy. Beauregard also changed his own story. He chose to ignore the matter of who gave orders to whom and insisted that it was his personal presence on the battlefield in the afternoon that turned the tide. In other words, that the victory was not the result of abstract decisions but of his own charisma.

Johnston sniffed, after reading this interpretation: "I gave every order of importance." It is a fact that much of the most important fighting was done by Johnston's Valley troops, and logic would suggest that Johnston took a special interest in positioning his own brigades and also that he was concerned about Beauregard's dangling left flank. In the contest over which of these two generals deserved the laurels, Johnston holds a slight edge, not because he himself controlled events, but because Beauregard remained blinded to reality far too long that morning, as the pace of events were picking up, and remained too wedded to his original plans.[128]

Philip St. George Cocke had decided to use the property of Francis W. and Fanny Lewis. Mrs. Lewis had just given birth to the Lewises' fourth child (whom they named John Beauregard Lewis); then she departed with her family to visit relatives. The Lewises had bought this home only three years earlier, when the house was already several generations old. It was not a stately mansion, but it was a fine-looking white Colonial, with two massive double-flue fireplaces, one at each end, both about sixteen-feet wide at the base. It had long been known as "Portici" (port-EEE-cee), after an Italian town not far from Vesuvius, famous for its fiery eruptions. General Cocke was drawn to its site because it sat atop a ridge, overlooking fields that sloped down to Bull Run, 650 yards away—and, beyond the stream, toward Centreville. Because of the house's elevated location, it could also be seen from far away, almost all the way from the railroad depot at Manassas Junction. A mile to its north was the stone bridge; three miles to the south was McLean's farm. The Lewis place, therefore, rested near the center of the Confederate left wing. The only flaw in its location was the paucity of nearby roads to tie together the separated Confederate units. A few farm paths passed by it, but the snakelike nature of Bull Run meant that men moving from one side of the Confederate army to the other had to swing wide around the stream and wriggle past intervening clumps of woods that blocked visibility. Men moving through this region found it easy to get lost in the confusing landscape.

After "Shanks" Evans sent Cocke the message that he was shifting his demibrigade away from the stone bridge, Cocke was concerned that Tyler's huge division might cross it and turn his left flank. He sent two guns to cover the position but remained unsatisfied. According to Cocke's after-battle report, Bee came to him and announced he was here to support him, and Cocke forwarded him and his brigade to the area behind the bridge. Cocke's report also indicated that Bartow came by a bit afterward, and Cocke told him to follow Bee. Then, Cocke said, Hammond came by, and he, too, was forwarded. Finally, Jackson came up, after spending the morning obeying Beauregard's disjointed orders, and was directed there. Even if Cocke exaggerated his own importance, which at most involved acting primarily as a policeman directing traffic, he deserves some credit for guiding reinforcements toward the area about to become the day's main battleground. In that sense, it was Cocke, not Johnston or Beauregard, who played some supervisory role in this sector. On the other hand, his directions about where the units should go were not precise, and the units in question arrived at Portici during a two-hour period and therefore trickled northward a piece at a time.

Bee was first.[129]

Virtually everyone who knew Barnard Bee admired him. One of his Union foes at Bull Run, Orlando B. Willcox, a cadet at West Point when Bee was there, later jotted in his journal: "He always stands out in my memory as the beau-ideal of a gentleman."

Born in Charleston, South Carolina, Bee had been imbued with the duties of gentility. He was of average intelligence (thirty-third in his class of forty-one), but he had far above average character. He was six feet tall, muscular, and fine-looking. Soon after graduation in 1845, he, like so many of his military generation, received a postgraduate education under Winfield Scott in the Mexican War. There, he was wounded and twice brevetted for conspicuous valor and boldness. Later, he served on the frontier at a variety of dismal posts, from Minnesota to Texas. He was on station in the Dakota Territory when he learned that South Carolina, his native state, had seceded.

Like many Southern career officers, he wrestled with his predicament. He was thirty-seven years old and had spent half his life in the army. Did he owe allegiance, he wondered, to his state, which he had hardly visited in the past fifteen years, or to the country and flag he had sworn to defend? He was a man who believed—profoundly—in "duty." Now he had to determine to which of the two rivals he owed his loyalty. Little of his correspondence from this period remains, but all other South Carolina officers during this time were bombarded with letters from people of their native state, and one can assume he was no different. Almost all South Carolinians resigned within days or weeks of their state's secession in December, but he did not, perhaps hoping a compromise could erase the "necessity." He was married and far from well-to-do. If he quit, he would be surrendering his only source of income. He finally resigned on March 3, one day before Lincoln's inauguration, and by doing so then, he could say he never served under a Black Republican president. The Confederacy made him a colonel—then, in June, a brigadier general, commanding one of Johnston's brigades in the Valley. A photograph of him, taken at the time, shows him still wearing his United States army blue uniform. Perhaps to alter that image, he had added around his waist a bright sash. In this picture his hair was of average length, but he may not have cut it afterwards, because an observer at the battle spoke of his "long hair."

General Bee and a portion of his brigade arrived from the Valley on Saturday. In the Valley his command had included a battery of artillery, but the guns had traveled separately from the infantry and had not yet materialized when he arrived. Then, at one o'clock that Sunday morning, after a grueling trek from Winchester, Captain John Daniel Imboden and his four smoothbore six-pounders bumbled into Manassas. Somehow in the darkness Imboden found Bee's temporary headquarters, a log cabin between the train depot and Mitchell's Ford, and reported. With that formality accomplished, Imboden and his men collapsed on the ground in exhaustion.[130]

Imboden's battery called themselves the "Staunton Artillery" since many of its 140 members came from the central Valley near Staunton. Imboden, thirty-eight, had been a lawyer and politician of little note, but he was about to play a critical role in this battle. He had only been asleep a few hours when Israel Richardson's guns opened up across Bull Run, the first shell landing not far from him and startling him awake. A few minutes later a courier rode up to him with a dispatch from General Bee: Imboden must hurry immediately to the general's cabin. When he got there, he found Bee in his shirtsleeves on the porch, obviously agitated and angry about a message from Beauregard he had just received that ordered him to move his brigade several miles north and act as a reserve, somewhere behind Cocke. Bee was also being given temporary supervision of Bartow's partial brigade, bivouacked not far away, but that was small compensation.

(Words like *regiment* and *brigade* ought not be taken too literally. For example, General Bee was a brigade commander, and he had also just been put in charge of Colonel Bartow's brigade. In theory he now commanded a *division.* But neither Bee nor Bartow actually was leading a full brigade since only portions of their commands had thus far arrived from the train depot at Piedmont. Bartow had with him two regiments from Georgia, the Seventh and the Eighth. The precise strength of the Seventh was uncertain, but officers of the Eighth, reviewing their rolls just after the battle, calculated that they had somewhere between 490 and 559 men, and the numbers of the Seventh would have been comparable. So Bartow had between a thousand and eleven hundred men. And even this estimate may be too high, because Bartow had marched his men quite vigorously that morning, and it is likely both regiments had sprinkled stragglers behind them. Bee's so-called brigade consisted of two regiments—the Fourth Alabama and the Second Mississippi, each with less than 600 men—and two isolated companies of the Eleventh Mississippi that had somehow gotten separated from their comrades when boarding the train at Piedmont. So the total enrollment of Bee's brigade was certainly little more than 1,300, perhaps less. His two-"brigade" division, therefore, numbered about 2,400 men.)

Bee was angry that morning because he was being moved away from where, he had been told, the real action was going to be—at Mitchell's Ford, as he understood it—and this seemed especially unjust since he had heard that Jackson would be allowed to stay down there. Now, in front of the log house, Bee advised Captain Imboden that he and his artillery could use the morning to rest because another battery had been temporarily attached to the brigade. Having said this, General Bee, a fairly perceptive individual, peered at Imboden and asked whether Imboden thought he could "stand that." "Not if I can help it," the younger man quickly replied. All right, Bee told him, then get your battery together as fast as you can; the infantry and I will start now, and you can catch up to us. Imboden said that his men and horses had not eaten in almost a full day. Too bad, Bee snapped, still testy about his own orders, adding sardonically Imboden's men would have plenty of time to eat where they would be going, since nothing important would be happening in their sector, except listening to the battle being fought far away.

Imboden returned to his bivouac, and twenty minutes later he and his artillerists were on the move toward Cocke's headquarters by a route slightly different from the one Bee's infantrymen were taking. Imboden was approaching Portici when he saw a horseman galloping in his direction. The courier stopped just long enough to tell him excitedly that a Yankee force of significant size was coming and pointed vaguely toward the north, then dashed away. Imboden halted his men and rode ahead to a hilltop. From there, he saw a large group of Yankees in the distance. He turned back toward his waiting battery and espied Bee approaching at the head of his infantry. Bee, apparently, had just spoken to Cocke who had sent him in this direction. After Imboden described what he had seen, Bee grew excited. Fully energized, he rode with the faster-moving artillery, letting his infantry trail along behind. Finally, Bee even grew impatient at the pace of the guns and spurred his horse ahead. He came to a knoll, from which he could see down to the turnpike passing left to right and, beyond it, a hill that sloped upward. He may also have witnessed the very beginning of the battle erupting on Matthews Hill, a mile in the distance. He examined the knoll he was on, made a decision, and galloped back the way he had come. As soon as he saw Imboden's artillery moving in his direction, he yanked his cap from his head, stuck it on the tip of his sword, and waved back and forth to signal: Come this way, quickly! Imboden sped to him and saw Bee's excitement. The general pointed at Yankees a mile away. "See the glistening bayonets of the enemy!" Bee exclaimed. "Here is the battle-field"—and he gestured toward the knoll, on which sat a small, undistinguished house owned by a Mrs. Judith Henry—"and we are in for it! Bring up your guns as quickly as possible, and I'll look around for a good position."

When the four smoothbores rattled up, Bee showed Imboden just where he wanted them unlimbered—in a gentle dip in the ground, fifty feet back from the crest, which rose five or six feet and so would serve as a natural parapet. From this dip, Imboden's gunners would remain almost invisible to the enemy. But the trajectory of their own fire would easily clear the crest. All the gunners would need was someone with a good eye—Imboden—to stand near the top and shout back directions and distance. As Imboden was placing his guns and ammunition wagons, Bee's infantrymen started arriving, and Bee assigned them spots on either side of the four cannon.

Bartow's men were still somewhere back on the trail. In fact Bartow's two regiments had gotten separated from each other, and both were wandering around, looking for the alleged left flank of the Confederate army. Including Bartow's two Georgia regiments that had not yet arrived, Bernard Bee's 2,400 men constituted a goodly number, but far less than Burnside alone had—and Burnside's brigade was only the first of at least five that were on their way straight toward this spot.

In addition to raw numbers, certain physical factors made Bee's position tenuous. His men were still travel weary because of their trip from the Valley. Given the haphazard nature of their recent meals, they would also have been somewhat weak from insufficient nutrition—though, when the battle began, the initial spurt of adrenaline would have maintained energy levels, but only for a while. In the past few hours they had marched five or six miles on dusty roads. They would be a bit dehydrated, and there was little available water nearby. Arrivals would send off a comrade, lugging a dozen canteens, hoping to get them filled at one of several muddy creeks that were within half a mile, then dragging them back. This was a problematic solution at best, and once real fighting began, even more dubious.

Though he lacked entrenchments, Bee had chosen an excellent position. The enemy would have to cross almost a full mile before reaching it, the last half-mile up a fairly steep hill into the teeth of artillery and musket fire. Bee had no way to guess how many Yankees he might face here, but he assumed he would receive reinforcements. Evans was somewhere out there in front of him, and could withdraw to this strong post. Bartow's Georgia regiments should arrive soon. Cocke was not far away, though Cocke's own position might require him to stay where he was. Maybe Jackson, maybe — someone. Bee could only hope, and wait.[131]

Imboden's four guns on the hill were not completely invisible; their presence soon became apparent to the Yankees. The Rhode Island battery turned its attention toward him. "Shanks" Evans also became aware of the arrival of Bee's command. The fighting near Matthews farm was becoming intense, and Evans's force was on the verge of falling apart. Most of the Tigers, after their last futile charge, had fled the scene. The Fourth South Carolina could not hold out much longer. Evans probably had fewer than 400 men by this time, and they were running low on ammunition. When he espied Bee, therefore, he saw his salvation. Those troops, he thought, must come *here*, and fight alongside their Confederate brethren. He left Colonel Sloan, the South Carolinian, in charge and galloped to Bee and pleaded for support. Their conversation is now lost. Bee might have expressed doubt about the wisdom of throwing more troops into that sector. He might have pointed out how much more sensible it would be for Evans to pull his men back. If he said such things, Evans could have reminded him how dangerous it was to withdraw troops in face of a foe. Whatever their words, Bernard Bee made his second critical decision of the day — to reinforce "Shanks." He ordered Imboden to remain there with his battery until he, Bee, returned. The evidence is muddled, but it seems probable that the Eighth Georgia had just arrived, though Bartow himself and the Seventh Georgia had not shown up. Poor Francis Bartow was terribly nearsighted and was apparently still wandering around on some dusty road, heading in this direction. He and the Seventh did appear eventually, but by that time Bee had already left.

The Battle for Matthews Hill

It was about eleven o'clock. During the next forty-five minutes, things happened very fast. Matthews Hill became like a whirlpool, sucking in units from both sides, men rushing toward the sound of the guns, the increasingly ear-shattering power of thousands of artillery shells and tens of thousands of cartridges all exploding at the same time inside a small space. Bee threw his 1,300 men into the maw. They were followed shortly by Bartow's two Georgia regiments. From the other side, Burnside pushed the rest of his brigade into the cauldron. Then appeared a battalion of South Carolina infantry, led by perhaps the wealthiest man in the South, Wade Hampton. And the Federal commander, Andrew Porter, brought up his brigade from Sudley. And Sherman splashed his way across Bull Run and appeared on the scene. And Thomas J. Jackson and his men marched to the top of the hill near Mrs. Henry's house. (Of them all, only Jackson — whether out of wise prudence or overcautiousness — refused to throw his men into the battle for Matthews Hill.) The pandemonium lured McDowell to the area, then Johnston, then Beauregard. Each of these generals would try to gain control over the chaos, or at least to make sense of it. Afterward, their reports about the events were, not surprisingly, muddy.

The soldiers who actually fought on Matthews Hill existed in a kind of cocoon, isolated from the outside world by noise and smoke and excitement and confusion. Orders were given and not heard, or simply ignored. More than six thousand men, pouring in from all directions, rushed onto the same fifty-acre plot of ground near the Matthews farm. It is impossible to offer a neat narrative, because some things fell apart, some came together — all simultaneously. Men who were there could make little sense of it at the time, or later. The accounts are rife with errors and gaps and riddles. One must use broad strokes, filled in here and there with a bit of pointillism, to suggest the probable pattern of events.

Bee pushed his 1,300 infantrymen down the slope toward the pike, then across it and up the opposite hill, tottering into and out of a sizeable creek called Young's Branch that meandered through this valley until it linked up with Bull Run. On the way Bee seems to have created two Mississippi "battalions," one by combining the two lonely companies representing the Eleventh Mississippi and another by splitting three companies from the Second Mississippi. He told them to go over and defend one or two nearby cannon. He ordered the other seven companies of the Second Mississippi, really now a battalion of about 400 men, to enter a clump of trees and wait. Two months earlier a Confederate army inspector from Richmond wrote a scathing description of this regiment: "The officers are entirely without military knowledge of any description, and the men have a slovenly and unsoldier-like appearance." These remarks were especially damning since the same report praised their Mississippi brethren, the Eleventh. The commander of the Second, Colonel William C. Falkner, had been a lawyer with little or no military experience. The losses of his men were about to be staggering — 25 killed and 82 wounded out of around 500 men, a 20 percent casualty rate. It does not seem to have been his fault; they were about to enter a meat grinder.

As the Mississippians moved toward their assigned positions, Bee rode ahead to examine things for himself. When he approached the battered men of the Fourth South Carolina, they cheered him, a fellow South Carolinian, mightily. He went back and led forward the troops of the Fourth Alabama.[132]

Meanwhile, the Union side was gaining strength. While the soldiers of the Second Rhode Island were grappling with Evans's troops, Burnside's other three regiments entered the scene and, on Hunter's odd insistence, stood in a field on the opposite side of the Sudley road. The Seventy-first New York and the Second New Hampshire stood next to each other, with the First Rhode Island behind them as a reserve. Waiting there, they came under rebel cannon fire, perhaps from Imboden's guns. This barrage disrupted their organization, a normal effect of incoming artillery fire on units with no satisfactory chance to retaliate. A soldier's staying in place while men around him get splattered into eternity wreaks emotional havoc. A few units in both armies stood such fire well this day; others grew disoriented or surly. The troops of the Second New Hampshire, in Burnside's brigade, were representative. Their colonel, Gilman Marston, forty-nine, was a lawyer and an ambitious politician. He had been a congressman from New Hampshire when the war began; in fact he retained his seat until 1863, so, officially, at this moment, he was still a member of Congress. He had raised the Second New Hampshire himself—presumably out of devotion to the Union rather than for any political gain. He may have been a competent lawyer, but he was not an effective military leader. One of his lieutenants, Ai Baker Thompson, thought Marston was "plucky and rash, but he was not born to command." (It should be noted that Lieutenant Thompson had scant respect for the regiment's other field officers.) When Marston was badly wounded and the doctors put his arm in a sling, the colonel promised to continue leading the regiment. His troops were apparently unimpressed. Lieutenant Thompson sourly wrote home that, even when unwounded, Marston had been "useless," and when the colonel finally gave in to his pain, climbed into an ambulance, and left for the rear, his command, the Second, remained stuck in the field, awaiting directions, taking artillery fire. A few of his men noticed rebel skirmishers in the distance. Without orders, they opened fire; then, a few minutes later, for no apparent reason, they stopped. When Burnside came up and tried to move them ahead to assist the Second Rhode Island, they proved so disorganized that he gave up and chose a different regiment. (In the afternoon the Second New Hampshire was sent into another sector of the battlefield. They advanced a bit, came under fire again, crouched immediately down, and stayed in that posture until withdrawn. Throughout several hours on the field, many of these men never saw the enemy or fired their muskets. Of the scores of units on both sides, its performance—as a unit, not as individual soldiers, some of whom performed heroically—was among the worst, though half a dozen others vied for that distinction. Yet one would not realize this from reading Burnside's report, in which he diplomatically declared that the New Hampshire men "rendered great service"—though he may have drawn this ludicrous conclusion from the report of that regiment's lieutenant colonel, Frank S. Fiske, who had taken over for Marston. In his own official report, Fiske would declare: "The men obeyed orders with coolness and precision during the whole day." Later in the war, in battles like Gettysburg, the Second New Hampshire would do well, but not this day.)[133]

Another of Burnside's regiments—the Seventy-first New York—had its own problems. At first they lay behind a small rise that protected them from rebel fire. While here, a Federal battery behind them—Captain Charles Griffin's—came hurtling through their right side, the horses' hooves stomping past the unwary New Yorkers and the heavy, rumbling artillery wagons threatening to crush them. The infantrymen scattered. After that experience, it took a while to reorganize the regiment. According to the *New York Times*'s cautious prose, its field officers, from Colonel Henry P. Martin on down, did not seem "notably brave leaders." To be fair, most members of the Seventy-first believed their term of service was already over and, unconsciously, they may have hung back a bit.

About this time, apparently, Burnside gave up trying to bring either the Second New Hampshire or the Seventy-first New York across the Sudley road. He was growing frantic. The Second Rhode Island was in trouble. So he tapped the First Rhode Island regiment, still in reserve behind the others. He rode up to it and shouted, "Forward, First Rhode Island!" These troops rose to their feet and began pressing forward. Almost immediately they bumped into the Seventy-first, still milling around. "Lie down, Seventy-first," Burnside ordered, "and let Rhode Island pass to the front!" Disgruntled by such rude arrogance, the New Yorkers took their time. But the Rhode Islanders successfully tiptoed through the sullen Seventy-first and moved ahead. They reached the crest of a hill, and in front of them stretched a cornfield. Several hundred yards across it they detected a batch of rebels. (It was Bee's Fourth Alabama, entering the battlefield.)

The First Rhode Island, strung out in a line on either side of their flag, stepped ahead.

The New Englanders started blazing away. In the confusion one Rhode Islander, aiming toward the enemy, felt something odd against his calves. He looked down. There behind him squatted one of his comrades, firing between his legs, perfectly content to use him as a makeshift embrasure. Their regimental color-bearer went down. Someone else picked up the banner, then he too was knocked down by gunfire, and a third man grabbed the flag. (By the end of the day, their flag was black with powder and pierced with thirteen holes.) During this phase of the battle, the twenty-four members of the Rhode Island brass band fluttered about the field like butterflies, caring for the wounded, carrying back those they could — a textbook example of the way battlefield medicine was supposed to work.

Governor Sprague stayed with them, giddy with excitement. Two of his horses, including Snowdrop, had already been killed. When the second one fell, he leaped to his feet, whipped off his hat, and, waving it back and forth, yelled, "Three cheers for the flag, boys; forward and give it to them!" A few minutes later, carrying a musket, he rushed to Burnside and offered to lead his "boys" in a charge; Burnside politely declined the offer. Later, when Burnside took most of his brigade's infantrymen off the field to safety, Sprague declined to join them, remaining, instead, with his own Rhode Island battery. Sprague would live a long life. He would marry the beautiful Miss Chase, become a senator, and build a splendid mansion. Then would come years marred by alcohol and divorce and money problems. In the end, however, he would turn his life around again and redeem it by his energy and high spirits. But this was his finest hour.

Back at the Seventy-first, following more confusion, the New Yorkers finally moved up until they were on the right of the First Rhode Island, facing the Fourth Alabama. Someone ordered them to open fire. The New Yorkers, glad for an opportunity to do something, did just that. But their organization had virtually disappeared. Moving to this spot, they had churned themselves into a clump six or seven files deep, rather than a line, so the men toward the back had little chance to shoot—which apparently suited some quite well since the wall of flesh in front offered comforting protection. Those at the rear of the clump who wanted to participate in the battle either banged away with little regard for their comrades in front (and without the slightest concern about accuracy); or they ran to the left or right to get a clear line of fire, scrambling the organization even more. Early on, someone began shouting excitedly, "You are killing our own men! It is the New Hampshire men!" The Seventy-first stopped for a moment, confused. Again Burnside appeared, this time to reassure them it was okay to fire; the men they were shooting at were indeed the enemy. They started again. They had brought with them two small howitzers, on loan from the navy yard in Washington, and began firing them as well.[134]

On the Confederate side, Evans's demibrigade had essentially crumbled. Sloan's Fourth South Carolina had somehow held on, and was still firing desultorily at the Second Rhode Island at the top of the hill when Bee's Alabamians and Mississippians joined them. Evans organized a last charge of his remaining men, but it, too, fell short. If Bee's reinforcements had arrived a few minutes earlier, the Confederates might have swept the outnumbered Second Rhode Island from the field, but now that the First Rhode Island, then the Seventy-first New York, were pushing toward the Matthews farm, the two sides again were about equal.

(Exactly what happened to the seven-company battalion of the Second Mississippi, stumbling through the trees, is unclear. But in a handful of minutes, their numbers much reduced and their organization in tatters, they were racing away. The brunt of the Yankee attack would be taken by the men of the Fourth Alabama.)

Bee, riding in front of the Alabamians, had reached a likely spot at a fence near a patch of woods and told them to lie down. He rode ahead even farther to reconnoiter the situation, then returned. He saw that Evans's last charge had failed and it was now up to him. When he returned to the fence, one of his men thought he "seemed very much excited." Some of them heard him yell in a strong military voice, "Up, Alabamians." He ordered out skirmishers, left and right, then yelled, *Go!*

Six hundred strong, maybe less, the men from north Alabama rose, clambered over the fence, and stepped forward, led by their colonel, Egbert Jones. Bee rode off, probably to hasten Bartow's Georgians or to check on the Mississippians. Colonel Jones, forty-one, a Huntsville lawyer back home, was imposing. A large man, six feet three inches tall, he seemed calm, almost serene, astride his big horse. Perhaps his steadiness gave the Alabamians courage. The ground from here to the crest of the hill undulated gradually upwards in waves five and six feet high so that walking men could not see far. The corn in the field was two or three feet tall, and it spanked against their legs as they walked. If a man dropped to his belly, the stalks waved far above him. These troops were certainly raw — "green," Lincoln might have called them. Some had come from Huntsville, a town of reasonable size, but most were from the rustic, piney woods world of northern Alabama. Some were dressed in overalls and straw hats and carried only shotguns. One later admitted they were "wild and undisciplined, but they were 'eager.'"

The Alabamians jogged forward, peering at the last Tigers scampering pell-mell back past them. They had not gone far when the Yankees (the First Rhode Island) opened fire. Like stones falling into water, the Alabamians crouched way down, where they were hidden by the cornstalks. Then, individually, one or the other would raise his head and, when he saw an enemy appear above the skyline, fire. They aimed especially at the Yankees carrying flags and picked off two. "I waited until I saw him good," one private wrote home, "that is, till I saw his body down to the hips. I drew as fine a bede on him as anyone can with a rifle, and pulled trigger, and down went the stars and stripes." More and more Yankees began to appear (the Seventy-first New York). The Fourth Alabama was now badly outnumbered. "But we thought," one later recalled, "of what they would say at home if we flinched, and how ashamed we should feel if, after all the big talk about 'whipping the enemy,' we let them whip us at the first chance." Through it all, somehow, Colonel Jones continued to sit on his horse, calmly giving out orders — till he was wounded in both hips. (After the battle his wounds festered, and he would die in September.)

One Alabama company, the Conecuh Guards, entered the field with forty-five men, perhaps fewer. Private George Anderson fell, shot in the head. His younger brother, fourteen, only a few feet away, saw him go down and ran to him, falling upon his brother's body, sobbing uncontrollably. Their captain, hoping to spur the boy to action, told him to stand up and avenge his dead brother, but the boy could not move and continued to weep.

The enemy's fire was fierce. An Alabamian had his shoe knocked off, another had his canteen perforated, a third lost his shoulder strap. In a few short minutes, four of the Conecuh Guards were dead and fourteen others wounded. About ten others were bruised by spent musket balls or shell fragments. In other words, two-thirds or more of this one company were at least touched by Yankee fire. All these men had been neighbors in the rural, sparsely populated county of Conecuh. Young women with children and hardscrabble farms did not yet know it, but they had just become widows—with all the poverty and loneliness that that implied. Afterward, Sergeant Reuben Kidd wrote home: "You who have never witnessed the horrors of a battlefield have no idea what its horrors are."

Following half an hour of this pounding, the men of the Fourth Alabama, one by one at first, began to pull back. Colonel Jones, in pain, holding his horse with one arm, pleaded for them not to run. He misunderstood. They were not fleeing exactly; they had simply taken as much as they could and were moving out of danger.[135]

It was now going to be up to Bartow's Georgians.

"VICTORY! VICTORY!"

I thought I had seen sights before, but I never saw nothing.
— JACOB S. CLOUTS, SEVENTH GEORGIA[136]

When Georgia seceded in January 1861, Governor Joseph E. Brown chose the politician Francis Stebbins Bartow to lead the Eighth Regiment. Bartow, forty-four, was a bright graduate of Yale Law School, a member of a prominent Savannah family, and a strong secessionist. But Governor Brown decided to name Montgomery Gardner as Bartow's second in command because of Gardner's military expertise. In appearance, Lieutenant Colonel William Montgomery Gardner, thirty-seven, seemed quite dashing, with a youthful, matinee idol handsomeness. In reality he was a conscientious officer but something of a dim bulb. He had graduated from West Point in 1846, almost at the bottom of his class, fought in the Mexican War with energy and courage, and then spent years in frontier service. He had resigned his commission in the United States Army as soon as he learned of his state's secession. By mid-July the Eighth Georgia, now part of Johnston's Valley army, seemed to be doing well. The Confederate War Department was planning to promote Gardner to the rank of brigadier general and give him his own command, but the department was swamped and had not yet executed the necessary paperwork. So, at this moment, Gardner remained at his rank of lieutenant colonel, even though he was now in total charge of the Eighth, since Bartow had been given an entire brigade, of which the Eighth was only a part.

On this morning the men of the Seventh and Eighth Georgia Regiments awoke, ate breakfast, and sat around. Their bivouacs, not far from each other, were well behind Blackburn's Ford. From that position, if they heard the first rumble of Richardson's artillery, the sound would have been muffled. Bartow, increasingly edgy, rode off to investigate what was happening. About eight o'clock he galloped back to camp. "Get ready, men!" he shouted. "The battle has been raging for two hours on our extreme left [the stone bridge], and we must go there at once."

The Georgia regiments took care of several details first. The Eighth, for example, had placed one of its companies out on picket duty almost two miles away. These men had to be tracked down and reeled in, and this took almost an hour. Then the chaplain of the Eighth led them in prayer, and they strapped on their accoutrements, picked up their guns, and prepared to march. Meanwhile, coffee was being heated over campfires and sandwiches slapped together to serve as a brunch to give the men strength before battle. It was about nine o'clock by the time the regiment started moving. The morning sun was high now and the day was getting warm. With the air so still, and no breezes to fan them, the marching men suffered, especially the ones just recovering from measles or those who were coming down with it. Bartow had departed for the railroad station to see if the remainder of his brigade had arrived, but he had indicated to Gardner he was anxious that the Eighth get "there" in time, so Gardner occasionally ordered the men to increase their speed to double-quick. This pace was too stiff for some, and men began dropping to the side. "My! how tired I was," one of them would recall, "and how the perspiration oozed from every pore." And then they heard the dull roar of artillery somewhere ahead of them — growing ominously like a terrifying waterfall downstream.

Unlike the troops who had fought earlier in the day — Evans's men, for example, and Burnside's — those who now moved toward the battlefield had to deal with two disconcerting facts: the sounds of battle, which grew in intensity as one approached it, and the ugly sights—the moaning, ambulatory wounded soldiers wandering past them toward the rear; then the corpses and human flesh littering the ground. Such sounds and sights chipped at a man's confidence. As one later said, when a soldier entered the fighting zone: "The shock was stunning."[137]

They marched up behind Mrs. Henry's house, where Barnard Bee told Gardner he wanted the Georgians in an open cornfield, not far from an apple tree. Gardner took them to the spot, ordered them to load their weapons, then rest. (Professional soldiers like Montgomery Gardner knew it was unwise to allow volunteers to load their cartridges until the last minute; accidental discharges were too common. McDowell had lost many men on his march from Washington to Centreville from such accidents.)

The men of the Eighth were glad to drop to the ground. One recalled: "Perhaps never before had I embraced mother earth so affectionately, as my weary head was softly laid in a freshly plowed furrow, and I pulled a stalk of succulent corn to slake my thirst." A few, however, eyed the apples dangling from a tree not far away, sweet-talking them with such ruddy allure. A handful of Georgians could not resist the siren call and ran to the tree. It was an old one, its branches too high above the ground to pluck off the fruit by hand. A few shinnied up the trunk to grasp the treasures, but others searched for rocks and clumps of dirt to plunk the apples down. Officers shouted at them to stay down, but Gardner, staring toward the Yankees in the distance, said mildly he did not think such orders were necessary. "I see a battery taking position over yonder."

Seconds later a Yankee cannon opened fire and a shell whizzed uncomfortably close. Gardner announced he considered such shooting amateurish. "That went a hundred feet over us," he said. But to the Georgians, this was really the first enemy shell ever shot at them. They reacted accordingly. "The boys dropped from the apple tree like shot bears," one man recalled, "and scrambled on hands and knees for their places in line." A second Georgian admitted to his diary he tried to burrow into the ground like some critter under attack, a squirrel or a possum. Another remembered that his first thought was: "This is unfair; somebody is to blame for getting us all killed." But to many of the Georgians, Gardner's confidence was reassuring as he sat calmly high atop his horse Brimstone, watching the enemy artillerists. Even the dozen or so members of the regiment's brass band got in the spirit and tootled away energetically—until the crashing of artillery entirely drowned out their efforts.

Time passed as the men of the Eighth lay there—some thought it a full hour, but it was probably half that. Bartow finally appeared, back from the depot, where he had been unable to find the rest of his brigade. He squinted at the Georgians myopically and asked, "Boys, what regiment is this?" He had organized these men back in Georgia and loved them like a father, and when they assured him who they were, he said, "My God, boys, I am glad to see you." In turn they felt a great warmth for him, and they broke out into cheers. A messenger from Bee arrived, asking for support. Bartow shouted to Gardner, "They have your range, Colonel, charge them!"

Gardner had already gotten off Brinstone and sent him back to safety. He had with him a sword he had owned since the Mexican War, and he picked it up and waved it in the air, shouting: "Rise, Eighth Regiment!" And the five hundred men stood, in anticipation, guns in their hands. "Attention!" he yelled. "Right face, double-quick, *march!*" It is not certain whether his specific goal was to charge the artillery that had been shooting toward the Henry house or was merely to assist Bee's men in some appropriate way.

He did not actually lead them in a straight line forward past the house. Instead, he marched them eastward a few hundred yards, in the direction of Bull Run, then turned them left till they faced down the hill. He stopped them for a moment. He was aware that, under such circumstances, commanders traditionally gave their men a pep talk, a speech that would stir them to acts of courage and honor. But he was a simple soldier, and he struggled to fetch the proper inspirational words from the scramble of half-forgotten phrases once heard. No magnificent oratory came to him. One of his men remembered him saying: "Men, I am no orator. I shall not attempt to make you a speech. Keep your ranks, do your duty, and show you are worthy of the State from which you came!" Another recalled his words thus: "I cannot make a speech, and haven't time now if I could. Keep cool, obey orders—follow me, and we will whip them, egad!" And down the hill they went—doing their duty, obeying orders—anxious to be worthy of Georgia.[138]

They crossed the pike and Young's Branch. Bee met them. He pointed toward the Rhode Island battery farther up the hill, and the Eighth started jogging in that direction. They went through a clump of oak trees and across a field. The Yankees saw them coming and started firing at them with cannon and muskets. Miraculously, only two of the Georgians were wounded running this gauntlet of fire. They headed toward a group of pine trees several acres in size. If they made it to that copse, they could creep through it toward the battery and emerge from the other side almost on top of it. But first they had to reach those tightly packed trees. The oldest of them, Jesse Dalton, was over sixty. The heat was affecting him, and the many hours of marching. A fellow Georgian saw the bullets pinging around the old man's feet: "Dalton was just too tired now to move faster. He fell just before he reached the thicket."

Then they were inside. And rushing headlong forward. The trunks of the trees and their haphazard branches shattered the Eighth's organization. The murk within the thicket and unexpected mounds of sharp-clawed blackberry bushes and a surprising ancient rail fence tumbled them about even more. Finally, some of them reached the thicket's far edge and peered out. Yes, it was true, the guns were not far away now! But there were also Yankee infantrymen between them and the battery—ten thousand Yankees, some imagined, maybe fifteen thousand. Between the two forces was an open field, in which stood an ice house and stacks of recently cut hay, and beyond the field a line of fencing. Past that was a farm house (the Matthews brothers'), with the usual assortment of outbuildings scattered about it.

The Georgians came to a sudden halt at the edge of the thicket. Forgetting their assignment, to attack the Union battery that was a few hundred yards away, they opened fire from the relative safety of the trees. The boles of the trees and the narrowness of the thicket made it impossible for all of them to get clear shots at the same time. The Georgians shoved at each other, those nearest the tree line not wishing to be pressed into the open by the anxiety of those behind them. Gardner shouted at his regiment to advance. Few could hear him. The trees blocked sounds and caused odd echoes. The bedlam of shouts and musket fire and exploding trees increased and grew almost palpable.

The Yankees, hiding behind the buildings and the hay and the fences, fired back at them, or at least at the clump of pines and anything that moved inside it. The Georgians began falling. Their regimental adjutant, John Branch, was shot in the chest and tumbled over. Two of his brothers, Sanford and Hamilton, were nearby, but only Sanford saw. A few days later Sanford wrote their mother. "I thought I would look behind me to see if any of my Company had fallen. But, Mother, just think of my horror to see John, Dear John, reel and fall. I dropped my gun and ran to him. I got there just after Dr. West [a physician in private life] and, who Dear John asked whether there was any chance or not. When told he must die, he replied, 'Very well — he would die like a soldier and a man'... I cannot write any more now, as I was taken prisoner standing by his body."

Colonel Gardner also went down, shot in the lower leg. He dragged himself to a stump, sat on it, and yelled encouragement — to men who could not hear his words. It was madness inside the thicket. "I kneeled at a sapling," one Georgian recalled, "fired, reloaded, and fired again; but it was impossible to see if my shots hit anyone." One of the captains tried to dress his "line." A musket ball smashed into his skull, and he crumpled to the ground without a word. Francis Bartow, still with them, was signaling with his sword when a Yankee bullet clipped off its tip. Above them, the trunks of the pines splintered as Yankee bullet after bullet picked away at them. Years later, one of the men, a veteran of the entire war, said, "I was never afterwards in as hot a place."[139]

Minute after crazed minute this madness went on. Any individual caught in a high-risk situation can grow disoriented when inundated by too many sensory details and enter an almost dreamlike state. The entire enemy army seems to be shooting at *him*—and *him* alone. Under such conditions, one man runs, another becomes robotic—not a "killing machine," but a man merely repeating the minimal tasks he has been taught: pulling out a cartridge, putting the twisted end inside his teeth and tearing it open, pouring the powder into the barrel of his gun, shoving in the ball, taking out the ramrod. Aiming—at least, pointing his weapon—toward the hordes. Doing this, over and over.

When the Eighth Georgia arrived inside the thicket, the two sides on Matthews Hill were still approximately equal—though those fighting would not have agreed. As each individual saw it, his side was outnumbered. Excluding the artillerists, who were mostly focusing on each other at this time or moving their guns around, the only Union soldiers in this stage of the battle were Burnside's men. Burnside probably had no more than 1,500 men now fighting, perhaps fewer. With the arrival of the Eighth Georgia, the Confederates had about the same. The Second Rhode Island, as a unit, hardly remained in the battle, any more than Evans's brigade. The Seventy-first New York and some of the Second New Hampshire had moved in and were still grappling with the Fourth Alabama and the Mississippians. So at first, the Eighth Georgia, although it did not realize it, was scrapping, head to head, mostly with the men of the First Rhode Island. And despite the nightmare of the thicket, in a sense, for the first few minutes, the Georgians had the advantage.

Since Burnside's men were on the offensive, by military standards of the day they ought to have had far more men than their foes. The usual rule of thumb was that an assaulting force ought to be about double the enemy's size, particularly if the enemy was well entrenched. The Confederates on Matthews Hill did not have entrenchments, of course, but they were using fences and the woods to their advantage. Moreover, many of Burnside's men carried only smoothbores, and seven companies of the Eighth Georgia had good rifles. The distance from the thicket to the farm house was a couple of hundred yards, the distance where a rifle was a far more accurate weapon than the shorter-range smoothbore. (Inside the thicket a number of Georgians were struck with spent balls that did little damage or buckshot that only stung.)

Moreover, the Seventh Georgia was approaching, and Hampton's Legion was heading toward the scene.

Burnside could see that his brigade was being decimated. It seemed as though the rebels were about to win the battle of Matthews Hill. He desperately wanted assistance, and he thought about a particular battalion that he knew was attached to Porter's brigade. Those men were not volunteers—like those of the First Rhode Island, whose terms were already over, or like those of the Second New Hampshire, who had had only a handful of weeks of half-hearted training. The soldiers Burnside wanted were the legendary "regulars"—professional soldiers.

West Point graduates like Ambrose Burnside spoke of such regulars with respect. During peacetime, even a year earlier, most Americans who thought about professional military men felt disdain. To a typical American of 1860, any enlisted man in the tiny United States Army was a contemptible figure—a loser no doubt, probably a drunkard, a foreigner, a thief, a laggard. But now that a real war had arrived, the volunteers—civilians at heart—tended to view the regulars with a kind of mixed awe and the resentment rookies in any profession often display toward professionals. McDowell had brought a single battalion of regulars and had assigned them to Porter's brigade that had spent the morning marching after Burnside.

Porter had arrived in the area of the battle and had taken his brigade into the fields on the opposite side of the Sudley road from Matthews Hill—the northeast quadrant. Griffin's battery was already there, unlimbered a few hundred yards from the Warrenton turnpike, not far away from another farm (one owned by John Dogan). Behind the guns were three New York regiments—of, as it turned out, uncertain quality—and seven companies of regular cavalry, also of untested ability. Marching near the rear of Porter's brigade came Major George Sykes's battalion of regulars, almost 600 strong.

Despite their reputation, many of these men had only recently joined the army, and almost all their officers were relatively inexperienced—either completely new to the service or just graduated from West Point. In Sykes, they had a West Point career officer in command, but so did a number of regiments, North and South. On the surface, therefore, the regulars seemed not dissimilar from the soldiers in many volunteer regiments. But their reputation turned out to be accurate; they were indeed different. They would prove themselves to be rock solid. Why did they do so well? Was it Sykes's leadership? If so, what was there about him so different from all the other hard-bitten professionals? Or was it the discipline of the regulars?

Major George Sykes, thirty-eight, was a simple man. Therein lay perhaps his greatest strength. At West Point he had been a middle-level cadet from Delaware, nicknamed "Tardy George" because of his casualness about schedules. But his classmates also noticed he had a straightforward, honorable candor about him. They liked him. After graduating in 1842 he served in the Mexican War, then on the frontier where he revealed his real style. He was "army" all the way, a born lifer, accepting its rules and traditions. Never known for much, perhaps any, imagination or wit, he was a person one could trust — if necessary — with one's life. A serious man. In 1861 George Sykes was lean as a swagger stick and just as sturdy. His small blue eyes were set in a red face, roughened by years of merciless Texas sun. He had let his brown curly beard grow long, and it hung against the rock-hard muscles of his chest. He was not exactly flinty, but he believed in discipline — not because he felt any sadistic need to punish but because he had learned discipline worked. One could not expect men to act like machines, he thought, but if one trained them correctly, when it came to a battle, soldiers who had stuck out the hardships of army life could be counted on to do the simple things right. It was he who supervised the whipping of the two deserters just the day before. (Apparently those two men were still marching with the battalion, their backs raw from the lash, their faces still bearing the burned-in *D*s, but history has lost their names.)

Sykes's battalion of eight companies was a makeshift group of regulars, temporarily pieced together to give McDowell's army some "spine." Some of its enlisted men had seen years of service, and one can suspect these old-timers — the sergeants and the corporals — along with Sykes, served as the unit's leathery backbone. But few were grizzled veterans of bloodied battlefields, the classic characters of countless movies and books. What made them, therefore, better soldiers than the volunteers—who were often older family men and better-educated? Perhaps the answer lay in their *expectations*. The volunteers expected to fight a bit, then go home as soon as the war was over. Inside their hearts, they remained "civilians" no matter what clothing they wore. The regulars saw themselves as "soldiers." This meant they accepted the standards of the profession. In a sense this is what separates lifers from part-timers in any profession. It is not so much how many years a person devotes to his or her job; it is whether he or she embraces the often unexpressed rules of behavior. One must, however, be careful not to exaggerate the devotion of army regulars before 1861. As we have seen, the army had been annually losing one-fifth of its enlisted men through desertion, men unwilling to accept that army discipline. But it is likely that the vast majority of Sykes's men had consciously or unconsciously accepted the "army" and the discipline which that acceptance suggested. It was almost certainly this attribute that made them the best soldiers at Bull Run.

Burnside sought out Sykes's battalion. He galloped to Porter and said, "Porter, for God's sake, let me have the regulars. My men are being cut to pieces." Andrew Porter was nothing if not controlled. "Colonel Burnside," he replied, "do you mean to say the enemy is advancing on my left?" (This, of course, was not at all what Burnside was saying. Burnside was exclaiming that *his* brigade was in trouble, while Porter seemed only concerned with how that might affect *him*. Porter had no desire to part with his precious regulars. Porter also had attached to his brigade an excellent battery, but his three New York regiments seemed potentially wobbly. Subtracting the regulars, therefore, weakened his brigade significantly.) Burnside realized it was best to try a different tack. "Yes," he said, "and you will be cut off if you can't stop him." Porter reluctantly acquiesced, and Burnside raced away.

Porter was not entirely pleased with his own decision. In his report he would say archly that Burnside's problems resulted from "attacking the enemy's right with, perhaps, too hasty vigor." It had been Porter's intention to sidle his brigade past the Confederate force that he could see in front of him. This was why he was on the western side of the Sudley road rather than on Matthews Hill. Without Sykes's regulars, this thrust would be weaker.

After Burnside left, Porter sent orders to Sykes to join Burnside's assault. Major Sykes gave his men a short speech. They would have some work to do, he told them; that was the extent of his address, even briefer than Gardner's little speech. Then Sykes jogged across the Sudley road, his men following behind him. They passed a battery, led by Captain James B. Ricketts, that was just arriving, and one of its officers waved his cap excitedly at them. The appearance of Sykes's regulars filled men with confidence. When they marched up to Burnside, the Rhode Islanders saw them and began to cheer. How, the Rhode Islanders wondered, could they lose with these regulars on their side? Burnside himself was delighted. "Good God!" he burst out with pleasure. "Major Sykes, your regulars are just what we want; form on my left and give aid to my men who are being cut to pieces!"

Sykes lined his men up, their left side about a hundred yards from the Matthews house. While they were getting into position, some of them seemed a trifle jittery. To inspirit the men, their officers stood behind their lines and reminded them they had just become the steel core of Burnside's brigade at a critical time. Besides, the officers added, if any man of them turned to run, the officers intended to shoot him. Then the regulars opened fire on the rebels. Despite repeated urgings from Sykes beforehand, most of the new troops, wobbly with excitement, aimed too high. But soon even they settled down. Their entrance onto the battlefield of Matthews Hill probably by itself would have sealed the fate of the rebels still there. But a great many more Union troops were about to enter the scene at that moment because of a decision made, miles away and much earlier, by General McDowell.[140]

McDowell's Headquarters

Irvin McDowell and his staff had spent much of the morning back at the blacksmith shop. It was a good central location for the commander of this huge army extending its tentacles out miles in several directions. The shop was about halfway between Centreville and the stone bridge, and halfway between Sudley Ford to the north and where Richardson and Davies had placed their batteries to the south. McDowell's respite here may have allowed him to cease his bouts of vomiting and diarrhea; it also permitted him to observe things, to receive information from couriers, to move units about as he deemed necessary, and to contemplate his next steps. Professional military men know that paper plans are as fragile as spider webs. A commander must keep his mind flexible and be ready to make changes as circumstances require. A battle between two equal foes is like a judo match where opponents know that mere muscle power by itself will not be enough; victory will often come from sensing when one's adversary is slightly off balance and then thrusting and heaving at just the right spot at the right moment. McDowell would be judged by how he now reacted. Would he be able to "feel" his foe's weakness and spin the enemy to the mat?

In the most general terms, McDowell's army by midmorning, just before the fighting began in earnest on Matthews Hill, looked like this: His eleven brigades were split into three parts. He had three brigades on his far left (Davies's and Richardson's, along with their batteries, a couple of miles from Centreville, with Blenker's near the village as a reserve). He had Tyler's three brigades (Sherman's, Schenck's, and Keyes's) not far from the stone bridge, ready to cross Bull Run as soon as the rebels on the other side had been pushed out of the way, permitting the engineers to drop their prefabricated bridge into place next to the presumably mined stone bridge. McDowell's other five brigades were moving to the right (north) and would soon be pressing southward. McDowell never said, but one senses he planned to cross Bull Run personally with Tyler. This would have put him in the center of almost 18,000 men. He would have moved his *mobile command center*—always a chancy thing to do during a battle—from the blacksmith shop to somewhere beyond Bull Run. It would be important to set up a *headquarters* so that couriers could find him and that quartermaster and commissary wagons, carrying provisions and ammunition, would have a specific place to go. Wagons were already lining up on the turnpike, preparing to cross.

McDowell made two important alterations to his original plans. By nine o'clock Hunter's division, consisting of Burnside's and Porter's brigades, had disappeared into the woods. Heintzelman's division of three more brigades was now passing McDowell, turning onto the path. In McDowell's mind something had gone awry. He had not been informed that the road to Sudley Ford was much longer than Major Barnard's calculations. He had expected to hear the sounds of battle from the far side of Bull Run an hour or so earlier. He had assumed that Burnside's brigade would have already crossed the stream and started fighting whatever rebels were up there. He also found it disconcerting that Tyler's guns near the stone bridge had elicited such a small response. A generation later Sherlock Holmes would deduce evidence from a "dog that did not bark"—in other words, from an expected event that did not occur. Since McDowell did not hear any fighting going on across the stream, he wondered if the rebels were about to unleash a surprise attack—probably in the vicinity of Mitchell's Ford. He suddenly decided it would be unwise to continue sending half his army northward, directly *away* from the place Beauregard might be just about to assault. On the spur of the moment, he halted Heintzelman's last brigade that was just passing him, the men commanded by Oliver O. Howard. He ordered Howard to remain here. From this spot, Howard could move his brigade in any of three directions, wherever it might be needed. Like Blenker, Howard was to stand as a ready reserve, but in an advanced position and with an assignment to be ready to move quickly.

As soon as he presented Howard with his new role, McDowell and his staff started riding north, along the path to Sudley Ford, still uneasy about not hearing any fighting. He rode past Heintzelman's marching men and nervously urged them to quicken their pace. McDowell and his staff emerged from the dense woods, eventually turned left toward Sudley Ford, and found themselves riding along a fairly high knoll. It was about this time that the battle began between Slocum's Second Rhode Island and Evans's demibrigade, the fight that McDowell had been listening for. He therefore knew that Burnside—the vanguard of Hunter's division—had crossed the stream and was moving south, according to plan. From this knoll, however, McDowell and his staff could also discern in the southwest, some miles away, several immense dust clouds rising far above the trees. They correctly concluded these clouds were made by large numbers of marching men, maybe thousands of them, moving in this general direction — which meant that a major force was heading toward Burnside. (Since the time was about 9:30, the clouds were almost certainly being raised by the tired, shuffling feet of Bee's troops and Bartow's Georgians, and perhaps Hampton's Legion, heading from the train station toward Cocke's position at Portici.) The sight of these dust clouds pushed McDowell into his second decision — the one that actually guaranteed the Union victory on Matthews Hill. He ordered an aide to rush back to Tyler, carrying a message to smash across Bull Run by any method, not to wait any longer for Hunter's or Heintzelman's drive southward to clear the way for him. It was critical, McDowell thought, to rush more men toward that spot (Matthews Hill, though McDowell had not yet learned its name). His ride here had convinced him it would be hours before Heintzelman's division could cross Sudley Ford. By then it might be too late. Tyler must move now.

The aide — Lieutenant Henry W. Kingsbury — found Tyler by a tall pine tree a few hundred yards east of the stone bridge. An agile member of Tyler's staff had climbed far up into its branches, was observing rebel movements with a field glass, and was shouting down what he could see. Lieutenant Kingsbury told Tyler what McDowell had said. Since these new orders contravened the old ones, Tyler wanted to be very sure they were exactly what McDowell wanted; it was far too common for orders to be misremembered or misstated by inexperienced aides. "What does he mean?" Tyler asked. "Does he mean that I shall cross the stream?" Kingsbury said he was repeating the exact words that McDowell had used. Tyler mused a second, then said, "I have a good mind to send [some troops] across the stream." (McDowell was so edgy about this matter he sent another aide to Tyler to reinforce his orders.)

In this second change in plans, McDowell made two errors. If he wanted Tyler to send across his entire division, he should have specified it. Since McDowell did not do that, Tyler forwarded only two of his three brigades. Also, McDowell ought to have then ordered Howard to link up with Tyler, less than a mile away. When McDowell did finally tell Howard to start forward, Howard properly assumed he was expected to rejoin Heintzelman's division. This required him to take the long, northerly route and, as we will see, unduly tire his men. They could have had a far greater impact crossing near the stone bridge at noon than they did when they arrived on the battlefield, exhausted, hours later, after a long hike in the heat of midafternoon.[141]

But for the rest of the morning, such critiques would seem nitpicking. Things were about to go very well for Irvin McDowell. By 11:30 the fight on Matthews Hill had already reached critical mass when Sykes and his regulars entered it. Also, the arrival at this time of Ricketts's battery, attached to Heintzelman's division, was significant. Ricketts's appearance meant that Heintzelman's front brigade — which included the three regiments of William B. Franklin — was entering the arena. Two thousand more Union infantrymen and Ricketts's excellent artillerymen could focus on the remaining rebels on Matthews Hill. One of Burnside's New Hampshire men would recall that Franklin's men came up, "shouting and cheering like madmen."

Just then, the vanguard of Sherman's brigade appeared from a different direction, their arrival the first result of McDowell's change of plans. When Tyler had received McDowell's new orders, he sent a dispatch to Sherman: Cross Bull Run and assist "Hunter" (that is, Burnside's men). Up to that moment, Sherman had spent the past hour or so watching rebels on the other side of the stream pass toward the north. He had directed his artillery to fire on them, but the rebels generally kept themselves out of range. He was impatient and unhappy. Tyler's message changed things. He immediately put his brigade into motion. They crossed precisely where the pugnacious rebel officer several hours earlier had foolishly indicated a fording place. The banks of the stream at this spot were too steep to permit the passage of his artillery, but Sherman's infantrymen had no trouble sloshing over. They clambered up the far side, went through a band of woods, and appeared in the fields beyond. There in front of them were a bunch of rebels, scurrying around like cockroaches caught in bright lights.[142]

It was the Fourth Alabama, one of the last Confederate units to leave the hill in a relatively coherent state. Moving away from the action, the Fourth had unfortunately just stumbled into one of Sherman's arriving regiments, the Sixty-ninth New York. Not expecting to see Yankees coming from that direction, the men of the Fourth attempted Beauregard's secret gestures and pass-words to signal to these presumed Confederates that they were friends. But as soon as their flag bearer unfurled their rebel banner, the New Yorkers opened fire. The Alabamians returned fire raggedly, then hustled quickly away. The Fourth Alabama's losses during the battle were about 40 percent of those who actually fought, the highest percentage of any unit on either side. There is an old military axiom, painfully learned: When a unit loses 30 percent or more of its total manpower, its organization almost always disintegrates (*losses* defined as those men killed, wounded, and missing). Both the Fourth Alabama and the Eighth Georgia fell into this category.

The men of the Eighth Georgia were still inside the thicket. One Georgian later recalled seeing Sykes's regulars rising up before them, "as if by magic from the ground." Another Georgian became aware that some Yankees had entered the brush and were coming toward them. (These, too, were the regulars, seen from a different angle.) Inside the thicket the fighting turned into hand-to-hand combat. The Eighth Georgia, as a fairly well-organized, articulated unit, now ceased to exist. Afterward, no one could recall how the retreat from the thicket began. Someone did overhear Bartow say, "We must get these men out of here," but few others caught it. "When the command to retire was given," one recalled, "I did not hear it, and soon found myself with none but dead and wounded around me." He heard someone sing out, "Rally, Rome Light Guards!" The regiment as such had disappeared, its men now moving as companies — or even as small groups of mere companions, clumps of five men, more or less, moving shoulder to shoulder alongside men they recognized from home, friends and family members. Fighting now became almost clan warfare. Here in the thicket, the "Confederacy" had disappeared.

Some Georgians, oblivious to everything, continued to fire for a few minutes, then even they began to pull back. A few officers gathered as many men as they could—as it turned out, little more than 10 percent of those who had entered the thicket less than half an hour earlier—and started to get away from the trees. As they reached the fresh air of the outside, their flag held aloft above them, they tried to maintain what little pride they had, but they felt desolate. They—representatives of the Confederacy, of "Dixie," theoretically stalwart "Southrons" protecting their noble hearths—were retreating. Their humiliation was oppressive. They tried to maintain some semblance of dignity by refusing, at least, to run. One officer wrote his father: "For the honor of the State we marched at a deliberate walk." A few of them stopped occasionally to fire back toward the satanic Yankees, but most shambled stolidly toward the pike.

A Georgian would recall years later his own departure from the thicket. "I saw it was 'all up' with us, and as everyone about me seemed to be dead or wounded, I determined to take my chances of saving myself by getting away as fast as I could." He was able to stagger from the brush and suddenly saw a comrade carrying the Eighth's banner, surrounded by a small cluster of moving men. He tried to catch up to them, a drowning swimmer desperate to reach a life raft full of friends, but he found himself so weary he could hardly walk, and he dropped to the ground to rest and watched his comrades with the flag disappear.

Then, stunningly, some Confederates (the men of the Seventh Georgia? Hampton's Legion?) noticed the Eighth emerging unexpectedly from the trees and opened fire on them. A few more Georgians fell to the ground. The rest kept moving.

Bartow, half-hysterical by this time, saw them some distance away and shouted out hoarsely, "Who is that officer who is leading off those men?" He stamped his foot and shook his fist at soldiers he considered cowardly traitors. A few men, standing near him, tried to call to the little group that were moving off, huddled protectively around their flag, but nothing could be heard over the noise. As a final insult to the wretched Georgians, a dashing officer with a handsome, colorful sash around his waist galloped up and challenged their courage. By some alchemy, a few of Evans's Fourth South Carolina were still fighting somewhere on Matthews Hill. This officer demanded to know how *Georgians* could be "running while the South Carolinians are fighting." The soldier holding the banner, already humiliated, was enraged. He cursed the officer and said he would shoot him off that fine horse, whoever the hell he was. Others in the pathetic little band also ran at the rider, shouting emotionally—perhaps secretly suspecting he was correct about them. For some reason, the officer retracted his statement; maybe it was something about these men. "I must admit that you are ready enough to fight; I withdraw the words I should not have used." And he rode off. Apparently, none of the men recognized him. It was General Barnard Bee, the man who had led them to this spot. This small band of Georgians and other dribs and drabs of the Eighth who had wandered out of the thicket from other directions kept moving, away from Matthews Hill.

(According to one story, a few minutes later, not far away, Bee and Bartow, each frenzied at what he had just seen and experienced, at the frightful losses of the men from their home states—South Carolina and Georgia—almost came to blows. Bartow, from Georgia, had seized the regimental banner from a South Carolina color-bearer to lead them toward battle, and Bee, seeing this, rushed up and wrested it away. The incident, if it in fact really occurred, was the result of the powerful emotions of that awful moment and perhaps of Bartow's resentment at the fact that Bee had been placed over him. And, ironically, the two were defending their state's rights: those of South Carolina and Georgia. One observer thought the squabble would have ended up in a duel between the two proud men had not fate decided to intervene in a different way.)[143]

Francis Bartow was particularly distraught. His Eighth Georgia Regiment, the one he had put together back home, had been pulverized inside the thicket. He felt discouraged and perhaps unconsciously embarrassed by the apparent rout of his Georgians. He was on his way back to the Seventh Georgia to bring it forward when his horse was killed. He was so drained he had to sit down to catch his breath. He was heard to say, "My men are nearly all killed and I care not longer to live." An hour or two later a passing courier gave him another horse, and Bartow rode off to lead the Seventh Georgia into action. Its regimental color-bearer had been shot, and Bartow picked up the flag himself and shouted to the Seventh, "On, my boys." Holding the banner aloft, high above his horse, he was a magnet. A Yankee ball smashed into his chest. A story—perhaps apocryphal—was soon told throughout Georgia and the rest of the Confederacy that his dying words were, "They have killed me, my brave boys, but never give up the ship—we'll whip them yet."[144]

But many Confederate soldiers had in fact given up all thoughts of further fighting, at least for now. Exhausted, they had stumbled off. Around noon, the elderly secessionist, Edmund Ruffin, saw a large bunch of Southern troops who seemed to have lost all purpose. He thought they numbered at least a hundred, maybe two. They had no reason to be where they were, nor did they seem to care. "I learned on inquiry of those nearest me," he wrote in his diary, "that they had been in the battle, & had left the field, some for slight wounds, but mostly because of exhaustion, & (as they said) by order, or by permission, to rest themselves, & then to return. But none seemed to have the least desire to return." These "stragglers" or "skulkers" made him uneasy. "I was struck by the strange fact, that of all these men reported as either wounded or worn down by exertion, not one was sitting or lying, as if to rest, but that all were on their feet." He called on them to join him in going to the fighting. "Not one replied, nor made any indication of hearing, except by staring at me in silence." He walked off by himself and farther down the road encountered other skulkers. They, too, told him the battle had been lost.[145]

As McDowell watched the retreating Georgians—and Alabamians and South Carolinians and Louisianans and Mississippians—it dawned on him, and his troops, that perhaps they had won. The ground was theirs.

The battle for Matthews Hill had been bitter and bloody. This morning's fight had been one of the greatest battles in American history, in terms of the numbers of men involved and the losses, and the Union side was victorious. McDowell rode up and down, a huge grin spanning his homely face. Jubilantly, he waved one of his yellow gloves in the air. The tiny spike jutting from his white helmet seemed proud and triumphant. Men stopped and gawked, then started to hurrah, "Victory! Victory!"

It was a wonderful moment for McDowell, for the "green" volunteers of Lincoln's army, for the Union. "Victory! Victory! The day is ours!"[146]

Intermezzo

As the fighting on Matthews Hill abated, Burnside spoke to McDowell. Most of his brigade was low on ammunition, Burnside said, and he asked to withdraw it to a quiet spot where his men could receive more ammunition and rest and recuperate after their fierce fight of the morning. McDowell concurred, and Burnside pulled back and settled down. It had been a long and trying day—with the fatiguing march followed by almost two hours of fighting. In 1861 a soldier in battle often ran forward and backward; he scuttled from one vantage point to another. He threw himself to the ground, then leaped to his feet. He loaded and reloaded his heavy rifle or musket. He climbed or hopped over fences and rocks and stumps and logs—and bodies. He picked up wounded companions and carried them to safety. Although each motion involved only a brief spurt, in combination the actions became a major physical workout. It did not take long before muscles grew tired and weak. A soldier's shoulders and biceps ached; his back and his legs felt spongy; his eyes were raw from sleeplessness and stress and billowing smoke. Around his lips was that ring of black powder from tearing open his cartridges. His mouth was dry, his tongue was swollen. In all likelihood, his feet were sore and probably blistered and bleeding. Any rest would be not only a relief but prudence. He could use some food, and his entire system screamed for water.

Wounded men had additional needs.

Dr. King, McDowell's chief medical officer, was a true professional, a physician who understood the army's rules, routines, and paperwork. He had recently visited the camps of the volunteers and concluded that some of them had the potential to become superb soldiers, while others represented the "worst material I had ever met with." The regimental surgeons, he thought, were generally men of good intentions but inexperienced in the byzantine ways of army paperwork. He gave them advice about how to requisition supplies and such arcane matters.

Dr. King had been pressing the army for ambulances. The War Department actually possessed a number of these vehicles. The four-wheeled variety were relatively efficient and could provide wounded men with some comfort, but, to save money, the Department had also purchased four times as many two-wheeled ambulances. The two-wheelers were little more than rickshaws, and they caused intense agony to any unfortunate wounded passengers, flinging them from side to side and sometimes even flipping them onto the ground. A few days before McDowell started toward Manassas Junction, his army received some of each kind, but not nearly enough. How these were distributed is a puzzle. The Second New York wound up with three and the Second Rhode Island had six, while many regiments had none. Ambulances were not the only medical deficiency. Dr. King had urged the Department to provide the army twenty wagons to carry medical supplies. These never appeared, so he divvied up supplies as well as he could, hoping for the best.

All in all, however, he was not terribly concerned. "My impression at the commencement of the battle," King wrote in his report, "was that there would be a brief skirmish, and then the Rebels would most probably fall back and take up a new position." He might be able, he thought, to deal personally with most of the casualties. In his saddlebags he carried medical instruments, a few dressings, and the sort of "stimulant" surgeons used on battlefields (probably brandy). He decided to write down each wounded soldier's name and his injury in his notebook. But when the battle opened, he found himself writing furiously. He also was increasingly dipping into his saddlebags for medical supplies. "Soon I became convinced that a most desperate engagement was at hand." In normal practice, each regiment should have had its own medical staff — including a surgeon, an assistant surgeon, and at least one steward or orderly and several men designated to act as stretcher bearers.

In theory, there should have been three levels of medical care for the injured. On the battlefield itself, a medical person — often an assistant surgeon, wearing a green sash to indicate his noncombatant status — would examine a wounded man. He would make what would later be called *triage* decisions: determining who could benefit from medical attention and who was past it. For those whose condition was serious but who could be transported especially long distances, the army had, weeks in advance, designated certain "hospitals" in the Washington area. Although each regiment had a "hospital" at its base camp — a tent or two, where a sick soldier could recuperate — the War Department additionally took over several empty hotels, seminaries, and infirmaries inside the District and in Alexandria, designating them *general hospitals.* These were relatively small, capable of handling no more than a hundred patients, but this capacity seemed more than adequate to cover the expected needs. Most of such "hospitals" were dank and dark — buildings that had been readily available for a reason. There was one good "hospital," in Georgetown. Once called the Union Hotel, it had fallen on hard times and grown seedy, but now, as a medical facility, it was surprisingly clean and efficiently managed. This came about because, since June, an energetic, no-nonsense woman, Dorothea Dix, had been entrusted with it. She was well informed about Florence Nightingale's work during the Crimean War and intentionally emulated those efforts. Fifty-nine years old, Dix had long been a health crusader, working particularly in caring for the mentally ill. She distrusted incompetents and treated ill-trained surgeons and good-hearted but unprepared nurses with brusque impatience. Union soldiers, wounded at Bull Run, were lucky if they fell under her watchful eye.

Between the cursory care on the battlefield and the "general hospitals" in the Washington area, were *field stations*. By tradition, these were set up about a mile from the fighting (near enough that the wounded could be carried there by men with litters, and far enough away to be out of artillery range). Tyler's division, near the stone bridge, suffered the first casualties that morning, and a four-room farmhouse next to the turnpike, owned by a Mary Spindle, became the day's first field station. (Mrs. Spindle actually stayed and assisted the Union surgeons.) Houses like hers were preferable to most alternatives for three important reasons: They provided shelter from the sun, they were generally cleaner than barns or shops, and they offered handy wells. Among other Union field stations that day were a two-room house owned by Maggie Lewis (not far from the Van Pelts' home) and the stone house that abutted the turnpike. But the most active field station was in the Sudley area.

As soon as Dr. King realized the fighting was more ferocious than he had assumed, he stopped writing names in his notebook and directed his assistant, Dr. David Lynn Magruder, to go back to Sudley and set up a station. There, Magruder quickly determined that the church would be best and ordered ambulances to rush to the battlefield and start collecting the wounded. Meanwhile, he began converting the church into a makeshift hospital. He had its seats removed, its floor covered with blankets and hay, buckets of water brought inside, and he improvised an operating table, with instruments handy. A few minutes later the first ambulances returned and dropped off their bloody cargo, then headed back for more. Soon the building was too crowded to accommodate the deluge of patients. Other nearby structures were taken over: a barn, a wheelwright shop, and at least two homes, including the one abandoned by the Thornberry family the night before. Still the dying and the mangled arrived — so many they were lined up on the ground, unattended, in a grove of oaks near the church, to survive as best they could. The entire scene was grisly. An observer recalled that the "blood trickled from the ambulances like water from an ice cart, and directly in front of the church door was a large puddle of blood."[147]

No one at the Sudley medical facilities kept accurate records, but after the battle the church's minister counted over three hundred wounded still there, and he, of course, could not guess how many had been sent there but had died or had then been moved somewhere else.

Soon after Magruder established his "hospital," other surgeons started showing up and pitching in. At least fourteen doctors eventually joined Magruder (including one physician from Boston, unconnected to any regiment, who just wanted to help). Hour after hour, these fifteen surgeons, along with their medical stewards, did what they could. Some, like Magruder, who was there all day, probably handled at least thirty or forty patients — sewing up a different man or amputating another limb every few minutes.

Every battlefield has heroes — only a few of whom receive recognition or medals. The man who hazards bullets to carry a wounded buddy to safety is a hero. So is the anonymous soldier who runs with a fistful of canteens, fills them with precious water, and totes them back to his comrades. But it would be hard to surpass the courage of the nine surgeons who volunteered late that afternoon, when the Union army retreated, to stay in Sudley with their patients (or of the other Union surgeons who did the same at other field stations). These men knew they were accepting imprisonment, or maybe worse, at the hands of outraged rebel troops. Not one of the surgeons who remained behind received a medal for heroism. Also deserving the title of "hero" were those countless soldiers who refused to abandon wounded comrades on the battlefield, knowing full well they would be captured, accepting that fate out of friendship, out of kinship, out of love. These mostly anonymous individuals truly represent "nobility," a value both sides claimed they were fighting to defend.

(When the war began, neither army handed out medals. Instead, the traditional honor was to be "mentioned in dispatches," which was why after-battle reports generally included lists of specific names. Seldom were enlisted men below the rank of sergeant mentioned. Several months after Bull Run, the United States Congress considered something eventually called a Medal of Honor. The first of these was handed out in March 1863, but by 1865 few individuals had received one. A generation later, however, a committee, culling through the official records of the Civil War, chose people whose actions, for various reasons, were deemed worthy. Twelve who were at Bull Run were eventually granted the medal, though seven of these were not officially recognized until the mid-1890s. One of the twelve, Lieutenant Charles Joseph Murphy, was cited because, although not a medical man, he stayed with the wounded of his regiment, caring for them until he was captured. By far the most fascinating recipient was a surgeon, Dr. Mary Edwards Walker, twenty-eight years old in 1861. She was a civilian physician under contract with the Army. Whether Dr. Walker actually reached the battlefield is unclear, but a Connecticut soldier did see a woman driving an ambulance toward the battle: "A woman, sure as you live — a solitary woman, a resolute, matronly looking body." If that woman was Dr. Walker, she probably did reach some section of the battlefield. It is certain that Dr. Walker was somewhere in the vicinity of the Bull Run fighting, but her medal, given her in 1865 at the urgings of Generals Sherman and Thomas, was granted to her for the totality of her four years of service during the war, including a four-month period as a prisoner of war. Sadly, this honor was taken away from her in 1917, along with that of 910 other recipients — in order, the government said at the time, to "increase the prestige of the grant." Dr. Walker haughtily refused to return her medal, wearing it each day until she died. Many years later, in 1977, President Carter and Congress rightfully reinstated her onto the Medal of Honor's roll of remarkable individuals.)

As far as medical care was concerned, the Confederates used the same basic arrangements as McDowell's army. But not as much is known about how well they utilized their system at Bull Run since there are no surviving after-battle reports by any of their surgeons. Some facts, however, are clear. In the weeks before the battle, the Confederates designated hospitals in certain relatively distant Virginia towns: Culpeper, Charlottesville, and Richmond —

mostly staffed by volunteer women. And it seems that during the battle, or perhaps even in the days before it, several farmhouses near Manassas Junction were chosen as places where wounded could be taken. At least four of these buildings were not far south of the turnpike. The combined armies of Beauregard and Johnston had a number of regimental surgeons, and after the battle at Blackburn's Ford, volunteer surgeons began arriving at Manassas Junction. The Confederates had some ambulances, though not as many as McDowell. One advantage they did have was that Manassas Junction was a railroad station, so men with serious wounds could be moved on freight cars to more distant hospitals. Lying in agony for hours on filthy straw inside a train was a nightmare, but better than being transported in a bouncing wagon all the way back to Washington. As to whether the Confederate surgeons at Bull Run had the same supplies as Union surgeons, any answer would only be conjecture. But both sides did practice the same medical techniques — for both good and ill.[148]

The medical procedure a soldier could expect went something like this: When an assistant surgeon scurried over the battlefield, he generally carried with him a medical knapsack or was accompanied by an orderly or steward who lugged it. Inside were a handful of useful things: one or two tourniquets; several splints and pins to hold them; ligatures and needles to close gaping wounds; a case of assorted instruments; sponges and a tightly packed pile of bandages to dress the wounds; and usually brandy — which was used, paradoxically, either to dull pain or revive the woozy. (At field stations some surgeons at Bull Run had chloroform and morphine, but apparently not much of it; its use only became common a few months later. Luckily, the wounded sometimes did not immediately feel the pain that would later come, because their bodies had supplied them with a kind of natural temporary anesthetic.)

The assistant surgeon who first encountered a wounded man somewhere on the battlefield also carried a canteen of water, sometimes several of them, slung across his shoulder. Wounded men generally cried out for water — and this was especially true at Bull Run because of the heat of the day, the exertions, and the dust. As the soldier took a few swallows of tepid, sometimes filthy, water, the surgeon glanced over him. If the soldier could walk, the doctor would help him to his feet and direct him toward the field hospital; if the man had an abdominal wound, the surgeon often gave him some brandy—and left him. Fatalities from such wounds were almost inevitable, particularly if the intestines were perforated, since peritonitis almost inevitably set in. The doctor looked closely at puncture wounds, especially of the limbs. These could be dealt with. Well-organized regiments, like the two from Rhode Island, had litter bearers who accompanied the surgeons to the field, often band members or drummers. Not surprisingly, these noncombatants sometimes became reluctant to run onto a battlefield where, unarmed, they were expected to pick up a wounded man on a stretcher and to totter with him slowly back across rough terrain while rifles and cannon fired around them.

Field stations at Bull Run (and elsewhere) became infamous. Soldiers passing by them were shocked. They were stunned by the whimpers, the screams, and the sobbing of those awaiting treatment, by the shrieks of men being examined by surgeons. But most riveting were the piles of arms and legs. Civil War letters spoke in awe of such sights. Some soldiers assumed that surgeons were mere butchers and hoped to avoid any personal contact with their operating tables.

It was true that most army surgeons were ill trained. Medical schools in the United States did not offer challenging curriculums. The better ones—all of which were in the North—only required a few months of lectures, though some schools did demand that students take a second term. Amazingly, during this second portion of their training, they would be forced to endure the same lectures, word for word. Medical students were given little or no clinical experience. Most states had laws prohibiting dissection. In fact, during the 1850s, the standards of medical schools actually sank. At some private institutions that were interested primarily in fees, a student could pocket a diploma in a few weeks. Some surgeons at Bull Run were as young as twenty-one and had virtually never practiced. Those men who did have medical practices at home often only had knowledge of conditions seldom found in the military. They knew about rickets, clubfoot, scarlet fever, and geriatric problems, but little about chest wounds. Except for setting broken bones and sewing up gashes, even the most experienced doctors were fairly unacquainted with what they were about to be confronted. Thermometers had been around for over two hundred years, but it is likely that not a single physician at Bull Run owned one. Their most serious ignorance involved bacteria. In Europe some individuals like Joseph Lister and Louis Pasteur were beginning to understand a few of the implications of germs and infections, but in the United States surgical antisepsis was unpracticed.

A gunshot wound was serious, not only because of shock and loss of blood but because of infection. The round balls used in smoothbores were bad enough, but wounds made by the conical minié balls were far more ghastly. The guns of that era were not high-velocity weapons, and when their balls, made of soft lead, entered the body, they flattened out and tore great gouges, often ricocheting off those bones they did not shatter. If the wounded man was lucky, the bullet passed through him—though seldom in a straight line from the entrance wound. Even in such a case, it had probably pressed bits of filthy uniform into the wound. So whether the bullet had obviously exited the body or not, surgeons usually felt they needed to probe the entire wound. To make this probe, surgeons could have used a metal instrument, but that was actually far less efficient than the doctor's forefinger, because the surgeon could utilize his sense of touch to detect cloth and bits of bones and bullet fragments that a metal tool would have missed. And his finger could turn corners that a rigid forceps could not. Surgeons understood that probing had to be done quickly. Wounded soldiers felt excruciating agonies when a surgeon plunged his finger, even his hand, into a raw wound. Stewards had to press the soldier down so the doctor could perform the search because any thrashing made the task impossible. Unfortunately, the result of such an examination, days later, was often death—from pyemia, erysipelas, septicemia, osteomyelitis, and "hospital gangrene"—among far too many other conditions. When the surgeon made his examination, the grime on his hands and beneath his unwashed fingernails had been forced deep into the patient's body.

In 1861 Dr. Frank Hastings Hamilton, one of America's leading surgeons, published a treatise on the topic of military surgery.

This book served as a kind of bible for doctors on both sides, as "Hardee" did for infantry officers. After four years of war, Hamilton wrote a much-extended version, a tome of about seven hundred pages. In it he admitted he and his colleagues still did not understand traumatic gangrene. "Perhaps," he mused, "it is due to nervous exhaustion." He had noticed that warm, even hot, water sometimes worked, though he did not know why. He suspected some patients were simply prone to "a scorbutic taint." One thing Hamilton was positive about. After examining thousands of cases: "No one doubts that hospital gangrene is contagious." He would have been aghast at the thought that he himself was the "contagion," literally carrying the infection on his fingers from one patient to the next. In this regard Civil War medicine remained medieval.

Over 70 percent of Civil War wounds were in the arms, the legs, the hands, or the feet. Some were simply gashes — serious enough, especially if they involved an arterial cut — but the worst normally involved the shattering of a bone. In such cases surgeons leaned toward amputation. Not because they were callous or because their medical knowledge was barbaric, but because of the likelihood of fatal infections in lengthy hospital stays for those who had not received amputations. Military surgeons agreed that, if amputations were going to be done, it was generally best to perform them immediately, partly because patients — already in shock — emotionally accepted the results more readily. Surgeons disagreed about the kind of amputation — whether they should leave a "flap" of dangling skin that could be sewn around the stump or they should perform a *circular amputation*, in which the cut was made directly across the extremity. The speed of an operation was critical in a field hospital — to some extent because of the overpowering demands of too many incoming patients, but mostly because the man on the table could only take the agony of the operation for a short time. An expert surgeon prided himself on his ability to saw off a limb and sew on its skin flap in under a minute. Then he would wipe his gory hands down his apron, pinch his scalpel relatively dry in a cloth, and shout, "Next!" Stewards would lug over the next soldier from the group lying on the sod. The scene, once observed, was hard to eliminate from one's mind. An orderly at Sudley described it: "Under a small table immediately in front of the pulpit was a heap of legs and arms that had been amputated . . . At the end of the table, to the right, lay the almost nude body of a man who had been shockingly mutilated by a round shot, and who had died in horrible agony before anything could be done to relieve him. The anguish depicted on the poor fellow's countenance, and the contorted attitude in which the death struggle left him, can never be effaced from my memory. But the cries of the wounded and dying were the most heartrending . . . 'Water, water for God's sake!' was the one universal cry, and 'Oh! for Heaven's sake don't step on me!'"[149]

Late that morning, far from the operating tables, reporters on both sides were jotting their preliminary stories. Representing the Southern journals were at least half a dozen correspondents who, throughout the morning, hovered close to Beauregard and Johnston, and therefore missing the real fighting, going on five miles away. Northern reporters were no more successful in seeing the battle. With few exceptions, they either hung around Centreville or they edged forward toward Tyler's position near the stone bridge, from which they could hear portions of the battle, but could see little beyond puffs of smoke and spirals of dust. They would ask passing couriers and wounded men passing to the rear what was happening on the other side of Bull Run. They received rumors and distortions.

Reporters were not the only civilians near the battlefield. Others, interested in the outcome, had been trickling in on both sides for quite a while. One was the photographer, Mathew Brady, draped in a long linen duster, a straw hat on his head, a large box strapped to his back. Already famous, he was here to record History. "I know well enough that I cannot take a photograph of a battle, but I can get a little glimpse of some corner somewhere that will be worthwhile. We are making history now, and every picture that we get will be valuable."

A crowd of civilians gathered on a knoll west of Centreville. Later this group would be famous. Southerners especially relished the scene. They would speak of it often as if they had actually seen it, expanding on it with each retelling. As they imagined it, hundreds of large and fancy carriages were lined up, wheel to wheel, their passengers dining on exotic foreign cuisine, dabbing at their lips with French lace napkins, guzzling champagne passed to them by waiters from Washington's most famous hotels and restaurants. In this fantasy a carnival atmosphere permeated the scene, a kind of Roman Colosseum populated by coarse, jolly Yankees come to watch the easy defeat of undisciplined rebels. One could almost hear the tittering laughter of women: berouged strumpets, the storytellers leered, playthings of Yankee financiers, scarlet women who had packed their trunks with fine dresses they expected to wear at dances in Richmond. The callousness of these civilians was a metaphor for so much that Southerners loathed about the "North." Given the alleged behavior of this flock of Yankee civilians, their comeuppance late that afternoon, when they scurried away just ahead of their own retreating soldiers, was triply delicious.

This imagery makes for a good story, but was the portrayal accurate? Not very. Civilians did arrive before the battle, and many settled themselves on one particular knoll, hoping to see the battle. The vast majority of those at the Centreville knoll were not caricatures, not gaping hordes gleefully strolling through P. T. Barnum's "museum" in New York, wanting to see geeks and freaks and other curiosities. The people of that era had no understanding of the realities of war. Most soldiers were volunteers, representatives of their stock. Folks from home wanted to know how they were doing. Most of the civilians were politicians who considered themselves ombudsmen for the men they represented, not very different from Governor William Sprague, who was at that moment leading his Rhode Islanders into battle. There was Senator Henry Wilson of Massachusetts, who cared deeply about this war and what it meant, who felt a personal sense of responsibility for his "Massachusetts boys." He had brought with him scores, maybe hundreds, of sandwiches, and he had an attendant hand them to members of the Massachusetts regiments as they marched by. Wilson did not mean anything by this act other than naïve generosity and the spirit of American democracy. The population of the nation was smaller then, and voters far fewer. Wilson's sense of "connectedness" to his volunteers was as real as the pride the ladies of Savannah felt when they darned socks or sewed havelocks for their "boys." In his mind he personally represented all those family members back home who could not be here. Another civilian was Senator Ben Wade of Ohio, and he felt about the same — as did at least eight other senators and twenty representatives. (Wilson returned to Washington so early in the day that when he arrived at Willard's Hotel and was asked the news, he admitted he could not yet guarantee the result, though things had been going well when he left the scene.)

Did they bring hampers of food for themselves? Certainly. Most of these politicians resided in Washington's hotels or rooming houses, since they did not expect congressional sessions to last more than a few weeks. They would have received official — and difficult to obtain — passes the day before, permitting them to cross the Long Bridge, and would have asked whatever establishment they were staying at to fix them eatables they could take on a day trip. The hotel or restaurant would have placed this food inside a "picnic" hamper, though the connotation in the word *picnic* was an unfortunate sidelight, since it suggested a kind of casual gaiety. Did some men bring intoxicants with them? Of course. Carrying booze was normal in that age — to provide small pick-me-ups or to pass around as a friendly gesture. Every regimental medical staff had it. So did countless soldiers — some of whom became noticeably tipsy during the battle.

Not surprisingly, most of the fifty or sixty visitors on the knoll came from places with important contacts inside the administration: states like Illinois, of course, and Ohio (Secretary Chase), and New York (Seward), and so on. No doubt some of these men came out of mere curiosity, but most appeared to feel genuine concerns and a desire to participate in some way. One congressman from Illinois, Isaac N. Arnold, served as a voluntary aide on the battlefield. An elderly civilian abolitionist named W. P. Thomasson, wearing a tall silk hat and carrying a gun, marched with the Seventy-first New York all the way to Matthews Hill, where he enthusiastically fired at the rebels. Another tough old abolitionist, Congressman Owen Lovejoy of Illinois, came to watch the battle but grew so caught up by his emotions that he picked up a gun in the afternoon and joined the fray, participating in part of the day's hottest fighting. Another civilian who took part in the battle, as we will see, was Javan B. Irvine, who walked along with the First Minnesota.

There were also fathers here, worried about their sons—including Daniel McCook of Ohio, who had two boys in Tyler's brigade. About noon, young Private Charles McCook, eighteen, who had been a freshman at Kenyon College a few weeks earlier, took a break from the fighting, came back, and had lunch with his father by a carriage. Charles returned to his regiment, and a few hours later was killed.

Among the civilians were two adolescents who had come to Washington from Boston, each to visit his own brother. They were still in the capital when they learned that one of the brothers had been killed at Blackburn's Ford. They obtained a wagon to get his corpse and by chance arrived on Sunday. While the dead soldier's brother went to find the body, his companion searched for the volunteers who came from his hometown. Asking around, he learned they were in Richardson's brigade, discovered where that unit was at this moment, and walked down there and found them. In his black funeral suit and his straw hat, he crawled up to where they lay, "and shook hands with nearly a hundred men whom I had known all my life." He told them gossip from home, promised to carry their messages back, and reluctantly left.[150]

Other civilians with the Union army were an unknown number of African-Americans, servants to some Northern officers. Reportedly, a few of these men participated in the battle in some way. At least one was badly wounded and died a few weeks later. Unfortunately, several seem to have been captured by Southerners. After the battle a South Carolinian wrote home with revulsion: "One of the most disgusting features in this war is the fact that Negro soldiers are brought into the field against us. There are many of them among the prisoners. I myself counted six among the first prisoners brought in." (Perhaps one of these prisoners was a boy, fifteen or sixteen years old, who had worked for the Second Vermont Regiment and had been given one of their uniforms to wear; he was unlucky enough to be captured.)[151]

Most striking among the civilians on the knoll was the reported presence of women, because they gave the scene a kind of unsavory jollity that did not sit well with folks at home reading about the battle. Sumptuous repasts, champagne, girlish laughter—an ambiance of merriment—were repellent. Especially when readers compared that image to screams and disembowelments and amputations a few miles away. Were there women on the knoll, or at least in the area? Yes. The most famous description was provided by William Howard Russell, who arrived late and stayed a while in his carriage atop the rise. "On the hill beside me," he noted, "there was a crowd of civilians on horseback, and in all sorts of vehicles, with a few of the fairer, if not gentler, sex." "The spectators," he said, "were all excited, and a lady with an opera glass who was near me was quite beside herself when an unusually heavy discharge roused the current of her blood—'That is splendid. Oh, my! Is not that first-rate? I guess we will be in Richmond this time tomorrow.'" Russell was a good reporter, but was not above adding a smidgen to spice up his stories. It is unlikely he fabricated this woman, but he almost certainly dabbled creatively with her words, which seem far too stagy, making her a caricature of a giddy female at a battle.

The females present at or near the battle were not such absurd creatures. They included, for example, a number of local women who brought foodstuffs, circulated through the crowd, and sold them. There was at least one unnamed mother of a soldier in the Thirteenth New York. She and her husband arrived at Centreville that morning, hoping to see their boy (who was in Sherman's brigade near the stone bridge when they arrived). Her son Sam would write a friend two days later that his parents were so determined to visit him that they followed Sherman's brigade—at least until it crossed Bull Run. Sam felt sure: "Mother was the only woman around for miles."

He was wrong. There was also Mrs. Richardson, the colonel's wife, whose husband's cannon were firing across Mitchell's Ford. And Jane Hinsdale, a paid laundress with the Second Michigan, married to Private Hiram Hinsdale. (According to army regulations, each company was permitted to hire four washerwomen—generally wives—who would be paid in "rations.") For a week after the battle, the unfortunate Mrs. Hinsdale was a prisoner of the Confederates. Other women connected in some way to the battle were Kady Brownell, eighteen, married to Robert, a private in the First Rhode Island, and Annie Etheridge, also eighteen, whose husband was in the Second Michigan. And Miss Augusta Foster, adopted by the Second Maine as a "daughter of the regiment." And Dr. Mary Walker, of course. There was also Sarah Emma Edmonds, who was passing herself off as "Frank Thompson" and was, during the battle, serving as a medical orderly in one of the regiments. No doubt there were others, but except in the vivid imaginations of gleeful Southerners and too many historians, there is no concrete evidence that any of the politicians were accompanied by some brainless bimbo. That creature seems to have been the stuff of legend, and William Howard Russell.[152]

Almost overlooked in the accounts was the fact that many civilians observed the battle on the opposite (Confederate) side of Bull Run. Three days earlier, Beauregard had ordered away from the camps all civilians who were not residents, though he said that they only had to go four miles. But on Sunday morning people began to drift toward the scene. These folks, Virginians all, were just as anxious and as curious as the far more famous group of civilians on the knoll near Centreville. When Porter's brigade poured into the northwest quadrant of the battlefield, heading toward Dogan's farm, they marched past a hill on their right. At that moment on its summit was a crowd of local citizens—men, women, and children—who watched Porter's men pass, then other stirring events during the day. The males in this group, mostly gray-haired gentlemen, discussed the prospects of victory for this side or that. The women, more diffident, spoke to each other in whispers, while the children played joyfully on the grass, laughing and frolicking as they would at any picnic. Not far away was a small school that local children attended when it was in session, and this hill was near their usual playground. Hours passed as these Virginians watched the contest. Their vantage point was much better than the Centreville knoll, and they could see more of what was happening. One of them was a boy of about twelve who sat silently on his horse. He knew his father was fighting over there, somewhere, and he wept.

Several locals saw more of the battle than they cared to. South of the turnpike were two houses, not far from Matthews Hill. The one nearest the stone bridge was owned by a free African-American named Jim Robinson, the illegitimate son of one of the Carters, the numerous descendants of Robert "King" Carter who had once controlled all this region. "Gentleman Jim" Robinson, sixty-two, earned part of his income from passing drovers. He maintained fenced areas on his farm, where the herdsmen could temporarily keep their cattle when staying at the stone house; he also manufactured some moonshine in his still and sold it to them. Exactly where he spent this day is uncertain, but it was not inside his home.

Sadly, the same was not true of his half sister, Judith Henry, who resided in the house just west of Jim Robinson's place. It was her small home, sitting atop a little hill, that Barnard Bee spotted and told Imboden to place his guns near. Judith Carter Henry, a white woman, had been born in 1777, only a mile away. In 1801 she had married a Navy surgeon. He died in 1829, and since then she was generally referred to as "the Widow Henry." Living with her were her semi-invalid son, John, fifty-six, and her unmarried daughter, Miss Ellen, fifty-four. The house must have been crowded. A young African-American servant (a slave named Lucy, owned by a local minister, Alexander Compton, and hired out to the Henrys) had been caring for the feeble Mrs. Henry, and she, too, may have been living in the place. When the artillery duel began between Imboden's guns and the Rhode Island battery, Mrs. Henry's two adult children wanted to move their mother, but she stubbornly resisted. She changed her mind, however, after one or two Yankee shells banged through her roof. Her children and Lucy somehow picked her up, using her mattress, and started off toward the home of Reverend Compton, about a mile away. But as they staggered along with their burden, the cannon fire seemed to get worse, and she, now terrified, begged them to take her back home. They did so. A few minutes later a shell burst inside her bedroom, killing her. The same explosion seems also to have wounded Lucy, who thereafter walked with a noticeable limp, and permanently deafened Miss Ellen.[153]

The Confederate side included uncountable other civilians. Some were the many slaves who served the soldiers. As usual, the presence of slaves remains shadowy, but they certainly participated in the battle in assorted ways, and some may have been killed. A few white civilians were also engaged in the fighting. The *Charleston Courier* was later pleased to announce that a "Colonel Newman McBain" had arrived at Manassas Junction from Georgia with his rifle and used it to "good service" during the battle; so, too, the newspaper said, had "Colonel Orr of Mississippi," who helped soldiers fire and load their guns and gave them cheerful encouragement. Edward Farley, a student at the University of Virginia, had felt a powerful need to see what was happening, and during the battle he wandered around, much like a tourist, to observe interesting sights.

According to her own testimony, a Southern woman participated personally in the fight. Years later, Loreta Janeta Velasquez wrote a mostly bogus account about how she passed herself off as a male during the war and served as one of Bee's volunteer couriers throughout the battle of Bull Run. Some gullible readers have swallowed her tall tales. It is vaguely possible she did do a few of things she later claimed, but unlikely.

More touching were stories about those who *listened* to the fighting, from far away. Colonel Eppa Hunton's wife lived five miles from the battleground. She was not feeling well that day and lay down and pressed a pillow against her ear to drown out the frightening noise. In Lynchburg, Virginia, 160 miles away, Mrs. Robert C. Saunders, whose husband was in the battle, was sure she could detect sounds from the battle. All day long she stood on a hill near her home, her heart's conceit "hearing" explosions at Bull Run.

Churchgoers in Alexandria first heard cannon fire while attending service. Across the Potomac, in Washington, by early afternoon the din of battle sounded like thunder. People in the city stared westward, wondering. Abraham Lincoln, apparently the latest in a string of mediocre presidents, heard it, too. Ironically, the morning's battle had proved that, in a sense, he *had* been correct. The soldiers on the two sides had been equal in grit. They had shown themselves to be amateurish in many ways. They often ignored orders; they wandered off to eat blackberries and rest when it suited them; they refused to follow the manuals with robotic precision; they aimed their guns more often at the sky than their foes. Despite all this, the men of the Second Rhode Island and of Hampton's Legion, of the First Minnesota and of the Fourth Alabama, of the Third Connecticut and of the Eighth Georgia—these had already proved themselves worthy of their famous Revolutionary forebears. Though weary from long marching, though weakened from poor diet, though dizzy from dehydration, they had showed they were capable of standing against artillery barrages, of charging entrenched enemies, of countless acts of courage and individual decency.

After service at the Presbyterian church on New York Avenue, Lincoln went to the War Department for news. Two young telegraph operators there told him what dispatches they were receiving from Fairfax Court House, where McDowell was sending couriers. General Scott also read the messages, which were cautiously optimistic, and reassured the president. Members of the cabinet dropped in. Generals there used maps to indicate what was likely happening near Manassas Junction. Seward smoked cigars and told the others with quiet self-congratulation that he had been right, the war would be over within a few weeks. After a while Lincoln, the man who had rolled the dice, went for a ride into the northern, sparsely populated sector of the District.[154]

BUILDING
STONE WALLS

The result is not certain at the moment I write.
Both sides have fought with terrible tenacity.
—DATELINE: "2 P.M., JULY 21, 1861, BULL RUN,"
The New York Times

Porter's Brigade, the Union Army

In the early afternoon, Andrew Porter—apparently acting
independently—ordered forward his three regiments of volunteers. One was the Twenty-seventh New York, led by that competent and tenacious West Pointer, Henry Warner Slocum.
Porter's other two regiments were the Eighth New York, really
just state militiamen (with all that that meant), and the under-
sized Fourteenth New York, a Zouave outfit with blousy red pantaloons, commanded by Colonel Alfred M. Wood, an officer with
virtually no military background.

Porter's three regiments started from the western side of
the Sudley road, near the Dogan place. Rather than marching
straight south, following the road from Sudley toward Manassas
Junction, they angled back eastward. Perhaps they intended to
follow the retreating rebels; perhaps they were avoiding the rebel
artillery that was still atop Henry House Hill, banging away in
their direction. Their movement brought them first to the stone

house, at the intersection of the Sudley road and the turnpike. Here, they came under heavy fire — not only from the rebel cannon but from remnants of the Fourth Alabama and the Eighth Georgia, as well as another South Carolina unit that had just arrived on the scene.

The Hampton Legion, the Confederate Army

In a sense, "Hampton's Legion" was medieval. Wade Hampton III of South Carolina, forty-three, one of the South's richest planters and owner of almost 3,000 slaves, had no military experience. But he was intelligent, well educated, a superb athlete, and a natural leader. Although opposed to secession and rather disenchanted with slavery, when the Confederacy was created, he went to Jefferson Davis in Montgomery and offered his support. He said he would place 4,700 bales of his cotton at the Confederacy's disposal, which could be used to trade in Europe for guns. He also proposed to raise a "Legion" in South Carolina, unlike any other small military force in the United States. First of all, it would combine into a single, integrated unit the three basic field functions: infantry, artillery, and cavalry. Second, like some Scottish laird, he himself would pay for its artillery and much of its equipment — then lead it into battle. Davis accepted this suggestion. Hampton returned to South Carolina and announced his plan. He had no problem finding volunteers, though their quality was, as yet, unknown. Two of his sons served as privates. Several of the enlisted men were only in their midteens, including a fourteen-year-old. After a few weeks of drill in South Carolina, the Legion left for Richmond — six companies of infantry, four of cavalry, an artillery battery, a veritable mountain of personal trunks and valises, and countless slaves. Military discipline in the Legion was relaxed. Officers and privates messed together, their meals prepared by their black servants.

The Legion was still in Richmond on the morning of July 19 (the day after the Battle of Blackburn's Ford) when Hampton was informed that Beauregard's position at Manassas Junction was in peril and he must take his soldiers there immediately by train. His men, when told of this, were excited. They struck their tents, packed their trunks, and were ready to march to the train station by early afternoon. They did not bother bringing extra provisions since they knew rations would be available in Manassas Junction. There were delays. It was evening before they arrived at the station and boarded some empty boxcars. It then turned out that no engines were available. They waited. Sometime after ten o'clock a train arrived from Manassas Junction, carrying some of the Blackburn's Ford wounded. Its locomotive was attached to the boxcars, but its engine was too small and frail to pull the whole Legion. After some discussion, Wade Hampton decided to bring only his infantrymen — fewer than six hundred men. It was almost midnight by the time this group left Richmond. Even then, things did not go smoothly. Off and on, the engineer would stop the train, get out, and tinker a bit. Finally they transferred to a different train. The men got quite hungry. At one station they bought a few cakes and pies and sandwiches from some black women.

They arrived at Manassas Junction after a dismal trip of more than twenty-seven hours. It was Sunday morning. Several miles away, though they were unaware of it, McDowell's army was on the move. They stumbled from the train, brought down the few horses that were to be ridden by field officers like Hampton. They built themselves fires, found rations near the station, heated up coffee, and were eating some crackers when they heard the rumble of artillery in the distance. Someone — perhaps Beauregard's adjutant, Tom Jordan — told Hampton to take the road northward, toward Cocke's position, and gave him general directions. Hampton and his men set off. They knew nothing about the region. They stopped along the way to ask passersby for clarification. After many miles of marching, which took them two or three hours, they reached a spot where they could see in the distance men fighting. But they could not be sure which were friends, which were foes. They suddenly came under a barrage from Yankee batteries on the far side of the turnpike. They were not yet in battle, but already their numbers were declining — from exhausted men dropping out, from the killed, from the wounded being carried off by companions. The remainder felt confusion. Hampton moved them down the hill and toward the right, away from the worst of the cannon fire. He could not know it, but he had just reached Jim Robinson's place. In military jargon, his men were "fresh troops," probably now numbering only four hundred or so. Retreating Confederates, coming off Matthews Hill, stumbled toward their position because it seemed to offer a kind of haven. Bee and Evans, fellow South Carolinians, came by to greet them. Bartow's Seventh Georgia also moved toward them, when it became obvious it was useless to cross the turnpike and get trapped by the masses of Yankees over there.

It was Hampton's Legion (which was now, in fact, only a battalion of infantrymen), supported mostly by Georgians of the Seventh and Eighth Regiments, that Porter's three New York regiments were moving toward. One of Hampton's captains, James Conner, wrote his mother a few days later: "At that moment a large body of Yankees were seen moving round." Hampton had his men move into a gully by the side of Robinson's driveway, and, using the wall and the gully as natural breastworks, they opened fire on the approaching Yankees. Much of Porter's firepower was instantly directed at them. Captain Conner stood at one side, Hampton on the other. They told their men again and again that they should stay cool and aim each shot with great care. Hampton himself was famous throughout the South for his marksmanship and shot at least one Yankee, perhaps more. Other members of his Legion were less skillful. In a letter home, one private described these long minutes. "My first shot fell about 200 yds too short, my second I missed a little higher and got about a hundred yds nearer, my third I aimed still higher and got within a few yds of them, my fourth and fifth were aimed a little above their heads." His sixth shot, he noticed, fell short again. Just then a Yankee bullet—or perhaps the recoil of his own gun—smacked him on the bridge of his nose. He tried to get up and reload but found himself too dizzy. "I gave it up and sunk down." He had fired six times at the enemy and missed each time. He departed in search of a hospital and some medical attention. He had quit fighting for the day.

The Legion's position soon grew untenable, and the men scrambled back. Hampton's second in command had been killed early in the action. Hampton himself fell, shot in the cheek. As a unit, the Legion fell apart—though many of its members still continued fighting. As one of them would recall, "After this the Legion fought in squads, sometimes under Company officers, but more often alone." (Their losses this day would be 121 men — a quarter of the effectives who had marched that morning from the depot at Manassas Junction.)

But the men of the Legion had temporarily halted the Yankee advance. Porter's three regiments stopped moving in this direction. One of the regiments — the Eighth New York — essentially collapsed and never recovered. The other two — the Twenty-seventh New York and the Fourteenth of Brooklyn — withdrew to lick their wounds and to consider the next step — which would almost certainly involve Henry House Hill.[155]

Henry House Hill

Ever since the Battle of Bull Run, many people have tried to understand the events on Henry House Hill that afternoon. Even the following day, soldiers who had just fought there wandered over that rather small ridge in wonderment. It seemed almost impossible to parse its intricacies. Those who wrote about it that week — in letters or newspaper articles or after-action reports — tried their best. Some attempted to present the chaos as though it contained neat patterns. The surviving generals ordered subordinates to submit memoranda, and these subordinates told those below them to give them their own reports so something could be pieced together that made sense. Newspaper correspondents for both sides interviewed participants and wrote accounts, and they printed, or at least drew from, the official versions of men like Beauregard and McDowell. Months later, the Joint Committee asked dozens of Union officers to tell their stories, but most of these men simply summarized the official reports they had already written. After the war writers began churning out regimental histories and personal stories about the great battle. But for the events on Henry House Hill, they mostly drew from the official records. This pattern meant a kind of repetition, an echoing of the same interpretations, even the same inconsistencies. In time historians provided more dispassionate analyses. The best accounts — like Richard Moe's *The Last Full Measure: The Life and*

Death of the First Minnesota Volunteers, George H. Gaff's *If This Is War* (a study of the Second Wisconsin at Bull Run), and Warren Wilkinson and Steven E. Woodworth's history of the Eighth Georgia, *A Scythe of Fire*—are intentionally narrow in scope, focusing on a fraction of those who clashed atop Henry House Hill.

Today, at the Manassas National Battlefield Park, the basic terrain of Henry House Hill is similar to what it was in 1861. But the ground has been softened by time and the tender care of the National Park Service. Gentle deer now graze on its sweet grass. Curious tourists stop, take photographs of the statues and the markers and the nicely lined-up muted cannon. As with all such re-creations, the scene is inevitably placid and antiseptic, and not really...true. Where are the trees that Jackson's men hid inside? Where is the orchard that the Georgians snacked upon? Where is the cornfield through which soldiers stumbled? Where is the chicken coop? And the outhouse?

The soldiers who fought there spoke confusingly about distances: "The guns were back a-ways." How can we determine where men stood? How long would it have taken to charge the enemy? A tourist can jog—that is, "double-quick"—the three hundred yards from Mrs. Henry's house southward toward where the Confederate guns probably stood. He can note that it takes him about a minute and a half. But such an experiment is absurdly unrealistic. Anyone now moving across that meadow is likely to be wearing comfortable clothes, and sneakers. One cannot truly replicate the physical realities of that afternoon—to say nothing of its emotions. The ground is gentle now. There are no trees to block the way, no serious dips to twist a person's ankle, no chunks of dirt thrown about by artillery shells, no dead bodies or writhing horses, no coppery odor of blood, no noisome stench of intestines. The tourist has probably not exhausted his body by making recent long marches. He is not dehydrated. His nasal passages, his throat, his lungs are not screaming and raw from breathing in clouds of Virginia's red dust. His eyes are not bloodshot, from weariness and dust.

There is another problem in trying to decipher what happened that day: the matter of timing. Many participants spoke about a "lull" in the battle, lasting an hour or two. But one should not take this word too literally; the spatter of musket and rifle fire was virtually constant somewhere on the battlefield as regiments moved from place to place. But it is true that in the early afternoon the major roar of cannon did subside for a while. On the Confederate side the reason was simple. Imboden, running out of ammunition, slackened his fire. On the Union side, McDowell decided to move much of his artillery forward, and this took time. The "lull," therefore, was the result of movement, not inactivity.

The Confederates

Beauregard and Johnston were still several miles away atop a knob (thereafter called Lookout Hill) not far from Mitchell's Ford. This hillock was fairly barren and offered a clear view to the opposite side of the stream, where the "real" battle was supposed to occur that day. The two generals had come here and were now surrounded by a swarm of aides and couriers, fifty or sixty men. Not far away, reporters stood, mostly apart from each other, in the shade of trees, making notes. Even without opera glasses they could see some Yankee movements across the way (Richardson or Davies's men). And it did not take the Yankee gunners long to notice this sizeable group of Southerners and to turn their guns toward this attractive target. A messenger from Beauregard scurried to the correspondents and politely told them to move. The explosion of a shell a few feet away gave them further encouragement. Besides, the heavy rumble of battle off to the north and the huge dust clouds rising in the air like genies from a bottle made the reporters decide to transfer their attentions there.

Beauregard was growing impatient. At dawn he had, or at least he thought he had, ordered an attack against McDowell's left flank. The assault should be well under way by now; the sounds of fighting ought to be drifting over here any time. He was aware, of course, that the Yankees were doing *something* in the direction of the stone bridge, but he assumed he had sufficient force there, especially since Johnston had already ordered Bee and Bartow and Jackson in that direction. The real question in Beauregard's mind involved the status of his own attack.

Sometime after ten o'clock a messenger arrived from Ewell, several miles to the south. The courier explained that General Ewell had been waiting for hours to receive the promised go-ahead order from Beauregard; that Ewell had finally sent someone to Jones, asking him if he knew anything, and had discovered that Jones had gotten orders, moved across Bull Run, and was waiting for Ewell to join him. This situation was confusing, the courier told Beauregard. What should General Ewell do? Two years later Beauregard would admit, "My heart for a moment failed me! I felt as though all was lost, and I wished I had fallen in the battle of the 18th." Then he pulled himself together. "I thus had suddenly or on the spur of the moment to change my whole plan of battle." (Assuming he was accurately recalling his emotions and his thought processes, until this moment, Beauregard was still intending to go ahead with his plan, which meant ignoring the growing sounds of battle on his left. Since Beauregard's watch had stopped earlier in the day, we cannot know what time Ewell's courier arrived at Lookout Hill, but it was almost certainly about 10:30 — well after Evans and Burnside had started grappling with each other a couple of miles away, after Imboden and the Rhode Island battery had begun their noisy duel.) "I soon rallied," Beauregard would say, "and I then solemnly pledged my life that I would that day conquer or die!" These recollections sound quite melodramatic and, even more, decisive. They were self-congratulatory, of course, and they were almost certainly inaccurate, or at least exaggerated. Beauregard may indeed have felt a wave of despair, but his reactions for the next hour remained frozen by uncertainty. He did send young Chisolm, who had returned to his side by this time, to contact Longstreet, Jones, and Ewell and order all three — wherever they presently were — to withdraw behind Bull Run. Chisolm rode off to track down all three men, widely separated from each other not only by Bull Run's serpentine shape but also by heavy trees and ravines. After giving each of them Beauregard's message, he returned and found Beauregard still waiting — for something — at Lookout Hill.[156]

As a French-speaking Creole, Beauregard had first grown interested in war as a boy, reading about Napoleon. He never outgrew this influence. Just as Napoleon had admired audacity, so did Beauregard. His mind was always intrigued by concepts of lightning movements, sudden thrusts—the unexpected assault. In the morning, when his right wing failed to initiate his planned assault, he had a feeling it was Ewell's fault. He never fully forgave Ewell for not reading his mind and throwing troops at the Yankee guns—later snidely saying that, although Ewell's inaction was "*technically* [emphasis added] not in the wrong," sometimes a commander with genius would contravene direct orders. As an example, Beauregard mentioned one of Napoleon's generals—Louis Desaix de Veygoux—who had done that very thing at Marengo in 1800 and crushed an Austrian army (though losing his life in the process). To rub this point in more, he added that, in retrospect, he could not "help believing that if [Stonewall] Jackson had been there, the movement would not have balked"—totally ignoring the fact that Jackson, an aggressive but ever obedient soldier, would have gone out of his way to avoid disobeying a direct order.

Blaming Ewell for timidity was not merely cruel; it was ludicrous. Ewell's orders from Beauregard had been to await a signal. By nature Dick Ewell was not a serene fellow. Having spent much of his military career on the frontier, he lacked urbanity. One observer said of him: "No man had a better heart nor a worse manner of showing it. He was in truth as tender and sympathetic as a woman, but, even under slight provocation, he became externally as rough as a polar bear." Another said of him: "General Ewell was at the time the most violently and elaborately profane man I ever knew...It was profanity which might be parsed." During the morning Ewell could not sit still. He paced, he mounted his horse, he got off, he paced some more. Late in the morning he received a message to cross the stream. He pushed his men over, then was told by a courier from a nervous Beauregard to come back (since the situation near Henry House Hill was heating up). More waiting. Ewell grew more agitated. So when Beauregard suggested that the failure of his own marvelous plan was Ewell's fault, the Creole had stepped far beyond the realities of that morning.[157]

———

Although Joe Johnston was officially in command of the combined Confederate forces, he had far less emotional investment in Beauregard's plan than the Creole. If sudden changes had to be made, so be it. Several facts were coinciding, and they helped Johnston make up his mind. It was becoming hard to ignore the din of battle drifting over from the left (Matthews Hill). Then, around eleven o'clock a scout came in from across Bull Run — probably sent by either Longstreet or Jones, both of whom had been on the far side of the stream and were just returning. Union axmen, the scout said, were cutting trees over there. The implications of this report were significant. Those Yankees were almost certainly felling timber to erect an abatis — which meant they were creating a *defensive* position. Therefore they were not contemplating an assault. Their cannon fire was a ruse. If that was so, then perhaps the sounds from the left meant McDowell was really moving most of his army into that sector.

Johnston then received another piece of information. Porter Alexander was still at his lookout station to the south where Beauregard had assigned him earlier. He had a number of couriers and kept sending them to Lookout Hill to advise Johnston and Beauregard that he was watching large troop movements far to the north (near Sudley Ford) and that he was also seeing huge clouds of dust (particularly now that the morning dew had dissipated). To Captain Alexander, these sightings indicated that McDowell was making a strong move in that direction. In the young signal officer's mind, the real battle was not going to be at Mitchell's Ford after all. But his couriers kept returning to his post and telling him the two generals remained standing at Lookout Hill. "At last I determined to go myself, thinking that perhaps my reports, being moderate statements of exactly what was visible, had not impressed them sufficiently." He arrived on the hillock and told the two generals what was worrying him. "Apparently Gen. Johnston was disposed to go there, but Beauregard seemed to hesitate." More minutes passed, perhaps half an hour.

In years to come, Beauregard would try desperately to prove that he maintained control over events during most of the day, that Johnston was little more than his stooge. But the weight of evidence is against this interpretation. For the first few hours that morning, Johnston had hung back, allowing Beauregard to remain in charge. After all, the plan of the day was primarily Beauregard's, and the men who would be carrying it out were almost all his troops. But as the plan began to fade like the Cheshire cat, Johnston started asserting himself, taking matters out of Beauregard's hands. In fact, Porter Alexander's recollections would indicate that Beauregard was still ambivalent, perhaps even indecisive, a full hour after he had discovered that his plan had failed.

With Alexander's new information in hand, Johnston wanted his left wing strengthened even more than it had been. Troops must be sent there immediately. Beauregard suggested the two brigade commanders, Early and Holmes, who had only been acting so far in a reserve capacity, could be started toward the stone bridge. Johnston concurred. (But these two brigades, miles to the south, would need several hours to march their men that far. Johnston wanted them to get moving immediately. Yet, for some reason, neither brigade started moving until about one o'clock — probably because they had to gather themselves together before starting out.) General Bonham was standing near Johnston on Lookout Hill, and Johnston ordered him to send two of his five infantry regiments and an artillery battery toward the still-amorphous "battlefield" in the north. This order was a powerful indication Johnston had given up entirely on Beauregard's notion of events, because Bonham, at Mitchell's Ford, had been holding the most critical position for the success of Beauregard's plan. Johnston's extraction of almost half Bonham's force meant Johnston had concluded that Mitchell's Ford could be virtually ignored. It also meant he was really taking charge.

Suddenly there was a great roaring of musketry from Matthews Hill (probably the arrival of Sykes's regulars onto the battlefield or the appearance of Sherman's brigade). "I am going there!" Johnston said decisively. He had made his final decision; it was idiocy to wait any longer. He walked to where someone was holding his horse, ordered his staff to join him, and rode off. He soon spotted his own chief of artillery, Colonel Pendleton, and told him to bring along all the guns as fast as he could. Back at Lookout Hill Beauregard stopped to tell Porter Alexander to

return to his post and to continue to send couriers with information about any changes that he noticed. (Clearly, even now,
Beauregard remained unconvinced the area near the stone bridge
would be the main scene of the battle.) Then Beauregard started
riding after Johnston. The two generals were soon side by side,
their staffs trailing behind them, the whole group cantering toward the sound of the guns. It was early afternoon.[158]

As they approached the area, things did not look promising.
Hundreds of stragglers littered the road, men who looked beaten,
who sounded beaten. The two commanders tried to make sense
of what had happened but could find no one in charge to offer a
definitive answer. And although the appearance of the generals
may have inspirited some troops, the two men had little initial
success in bringing order to the chaos. As Beauregard would recall it, "Every segment of the line we succeeded in forming was
again dissolved while another was being formed; more than two
thousand men were shouting, each some suggestion to his neighbor, their voices mingling with the noise of the shells hurtling
through the trees overhead." Jackson was on Henry House Hill,
still getting his brigade into position. Johnston did notice the
Fourth Alabama — or at least remnants of it — standing about. He
recognized these troops; they had arrived with him at Manassas
Junction just the day before. He discovered they had lost all their
field officers and clearly lacked direction. He thought they would
be better positioned if they moved forward a couple of hundred
yards, and he rode up to the man holding their banner. He said he
would lead them to the spot where he wanted them, and he offered to carry their flag on the way. The color-bearer said he
would prefer holding it himself. So Johnston led them ahead a
bit, pointed out the position, then rode away.

About this time Johnston and Beauregard discussed how
best to divvy up the responsibility. Beauregard suggested he
would stay near this particular battle zone and run things, while
Johnston could ride back to Portici, which they had passed on
the way. That place was central to this region (the southeast
quadrant), and someone in authority could establish the entire
army's headquarters there, then shovel ahead reinforcements as

they came by. Beauregard would later admit that Johnston was "disinclined to leave the battlefield" but was persuaded by Beauregard's reminder that he, not Johnston, best knew the terrain. In his several memoirs, Beauregard might have left the matter at that. But his seething hatred of Johnston made him continue. He offered this aside: He, Beauregard, really only proposed that Johnston go to Portici because his aide, Tom Jordan, was too busy at Manassas Junction to do so. In other words, in Beauregard's mind whoever was at Portici would be performing a mere adjutant's role. The Creole made his contempt for Johnston even clearer. He said: "The writer [Beauregard] does not believe that military annals will furnish an instance, in similar circumstances, where the actual commander ever left the command of the line of battle to go back upon such a service." In this sarcastic sentence, Beauregard implied several things: that the great victory about to occur was due solely to *his* efforts, that he had sent Johnston on a mere secretarial mission, and that Johnston's willingness to go was a sign that, deep down, he was a coward. In all his accounts of this battle, Beauregard was, quite simply, a glory hog. Ever since mid-April, he had been touted everywhere he went as the Hero of Fort Sumter. The pleasures of such idolatry had tasted delicious. That level of fame could be increased right now. He had no desire to share it with anyone.

Johnston, however, was far more generous. In his official report he said he rode to Portici since that position gave him control over "the whole field" and that he "had full confidence in the skill and indomitable courage of general Beauregard."[159]

About noon John Imboden realized he must withdraw his four guns from their position. He had been on Henry House Hill since Bee had placed him there in midmorning. Part of the time he and his battery had been virtually alone. After dueling with the six-gun Rhode Island battery for an hour, he had watched the arrival of a second Union battery (Griffin's), then a third (Ricketts's). The din around him was awful. He shouted orders to his men, many phrases going unheard, his words disappearing into the explosions. His gunners, he noticed, were starting to collapse — from wounds or physical exhaustion. In the best of circumstances, handling field artillery is grueling. A cannon's barrel sat atop a two-wheeled contraption called a *gun carriage.* To move it any distance, a gunner connected the carriage to a second two-wheeled vehicle called a *limber.* Together they formed a relatively mobile, four-wheeled, flexible, wagonlike thing, with the limber's wheels serving as its front and the gun bouncing along at the back, its barrel facing away. Once a gunner arrived at the spot where he wanted to start firing, he turned this vehicle 180 degrees and disconnected the limber (he *unlimbered*). A large ammunition chest was normally bolted onto the limber, and the gunners drew the cartridges and shells, as they needed them, from this box. The back of the gun carriage (called the *trail*) fell to the ground, where it served as a brace. But each time a cannon fired, the carriage on its wheels recoiled backwards several feet, and the tail dug a trench. After each shot, the gunners ran to the cannon and, using the muscles of their legs and back, picked up the trail and pushed the gun forward again. Often they also turned the trail left or right a foot or two to aim at an always moving enemy. Since their previous shots had indicated the range of the enemy's position, one of the gunners could turn a screw mechanism to elevate or lower the barrel, to shoot farther or nearer.

Aiming a cannon required a combination of complex skills. A good gunner had to be able to eyeball the distance to the enemy, to feel the wind velocity and direction, to understand that cannon powder loses some of its power whenever it gets damp and that the sweat on a man's chest and hands as he totes a cartridge to the gun dilutes its force somewhat. The gunner had to know that *shot,* which is solid, is most accurate and can be purposely ricocheted, especially against infantry in columns. *Shells*—officially called *spherical case*—were much more difficult to fire accurately because they often exploded too soon or not at all. Much of their usefulness derived from the terrifying shrieking sounds they made in the air and the frightening power of their explosions. American field artillery no longer fired *grapeshot,* but they did fire *canister,* which, as its name implies, was a tin can filled with balls. At fifty yards, a single canister's deadly charge spread a sixteen-foot swath. If charging infantry came near, gunners could stuff more than one canister at a time into their guns. "Triple-shotting" was not unheard of. Knowing how to perform all these tasks, and when, required part mathematics, part mechanics, part voodoo instinct.

In action, a gun was usually swabbed clean and cooled down with water after each shot. Then gunners carried the next bag of powder to the mouth of the barrel and rammed it deep inside, hoping it would not explode prematurely. They brought a solid shot or a shell or a canister from an ammunition box. A single battery might consist of two or three different kinds of guns, each of which fired a different gauge, requiring a different cartridge. So the gunners had to be sure they did not get confused and use the wrong cartridge or shell. Farther behind them — perhaps forty feet, sometimes as many as two hundred — sat another vehicle called a *caisson,* which had accompanied them to this position. It carried three more ammunition boxes with cartridges, shot and shell and canister, and an assortment of tools.

A well-equipped battery, like several on the Union side, also had a forge that could be used to make on-the-spot repairs. A gunner had to assume things would go wrong, and it was wise to be prepared. When in motion, a horse sometimes lost one of its shoes, which needed to be replaced right away, before the horse went lame. The terrain of a battlefield was seldom smooth. It almost always contained rocks and ditches and channels cut by creeks. A battery's drivers tended to gallop from place to place, shouting and swearing at infantrymen to get out of the way. A battery's vehicles bounced about accordingly. Their wheels were somewhat fragile, and rocky terrain could rip them apart. A wheel — on the gun carriages or the limbers or the caissons — might break and need to be replaced. So batteries carried spare wheels. In theory all their wheels were the same size and could be exchanged with each other. During a battle it was normal to see gunners, while being fired at, heaving up one side of a caisson with a broken wheel and muscling it off and sliding on a replacement. (Most Confederate caissons at Bull Run had been farm wagons a few weeks earlier, converted to their new uses with hammers and nails. They tended to be higher than regulation military vehicles and therefore harder to use. And their wheels were irregular in size.)

During peacetime drills, when artillerists were well rested and well fed, they still tired fairly quickly. The tasks they needed to perform involved a combination of weight lifting and ballet. Battles intensified everything. Their horses and vehicles made them obvious targets. Ammunition boxes often exploded. Gun barrels grew intensely hot and sometimes shattered. Being an artillerist was not a job for the weak or timid.

As for Imboden and his men, they had hardly slept in days and had eaten badly. How they were able physically to continue firing their guns for almost two hours is a mystery. Their sinews must have screamed in protest; their parched throats, caked with dust and gunpowder, would have made their voices crack and squeak. Although, amazingly, Imboden's battery only lost three men to wounds, by noon at least half of the gunners had collapsed to the ground, their physical limits reached. Imboden himself was a mess. He had been nicked here and there and was bruised. Blood spattered his clothing. At one point he had his head too close to a gun that fired, and blood spurted from his eardrum and ran down the side of his neck. Sweat cut ridges in the filth that encrusted his face. One of his guns was now out of action — temporarily spiked by a priming wire. A Yankee ball cracked the axle of another. A quick tally told him he only had three more shots for each cannon. He had started with a supply of 460; he had no more than ten left. (This means each of his active guns averaged more than a shot per minute, an amazing statistic if one takes into account the time spent between each shot, when the gunners moved the gun, aimed it, swabbed it, loaded it.) Many of Imboden's horses were dead. Men can only physically push a gun so far by hand. For any real distance, a man must utilize genuine horsepower. Without sufficient horses, a battery becomes as immobile as a boat with its side caved in.

Low on ammunition and horses, his men dizzy from exhaustion, Yankee infantry approaching, Imboden started toward the rear. He was maneuvering his battery through some scrub pines that lay between the Robinson house and the Henry house when he bumped into the front of Jackson's brigade, just arriving after their long morning's peregrinations. Imboden was in a foul mood. In his estimation, he and his men had been allowed to dangle too long on that hill back there. Where the hell was Bee? Why had he not relieved them? At his best behaved, Imboden was not a completely polished gentleman. Now, facing Jackson, he began to curse Bee, the absent South Carolinian, until it dawned on him that Jackson did not approve of swearing and that, after all, General Bee was Imboden's superior officer and that Jackson was nothing if not militarily punctilious. Imboden shut his mouth. Jackson said he understood how fagged out Imboden's crew was, but he did not care. He ordered Captain Imboden to remain here with his battery a while longer. Even though they had only a few more shells, they could protect Jackson's infantry as the foot soldiers got into position and could hold the ground till Jackson's own artillery got themselves unlimbered. As for the approaching Yankee infantry—which Jackson had not yet seen—Jackson was confident his five regiments could sufficiently protect Imboden's battery. Imboden could only reply, Yes, sir! He turned his guns around and set them in place. His men fell upon the ground, bone weary, blackened with smoke and dust, too spent to move. Luckily, they were hardly called upon to load and fire their cannon, since the Yankees did not approach right away.

Jackson saw to the placement of his regiments. He rode back and forth, getting the lay of this landscape, then told the regiments where he wanted them to go. Each marched to a designated spot and lay down, many of them sheltered from the sun by the trees that spread across this southern slope of Henry House Hill. By the time they got settled, they were spread out in a half-mile arc behind the Henry and Robinson places. Jackson also took great care in placing his cannon. Artillery usage was a subject he had taught in Lexington, and he knew its manuals and mathematics well.

It took almost an hour for Jackson's brigade to get itself set. He then told Imboden the captain could leave with his battery. The gunners withdrew, but Imboden stayed for a while, to see if his advice could help. When he finally departed, he passed some of Hampton's Legion. At that moment a Yankee shell landed in the Legion's midst, and they started to stampede. He tried to stop them, raising his sword as a gesture of authority. One large South Carolinian, crazed by terror, thrust at Imboden with his bayonet, jabbing into Imboden's left arm and smacking him with the musket itself, knocking Imboden down — then finally running away. Imboden rose painfully to his feet and went on to Portici, where he found his battery.[160]

Johnston and Beauregard and their staffs rode up, apparently before Jackson had finished positioning his men. Other Confederates began arriving and were placed by Johnston or Beauregard on either side of Jackson's position. Some of these were makeshift groups like the curious battalion of Colonel William "Extra Billy" Smith — his nickname the result of his tendency, when he had been a politician, of making sure his constituents received plenty. Smith was sixty-three years old, as tough as leather, and a week earlier he had been appointed to take charge of a new Virginia "regiment." Although it still consisted of only three partial companies, it was politely referred to as the "Forty-ninth Virginia" or, sometimes, "Smith's regiment." As one of Beauregard's aides recalled about Smith: "He did not know any words of command, and his men would not have understood them if he had." His "regiment" was but a tiny cog in Cocke's brigade, yet his high energy in the early afternoon changed things. He wanted action, and Beauregard saw to it he was guided toward Jackson's left flank. Three other groups were placed on Smith's left. One was a makeshift battalion, which Johnston put under one of his aides, Colonel F. J. Thomas, consisting of the frazzled remains of Bee's and Evans's brigades. The other two were the remnants of the Second Mississippi that had retreated from Matthews Hill and the Sixth North Carolina that had just arrived at Manassas Junction by train and had wandered around for a while, totally lost. The left wing of the North Carolinians almost touched the Sudley road.

In reality the Confederate "line" was never as neatly placed as this description suggests. In fact, with the exception of Jackson's brigade, units arrived haphazardly, and the records are not clear about the times. When fighting started here, there was much rushing about, and units, or sections of them, fell back and sometimes evaporated. But one can estimate that at most the Confederate "army" on Henry House Hill numbered fewer than 6,000 men, probably fewer than 5,000. Altogether they had 20 cannon, but probably never more than 13 at any one time—once Pendleton's guns arrived to join Jackson's. On the other hand, Beauregard, who was in nominal command of this force, was only vaguely aware of the fact that by one o'clock he had a dozen more Confederate regiments (about 8,000 men) marching toward him from widely separated spots—from the Manassas Junction train station on one side, from McLean's and Mitchell's Fords on the other.

During the afternoon Johnston at Portici performed a critical task, forwarding to Beauregard as many men as he could—much like Eisenhower in England sending reinforcements to Omar Bradley. Curiously, despite Beauregard's insistence on remaining in charge of the hill, he actually did little of vital importance beyond indicating to the new arrivals approximately where he wanted them. He did ride around and buck up the troops with encouraging words. He was not by nature an effervescent person. He was normally unsmiling and solemn, if not dour. But on this day he acted the cheerleader. And a few times his words did provide great emotional value. (The best sentence he ever uttered was to the battered men of the Eighth Georgia. He could not have been aware what a nightmare they had gone through inside the thicket on Matthews Hill, but he must have seen something in their posture as they passed him. They themselves felt like failures, for they had run. Perhaps only fifty of them were now still clumped together, shuffling along next to their flag. But as they went by, he said he saluted them. Some thought he said, "I salute you with my hat off," while lifting his cap in their honor. Perhaps he did. If so, it was only what they deserved. Whatever he said on this occasion, his words gave them back their pride—and would, forever after, be remembered and appreciated in Georgia.)

One of the most famous—and controversial—moments in the entire war occurred sometime during this Confederate maneuvering. Four days later an article appeared in the *Charleston Mercury*, wired to it by one of their correspondents in Richmond. The story involved the South Carolinian, Barnard E. Bee, whose exploits at Bull Run caused the reporter to write: "The name of this officer deserves a place in the highest niche of fame." The ar-

ticle described how "the brunt" of the morning's battle had fallen
on Bee's command, until his men, facing overwhelming Yankee
numbers, had been forced to retreat. The article told how Bee, in
the early afternoon, then rode "up and down his lines, encouraging his troops." Finally, when their numbers "dwindled to a
mere handful," he went up to an obscure Virginia officer named
Jackson, who was just arriving on the scene. Bee expressed to
him his concerns, and Jackson laconically replied, "Sir, we'll give
them the bayonet." The calm terseness of this statement, according to the tone of the article, made Bee ride to the paltry remnants
of what had been his brigade and say, "There is Jackson standing
like a stone wall. Let us determine to die here and we will conquer." Then, the article said, Bee led his men back into the fray,
yelling, "Follow me." Beauregard was heard to remark about
Bee's leadership that he had "never seen such gallantry." The
story, in other words, in this Charleston newspaper was about
that South Carolina hero, Barnard Bee. It was certainly *not* about
Thomas J. Jackson, a man whose name was virtually unknown
in Charleston. During that week newspapers across the United
States had tales—many of them quite tall—about local boys who
had allegedly done something at Bull Run worthy of note. This
story about Bee was merely one of these, written by either
Leonidas W. Spratt or George W. Bagby, neither reporter especially reliable.

Four days after this article appeared, the *Richmond Dispatch*
reprinted it word for word, the sixth of fourteen items listed
under the headline, FACTS AND INCIDENTS OF THE BATTLE. Then,
thereafter, little by little the tale mutated until it no longer resembled the original account. The transformed story became part
of that vast, semifictionalized Americana that includes Betsy Ross
and her flag and Teddy Roosevelt "riding up San Juan Hill."

Did any part of this story really happen? Particularly that
line about "stone wall"? If Bee really said those words, did he
mean the brigade of Virginians or their general? If he meant
Jackson, was it a compliment, or was he raging over the fact that
Jackson had not brought his regiments down from the hilltop to
join Bee at the critical moment when Bee's men were being
slaughtered on Matthews Hill? After all, Jackson was simply one

of Joe Johnston's brigade commanders from the Valley, just like Bee himself. There is no question Jackson spoke of "giving the bayonet" to the enemy. He repeated this phrase as a kind of mantra several times to his colonels during that afternoon, so whether he said it to Bee is immaterial. Porter Alexander later said he had heard General *Johnston* compliment a single one of Jackson's regiments—the Fourth Virginia—as standing "like a stone wall" and that he, Alexander, believed that the *Mercury*'s reporter had got the story scrambled—or had given the line to Bee, the South Carolina hero.

An observer of that conversation between Jackson and Bee was a captain in one of Jackson's regiments, Captain Asher Harman. He saw Bee come up and speak to the regimental colonel, William H. Harman—the witness's brother—asking him to advance his regiment. When the colonel seemed to hesitate, Bee ordered him to do so. But Harman kept saying he couldn't, General Jackson's orders had been explicit about staying right here. Bee finally departed, very dissatisfied. The witness of this conversation later said, "I'm not the least sure Gen. Bee's remark— 'There stands Jackson & his men, like a stone wall'—was meant as a compliment."

Unfortunately, Bee could not be asked. When the battle on Henry House Hill began, he did ride to some of his men—mostly members of the Fourth Alabama and the Second Mississippi, who had already fought for hours and were now resting several hundred yards behind Jackson's position—and he offered to lead them back into battle, since Jackson's men seemed to be *in need of assistance.* On their way forward, a Confederate battery galloped forward from behind them, hurtling down the narrow path Bee and his men were taking, forcing them to scatter to either side. After it passed, most of Bee's men headed through the woods in one direction, while he, not noticing, led a handful in another. A few moments later he was shot in the lower abdomen or groin.

He knew it was a fatal wound, belly wounds being killers. But he lingered into the next day, and as he lay dying, he heard that Captain Imboden was angry at him for letting his battery stay on Henry House Hill so long unprotected, and he sent assurances to the artillery officer that he really had sent a courier to relieve him. Friends with Bee on this day were convinced Bee was still furious at Jackson for his lack of support, and remained so to the end.

Ultimately, the nature of Bee's real feelings is unimportant. Jackson had just acquired a memorable nickname. Few have ever heard of the man Temujin, but everyone knows his nickname, "Genghis Khan" ("great chieftain"). History offers many colorful names: "Mad" Anthony Wayne, Ivan the Terrible, Honest Abe, Catherine the Great, Babe Ruth. Each of these nicknames has some core of truth in it. So, too, did Jackson's new label. His performance at Bull Run was actually no more courageous or resolute or dogged or unyielding than that of dozens of other officers on both sides. He did ride back and forth before his men, trying to keep them cool by his unflappability—even after receiving a painful wound in one of his fingers and wrapping it in a bloody handkerchief. But other officers calmed their soldiers in the same way—Sherman, for example, and Beauregard. Officers learned this technique at West Point, and many military manuals emphasized its importance. Nor did Jackson's stern resolve win the battle. Hundreds of factors went into its ultimate result. The men of his brigade were later proud to say they served in "the Stonewall Brigade," but several times that afternoon bunches of them ran away as fast as they could. And the men of Eppa Hunton's regiment, for example, and "Extra Billy" Smith's makeshift battalion and the Hampton Legion were just as firm as any of Jackson's five regiments.

But the nickname stuck—to him and to his men. At first, it was certainly just a press gimmick. The Confederacy needed heroes. There was also the subtle matter of state pride. Georgians could be proud of Bartow, South Carolinians had Bee, Louisianans had Beauregard, Mississippi had Jefferson Davis. That took care of those states. Virginians wanted a favorite son of their own. Robert E. Lee was only a paper shuffler in Richmond; Joe Johnston had done well at Bull Run, but he did, after all, spend much of the battle far from the action. Jackson was the highest-ranking *Virginian* in the battle's hottest sector. Moreover, he represented an important clientele. He was a Valley man, a bit rough around the edges. In a sense, therefore, he represented "the people" of Virginia—not the Tidewater cavaliers of Lee and Johnston and Cocke. Northern Republicans liked emphasizing Lincoln's "log cabin" background, conveniently overlooking the fact that Old Abe had made himself into a well-to-do, successful lawyer, whose career had primarily involved defending large Midwestern businesses. In the same way, Jackson's "common" background was politically convenient to Virginians who wanted to retain the support of the state's average citizens. So was Jackson's obvious religiosity, his simplicity, his love of his wife, his quiet dignity, even his eccentricities. Such traits made "Stonewall" seem a man of the people. Virginia's newspapers, which were about to make him famous, were lucky he turned out to be as brilliant and gritty a fighter as his nickname—though it might be noted that his best fighting would be done at home in the Valley or near it.[161]

By about one o'clock Johnston and Beauregard and Jackson and the other high-ranking Confederate officers had done about as much preparation as they could with the men and artillery they had immediately on hand. Most of their infantrymen were lying down behind brush-covered fences or were hidden within the pine trees on Henry House Hill. Their positions, several hundred yards behind Judith Henry's place, put them on a slight downslope and therefore mostly concealed them from Union observers on the northern side of the turnpike.

Take the
High Ground

Terrain exercises a tyrannical influence on every maneuver.
—French Military Maxim

*We fired first, and advanced. We then charged
bayonets, yelling like savages, and they retreated,
and our regiment took their artillery.*
—Private John O. Casler, Thirty-third Virginia[162]

The Union Side, Keyes's Brigade

When Sherman's four regiments began wading across
Bull Run, closely followed by Keyes's brigade, General Tyler left
behind Schenck's three regiments to protect the engineers who
had still not placed their trestle bridge across Bull Run or hacked
through the abatis. In the morning, following Tyler's orders,
Schenck had ordered his brigade to press southward along the
Centreville side of the stream, where many rebels were reportedly camped. Almost immediately, Schenck's regiments bumped
into a "masked" rebel battery. As the Confederate gunners opened
fire, they were heard to shout: "Now, you Yankee devils, we've
got you where we want you!" Schenck urged his troops to attack
the guns, but his officers remonstrated. Colonel George W. B.
Tompkins, in command of the Second New York, simply refused
to obey, and the commanders of the two Ohio regiments concurred. It was a mini-mutiny, no doubt the residue of the dis-
gruntlement that permeated this brigade from the semimutiny of

the day before. Schenck had no choice but to withdraw his brigade to its original position near the stone bridge. After this, until late afternoon, their only real service was guarding the engineering detail at the bridge, three regiments involved in a task where one would have been more than sufficient. McDowell might have insisted that Schenck send over his two Ohio regiments, but he did not.[163]

General Tyler accompanied Keyes's brigade when it crossed Bull Run. They arrived just as McDowell's aides were gleefully yelling about their "victory." Tyler, instead of going to McDowell to consult about the next step, ordered Keyes to march his brigade away from this scene, to slide along the eastern side of Bull Run, south of the stone bridge. It was not a bad idea. Clearing the area by the bridge was critical. Soon Federal artillery batteries would be crossing over to this side, and so would wagons with important ammunition and provisions, and ambulances to carry back the wounded. The "masked battery" that had fired on Schenck earlier and Cocke's infantry ought to be pushed aside or isolated. Most of all, there were the rebels who were increasingly visible on the ridge south of the turnpike (Henry House Hill). Keyes's four regiments could charge up the side slope of the hill while McDowell sent men up its front. Tyler's decision to order Keyes south, therefore, was reasonable. His error lay in not informing McDowell what he had in mind, preventing any sort of coordinated assault. Tyler's choice to act alone was, at the least, arbitrary. He did not even tell Sherman, one of his two brigade commanders on this side of Bull Run. This lapse was even more egregious because Sherman was only a few minutes' ride away. Some historians have believed that Tyler was acting spitefully, that his animosity toward McDowell had intensified since the Battle of Blackburn's Ford because of McDowell's obvious displeasure. But reading such childishness in Tyler's actions and inactions is based only on conjecture — and fails to explain why Tyler omitted Sherman from his plan. Most likely, Tyler was merely unable to mentally grapple with the size and complexity of his command — like every other commander that day. It is revealing that six months later, when testifying to the Joint Committee and recalling this moment, he said he now moved southward with "my division"—when, in fact, Keyes's men only represented a third of it.[164]

It was about 12:30 when Tyler and Keyes set off. Their regiments—the Second Maine and the First, Second, and Third Connecticut—crossed the turnpike several hundred yards west of the stone bridge. They moved carefully because they could not be sure where the enemy was. It took them at least half an hour to get to the base of the slope below Jim Robinson's place, and another half hour to organize themselves. The men of the Second Maine and the Third Connecticut were placed side by side, with the two other Connecticut regiments backing them up. About 1:30 they started jogging up the slope toward the house. They had done no real reconnaissance, nor did they have any artillery support. But Daniel Tyler was upbeat. One of his men saw him "smiling and happy, full of hope." He announced to his fellow Nutmeggers, "Now, Connecticut, do your duty. The day will soon be ours." He pointed to a battery he espied on the hill and ordered them to take it.

The four regiments advanced, and, after about a hundred yards, they lay down inside a dip in the terrain and finally loaded their muskets (meaning that they had double-quicked across a mile of enemy-controlled territory with unloaded guns). When they rose to their feet and charged, their front line was a third of a mile across. "We went up that hill," one would recall, "shouting and yelling as if two thousand demons had been suddenly let loose from Pandemonium."

Just in front of them were remnants of rebel units that had been flung off Matthews Hill—Bee's men, Hampton's, Evans's, mostly unorganized and shattered. These turned and ran. The core of rebel resistance near Robinson's farm now was the battery that Tyler wanted to take and an infantry regiment that Jackson had just placed here, the Fifth Virginia (the very regiment that Bee had wanted to move, whose colonel had refused). The Virginians were partly sheltered behind some bushes, a fence, and the house. Some historians have suggested that this charge of Keyes's men might even have successfully rolled up Jackson's flank. This is absurd. The farther up the slope they ran, the more exhausted, the weaker, they became. Even had the Fifth Virginia dissolved, Jackson himself had many cannon atop the hill, along with four additional infantry regiments. Jackson was not about to panic. Keyes's men would have arrived at the top, essentially entered a trap, and been slaughtered. To succeed against Jackson's brigade, the charge would have had to be part of a much wider and coordinated assault—an implausible prospect, since Tyler had not told McDowell what he planned.

The soldiers of the Fifth Virginia were unsure who these running men were. They might be Confederates moving in this direction, like the others who had previously come this way—Hampton's Legion, for example. The troops from Maine wore gray uniforms. Besides, by this time in the afternoon, all the uniforms, covered with a thick layer of Virginia dust, looked much alike. But the Virginians finally decided these approaching troops were Yankees and opened fire. So did the battery near them.

At the center of the Second Maine's front line was a platoon of men surrounding the color-bearers carrying three flags: a Maine flag, a United States flag, and a brand new banner given them the night before, sent by folks originally from Maine who had settled in San Francisco. Because rough ground often threw off a soldier's strides and because thick smoke often enveloped him in battle, an individual could easily grow confused about his situation. That was the importance of flags. The men of the Second Maine only had to look around, and there were their banners, moving inexorably forward. The color-bearers—men like Sergeant William A. Deane—were proud to hold them aloft. When Deane went down, shot in the throat, Corporal Americus V. Moore picked up the "California" flag, climbed over a fence, and continued moving toward the rebels. The Virginians retreated a hundred yards, maybe more. General Tyler rubbed his hands together in glee. A Connecticut officer grabbed his own regimental flag, leaped onto a fence, and urged his men to "rally 'round the flag," but as one of them wryly recalled, "It ain't half as easy to do under such circumstances as it is to sing about."

Then Americus Moore went down. And another flag bearer fell. The Second Maine broke and ran back behind the fence. On the field behind them lay their wounded, and their flags. General Tyler became semihysterical. He wanted them to go back, to charge again up the hill. This time he suggested a bayonet charge. In his excitement he was heard to say, "Men! Can't you take that bayonet at the point of the battery?" One of his aides, Lieutenant Emory Upton, twenty-one, rode to the Second Connecticut, not yet in action, and shouted, "Boys of Old Connecticut! There is a battery on the brow of yonder hill; I want you to follow me, and you shall have the credit of capturing it. Will you follow?" The Connecticut men began to cheer mightily. They took off their caps, placed them on their bayonets, and waved them about. But Keyes and the other colonels took Tyler aside and persuaded him the idea was impractical. They told him, No, the brigade could *not* take that battery—with bayonets or bullets.

The Second Maine was ordered to pull back. One man, however—Corporal Benjamin F. Smart—looked across the fence and said he was not leaving, not without those banners. His colonel, Charles D. Jameson, standing nearby, agreed. Jameson also felt the same about their dead and wounded. He turned and asked for volunteers to go with him—up the hill, across the fence, and into that field. Nine men stepped forward, a captain and eight enlisted men—including Corporal Smart. As their companions watched in amazement, these ten men dashed up into the field, through musket fire and artillery shells. Miraculously unscathed, they accomplished part of their goal, snatching up the flags and some of the wounded, then racing back. There were too many wounded to carry all of them back, but the attempt by this little band was magnificent. (Ben Smart would write his father two days later about his feelings for Colonel Jameson: "Oh, Father, words are inadequate to express my love for that patriotic hero.") Officially, the Second Maine lost over 27 percent of its aggregate manpower; in fact, discounting stragglers and noncombatants of various types, like band members, the losses of the Maine soldiers who actually charged up the hill perhaps ran as high as 50 percent. The Confederates would later find and capture twenty-five wounded members of the Second Maine on the slope, along with their chaplain, John Mines, who had heroically remained with them.

With the failure of this assault, Tyler had to rethink his plans. He finally contacted McDowell, sending a courier with the cryptic message that he, Tyler, and Keyes intended "to turn the batteries on the plateau by a movement below the Stone Bridge"—whatever that was supposed to mean, since the rebels had various batteries. McDowell ought to have sent the courier back with an order to return to this part of the battlefield, but he did not. During the next two hours, Keyes and Tyler and the four regiments crept carefully southward, along the base of the hill, not far from the stream. It was slow going. The area was cut by gullies and ravines and was thick with trees. About four o'clock they finally reached a quiet spot, from which they decided they could launch another attack—and were about to do so when they were told they must return to Centreville, the battle was over. They were stunned. They had had no inkling what had been going on behind them.[165]

McDowell's Decision

Despite Tyler's mostly ineffective activities, by early afternoon the outlook for McDowell's army seemed favorable. The Federals had been in control of Matthews Hill since noon—that is, they controlled both northern quadrants. Discounting Burnside, whose brigade was now resting, and Keyes, who was off on Tyler's odd mission, McDowell already had three fresh brigades on the scene—Sherman's, Franklin's, and Porter's. Heintzelman's other brigade, the one commanded by Orlando B. Willcox, was in the process of passing across Sudley Ford. This meant that four mostly unbloodied Union brigades would be on Matthews Hill, or near it, by twelve-thirty or one o'clock. If McDowell acted promptly, and if his brigade commanders could manipulate efficiently the thousands of troops in each of their commands, the Union army might still capture the depot at Manassas Junction before nightfall.

But McDowell would have to coordinate the movements of his unconnected brigade commanders and their scattered artillery batteries. This would be difficult. He lacked sufficient staff to maintain close communications with his subordinates. Also the contours of the ground and the thick clumps of trees made it impossible to know the next best step to take. He could see that the rebels had placed some guns on the hill beyond the turnpike (Henry House Hill). But he could not discern exactly what was over there, how many guns, and how many infantrymen were up there to defend them. Should he take immediate advantage of the rebel retreat from Matthews Hill and press his army forward? If he dawdled and waited for reinforcements (Runyon's division?), could he not be later charged with failing to aggressively follow up his morning victory? Suppose he instantly ordered Sherman and Porter to charge Henry House Hill? They might run right into a slew of rebel artillery. Would it not be wiser to push some of his own guns up there first? Perhaps he ought to ignore that hill entirely and move his army toward his right, in the direction of the railroad station, through the southwest quadrant. But if he did that, he would be spreading his army into two wings, increasingly far apart—those units going toward the depot and those still on the other side of Bull Run. What was Beauregard doing? Was he in the process of swinging most of his army across Mitchell's Ford and perhaps already assaulting Richardson, Davies, and Blenker? If the rebels were doing this, they might take Centreville and cut off McDowell's supply line. (McDowell could no longer ignore the fact he was facing at least some of Johnston's force; prisoners from Johnston's Valley army had been taken. But he still could not be sure how many of Johnston's men had arrived.)

Another possible tactic involved waiting at his present position near the stone bridge. In a few hours at most, his engineers could cut through the abatis there and erect their pontoon bridge. As soon as this was accomplished, ammunition and provision wagons, lined up on the Centreville side, could speed across, to say nothing of Tyler's artillery, which was still stuck on the far side. The disadvantage of waiting would be that, by the time this was accomplished—assuming the rebels permitted it—precious hours would have passed. It would be early evening, perhaps too late to attempt another assault. He was in "enemy territory," and he did not have the advantage his foes had of a railroad supply line. Every passing hour meant the rebels might be increasing their strength. Besides, why wait? At this moment it seemed plausible that he had already won. But was the rebel army retreating? Or were they gathering their forces inside the woods on the hill over there? Were they preparing for some desperate measure of their own?

McDowell's thinking at this critical time—noon till two o'clock—remains unclear, but he certainly would have considered all or most of these questions. But contemplating them in the abstract would not, by itself, be enough. Most of the answers could only be gotten by solid reconnaissance. Porter's brigade did include several hundred cavalrymen. McDowell might have sent them ahead, but he probably thought they were too inexperienced to hazard them in that way. Without using a cavalry probe, therefore, the only practical way to know the approximate strength and resiliency of the rebel army was to attack it. And so the real question was when. Should he wait until he had all four brigades ready—those he knew should be on hand within the next hour or so?

He had always been something of a desk-bound bureaucrat, yet his mind was usually good and analytical, and he had shown himself capable of arriving at reasoned decisions. But during the past two days, he had seemed mentally lethargic. His willingness to allow his chief engineer, Major Barnard, an extra day to scout Bull Run is an example. Or, on Saturday afternoon, when he permitted Burnside to convince him to postpone the attack for eight hours, altering the plan significantly, he seemed indecisive. His later claim that Burnside's rationale had sounded logical would have been more persuasive had he not also been wishy-washy throughout the day of the battle. His irresolution became particularly evident on Sunday afternoon, when none of his decisions were confident or crisp. He had been working extremely hard, under enormous pressure, for weeks. He had hardly slept in the previous few nights. And perhaps not at all Saturday night, because of his illness. Near the blacksmith shop that morning, he had laid on the ground part of the time, still vomiting. Some passing soldiers, seeing him in that condition, not realizing he was a teetotaler, assumed he was drunk. When he had pulled himself onto his saddle and ridden to the battle, few commented on his presence — except when he announced the army's "victory" about noon. At that moment he was undisguisedly elated. It is possible that, thereafter, a physiological reaction came over him. Euphoria can be draining. Following an uptick of gaiety, a feeling of exhaustion can set in. Perhaps something like this happened to McDowell. It is true that his thinking now was muddled. Months later, when questioned by the Committee, he could not clarify his mindset on the afternoon of the battle — or even where he was during those hours. We can, therefore, only apply deduction, using mostly the testimony of others.

In July 1861 Lieutenant William Woods Averell was a moderately bright and quite aggressive officer, temporarily assigned as an assistant adjutant general for Porter's brigade (that position often little more than a courier). But when Hunter, the divisional commander, was wounded and Porter took official charge of the division, Porter departed, leaving command of the brigade, de facto, to Averell, a mere twenty-eight-year-old cavalry lieutenant who had graduated near the bottom of his class at West Point.

Attached to Porter's brigade was the six-gun battery of Captain Charles Griffin. Griffin had entered the battle almost an hour after it began. As we have seen, his guns had hurtled down the Sudley road, pulled into the field on the right, unlimbered, and begun firing. Five days earlier Averell had told Major J. G. Reynolds, in command of the marine battalion that was also part of Porter's brigade, to stick with this battery. The marines, being especially raw, were not in excellent physical shape. During the march from Washington, they had found it difficult to keep up with the artillerymen, who made no attempt to accommodate their pace to their infantry escort. Now, as Griffin whipped his guns into battle, the panting marines found it impossible to stay with them and had to pause to catch their breath. Averell was riding past Griffin's battery, and Griffin shouted to him that his guns now had no infantry support. Averell rode off to see what he could do, looking for other men from Porter's brigade whom he could assign to back up Griffin's battery. He spied one of the brigade's three volunteer regiments doing little: the Fourteenth New York, the red-pantalooned unit from Brooklyn. He rode to them and guided them to Griffin.

Another staff officer also played a key role during these minutes. Captain Amiel Weeks Whipple, forty-three, West Point, 1841, was highly competent. Among his many accomplishments, he had recently been responsible for preparing the army's best maps of this region. Although a topographical engineer, he had been assigned to act temporarily as Hunter's assistant adjutant general. Now, with Hunter departed, Whipple, like Averell, was in a position of great potential importance — since it had been essentially Hunter's division that had won the battle for Matthews Hill. About noon Whipple and Averell — and perhaps Porter — talked about what they should focus on now. They decided, to use Averell's later words, that Henry House Hill seemed "the keypoint of the enemy's position, and must be taken" — if nothing else, to solidify their victorious position on the battlefield. To accomplish this, they glanced around at the available soldiers in their vicinity. They thought Griffin's battery could act as the core of the assault, backed by the Fourteenth Brooklyn. When the missing marine battalion arrived, it could also join. Heintzelman's division was just arriving on the scene, and his front brigade, led by Colonel Franklin, seemed fresh: two regiments from Massachusetts, the Fifth and the Eleventh, and the red-shirted stalwarts of the First Minnesota. Just behind them were the four regiments of Orlando B. Willcox, including two from New York that had a reputation for manliness: the Thirty-eighth (the so-called Scott Life Guard) and the Eleventh (nicknamed the Fire Zouaves). Averell and Whipple also thought one or two of Sherman's regiments that had just come across Bull Run could assist. They had in mind, Averell would recall, an attack across the turnpike and up the hill by Griffin and five or six of these ten regiments. The two officers started to put this force together. They found Colonel Franklin not only sympathetic with this goal but very helpful. They were also assisted by McDowell's aide, James Wadsworth, who was anxious to help.

All this organizing activity took time. As it was progressing, Irvin McDowell had come to a decision on his own—a bafflingly wrongheaded conclusion, only explicable as the fuzzy thinking of a tired mind. He ordered his chief of artillery, Major William F. Barry, to send twelve guns to the top of Henry House Hill. He mentioned the two batteries he had in mind, those of Griffin and Ricketts. (McDowell also had twelve other cannon nearby, but for some reason he did not mention these to Barry.)

So here were Whipple and Averell planning to send 4,000 infantrymen simply to accompany Griffin's battery. But McDowell seems to have said nothing about infantry support for the two batteries he proposed to push against the visible enemy guns that were beginning to arrive and that obviously were going to be defended by an unknown number of rebel infantrymen. Averell would recall that, when he learned of McDowell's notion, he realized how vulnerable the two batteries would be and rushed to the general and explained his concerns. McDowell, Averell said, "raised both hands and in a weary voice said, 'Go and give any orders you deem necessary, Mr. Averell.'" Off Averell rode, to scoop up whatever infantry he could and send them forward immediately: the Fourteenth Brooklyn, the Fire Zouaves, and the marines. Heintzelman also told the First Minnesota to hurry up and go along with the guns. But this entire operation had not been thought out. No reconnaissance had been made of Henry House Hill. The two batteries were not together when they started, and they took separate routes. The infantrymen who theoretically "accompanied" them came from different directions and had no central command or plan. The result was this: The Union army was ordering about 2,400 infantrymen and 12 cannon directly into the lair of at least 4,000 Confederates and 13 cannon.

Whatever was about to happen up there would be brutal.[166]

After General McDowell ordered Major Barry to send the two batteries to the top of the hill, Barry rode off. Had he not just made a serious mistake? He had only joined this expedition after it had left Washington, its second day out, when McDowell had named him his chief of artillery. Barry did not now serve McDowell well. Any courier, any flunky, can carry orders. Whether Barry realized the general was overly tired or ill or simply confused, it was his duty as chief of artillery to offer expert suggestions. Before departing to carry out McDowell's wishes, he ought to have pressed the general for two things: adequate reconnaissance and sufficient infantry support. He apparently suggested neither.

The Joint Committee would later ask both Griffin and Ricketts if artillerymen used a rule of thumb about how many infantrymen should accompany a battery. Griffin said, "There ought to be at least 1,000 men to every gun." (Since McDowell had just ordered twelve pieces up, they would have required far more men than McDowell had available.) Griffin did add, "At least there ought to have been not less than 4,000 men to support those batteries." When Ricketts was asked the same question, his response was more reflective, but he offered a similar conclusion. It would depend on circumstances, he said, but: "To go into such a place as that there should have been two full regiments to have supported my battery [by itself]." Both officers, therefore, agreed they were not provided proper support at the time they went up the hill, as they entered an unexplored enemy territory, a potential hornets' nest.

Given McDowell's repeated willingness to listen to advice, Major Barry's failure to advise him was appalling. Barry would insist to the Committee that he personally saw to it that two regiments—the Fourteenth Brooklyn and the Fire Zouaves—were sent along with the guns, but this statement was disingenuous. In fact, other officers, as we have seen, were in the process of doing that very thing, but they were not given sufficient time to organize their efforts properly. When the Committee asked Barry why the guns were lost, his answer was, "The infantry support abandoned them." The fault, he was suggesting, was certainly not his. It was the fault of infantrymen, not artillerymen. (By the end of the Civil War, Barry would become one of the army's highest-ranking artillerymen, and he generally would perform his job well. Bull Run was not one of those occasions. McDowell had two main advisors in his army: Major Barnard, responsible for coordinating the planning, and Major Barry, in charge of the artillery. Both served him ill.)

Barry told one of McDowell's aides, Lieutenant Kingsbury, to find Captain Ricketts and tell him to move his guns "there" — though of course Kingsbury could not be certain where the best spot would be. (Compare this to Bee's very precise placement of Imboden's guns four hours earlier or Jackson's careful positioning of his own artillery at this very moment.) Ricketts was unhappy with these orders but obeyed them. He took his six guns straight up the hill while Confederate artillery constantly fired on him. He did stop briefly when one wheel broke while passing over a ravine, but his men quickly replaced it, and he continued on. He reached the top and unlimbered his guns just past Judith Henry's place. He was immediately aware that some rebel infantrymen were firing at him — either from inside the house or just outside. He decided to put a stop to it. He turned his guns on the building and blasted it. This was almost certainly when Mrs. Henry received her fatal wounds. The time was probably two o'clock, perhaps a few minutes before.

Ricketts was asked by the Committee, "Was Griffin's battery near you?" His response was astonishing: "I do not know, except from what I have heard. I know there was a battery a little to the rear on my right, and from all accounts I suppose that to be Griffin's battery." This means that the two Federal batteries had absolutely no coordination of their actions — in fact they seemed to have had no contact with each other while atop Henry House Hill. Ricketts's six guns, along with his limbers and his caissons, would have taken up a large rectangle. And Griffin was somewhere outside that box.

Although often overlooked by historians, two Rhode Island guns, after spending all morning firing, joined the fray on Henry House Hill. The idea was Governor William Sprague's. He had been watching the preliminary action up there and thought maybe his beloved guns could assist the two Federal batteries. At some point during the fighting, the two Rhode Island cannon moved up the hill and pulled next to Ricketts's right. It is possible the

Rhode Islanders were the guns that Ricketts testified were "to the rear on my right," though probably not, because they had hardly arrived when — *Bang!*: "Thick and fast their bullets came in upon us." The Rhode Island gunners suddenly saw a large body of rebel infantrymen preparing a charge at them. So, firing not even a single shot, they limbered up and beat a hasty retreat.

For thirty minutes the opposing artillerists on the hill — Union and Confederate — dueled each other. Some of their guns were less than three hundred yards apart. Amazingly, they did remarkably little harm to each other. A Confederate battery commander would later report that only one of his men was injured during the entire battle. Some analysts have suggested that the Confederate guns, made up of eleven smoothbores and two rifled guns, were actually more suited to close work than the nine rifled and two smoothbore cannon of the Union batteries. But since neither side suffered much damage during this duel perhaps the reason was that the gunners were as amateurish as the infantrymen. It might be noted that their fire, however, killed and maimed many infantrymen, squatting or lying behind the guns. A Federal marine lieutenant had just remarked, "Those cannonballs are flying pretty thick," when a ball, ricocheting along the ground, literally knocked his head off. (The sight of his headless form startled many of those who wandered the battlefield the following day, persuading several witnesses of his corpse to discuss the meaning of the phrase, "the horrors of war.")[167]

The Union Side on Henry House Hill

Three Union infantry units — two regiments and the marine battalion — soon settled into the high grass behind and to the right of the guns. The regiment nearest the cannon was the Eleventh New York, the Fire Zouaves.

At this moment of the war, these men were the most famous volunteer regiment in the Union army, and many people expected big things from them. They had sprung from the mind and energy of one individual: Elmer Ellsworth. A twenty-four-year-old friend of President Lincoln, Ellsworth rushed to New York City immediately after Fort Sumter and announced he was organizing a regiment drawn from the city's firemen. It was an intriguing notion. Most firefighters could be assumed to be physically fit and, unlike many Americans of that era, used to highly organized activities. Ellsworth was already nationally famous from the previous summer when he had led a Chicago militia company across the northern half of America, giving demonstrations of a "Zouave" routine he had devised. Militia companies traditionally wore tight uniforms, but he had designed one based on a French model, with wide pantaloons and loose jackets. He claimed these outfits were less restricting so their wearers could move more gymnastically. The kinetic activities of his troupe, in tightly knit group movements like a Busby Berkeley routine, seemed to prove it. Following intricate patterns, they sprang about the stage or field, energetically flipping around their muskets and swords. Audiences watching them were awed; even Winfield Scott was impressed. Newspapers and magazines found Ellsworth and his Zouaves great copy. At the end of that summer, following their tour, he disbanded that small troupe. Eight months later, in April 1861, with the war frenzy sweeping the nation, he was deluged with applications from firemen as soon as he arrived in New York. He had to turn away more than a thousand applicants. The men he did accept became instantly famous, mainly because he brought to them his own celebrity and because an entire regiment made up of firemen had a certain panache.

In the next few weeks his men brought even more attention to themselves by some of their activities. In one incident in Washington, they helped douse a fire right next to Willard's Hotel that threatened to destroy that landmark. There were other, less admirable public shenanigans by a dozen or more of its members with predatory natures. Those exploits, too, were widely reported. Ellsworth sent the larcenous individuals packing, but damage had been done. Lincoln's most famous volunteer regiment now had a reputation for lawlessness and a kind of swaggering disorderliness. During the next few months, whenever any soldier in Washington committed a crime, the fault was frequently laid at the doorstep of Ellsworth's "pet lambs."

At first he had dressed them in rather eye-catching uniforms, but those suits fell apart quickly, and his men were soon clothed in less exotic outfits, in which only their bright red "firemen's" shirts, each with a buttoned bib in the front, really set them apart. Although their new uniforms were no longer truly "Zouave," their nickname lingered. Most Americans continued to imagine them wearing extraordinarily distinctive uniforms. And the troops of the Fourteenth Brooklyn, with their red pants, and the First Minnesota, with their red shirts, were often confused with them.

On May 24, 1861, when Lincoln's troops had first crossed the Potomac, the Fire Zouaves were ordered toward Alexandria. Less than an hour after arriving, Ellsworth was shot and killed by a hotel keeper. Newspapers reported that some of his men wrote, "Remember Ellsworth," in their caps and had revenge in their hearts. Throughout the Confederacy, the Fire Zouaves now became infamous and were used by creative Southern editors to represent Northern evil. Letters written by Confederate soldiers, referring to them, revealed an astonishing loathing for this one regiment. Ironically, professional Union officers—like Griffin— tended to despise them also, without ever laying eyes on them, because of the sordid reputation that the war's early newsmen had given them. (In his testimony to the Committee months later Griffin said, "I do not think that any troops that will go through the country in a disorganized state, thieving and robbing, are brave men." This inaccurate characterization indicates he had accepted the exaggerated news accounts.)

Both the fame and infamy of the Fire Zouaves were misplaced. As a group, they were no different than many other regiments on both sides. Ellsworth's theory that their common background would give them special cohesion was wishful thinking. Although almost all its members had once been firemen, the many fire companies of New York had competed with each other more than they had worked together. Also, at a fire, firefighters tended to act as individuals or in small teams. Could firemen be molded into a well-organized unit? That question had not yet been answered. After Ellsworth's death, the command was turned over to Noah Farnham, thirty-two. Colonel Farnham had been a New York fireman/engineer and had also had years of militia experience. He was a solid man, but he lacked Ellsworth's charisma. Worse, during the weeks before the battle, he was quite ill and bedridden. When McDowell's army started marching toward Manassas Junction, he had pulled himself from his sick bed and rejoined his regiment—but he was still unwell.[168]

When Major Barry recalled to the Committee sending the Fourteenth Brooklyn and the Fire Zouaves toward Henry House Hill, not even remembering the marines trailing after Griffin, he seems to have forgotten the interest that their divisional commander "Grim Old Heintzelman" displayed in the events on Henry House Hill. The Fire Zouaves and the First Minnesota were part of Heintzelman's division. When Ricketts's six guns started forward, since they were also part of his command, Heintzelman ordered his two brigade commanders—Willcox and Franklin—to follow with all their men. He himself accompanied Ricketts's battery. Meanwhile, the Fire Zouaves' march had been slowed by having to cross some fences. As they approached the Henry house, Heintzelman saw them. He rode over and escorted them to where he wanted them. He left two of their companies well back in reserve, then placed the others directly behind Ricketts's cannon. Most of these men sat down in the high grass, a normal position for infantrymen when supporting artillery.

Then the First Minnesota marched up, led by its commander, Colonel Willis Arnold Gorman. Heintzelman put this regiment off to the right of the Fire Zouaves, near a tree line. Heintzelman told the two right-hand companies to check the woods near them. A few of its skirmishers apparently went in and may have started tussling with some rebels, but most of the Minnesotans saw fit to fire into the thicket rather than gamble entering it. Immediately one man popped from the woods and told them to stop firing at their "friends." He was Lieutenant Colonel Bartley B. Boone of the Second Mississippi, who were sitting in the woods. His regiment, part of Bee's brigade, was well-acquainted with the Fourth Alabama, who wore red shirts like the Minnesotans (and the Fire Zouaves). He had, therefore, reached the conclusion that the Minnesotans were simply confused. By the time he realized his mistake, he had been taken prisoner—amazingly by the civilian Javan B. Irvine, who had been marching along with the First Minnesota. Bartley Boone would turn out to be the highest-ranking rebel captured and taken back to Washington this day, and Javan Irvine would be rewarded by being made a lieutenant.[169]

No one later on could really make sense of the next hour. The official records and the recollections are messier than usual about when things occurred, or in what order. Many things happened simultaneously. Units arrived, twisted about for a while like dancers in a mosh pit, then spun away — generally leaving behind some men still fighting, so that companies, even squads, "represented" units as though the entire unit (regiment or battalion) were still active on the battlefield. When regimental and brigade commanders tried to piece together after-action reports, the results were confused and contradictory. If part of a regiment did one thing and the rest did something else, which was normally the case, the commanders did not know how to explain what had occurred — even assuming they grasped the details. The fight on Henry House Hill was a donnybrook between half-crazed volunteers. Reporters, trying to decipher the story, tended to use one of two techniques. They either asked high-ranking officers for big-picture clarification or sought out individuals for human interest anecdotes and pithy quotations. The Joint Committee tried to form a picture of the fighting on Henry House Hill and only added to the abundant confusion. Did Stuart's cavalrymen charge the Fire Zouaves before or after the Thirty-third Virginia fired? Where were Griffin's guns? Which group of trees did the Fourteenth Brooklyn enter? Historians, piecing these events together, agree on almost nothing.

Take the example of the Confederate cavalry charge against a bunch of Fire Zouaves. Some people have viewed this rather famous incident as not only colorful but as a critical event, helping to decide the battle. Others do not concur.

Stuart's Cavalrymen

Cavalry was not very useful in this kind of battle. Colonel Jeb Stuart had spent the morning in frustration. He had, he later calculated, 300 troopers with him, but probably he had fewer than that. He sent repeated messages reminding his commanders that he and his men were available for any sort of action. He even rode off and found Beauregard to reiterate his presence and interest in action. Beauregard said he would let Stuart know if his services were required. Then, in the afternoon, a courier galloped up to Stuart and announced that General Beauregard wanted him, now. Stuart's bugler played "Boots and Saddles," the call to horsemen to get moving, and Stuart's troopers climbed into their saddles and started off. They had not traveled far before they passed through a Confederate open-air hospital. The screaming patients, the blood, the stench, the flies proved too much, and many cavalrymen leaned from their saddles with projectile vomiting — and continued riding. They soon encountered Jackson, who told Stuart he was concerned about his flanks, so the cavalry commander split his men into two pieces, putting half along Jackson's right flank, near the Fifth Virginia. He and the rest crossed some fields behind the infantrymen until they were in a wooded area near the Sudley road.

Stuart moved his men forward until they saw some Yankee soldiers a few hundred yards off in a field. He sent two companies to lead the way, intending to follow with the rest. The forward troopers (thirty-three or thirty-five strong) called themselves the Loudon Company, since most of them came from that county. The second, the so-called Clarke Cavalry from Clarke County in the Valley, brought up the rear. As Stuart stopped to reorganize the rest of his men, who had grown confused in the woods, the two front companies started off, riding four abreast. Some of them gripped sabers, others held pistols or carbines. Their horses jumped a fence, and the cavalrymen saw before them a group of Yankee soldiers, the two reserve companies of Fire Zouaves that Heintzelman had assigned to stay here, numbering about a hundred men. Some red-shirted men of the First Minnesota were nearby — probably also acting as a reserve.

The Loudon Cavalry charged, the Clarke Cavalry in their wake — altogether, sixty or seventy horsemen. For cavalrymen, a charge like this was the stuff of legend, wielding their sabers left and right, shooting, breaking the enemy line. In reality, the Fire

Zouaves saw them coming, turned, and fired. All four of the first row of Virginia troopers fell or were wounded. The horse of their captain, R. Welby Carter (who would, later in the war, be cashiered for a variety of transgressions), stumbled, and he tumbled from the saddle. As he went down, he yelled to his men to keep riding. Some of them reached the Zouaves and began hacking and shooting their way through. Several Yankees reached up to yank them from their horses; others tried to spear them with bayonets as they passed. "Ellsworth! Remember Ellsworth!" some New Yorkers shouted. Remnants of the two cavalry companies did make it entirely through, then rode a bit farther, saw another formidable Yankee force past another fence, spun their horses about, and charged back, going the other way. During all this, Jeb Stuart remained back in the trees. Whether he actually observed any of the charge is unclear. He considered ordering the rest of his men forward, then thought better of it, and moved away. His report, amazingly, called the charge "handsomely done" and suggested it might have been responsible for the Confederate victory of an hour later, since he thought it possible the charge completely dispirited the *entire* Yankee army. He would write his wife Flora that he hoped his actions this day would lead to his promotion to brigadier general. One of the men who participated in the charge would always believe this cavalry action "saved the day." Confederate newspapers wrote glowing reports about it. Southerners who liked hearing tales of their own "gallantry" would romanticize this event and exaggerate its importance. The incident made them feel as though their Cause, somehow, represented a novel by Sir Walter Scott. They were certainly not "rebels," nor merely "Confederates," they were *Southrons*, members of a unique and genteel culture.

Unfortunately for legends, the charge probably had little or no effect on the organization of even the Fire Zouaves, or of its will, to say nothing of the rest of the Union army. Most of the Fire Zouave regiment was not in the vicinity. On the other hand, the losses for Stuart, especially the Loudon Cavalry, were high. Eight of the troopers from Loudon had been killed, nine others wounded — half that company's complement lost in a dubious action of no particular merit. (The losses among the Clarke company were not as severe.)[170]

Griffin's Battery

Another often debated incident on Henry House Hill involved Griffin's battery. Its movements and its positions there have always been unclear. Much of the confusion was due to Griffin's own vagueness. His after-action report was brief. He said that during the morning he moved his guns several times before Major Barry gave him McDowell's orders. (He actually left one of his six guns back behind the turnpike because it had developed a snag in its barrel.) He started toward the hill, got lost, started again, stopped, and rode back to Major Barry, saying that the Fire Zouaves that were supposed to support him were nowhere to be seen. Barry reassured him about the infantry support. Then, as Griffin recalled their conversation to the Committee, he told Barry, "I will go; but mark my words, they will not support us." He advanced his guns again.

Where on the hill did he place them? Lieutenant Adelbert Ames would win the Medal of Honor for his heroics at Bull Run. He was in command of part of Griffin's battery (what he called the "left section," though it may not have remained always on the left). During the morning Ames was badly wounded in the thigh and could not ride his horse. Griffin told him to get medical treatment, but Ames refused. Although he had just graduated from West Point a few weeks earlier, he was already twenty-five, having spent years working on a clipper ship. He certainly had pluck. With a tourniquet tied around his leg, when Griffin's battery started up the hill, he hopped onto one of its caissons, leaning against one of the gunners to cushion the shocks as the wagon jostled about. His right boot filled with blood that flowed down his leg. He grew dizzy, but his later recollections were specific: He said he *never* saw Ricketts's guns or even Mrs. Henry's house. He thought his section of guns remained somewhere on the other side of the Sudley road from the Henry house, and west of it. Perhaps he was confused because of his wound. Most historians agree that Griffin first placed his five guns north of Mrs. Henry's house — that is, on the turnpike side of it. Assuming this to be true, the house would have blocked it from Ricketts's view and may explain why Ricketts never saw Griffin's guns on the hill.

The battery was there about half an hour, dueling with rebel cannon. Then Griffin had an idea. He would split his battery in two. He told Lieutenant Charles Hazlett to stay here with three of the cannon; he intended to move the other two — a pair of howitzers — to the far side of Mrs. Henry's house, where he could apply pressure to the rebel artillery from a different angle. Splitting batteries was normal practice. To artillerymen, a single gun (along with its equipment and horses) was an independent unit, just as a ship is to sailors. For example, during the morning's battle the two guns connected to "Shanks" Evans's demibrigade worked quite separately from each other, often a mile apart. Generally, however, artillerymen thought in terms of two or three cannon working together; they referred to this as a *section*. In their eyes a normal battery was either two or three sections (four or six guns).

When Griffin moved his two howitzers, it is unclear what route he took, but he passed around the house and unlimbered them somewhere off to the right of Ricketts's battery. Here, his official report said, he got to fire only two rounds when he was suddenly charged by rebel infantrymen coming from the woods — whose guns "cut down" every one of his cannoneers and thirty or forty horses, "leaving the battery (which was without support except in name) perfectly helpless." In this statement Griffin was, at the very least, exaggerating. Several of his men had been killed during the morning's artillery dueling, and during the entire day his ninety-five-man battery lost only a total of seven men killed.

Six months after the battle, Griffin and Barry testified to the Committee about the moment when Griffin lost his two howitzers. Griffin's recollections were particularly vivid, and his words have often been quoted by historians, but his testimony was badly confused. When he spoke to the Committee, his emotions were still raw. He still seethed. During that battle his guns were lost. He blamed Barry. He blamed the Fire Zouaves. He refused to blame himself. He told the Committee his two guns were at this new position about five minutes, getting off those two shots. He recalled seeing then "a regiment of Confederates go over a fence" in front of his position. He said, "Some officer (I took it to be the colonel) stepped out in front of the regiment, between it and my battery, and commenced making a speech to them." Griffin recalled that he decided these were rebels and ordered his guns loaded with canister "and was just ready to fire on them, when Major Barry rode up to [him] and said, 'Captain, don't fire there; those are your battery support.'" Griffin told the Committee he replied to Barry, "They are Confederates; as certain as the world, they are Confederates." Major Barry repeated that he was confident they were Union troops, arriving to support the guns. Griffin, unconvinced, ordered his men "not to fire there." But he continued to stare at the unknown officer who finished speaking to his men, who then began marching them to the left a bit, then the right, until they were only about forty yards away. He said, "And then, [they] opened fire upon us, and that was the last of us." Griffin recalled he was so convinced they were the enemy that he used those minutes limbering up his guns. (He did not mention to the Committee that, by doing so, he had just placed his guns in their least defensible posture.) Despite his opinion that he himself was in no way responsible, he had not taken one simple precaution: If he really was confident in his opinion, during the few minutes that the strange, blue-clad troops marched around, Griffin might have kept his guns packed with canister and trained on them. If those infantrymen started aiming muskets in his direction, he could then have reasonably assumed them to be foes and opened fire.

Barry did not recall events this way. He said he had just ridden up to Griffin's new position after checking with Ricketts. He remembered "a very tall Virginia fence, eight or nine rails high," some distance away. Griffin called his attention to a bunch of soldiers, but, Barry told the Committee, all he could see were some bayonets on the other side of the fence. Barry, who gave his testimony a week before Griffin, was asked by the Committee if Griffin wanted to fire on these newcomers. "Not that I remember," Barry said carefully. "If he had chosen to do it, he was competent to do it." The Committee asked if he gave Griffin specific orders not to fire. "No sir; I gave no orders not to fire." One of these two artillery officers was, obviously, misremembering.

When and where did this assault take place? Who were the rebels who opened fire on the Union guns? Griffin said that the Fire Zouaves were near him when the attack came, but he did not mention either the marines or the First Minnesota, who were sitting next to the Zouaves. Before starting toward Henry House Hill, Barry had told Griffin he would be supported by the Fire Zouaves, but that regiment was actually situated behind *Ricketts's* guns, not Griffin's. Heintzelman was on horseback near the Fire Zouaves and did not remember, or at least never mentioned, seeing Griffin or his guns. In Heintzelman's private journal the focus of the rebel charge that he saw was Ricketts's battery, not Griffin's two guns. It is highly unlikely Heintzelman confused the two sets of artillery. For one thing, two cannon do not look like six. For another, he felt personally responsible for Ricketts's men because their battery was part of his division. He was well-acquainted with Ricketts and had spoken to him before placing the Fire Zouaves behind him. When the rebels started shooting Ricketts's men and horses, Heintzelman rode to the Fire Zouaves and pleaded with them to support Ricketts. No mention of Griffin. It is a puzzle. (One possible explanation is that Griffin, like so many others, had confused the red-shirted Minnesotans with the scarlet-bloused Fire Zouaves, who were in fact sitting rather far away, or even with the red-pantalooned Fourteenth Brooklyn who were about to arrive. Given Griffin's innate bias against the Fire Zouaves and the fact that many of the infantrymen around him now ran away, he may have jumped to an incorrect conclusion.)

Another matter confuses clear analysis. Captain William Woods Averell, Porter's staff officer, had escorted the marines here, positioning them to the left of the Fire Zouaves. He also later described "the assault." After placing the marines, he recalls riding up to Heintzelman and seeing Griffin right next to him. According to Averell, when Heintzelman saw the strange soldiers appear from the trees, the general asked Averell what his reaction was. Heintzelman later described the rebels in his unpublished diary as dressed in "citizen's clothes." At first he thought they were Union men, perhaps one of his own regiments sent by Franklin or Willcox. (Not far away, Colonel Willis Gorman, commanding the First Minnesota, was telling his men that those fellows, now about a hundred yards distant, were friends not enemies and not to be concerned.)

Averell scrutinized the newcomers and concluded they were rebels. Heintzelman still disagreed. According to Averell, the general unconsciously put his hand on Averell's arm, perhaps to emphasize his point. When the rebels opened fire, one of the bullets hit Heintzelman in the forearm, just below the elbow, breaking a bone. Averell said he remembered the moment clearly because Heintzelman still had his hand touching him when the shot came. (Six weeks later, after Heintzelman had recovered a little, he wrote in his diary that he received this wound just after the Fourteenth Brooklyn arrived, which would have been about fifteen minutes later. Maybe Averell's account was using dramatic license.) Heintzelman was the second of McDowell's four divisional commanders to be wounded in action, though, unlike General Hunter, he stayed and contributed for much of the rest of the battle.[171]

Colonel Orlando Willcox, one of Heintzelman's two brigade commanders, was also at the scene. The Fire Zouaves were part of his brigade, and he had ordered his other two regiments, the Thirty-eighth New York and the First Michigan, to come support the guns here. After giving that order, he decided to ride quickly and stay with the Fire Zouaves. (The Thirty-eighth marched up behind Hazlett's guns on the opposite side of Mrs. Henry's house and lay down to avoid being hit by the rebel artillery in the duel still going on. The First Michigan, at this moment, was somewhere along the path.) When the rebel infantry assault began, Willcox was on his horse, just next to Heintzelman. His own journal does not even mention the presence of Griffin at the time of the attack.

According to Heintzelman's diary and Willcox's journal, when the unknown rebels opened fire, it was Ricketts's guns nearest them that received the full shock. Willcox saw the confusion among Ricketts's gunners and ran over to help. He himself aimed one cannon because all but one of the gunners were down. Ricketts would later claim that the power of that blast carried away most of his horses and his gunners. Like Griffin, he, too, was exaggerating. He entered the day with fewer than a hundred men. During the entire battle, including the morning's artillery dueling, he lost only six men killed and seven wounded. (Seven others were captured, and two of his men were listed as missing and may have been killed.) But the blast at Ricketts's battery did have an important effect. Several horses were knocked down. This would make it difficult for Ricketts to maneuver.[172]

Griffin would sneer that the Fire Zouaves *immediately* disintegrated, leaving the impression that they all, or most of them, fled the battlefield as soon as the enemy infantry opened fire. Even if Griffin was correct in his recollection that it was the Fire Zouaves near him, their "flight" did not occur just like that. There was, of course, much confusion. The noise was terrific. Willcox would write in his journal: "Amid the din not an order could be heard. I shouted 'charge bayonet!' but although [I was] among the file closers, my voice could not reach to the files in front of me & the whole regiment was swept back as by a tornado." He and Heintzelman and Wadsworth worked to maintain some order among the Zouaves. Heintzelman kept screaming at them to charge. Some Zouaves were frozen by the unexpected assault, but many did move twenty yards or so toward the Virginians and fired into them. A curious thing then occurred: both sets of infantrymen, Northerners and Southerners, then pulled back from each other, leaving Heintzelman, somewhat baffled, in the middle.

What the Fire Zouaves had just done was typical of the behavior of so many volunteers this day. As individuals, these ex-firemen had previously proved themselves brave enough to enter burning buildings, but as soldiers, they had not yet been "hardened" to act like robots. After firing a single blast, they were not fleeing; they were only moving back a bit. It was a natural instinct. They knew it would take their clumsy fingers time to reload their guns, and since the enemy had fired first, the rebels had a head start in reloading. Emotionally, a normal person — still desiring to fight — would want to find someplace where he could safely reload. Professional soldiers had had one lesson drilled into their heads about this kind of situation: Do *not* step back. It was General Jackson's knowledge of this instinct that had led him to repeat his mantra for the previous two hours, that his troops must fire once, then immediately charge with their bayonets — that is, they must forget about reloading their guns. When the Fire Zouaves, who had pressed forward to fire at the enemy, now stepped back to reload, although this action involved only a momentary gesture, it had an echo effect. Many of their comrades, who had not yet fired, started to run. The marines, off to their left, who had also been sitting down when the Virginians opened fire, were just as confused. They sprang to their feet, and several of them shot in the direction of the rebels, but when the Zouaves started to melt, so did they. To their right, the Minnesotans reacted in exactly the same way. Some dropped into the grass and lay there a moment; others started running; still others took time to fire four or five rounds, then drifted away, while others remained to fight and were still there an hour later.

Like other units, the organizational cohesion of the Fire Zouaves, as a *regiment,* soon fell apart. Firemen, trained to assist injured comrades, automatically helped wounded friends from the field. Some lost all semblance of courage and skedaddled. But as individuals, many were still participating in the battle at the end of the day, hours later. Observers from other regiments like the Sixty-ninth New York and the First Wisconsin, who arrived quite a bit afterward, would describe numerous acts of courage on Henry House Hill performed by Fire Zouaves — including one incident when a bunch of them charged rebels who had grabbed the bright green flag of the Sixty-ninth, and wrested it back.

Willcox, the brigade commander, pasted together a company-sized unit, made up of men from several regiments, including some Fire Zouaves, and led it into the woods to attack rebels there. "We made three attacks," a Zouave wrote his father. Other Fire Zouaves mentioned that same number. What probably happened was that some individual companies with strong leadership stuck together and began acting semi-independently. As with many volunteer regiments, their regimental organization was not strong enough to hold together under pressure, but companies could. In a moment of chaos, one turned to one's friends. It was also true that a company officer, leading forty to eighty men could keep his eyes on them and generally be heard by them, unless the noise was deafening. But regimental leaders lacked this close connection. Losses among the Fire Zouaves were heavier than those among any other Union regiment, and most of the losses occurred in the first half hour.

Who Were the Mystery Confederates?

Experts have wrestled with the mystery of the "surprise" attack. For example, in her 1999 book on the battle, *"We Shall Meet Again,"* JoAnna M. McDonald said that the Thirty-third Virginia regiment fired at both Griffin and Ricketts at the same moment. John Hennessey, after being employed for an extended period at the Manassas National Battlefield Park and tramping about its area, thinking about the confusion, concluded—in his 1989 book, *The First Battle of Manassas*—that the Thirty-third Virginia attacked the Zouaves and the First Minnesota and scattered them, well *before* Griffin's two guns appeared. He believes that it was another second Confederate unit—Colonel "Extra Billy" Smith's little battalion—that opened fire on Griffin's guns, which arrived some minutes after the Thirty-third's attack. Hennessey decided that some members of the Thirty-third, still in the area, observing the effect of Smith's fire, rushed at Griffin's now undefended guns and captured them. Ethan Rafuse, in a 2002 book on the battle, *A Single Grand Victory,* offers a third interpretation. He accepts some of Hennessey's theory, but thinks members of the Thirty-third joined with Smith's little battalion in the second attack. Neither Hennessey nor Rafuse explain why Griffin never mentioned a fairly significant firefight still going on when he unlimbered his two guns.

Another scenario is plausible. There is no question both Ricketts's battery and Griffin's two guns were attacked and in the attacks suffered casualties—which in both of the commanders' minds, this early in the war, seemed devastating. Some of their men no doubt ran away, and many of their horses were probably killed or wounded, making the thought of moving the guns problematic. Perhaps, as Hennessey has suggested, there were indeed two similar infantry assaults, one on Griffin's two guns, the other against the right flank of Ricketts's battery. Since Griffin had positioned his guns so far away that Ricketts did not notice them, perhaps both the Thirty-third Virginia and Smith's "Forty-ninth" happened to emerge from the thicket at almost the same moment, separated by about one or two hundred yards, possibly hidden from each other by undulations in the terrain. They may well have fired at about the same time, without even noticing each other's presence.[173]

The truth about what happened is likely to remain a riddle, or at least a matter of conjecture and disagreement. We have the recollections of a number of participants, and part of the problem is that no two of them agree; it is always easier to write about history when the historian has the account of only one person or two. But one thing is clear: the ground around Ricketts's battery and Griffin's howitzers was about to grow more chaotic with each passing moment.

For the past hour and a half, there had been little concentrated fighting. When the mysterious rebel force came from the woods and started firing, it was as though two packs of cards, held frozen in a dealer's hands for a long time, suddenly shuffled together, very fast.

ENTROPY

During this whole battle we saw more dirt and trees than enemy!
— PRIVATE GUSTAV HOLLENBRECK, SECOND WISCONSIN

My observation was confined to my own company, and I am sure my vision was not particularly clear . . . I know we went in. My part of the line was driven back at first; then we went in again and fought it through, and found, when the smoke cleared and the roar of artillery died away and the rattle of musketry decreased into scattering shots, that we had won the field and were pursuing the enemy. This is not very historical but it's true.
— SERGEANT HENRY KYD DOUGLAS, STONEWALL BRIGADE[174]

The Stonewall Brigade

The Thirty-third Virginia, part of Jackson's brigade, was a stunted regiment, really only a battalion. It had purposely left behind in the Valley two full companies and hundreds of other men, too sick to make the trip. It likely lost more of its complement on this Sunday morning, marching back and forth. Estimates of its size that afternoon ran from 375 to 450. Most of these men had had only a few weeks training. Even their commander, Arthur Campbell Cummings, a lawyer from the Valley who had seen some action in Mexico, considered them raw and undisciplined. The uniforms of some of his troops did not match those of others, and a portion of the regiment may still have been dressed in civilian clothes.

When Jackson led his brigade to Henry House Hill, his first concern had been his cannon, but after he positioned them, he placed his infantrymen so that his strongest regiments were just behind the guns. He put the Thirty-third, the runt of the litter, off to the far left side, in a thicket. From that spot, Cummings's troops were on a rather severe slope and could see only the top of Mrs. Henry's house if they stood up and stepped beyond the tree line. Jackson ordered all five regiments to rest—and wait. He assumed the Yankees would come here, eventually.

Meanwhile, from across the turnpike, most of McDowell's two dozen cannon had begun concentrating their fire on the recently arrived Confederate batteries. The Yankee gunners aimed high to get their shots above the crest of the hill, which meant the shells often flew over the batteries and landed among Jackson's infantrymen. As we have noticed, being beneath such a bombardment can rattle a soldier's confidence. Jackson worked hard to calm his troops. Wait, he repeated over and over, wait. Wait until the enemy gets *very* close. Only thirty yards away. At that distance, Jackson knew, even his ill-trained infantrymen could probably hit their targets. Colonel Cummings of the Thirty-third heard Jackson's cautionary words and understood them, but he worried his men might crumble under the shelling before the enemy infantry got that close.

When Ricketts and Griffin arrived on the hill and started firing, the thicket hid the members of the Thirty-third. The Yankee guns focused on the Confederate artillery and, to a lesser degree, Jackson's three middle regiments—the Second, the Fourth, and the Twenty-seventh Virginia—which were mostly visible in the open. With the arrival of the Yankee artillery, Cummings knew that Yankee infantrymen would also be appearing shortly. Several times he walked up the slope, the mid-July grass reaching above his knees, and peered out. Finally, he saw them approaching not far away. He returned to his regiment, a "grim smile" on his face, and said, "Boys, they are coming now." One of his soldiers would always remember seeing the pointed tip of the Union flagstaff rising above the skyline, held high by its color-bearer; then the heads of the enemy; then their shoulders; then their guns.

Two things convinced Cummings to ignore Jackson's orders about waiting. One was that some soldiers, "dressed in red," according to his report, unexpectedly entered the brush on his regiment's left flank. A few of his men began firing at these mostly invisible foes. (These intruders may have been some red-shirted

Alabamians but more likely were skirmishers of the just-arrived, red-shirted First Minnesota.) At almost the same time, the Yankee artillery now turned and aimed some shots toward his now visible position, hitting the tree limbs overhead and the ground nearby (perhaps these were the two shots Griffin remembered firing). Cummings's men grew even more spooked, and he was sure they were emotionally cracking. He decided they were too raw to follow Jackson's schoolmaster's rigidity. Despite their soon-to-be-famous nickname, these men were not built of stone.

Cummings would later admit he had previously maintained a "reserved" demeanor with the men of his regiment. Now he was impatient to get them started and gave them no words of advice (meaning that the Thirty-third was probably not the one spotted by Griffin, who described its officer giving his men a rather lengthy address). Cummings brought his men out from the tree line and lined them up. He saw a bunch of infantrymen, not far from the Yankee guns (presumably, the Fire Zouaves) and felt a spasm of doubt about whether they were friends or foes, but when a few of his men took potshots at them and some of them replied, he ordered all his troops to fire, then charge.

Cummings was an amateur soldier, and he may or may not have correctly analyzed his regiment's mood. His men might well have been able to hold their position longer. Jackson's other regiments did. From a military viewpoint, his decision was almost suicidal. He was asking his few hundred men to run at the mouths of cannon and against at least one full Union regiment, perhaps several. He had no reason to assume the Yankee artillery would not fire at him (which, of course, it should have). At that distance, if the artillery used canister, the slaughter of his men would have been horrific. This could have led to a ripple effect. The sight of his losses might have frightened Jackson's other regiments and convinced them to turn and run, or at least have made them hesitant. The whole battle might have tipped right here, with no follow-up legends about "stone walls."

As it was, the charge of the Thirty-third was ragged. Although Cummings would remember it as "gallant," he also admitted his men did not move ahead "in a good order." In fact, they fired from near the woods line, reloaded, then rumbled forward like an armed mob, shooting at gunners and horses and nearby Yankee infantrymen. Like the Fire Zouaves, they tended to run back to reload after each shot, then dash forward again, and since each man reloaded at his own tempo, there was no way to make one single, all-out bayonet assault, despite Jackson's urgings. One member of the regiment would recall that much of their fire was aimed toward the sky and was unlikely to have hit many Yankees "unless they were nearer to heaven than they were generally located by our people."[175]

A few of Cummings's troops may have actually reached Griffin's guns and begun celebrating, or at least got close enough they could later claim to have "captured" the two cannon. If so, they certainly did not hold the guns long, because the Fourteenth Brooklyn arrived on the scene a few minutes later. Its colonel was down, so Heintzelman intended to lead them, but because of the wound he himself had just received in his arm, they were guided by McDowell's aide, the elderly lawyer Wadsworth, who lined them up, along with some nearby Fire Zouaves, grabbed their flag, and led them in a charge at the Thirty-third. The Virginians scattered. Their attack at the guns had actually disorganized them. Now their flight from Wadsworth and the Fourteenth Brooklyn dispersed them for the rest of the day. One of Jackson's five regiments, therefore, had just virtually disappeared. The importance of Cummings's charge at the guns was not its "success," but that it jiggled other Confederates into action.

Colonel James Walkinshaw Allen commanded the Second Virginia, the regiment against the right shoulder of Cummings's regiment. When the Thirty-third started to flee, two of its companies crashed into the left of Allen's regiment, disrupting the men there. At the same time, apparently, some Yankees unexpectedly began coming through the thicket (almost certainly Willcox's makeshift little battalion, made up Minnesotans and Fire Zouaves and assorted others—possibly still moving after startling Cummings's men earlier). Allen's after-action report said: "My left was turned. Not seeing the enemy in front, I directed that the three left companies be drawn back to meet them. This order was partially misunderstood by the center companies for a general direction to fall back, and all the line was turned. I at once gave the order to charge, but the thicket was so close and impenetrable only a part of the right wing...could be formed." So, Allen ordered everyone to move back. Many did not hear him. Then suddenly he himself—already blind in one eye—was completely taken out of action when a falling limb smacked his only good eye. Most of his Second then turned and raced off, shouting they had been "cut to pieces." In a matter of minutes, therefore, Jackson had just lost two regiments. (On Jackson's right flank, the Fifth Virginia had been somewhat battered by Keyes's attack an hour earlier. It was still together but had been damaged. Near it was a portion of Hampton's Legion that had refused to fall apart.)[176]

After this day, Stonewall Jackson wrote his wife: "Yesterday we fought a great battle and gained a great victory." He felt proud, though he hated to admit it. "Whilst great credit is due to other parts of our gallant army, God made my brigade more instrumental than any other in repulsing the main attack. This is for your information only—say nothing about it. Let others speak praise; not myself." His official report was more tempered. It noted that after Cummings's Thirty-third fell back, Jackson watched the Yankee infantry "advance." (What he was actually seeing was the move of the Fourteenth Brooklyn *beyond* Griffin's guns, toward Jackson's position—an intemperate move by the New Yorkers, who were overly excited by their easy "victory" over the Thirty-third.) Seeing the approaching Yankee infantry, in Jackson's mind, the time had come. He ordered his artillery to move out of the way, and they shuffled off, a few guns stopping on a crest to the rear, from which they continued to fire at the Yankees.

Jackson now had only two infantry regiments lined up directly behind him—the Fourth Virginia in the front and the Twenty-seventh in the back. These men—perhaps 1,200 of them—had waited here for two hours while Yankee artillerymen fired potshots at them. Although Jackson had been reassuring them—"All's well, all's well"—shot and shell had mangled some, killing others. One of their own caissons, near them, exploded with a mighty roar, startling them.

Some soldiers, as the saying went, tried to "get right with the Lord." One man, bleeding to death from a gash made by a piece of shell, said, "Oh, Lord, have mercy upon me, a poor sinner. Boys, pray for me." "I was scared," another man recalled. "I said all the prayers I knew, even to 'Now I lay me down to sleep,' and threw in some shorter catechism and scripture for good measure." One Virginian, overcome with terror, began to pray audibly. "Oh, Lord!" he muttered, "Have mercy upon me! Have mercy upon me!" A few feet away a comrade chirped up, "Me, too, Lord! Me, too, Lord!"

Jackson turned his horse and rode to his two regiments. One observer would remember that Jackson simply told the colonel of the front regiment, Colonel James F. Preston, to order his men to stand, but another man recalled Jackson shouting, "Up, Fourth and Twenty-seventh!" His injured hand—which would cause him considerable pain for months—was wrapped in a handkerchief. Using his other hand, he pulled his sword and pointed it toward the enemy. Someone recalled him saying, "We'll charge them now and drive them to Washington." Another claimed his words were, "Reserve your fire until they come within fifty yards, then fire and give them the bayonet; and, when you charge, yell like furies!" (Some Southerners would long cherish the silly legend that Stonewall had just created the "rebel yell." Actually, men on both sides had been screaming all day. As anyone who has ever taken a martial arts class knows, yelling increases the input of certain chemicals into the body and provides a momentary rush of strength and willpower. Primates entering conflict make noises, and so do dogs and cats and others. Zulu warriors shouted, "uSuthu." The later famous "rebel yell" went something like, "Who-ey! Who-ey!"—high-pitched and sounding much like the yell of British foxhunters. Yankee soldiers, charging into battle, often yawped a kind of long single-syllable sound: "Yaaaahhhh!" or rhythmically yelled, "Hoo-ray! Hoo-ray!")[177]

Despite dramatic imaginings, Jackson's two regiments did not now "charge" across an open field toward the Fourteenth Brooklyn and toward Ricketts's guns beyond. Various impediments stood between them and the enemy. These slowed them down and even interfered with what they could see. They had to pass through a patch of corn, the stalks as high as their bellies. They also had to go around numerous pines here and there along their route. (One lieutenant wrote a friend that he halted part-way, hid behind "a small tree and commenced firing.") And they had to cross a washed-out old farm road that angled across their path, on the far side of which stood a fence. The Fourth, leading the way, arrived at the fence. Colonel Preston, riding in front, looked around, saw a gate, and ordered his men to pass through it. This maneuver threw them off. They had had little training in such field exercises, and this one was like squeezing a pound of butter through a keyhole, hoping it would remold itself on the opposite side. The Twenty-seventh, on the other hand, ignored the gate, clambered over the fence, and as a result took the lead. The Yankee fire against them was ferocious. The Virginians leaned forward unconsciously, as if trudging into a gale or hail-stones. The Twenty-seventh, commanded by Lieutenant Colonel John Echols, crashed against some of the men of the Fourteenth Brooklyn. These Yankees fought briefly, then tumbled backward and off to the left. Echols's Twenty-seventh kept going, heading toward the guns.

Ricketts was down on the ground now, shot in the thigh, but most of his gunners were still active. They threw canister into their cannon and blasted toward Jackson's on-stumbling regiments. The Fourth, apparently still confused and unorganized, dropped to the ground and did not move for some minutes. The Twenty-seventh itself began to fall apart. In the confusion Echols's leadership vanished. Jackson's "charge" had come to a halt. Thousands of Yankee reinforcements were minutes away, jogging in this direction. The Yankee loss of Griffin's two howitzers — mostly the horses — might only turn out to be a minor blip if McDowell's regiments could hold Ricketts's battery.

At this crucial moment, one Virginian, a captain in the Twenty-seventh, refused to be cowed. His name was Thompson McAllister, a well-to-do forty-nine-year-old from the Valley. He heard someone shout that they ought to retreat. "Never do," he shouted, "never do — if you can't stand up, lie down, but keep on shooting." Sometimes a single individual can make a difference. This seems to have been one of those occasions. Perhaps if he had not taken the actions he did, someone else would have — maybe. Three months earlier, a week after Fort Sumter fell, McAllister had raised a company of local boys — including his own eighteen-year-old son, William — and offered their services to Governor Letcher. He knew little about military matters. His money came from a flour mill, from planting, from railroads. On this day, his brother was a lieutenant colonel of a New Jersey regiment, part of Runyon's division that was just now being ordered by a courier from McDowell to start toward Centreville. McAllister had dark hair and light blue eyes. He wore a stubby beard under his chin and kept his upper lip clean shaven. He looked much like an Amish farmer, misplaced on a battlefield. His little company, which called themselves "Alleghany Roughs," had been told this day that it was their responsibility to carry the regimental flag, and so they had been in the lead. Now, if they retreated, the entire regiment might do so.

When both of Jackson's two charging Virginia regiments stopped, McAllister's company, like others around it, began to splinter. Some men died; others pulled back instinctively from the terrible Yankee fire. Others wandered off to the side in a heedless desire to fight, even on their own. A few of the wounded retreated, helped by friends. Those remaining with Captain McAllister lay on the ground, awaiting his orders. Without any military training, he had no notion what he should do. He wandered about, searching unsuccessfully for the regiment's field officers, his superiors, but could find no one to tell him what he ought to be doing. He did espy the regiment's acting adjutant and asked his advice. The adjutant told him that all he knew was that he had heard General Jackson say they were supposed to charge the enemy. That was good enough for McAllister. He was not a subtle man. He stood to his feet, leaped in front of the remnant of his company, his sword in his hand, and shouted, "Get up, boys, get up! Come on, come on, forward, charge them, that's the order."

His decimated company rose to their feet, surrounding the flag of the Twenty-seventh. There were probably only about twenty of these men. Around them troops of other companies stood. They stared toward the Yankee cannon. Men of the Fourth came forward now and joined them. So did a hundred-man vestige of the Second that had refused to run away. One of Jackson's soldiers would recall that the Yankee guns, not far off, looked "big as flour barrels." But the Virginians started trotting, the troops in the front racing so fast McAllister had to speed up to keep pace with them, making sure to keep on their right, as a leader, he thought, was supposed to do. This middle-aged planter, his son by his side, ran directly at Ricketts's cannon. Then, amazingly, all of a sudden, they were at the mouths of the guns—and past them. Thereafter followed a hand-to-hand battle. In a few minutes the guns belonged—for the moment—to the Stonewall Brigade. "It was the happiest day of my life," a member of the Twenty-seventh wrote his wife, "our wedding day not excepted." (A few weeks later, Colonel Tom McAllister, his health sapped by sickness, left Stonewall Jackson's army and returned home to the Valley. He would never fight again.)[178]

But the story of the six guns of Ricketts's battery and Griffin's two howitzers was not over. They drew men as flames draw moths. Each side tried desperately to grab and hold them—as much, it seems, for their symbolic value of "victory" as for their potential power, the two armies acting like crazed scrums grasping at a rugby ball.

Even though Jackson's Virginians held Ricketts's cannon, the Fourteenth Brooklyn still controlled the area near Griffin's howitzers. Then out of the thickets roared another wave of Confederates: the just-arrived Sixth North Carolina and the seven companies of the Second Mississippi—almost 1,000 men. They fired into the side of the unsuspecting New Yorkers, who raced back toward the Sudley road. A few minutes, or seconds, later the Confederates were celebrating their second "capture" of Griffin's guns when more Yankees arrived and opened fire. Charles Fisher, the colonel of the Sixth North Carolina was instantly killed, and his regiment and the Second Mississippi dissolved.

Madness on Henry House Hill

The southeast quadrant—dominated by Henry House Hill—began to resemble a butcher shop. Bodies lay everywhere. Dehydrated soldiers on both sides reeled about in search of water. The many hours of heat had taken their toll. Each tiny rivulet, especially Young's Branch, attracted gasping men. Wounded soldiers added their blood to the filthy waters, and one poor fellow died sipping from a stream, his head slumped entirely under the water.

Union troops, taking breathers, tended to retreat to the relative safety of the roads. Both the Warrenton pike and the Sudley road went through shallow troughs in the landscape, which now served something like World War I trenches. Wounded and dying and frightened soldiers found their way to the ditches along the roads' edges. Union troops, approaching the fighting, could hear the sounds of battle ahead—drums beating and bugles blaring orders to some unit or other, men shouting, the rattle of heavy musketry. Arriving soldiers also had to march past the forms lying within the ditches. The new arrivals realized these mounds of flesh—alive and dead—represented the detritus of regiments that had preceded them. Some arrivals were completely unmanned by such shocking sights and sounds. When ordered into that bedlam, they found themselves unable to find the courage. Others had the opposite reaction. The expectation of danger and the ghastly sights of the outdoor hospitals they had passed had made them uneasy, but when ordered to fire at the enemy, they felt a curious relief. Afterward many men wrote in wonderment about a strange calmness that flowed through them as they actually entered battle. One Union soldier recalled being terrified as he marched up the Sudley road. "I might be killed," he thought to himself, "or, what seemed worse even, badly wounded, and left on the field to be trampled by horses or crushed by battery caissons or gun carriages." He wished he were somewhere else. He would have run away, "if it hadn't been for fear of being called a coward." But once in battle: "I seemed to forget about myself entirely." Some men even felt a kind of bliss. "Battle fever," old soldiers sometimes called it.

Things on the hill, already confused, grew more turbulent. The accounts of soldiers who were there seldom agree on specific details. Not on the time or on which units they faced. They speak about "entering the trees" or "attacking the guns" but do not, or cannot, specify which ones. They say "we" loosely—and it is often unclear who they mean—a few men, an entire regiment, or their entire army. In his journal, Orlando Willcox recalled the "First Michigan" charging, then retreating, yet he also noted that its "right wing" did something else entirely, so what did "it" really do? We know that the First Minnesota and the Thirty-third Virginia fell apart early, but the accounts assure us that "some" individuals in both regiments actively participated in charges well afterward. When "Extra Billy" Smith's men entered the fray, how many men did he have? Two hours earlier, near Bull Run, he had had about 200, but since several assorted units had tagged along with him, he thought he might now command 450—though he certainly did not take the trouble to count them. Besides, before actually joining the fray, most of his additions were temporary and were soon turned over to someone else. When Smith, therefore, attacked the Yankees, did he have 200? Or maybe fewer, because of the natural tendency of units to sprinkle stragglers behind? Or perhaps more, since men of other—defeated—units, who refused to quit, had glued themselves to his battalion? We know both Bartow and Bee lost their lives on the hill, leading their men. But where? When? Markers now on the Manassas National Battlefield Park indicate spots where both men allegedly fell, and maybe these stones are situated near the right places—but one can wonder. History, it has been correctly said, is often only agreed-upon myths.

We do know there was a rich brew of madness on Henry House Hill. As fresh Federal units arrived, usually marching from the Sudley road toward the guns, the first thing they often saw streaming toward them from the smoky battlefield were bunches of strange men, mouths smeared with gunpowder, eyes red from smoke, seemingly deranged. Often, the arriving newcomers, thinking these must be rebels, fired into them. Many troops on both sides were killed this day by friendly fire. Gray uniforms? Blue? Zouave? Completely dust-covered? By this time both armies' uniforms looked quite the same.

The scene had a bizarre quality. Two comrades were side by side firing. One was shot, and his gun flew into the air and knocked his companion unconscious. Another soldier was sent reeling when a comrade's arm, ripped off by cannon fire, smacked into him. And there was the fellow who was hit on the eyebrow by a spent bullet and was positive he had just died, shouting that fact repeatedly, "O Lordy! I am killed! I am killed! O Lordy, I am dead." Over and over, he screamed these words, quite annoying those around him. And there was the soldier who was shot on the side of his neck, and the bullet came out his open mouth — and he kept fighting. And the man who was loading his rifle when the infantryman behind him was killed and fell forward, his bayonet lancing down and pinning the front man's foot to the Virginia soil. And there are at least a hundred eyewitness accounts, from both sides, asserting positively that the enemy used an underhanded ruse, waving a stolen flag to indicate they were friends, then suddenly opening fire — though almost certainly such tales were mistaken. In the dead-calm air of that afternoon, the two flags looked far too much alike. (The Confederacy would soon consider alternative banners.)

One can compare the actions on Henry House Hill of two Massachusetts regiments. When ordered into the fight, the men of the Fifth Massachusetts advanced in neat companies, one company at a time. Each company fired a single round, then stepped aside to allow the next company up. This did not provide much firepower, but it looked quite crisp. Not far away, the troops of the Eleventh Massachusetts stayed all bunched together and rose as one to fire, the men at the back often blasting those in front. Yet the Fifth ran away when its colonel — its only field officer — was wounded, and the troops of the Eleventh recaptured Ricketts's guns from Jackson's men, so that, once again, McDowell's army controlled the guns.[179]

During the weeks after the battle, the Union army analyzed what had gone wrong and concluded that one critical problem was the officers. Too many of the volunteer regiments were led by men ill-equipped to handle the challenges of battle. With this in mind, the Federal army would become more rigorous about examining volunteer officers. This decision was reasonable. But it is hard to fault most of those leading troops on Henry House Hill. McDowell arrived at the hill too late to do much more than provide encouragement. But General Heintzelman, whose division did much of the fighting, was active and forceful, even after being wounded. His two brigade commanders, Franklin and Willcox, proved to be brave and solid soldiers. In fact for a while Willcox seemed everywhere. McDowell's aide Wadsworth was a virtual whirlwind, leading and encouraging regiment after regiment. Thirteen Union regiments reached the hill. About half their commanders did well. At the regimental level, some field officers and many company captains acted timid or became confused, but this was equally true of Confederates at those command levels. Almost half the Union colonels who came to the hill were either wounded or killed, often in the act of rallying their men.

In terms of leadership the real problem lay in inexperience. No one represented that weakness more than William Tecumseh Sherman. Some Civil War historians have been somewhat disdainful of Sherman's military abilities, but an argument can be made that he was the best general in the war—accomplishing more with fewer losses than any other general on either side, and a few years after the war he would be given command of the entire United States army and would perform that assignment with distinction. At the very least, Sherman was a courageous and normally strong leader. At Bull Run he personally led his four regiments to the top of Henry House Hill. When the retreat began, he did more than any high-ranking officer to hold McDowell's army together until it got back across the stream. Despite all this, his memoirs provide a revealing tidbit. A few weeks after the battle, deciding that the war, as he had feared, would be both long and hard, he started putting his brigade through "a system of drills, embracing the evolutions of the line, all of which was new to [him], and [he] had to learn the tactics from books." It is fascinating that this West Point graduate, who had spent years in the army, only *after* Bull Run turned to manuals to learn "the evolutions of the line."

When Heintzelman first ordered Franklin and Willcox to bring their commands to the hill, those two brigades, through no fault of their commanders, were already fragmented because of assignments from above, so it would be unfair to censure either officer because his command arrived piecemeal. But Sherman's brigade was still together when he set out with it toward Mrs.

Henry's place. On the way he ordered one regiment, the Thirteenth New York, to head up the slope to the left of the battered house. The Thirteenth approached the left side of Ricketts's guns and banged into Hampton's Legion, a part of which, amazingly, was still actively fighting. The New Yorkers stopped, lay in the high grass, and for almost half an hour kept up a sporadic but rather ineffective fire. Meanwhile, Sherman was taking his other three regiments toward the opposite side of the house. When he had them lined up, back to back on the Sudley road, one at a time he sent them in.

First came the Second Wisconsin, led part of the way by the ever present Wadsworth. They drew themselves into ragged lines and climbed the three-foot bank from the road. "The woods in front of us was full of men firing on us," one of them would write home. "The smoke prevented us from seeing the length of our line and the noise from hearing commands even if any were given." They started their "charge" by a kind of "mutual consent." Private Elisha R. Reed recalled the pandemonium. "Guns were discharged so close to my face that my mouth was several times filled with smoke." After his second shot, he was stooping over to reload when he was shot in the back. "My wound was of course from our own men on the hillside below me." The commanders of the Second Wisconsin finally ordered a retreat back to the road, but many of the troops failed to hear it and stayed and fought. Those who did go back were fired into by nervous members of Sherman's Sixty-ninth New York, still waiting in the ditch.

In his report Sherman described what happened next: "By this time the New York Seventy-ninth had closed up, and in like manner it was ordered to cross the brow of the hill and drive the enemy from cover." The Seventy-ninth was nicknamed the "Highlanders," since they had, before the war, been a militia group made up mostly of men of Scottish descent. They had even sported kilts for a while. But the war had changed their character. To fill their ranks they had had to enroll many non-Scots, and they may now have had more men of Irish background than Scottish. Their colonel, James Cameron, however, was not only of solid Scottish heritage but was also brother of the secretary of war. They were the second of Sherman's brigade to charge from the road toward the foe, led by Colonel Cameron. They were thrown back and made a second charge. Then a third. Wade Hampton of South Carolina, watching from a distance, was heard to mutter, "Isn't it terrible to see that brave officer trying to lead his men forward, and they won't follow him." Sherman's report says: "For a short time the contest was severe. They rallied several times under fire, but finally broke." Colonel Cameron was killed just a few paces from the house.

Now it was the turn of Sherman's last regiment, the Sixty-ninth, the determinedly Irish unit carrying their bright green flag, commanded by Colonel Michael Corcoran. It happened to be joined by Willcox's Thirty-eighth New York that had finally left its perch on the grassy slope north of the house and had swung around to this side. These two Union regiments worked, more or less, side by side. Their pressure pushed back Jackson's last regiment, the Fifth Virginia and, at last, the amazingly doughty warriors of Hampton's Legion. Once again, Ricketts's guns were in Federal hands—for the third time that afternoon. Like their predecessors on both sides, the new troops celebrated. But their glee was short-lived.

Another wave of Confederates—Eppa Hunton's Eighth Virginia and Robert Withers's Eighteenth Virginia—came through the woods and ran at the guns. Both of these Confederate regiments, part of Cocke's brigade, had been coming in this direction for some time. When Joe Johnston had first arrived at Portici, he had spoken to Cocke about sending his whole brigade toward Henry House Hill, but Cocke had pointed out his men were facing at least one Yankee brigade across Bull Run (Schenck's). When it finally grew obvious those Yankees had no intention of driving across the stream, Johnston or Beauregard ordered Cocke to start forwarding some of his regiments toward the fighting. Hunton's and Withers's men, therefore, started trotting toward the sounds of battle. When they came onto the scene, the fighting in front of them was so intense their officers ordered them to lie down for a moment—apparently to permit the commanders to get their bearings, while letting the men who had double-quicked to this spot catch their breath. (Two of the enlisted men, who had only just arrived at their regiment this morning and had therefore had zero training, must have been pleased.)

The Virginians lay themselves flat inside a depression as musket balls flew above their heads. One fellow was curious and decided to take a look. He raised his head and was instantly killed. Finally the men were told to stand and "charge bayonet." "We did so," one recalled, "and our loud huzzas and rushing charge decided the day." (In their wake another of Cocke's Virginia regiments, the Twenty-eighth — which had actually begun the day on the Centreville side of Bull Run — crashed through the woods and encountered Willcox's jerry-built battalion and threw its men all the way back to the Sudley road, in the process wounding and capturing Willcox himself.)

"The firing was very severe," Sherman reported, "and the roar of cannon, muskets, and rifles incessant." The Thirty-eighth New York withdrew to the Sudley road. The Sixty-ninth, Sherman said, fell back "in disorder" — though, again, as with almost all the other regiments, many stayed on the hill and continued to fight for a while. Sherman did not care much for the Irishmen of the Sixty-ninth — for most of his brigade, in fact. Many of his men felt the same about him.

As a brigade leader, Sherman had just failed in this, his first battle. His brigade, he admitted, had been "repulsed regiment by regiment." Sending in one regiment by itself, followed later by another, was wrong. It would be like members of a mob, facing a famous karate master, coming toward him one at a time. Sherman considered his men far too green and undisciplined, but he recognized their failure to hold the hill was as much his fault as theirs. He had never been in a battle. Its tumult — its "havoc," to use his word — awed him. "Then for the first time I saw the carnage of battle, men lying in every conceivable shape, and mangled in a horrible way." The sight of dead and dying horses especially moved him.[180]

In a few more minutes, the last remnants of the Union regiments pulled back from Ricketts's guns. It was for the final time. The Confederates now held them — and the hill. Some Confederates even turned one or more guns on the retreating Yankees and fired a round or two. The Union army had lost the battle for Henry House Hill.

A private in the Sixth North Carolina wanted to tell his father what the battle had been like, but he had problems finding the proper words for the images. "I have turned threw that old book of yours," he said, "and looked at the pictures and read a little about war, but I did not no anything about it." He could only say what veterans often feel when trying to relate to civilians, "You have no idea how it was."

Which Confederate or Confederates won the battle for Henry House Hill? In truth, the victor's wreath did not belong to a single leader. The victory was due to the efforts of thousands of soldiers—and more than a dozen high-ranking officers. Southerners would eventually conclude it was Stonewall Jackson's resolve that turned the tide—a convenient answer to those who demanded heroes. Beauregard did not see it that way. During the war he would participate in a number of battles, large and small—Shiloh being the most famous. But when the Civil War was over, he retained a special feeling about this one battle, a sense that it was his, that he and his own genius won it. Beauregard did admit that Jackson performed in a "veteran-like and unwavering" way. In one of Beauregard's accounts, the Creole said that at a critical stage, he "ordered a charge of the entire line of battle, including the reserves, which at this crisis [he himself] led into action. The movement was made with such keeping and dash that the whole plateau was soon swept clear of the enemy." Other men said he sang out, about the time the Sixty-ninth New York fled from the guns, "The day is ours! The day is ours!" Sometime after that, he would recall, "I went to the Lewis house, and, the battle being ended, turned over the command [*sic*] to General Johnston"—implying he personally had been in command before that, a fact Johnston would have denied.[181]

The fight for the guns lasted almost two hours and sucked in between 12,000 and 15,000 men. Almost 500 Americans died near the house, including Judith Henry herself. To put this in perspective, during this single *phase* of the Battle of Bull Run, more Americans lost than lives than perhaps in any previous battle in American history. Far more died on that hill than in the whole Spanish-American War. About as many American soldiers were killed there as perished during the first day's fighting on Omaha Beach on D day, 1944.

THE END OF THE DAY

It was the turn of the tide.
—SERGEANT ABNER R. SMALL, THIRD MAINE

We ganed the battle and driven the damyanke back.
—PRIVATE JOHN L. HANEY, THIRD TENNESSEE[182]

McDowell's Situation

But the battle was not over. McDowell's situation was still far from hopeless. The permanent loss of the cannon on Henry House Hill was a dramatic moment but by itself did not guarantee a Confederate victory. To be sure, McDowell's army had been repulsed from holding a specific bloody piece of ground, but he still had sixteen guns on this side of Bull Run and another thirty-two on the far side. His losses in killed and wounded were severe, but the rebels had lost about as many. Many of his regiments had become scrambled in the fighting, and perhaps six had lost so much cohesion their officers could no longer keep them together. The same, however, could be said of the Confederate army, and it is possible its organization was more disrupted. McDowell could have no idea how many "fresh" regiments the Confederates yet had available, but he knew his army was still potentially strong. On the other side of Bull Run, he had two full divisions — Miles's and Runyon's. Runyon could not arrive at Centreville for some hours, some of his troops until the next morning, but their appearance would mean an additional 5,000 troops. Scott had dozens of regiments he could forward to Centreville. Tyler's division — that is, Schenck and Keyes — could still provide plenty of muscle, and even Sherman had been able to hold most of his brigade together and should be able to fight some if it came to it. The abatis by the bridge was almost gone now, so Schenck could come across, followed by dozens of cannon, by supplies and provisions — and, perhaps, by one or more of Miles's three brigades. Burnside's brigade had recovered somewhat from the morning's fracas. McDowell also had Sykes's rock-solid battalion of regulars. But of all the potential reinforcements, the first to arrive on the scene was O. O. Howard's brigade.

Earlier, after McDowell had ordered Howard to hurry from where he had been waiting near the blacksmith shop, the men of the brigade had trotted through the swelter toward Sudley Ford, splashing across there just before the fighting on Henry House Hill reached its crescendo, two miles away. When McDowell learned of their presence at Sudley, since the battle on the Hill was still in an uncertain stage, he sent an order to Howard to move west of the Sudley road into the northwest quadrant near the Dogan farm, then swing south from there, passing over the turnpike into the southwest quadrant. Thus far there had been little fighting in that sector. A man named Benjamin Chinn owned a farm there whose position dominated this quadrant, sitting near the top of a ridge across the road from Mrs. Henry's place. McDowell thought that Howard should push his men up the spine of that ridge, putting them on the left flank of the Confederate line. From there, Howard could roll up the rebel side, as McDowell's other brigades pounded at the Confederate solar plexus. When McDowell sent this order, it made sense. His army had just stymied a rebel counterattack on Henry House Hill. It seemed the moment for an all-out assault.

McDowell apparently then ordered his cavalry to join the action, because some of them did start toward the fray. We know that one cavalry detachment collided with some of Stuart's men and captured a few. Custer may have been with this group. He has left us a delightful description of moving into action. Since

Custer was a West Point graduate, one of his fellow cavalry officers, a mere volunteer, assumed Custer would know what to do and aped his every movement. But Custer himself, as he later admitted, had never "ridden at anything more dangerous or terrible than a three-foot hurdle," so as they trotted into battle he was unsure whether he should use his pistol or his sword. He knew that cavalry charges in paintings showed men wielding sabers, so he reached for his. Then he thought about the fact that his pistol was not only a repeater, but it could also allow him to remain farther from the foe, which seemed quite sensible, so he sheathed his sword and pulled his gun. Then he reconsidered, deciding it was likely he would be unable to aim the pistol properly, sitting on a jiggling saddle, so he shoved the gun back into its holster and retook his saber. Each time, his companion, watching him, mirrored his wise choices. Custer's recollections of the next few minutes are less clear. We know his group of cavalrymen approached their objective, wherever it was, came under fire — and immediately crumbled. Governor Sprague, the scrawny and unprepossessing civilian, was there and tried to rally them, but the cavalrymen became demoralized and retreated. When? Where? Unknown.[183]

The Fight for Chinn Ridge, Howard's Position

Colonel Howard hurried his infantryman forward, but his brigade was leaking troops like a rusty pail. His men were from Vermont and Maine. It sometimes gets warm in northern New England, for a few hours now and then, but it is seldom sultry — hot and humid — day after day. Howard's men had risen early that morning like everyone else. They had started off, expecting to fight, then McDowell had told them to wait by the turnpike. They had sat around, baking in the midday heat, waiting. When the call had come, they pushed hard to reach Bull Run. This drained their energies more. The brigade probably lost almost half its manpower in this hurried march. And the sight of the hospital at the Sudley church — "the dead and the dying limp on the ground" — mesmerized them. They lost another sizeable chunk when they virtually sprinted the last mile to get into position,

Alpena County Library
Phone: (989)356- 6188
www.alpenalibrary.org

Date due: 12/4/2015,23:59
Title: Dance of the bones : a Beaumont and
 Walker novel

Date due: 12/4/2015,23:59
Title: Incredible victory [large print]

Date due: 12/4/2015,23:59
Title: California - Eyewitness Travel Guid
e

Date due: 12/4/2015,23:59
Title: Donnybrook : the Battle of Bull Run
, 1861

***
***
****
****
****

passing broken regiments which drifted past them in the opposite direction. Some of their own stragglers rested along the way, pulled themselves together, and rejoined their companies. "I set myself down to rest with some of the boys," a private from Maine wrote home, "for with the march the nigh[t] before I was intirely existed [exhausted], so that I could do nothing if I was there. We set there about half an hour to we recovered sronth [strength] enoff to walk. Then we sarted for the battlefield."

In theory Howard's brigade of four regiments numbered about 2,500 men. But by the time he approached the enemy, according to his own after-action report, he had lost half his manpower. This estimate was still wide of the mark; he had lost far more than that. An enlisted man from Maine would write home that his company entered battle with only fifteen men, and he estimated his entire regiment at under two hundred. A lieutenant told his father his company consisted of eight troops. And the men Howard did have were emotionally and physically drained, like distance runners at the end of a race.

Moreover, in the time since he had first been ordered to rush toward this spot, the situation had changed, drastically. McDowell's notion had involved Howard *supporting* the main attack atop Henry House Hill, but Howard now found himself in a position where his enfeebled men were the only coherent assault force. Yet he felt he had no choice. He placed two of his regiments in the lead — the Second Vermont and the Fourth Maine — backed up by the other two Maine regiments, and marched them ahead. They crossed the pike and the ravine made by Young's Branch, then moved up the slope of the ridge. So far, they were unopposed. The front two regiments pressed through a deep thicket and came to the top of the hill.

Had McDowell had a larger staff, he might still have been able to juggle an attack by three relatively fresh brigades. He could have told Howard to move more slowly to prevent his men from becoming debilitated. He could have used the time to bring Schenck across the bridge and Keyes back into the scene. These, along with the cannon he still had available, might have enabled McDowell to try a combined assault. Exactly what would have happened is unknowable. Conceivably, the eventual Union defeat might have been worse, because even more regiments could have been whipped. On the other hand, Johnston's and Beauregard's soldiers at this time were in no better shape than McDowell's. They, too, had done either a lot of marching or much fighting, or both. They were just as tired, just as thirsty. Their giddiness at holding Henry House Hill was similar to what McDowell's men had felt a few hours earlier when they had taken Matthews Hill. Their momentary euphoria could have dissipated had they suffered a powerful assault.

But any planning that would require crisp Union organization was impossible. At this moment Joe Johnston's energy and staff work proved superior to Irvin McDowell's. Neither Keyes's brigade nor Schenck's came to the fore. The potential "success" of the Union army lay in the shaky hands of Howard's pitiful "brigade."[184]

The Fight for Chinn Ridge, the Confederate Position

Coming toward Howard's men was a massive force of Confederates, pieced together — by chance, by proximity, and by the imagination of Joe Johnston. Confederate units had been moving in this general direction all day, but Johnston's recognition that this spot was, de facto, going to be the *battlefield* had accelerated things. With the exception of two and a half brigades to hold the nexus of Mitchell's and McLean's Fords, all Confederates were on the march by early afternoon. But they, of course, were not coming as a single mass. They had started at different times, from widely separated positions, using different roads. Ewell's and Holmes's brigades were still miles away and could not expect to arrive until after five o'clock. But the rest, one by one, arrived at Portici. Johnston pointed them toward the fighting and urged them to press ahead. These troops — untested in battle and almost as worn-out as Howard's men — found themselves passing addled comrades who told them the battle had already been lost. "We are whipped!" the newcomers heard over and over. "We are whipped!" These naysayers were the residue of units beaten earlier in the day. The officers of the marching units urged their men not to listen to these sirens of defeat but to hurry on.

Two regiments from Bonham's brigade led the way for this next wave: the Second and the Eighth South Carolina, led by Colonel Joseph Kershaw (the officer who had revealed his energy and military acumen four days earlier in the withdrawal from Fairfax Court House). Once he had received his instructions from General Johnston, Kershaw and his demibrigade skirted along the southern slope of Henry House Hill. On the way they brushed against some Yankee soldiers in the woods, who had wandered south from the battle. Several of these men were Fire Zouaves who had blithely stopped to pocket some mementos of the fighting to carry home with them; others included a remnant of the Fourteenth Brooklyn. When Kershaw saw this latter bunch, he shouted, "There they are, those damned breeches fellows! Down with them, boys!" A brief firefight scattered the Yankees, and Kershaw kept moving westward until he reached the Sudley road, about half a mile south of Mrs. Henry's house. Since Kershaw clearly represented an organized Confederate force, sprinkles of other units joined him — including the last tiny nucleus of the Hampton Legion, led by the indefatigable James Conner. Conner's little band of South Carolinians had just participated in the final victorious charge against Ricketts's guns. Unsatisfied with that success, while other Confederates stopped to celebrate, Conner re-formed his men and moved with them until he joined Kershaw.

Kershaw brought his expanding force into line, west of the Sudley road, not far from Benjamin Chinn's house. As he was getting them into position, he spotted a large body of Yankees, appearing on the ridge in front of him (Howard's regiments). Most of Kershaw's men were armed with smoothbores that could not reach the enemy, and the Yankees had rifles that started to spatter his men. A member of the Second South Carolina felt himself shot near the groin and realized his life's blood was coursing down his leg from the severed artery. He stumbled off to die, then discovered that the warm liquid was tepid water from his canteen. He vowed not to fight anymore — and didn't. He walked

off, left the battlefield, and settled down far from all other battlefields for the rest of his life. Another soldier, shot in the chest, fell
roughly to the ground. A comrade opened his jacket to see if
there was anything that could be done for him and discovered a
round flattened piece of lead that had been greatly slowed first by
some other object—perhaps a fence rail—before striking the soldier. But when the quite lively fellow, apparently a true man of
steel, was shown the mangled ball, he concluded, "It got mashed
when it hit me."[185]

Kershaw told his infantrymen to lie down, and he ordered
Captain Delaware Kemper, the artillery officer with him, to open
fire with his cannon. A few moments later, Kershaw was joined
by a whole brigade of new arrivals, who had come all the way
here from the Valley.

On Saturday, when Joe Johnston had boarded the train at the
Piedmont station, he had turned matters there over to Brigadier
General Edmund Kirby Smith. After many long hours at the
depot, Smith himself left Piedmont, accompanied by several regiments. They had arrived at Manassas Junction at noon on Sunday—about the time McDowell was declaring the Union victory.
As their train pulled toward the station, the men in the boxcars, the
doors open for ventilation, could easily hear the din of battle. While
they scrambled stiffly down from the cars, Smith mounted his horse
and rode off for orders. He stopped at Beauregard's headquarters,
not far away, and was told by Jordan to go directly to Portici.

The new arrivals were still putting their knapsacks into piles
when Smith rushed back. "This is the signal, men," he yelled, banging the back of his hand against the bill of his cap. "The watchword
is 'Sumter.'" His men cheered. They had the secret hand gesture
and the password; success could not be far away. He left one of his
four regiments behind at Beauregard's fortification. (Jordan had
probably told him there was some concern McDowell was launching an attack at this very moment across one of the lower fords and
swinging toward the station.) The rest of Smith's brigade started
into motion. At first they marched at a normal pace, then picked up
their speed, quick-stepping a while. But already weary from their
train ride, the afternoon heat greatly affected them. And they faced

another problem. "The dust was very deep in the road," one soldier wrote home, "and rendered it a perfect impossibility to see the man before you, so that we had to be guided by the shouts of the front man alone." They also passed wounded Confederates and discouraged stragglers who assured them they were too late, their side had already been "cut to pieces" and was "catching hell." They slogged on. The march became torture.

Smith, riding ahead, arrived at Portici about 3:30, just after Kershaw departed. Johnston pointed Smith in the same direction and told him to hurry. The battle on Henry House Hill was reaching a critical stage, Johnston said. Chase Whiting, a member of Johnston's staff, privately admitted to Kirby Smith that things looked so gloomy at this moment that Johnston's staff was drawing up plans for a retreat, just in case. Smith urged his brigade on. Like Kershaw, he avoided the top of Henry House Hill, pushing along south of that ridge. When the front of his brigade arrived at the Sudley road, he rode ahead to scout out the best position. He saw Kershaw and asked him. Kershaw was just directing him to the left side of his own line when a stray bullet entered Smith's chest. Immediately, his second in command, General Arnold Elzey, took charge. (Kirby Smith would survive this wound to fight another day, but for him this battle was over.)

Elzey accepted Kershaw's renewed advice and shuffled his three regiments toward Chinn's house. Reaching what Elzey decided was a likely spot, they turned until they, too, faced Howard's little force on the ridge. When Elzey first pulled his brigade into place, he found himself somewhat separated from Kershaw. He stared at the top of the ridge and saw soldiers there but could not be sure which side they were on. He could see they had a flag, but the lack of any wind kept it limp. "My glass," he yelled at an aide, "quick, quick!" Then a slight breeze convinced him. "Stars and Stripes! Stars and Stripes! Give it to them, boys!" His men fired once or twice, probably without much success.

About this time another orphan regiment—the Twenty-eighth Virginia that had recently participated in the last charge on Henry House Hill—appeared at Kershaw's position and asked to join; then, so did Withers's Eighteenth Virginia.[186]

Howard's troops were about to confront even one more Confederate brigade, this one led by Jubal Early. All morning Colonel Early had waited near McLean's farm. His assignment had been to support either Longstreet or Jones, as the need arose, and it turned out this had involved sending out or bringing back portions of his command every time it appeared Yankees across the stream might be advancing. After hours of charging about at the whims of various generals, Early received word that Beauregard wanted him to hurry in this direction as fast as he could. Jubal Early started immediately with three regiments, about 1,500 men. He had no idea where he was heading. The note from Beauregard, written in pencil, merely said, as Early later remembered it, "Send Early to me." It was about one o'clock. Along the road Early received instructions to move to "the front... guided by the roar of the cannon." He pushed his brigade "as fast as [his] men could move."

Jubal Early was not by nature a patient man. A West Point graduate (Class of 1837), he had left the army to become a successful lawyer in western Virginia. Generally scruffy, his shirt front spattered with tobacco juice, he was far more spit than polish. He was also remarkably proficient at three-dimensional profanity and had a hair-trigger temper. The word "abrasive" was often used to describe him. On the other hand, he was intelligent and totally honest.

Like those who had preceded them, Early's troops passed wounded men along the roadsides. Some of these men encouraged them: "Go it, boys! Go it, boys, goddamn their souls!" They passed a young soldier who was crying, saying he had been fighting all day and his regiment had been "shot to pieces" and now he was "all tired down." Then even he added, "Go it, boys, and I will be with you soon as I get some water and rest a little, for I am tired down now." When they reached Portici, Joe Johnston gave them directions to Henry House Hill. Early's troops started marching there when they saw an officer galloping toward them from the hill. He wore no hat and his face was ruddy with excitement. He windmilled his sword around in glee. "Glory! Glory! Glory!" he yelled. "We have captured Ricketts's battery, and the day is ours!" And off he rode. Early pressed his brigade onward.

He skipped Henry House Hill and instead brought his force to where Kershaw was, placing his men next to a battery on the left of Elzey's brigade. He knew that his men "were much blown." His troops, originally from Mississippi, had only arrived at Manassas Junction from Richmond the day before. Their weapons were altered flintlocks and their uniforms were shoddy. The leader of their brass band later wrote his wife that, after that day's march, the men of the Thirteenth Mississippi were not "in any condition to fight unless required by urgent necessity."

Stuart had brought even some of his troopers to the scene, along with a few cannon of his own. This rather immense force now faced Howard: almost a dozen regiments of Confederate infantrymen, a half-regiment of cavalry, and a passel of cannon — confronting about 500 Yankees. Howard's New Englanders were outnumbered at least five to one and they had no artillery.[187]

The Fight for Chinn Ridge, Howard's Position

Luckily for Howard's men, the rebel units arrived one by one. Despite this, the New Englanders would have been quickly obliterated except that Howard held the high ground and most of his troops had rifles, far better weapons for this situation than the rebels' muskets. His front two regiments blazed away at the enemy — mostly Kershaw's men — for perhaps fifteen minutes, some Federals firing as many as twenty shots. They found it hard to see their foes because of the trees and the smoke, but they did the best they could.

Howard, feeling the pressure, decided to bring up his two reserve regiments that were waiting on the other side of the thickets. He went back to search for them. But in his absence they had come under disconcerting artillery fire from somewhere and, unable to respond, had started falling apart. When he arrived, he tried to reorganize them but had only minimal success. Most of one regiment — the Fifth Maine — had run away, spurred into speed after catching sight of some cavalrymen and, mistakenly, believing it was the enemy. Howard was able to bring ahead the other regiment and the few remaining companies of the Fifth Maine. Yet, in the handful of minutes he had been gone from his forward regiments, things there had also started coming apart. The gunfire had grown so savage that the colonel of the Second Vermont, Henry Whiting, ran into the woods and hid.

Howard told the Vermonters to retreat through the thicket; he intended to try holding back the rebels with the Maine troops he now had on hand—his few hundred remaining troops about to confront 5,000. One of his soldiers recalled: "There was a wild uproar of shouting and firing. The faces near me were inhuman." Making their situation seem more surreal, Howard's men could hardly see their foes. The cannon smoke lay heavy near the ground, and through this murk "flashed and crackled the rebel musketry." Suddenly they saw a huge force, a human tidal wave, charging them with bayonets.

Most of this assault came from the brigades of Early and Elzey—who had, without consulting each other, both ordered their men to "charge bayonets." (This was charmingly ironic since many of Elzey's troops did not even have bayonets, though they happily joined in the rush up the ridge, cheering.)

"It was," recalled a soldier from Maine, "the turn of the tide." Howard ordered part of the line to pull back a bit, but virtually everyone spontaneously concluded they had had enough. Some officers tried to slow the retreat, but without success. Colonel Mark Dunnell of the Fifth Maine was immediately—to use Howard's gentle phrasing—"exhausted by an attack of illness."

They had a quarter-mile head start on their oncoming foes and were energized by a desire to escape, but they might still have been crushed except for two factors. The rebels themselves were exhausted and poorly disciplined.

Once again, the lure of blackberries proved too inviting. "We pressed forward with a cheer," one of Elzey's men recalled, "not in a very regular line but each one striving to be foremost. But in passing over the stubble or pasture we discovered it bore an abundant crop of blackberries, and being famished with hunger and our throats parched with thirst, the temptation was too strong to be resisted, the men stopped with one accord and the charging line of battle resolved itself into a crowd of blackberry pickers." Their officers tried to get them moving, some by swearing, others by pleading. Finally the troops started—until they saw another blackberry bush, when again they paused to jam the sweet nectar into their mouths.

The men of the Thirteenth Mississippi faced a different problem. Their commander, William Barksdale, a fat lawyer known to imbibe freely and possibly at this moment somewhat drunk, was urging his troops to greater speed when a group of them rammed into a large wasps' nest hidden inside some persimmon sprouts. The entire right company broke ranks and fled from this new enemy. Barksdale, not seeing the cause, rode to the spot to reorganize his wayward soldiers, and the angry wasps began stinging his poor horse. One of his soldiers later told a comrade, "It beat a circus."[188]

By the time the Confederates reached the crest of the ridge, Howard's men had disappeared from sight. It was not exactly that they had fled in abject terror, just that they had moved quickly enough they had passed through the thicket behind them and reached the turnpike. Here they had bumped into other Union groups, such as the marines, whose officers had been working to reorganize. Various units began caroming off each other. Luckily, for the fate of McDowell's army, just now Sykes's crew arrived on the slope of Chinn Ridge. There they stood like firm sentinels while Howard's beaten volunteers streamed past. Major Sykes put his men in lines and had them fire carefully, methodically, and accurately at Elzey's charging brigade. This slowed the Confederates' momentum for a few minutes.

McDowell Makes a Decision

McDowell held a hasty conference of some officers not far from the Matthews farm. Could their army make a stand? The consensus was: No. Although, as a whole, the volunteers had not exactly been "routed," many regiments had lost cohesion. The repulses from Henry House Hill and now Chinn Ridge had shuffled most of them up too much. It would be prudent to return to their base at Centreville and regroup. Wadsworth, the white-haired lawyer, spoke up. He said he would lead any regiment back into battle, but McDowell finally said, "Gentlemen, it seems evident that we must fall back to Centreville. Colonel Porter, you will please cover the withdrawal with your division."

Word of this decision spread rapidly. Although troops had already been drifting back in a kind of blind need for rest and water, this was different: It was orders. When the men of Keyes's brigade, off on the east side of Henry House Hill, heard about it, they were shocked. They had just been planning their attack. Why, they wondered, must they retreat? Burnside's men, still resting in some woods well behind the Matthews farm, were equally puzzled. The troops of Henry Warner Slocum's Twenty-seventh New York were positively angry. "We are not whipped," they yelled, shaking their fists in the air, "don't let us go away." But even they finally started from the field, still dissatisfied, their own lines strong and proud. McDowell tried to get some of the disorganized regiments—probably Howard's men—to mimic them. "Soldiers," he called out, "form on that noble regiment!" The New Englanders paid no attention and continued to slump slowly along. They were not running, but they had no intention of fighting any more this day. It was almost five o'clock.

McDowell rode several miles ahead to Centreville, where he penned a telegram to Washington. He told his superiors that his army had defeated the rebels twice—once in the morning, then again, after being repulsed, in the afternoon. But the appearance of Johnston's "reserves," he said, had finally done them in. His troops were now too "exhausted with fatigue and thirst and confused by firing into each other." They could no longer be rallied. He intended, he said, to hold Centreville—at least until all his men were safe there.[189]

Near Centreville: Dixon Miles and His Outposts

For the previous few hours, events near Centreville had been moving at a rather leisurely pace. Civilians continued to arrive and pull carriages onto the ridge. They chatted and ate, they wandered about, they asked passing soldiers for gossip. Colonel Miles spent part of the morning sitting on the front porch of his hotel headquarters, then decided to activate himself. He checked on Blenker's brigade nearby, then rode out to Davies and Richardson, a mile back from Bull Run. He went first to Richardson's position.

A decade earlier, both of these soldiers had served at the same isolated post in New Mexico for two years. Richardson at the time had been a captain and Miles was his superior officer. Both men were quick-tempered. Dixon Miles was a stickler for military punctilio, and Richardson found this trait a constant annoyance. They had exchanged increasingly hot words, and eventually each was transferred. McDowell probably knew about their mutual enmity when, on Saturday, he had put Richardson's brigade under Miles's supervision, but had decided to ignore it. Now, as Miles examined Richardson's placement of his regiments and guns, he expressed himself satisfied. (Things were so quiet at Richardson's position that mail arrived about noon and was distributed. During the afternoon men there read their letters and took naps.) Miles then rode over to Davies's brigade. This conversation did not go as well.

In the previous few hours, as Davies's battery desultorily flung shot and shell toward the enemy, he had examined the area with a local man as his guide. Davies was concerned when he discovered a path that approached his position from the left. He asked the guide if a rebel force could use it to sneak up on him. Yes, the man replied. So, as a precaution, Davies placed two of his four regiments along that road, with two guns. Then, as Davies told the Joint Committee, "When Colonel Miles came down in the morning he was in a terrible passion because I had put these two regiments there. He gave me a very severe dressing down in no very measured language, and ordered the two regiments forward [that is, back to the front], without knowing what they had been put there for. I complied with the order, and said nothing." (Davies was not normally a shrinking violet. He had a rough and profane tongue of his own, as well as an explosive temper, so it must have required much restraint for him to maintain his self-control.) After Miles rode away, Davies remained worried about that side path. He therefore ordered a crew of pioneers to cut down trees and create an abatis to block it. "As I expected," he told the Committee, "the enemy made an attempt to go up that road, but finding it obstructed by trees, and protected by a few pickets, they went back." (Which Confederates performed this probe or when it occurred is uncertain.) Richardson, meanwhile, had built an extensive entrenchment directly across the path in front of his position. That barricade was made of thick trees, two feet across, fronted with a dozen feet of dirt berm.[190]

The erection of those abatis led to a delightful byplay between crusty Dick Ewell and a young woman, a local girl, about seventeen, who saw the two barriers being built. She rode to the Federal pioneers and asked, "Why are you obstructing our road?" They told her the purpose, and she went away. In the previous few weeks, Southern newspapers had carried heroic stories about two young ladies who had performed good service to the Confederate army in western Virginia when they carried word that Yankee soldiers were approaching. Perhaps this girl near Centreville had those two heroines in her mind when she galloped to Ewell's camp on the far side of Bull Run and breathlessly explained what she had seen. He tried to be patient but finally blurted out, "Look there, look there, miss! Don't you see those men with blue clothing on, in the edge of the woods? Look at those men loading those big guns. They are going to fire, and fire quick, and fire right here. You'll get killed. You'll be a *dead damsel* in less than a minute. *Get away from here! Get away!*" She turned, glanced calmly at the Yankees a moment, then turned her back on them and continued her report. Ewell stared at her in disbelief and said to a companion standing there, "Women — I tell you, sir, women would make a grand brigade — if it was not for snakes and spiders!"[191]

In early afternoon Dixon Miles returned for the second time to check up on his two outposts. He had probably had lunch by now, along with some alcohol. Like many old soldiers, he was known to be a fairly heavy drinker, though apparently not an alcoholic. Military rules about drinking on duty were quite specific: "Any commissioned officer who shall be found drunk on his guard, post, or other duty, shall be cashiered." Three weeks after the Battle of Bull Run, the army would hold a court of inquiry about Miles's condition on this afternoon. Miles admitted to the court that he did have a drink or two during that day but said, in expiation, he had been ill and was under a doctor's orders to take a particular medicine. He did not name it, but the dosage no doubt contained opiates, as many did in that era. Combining such a chemical with alcohol could easily explain his somewhat aberrant behavior. Some soldiers who saw him that afternoon were shocked that he was now wearing two straw hats, one mashed atop the other. But the day was hot and sunny, and, like many who had served in the Southwest, Miles had learned that trick to moderate the sun's rays. Blenker spoke to him in midafternoon and later told the Committee that Miles showed "nothing like intoxication." (It should be noted that Blenker himself liked his beer. He said about Miles: "He took, once in a while, a drop. Never mind, that is nothing.") The military court, however, did find Miles guilty of being drunk on duty. It permitted him to remain in the army, though it took away his command of a division.

Miles arrived the second time at Richardson's position and stared over toward the enemy. He apparently saw little activity across the stream and decided the rebels had moved away. He was right, of course; Beauregard and Johnston had withdrawn most of their forces from that sector — though at this time they still had a sizeable crew there, or at least not far away. Miles told Richardson that it was his conclusion the rebels were fleeing toward Manassas Junction and that this was a propitious moment to throw both Davies and Richardson across Bull Run to drive out anyone remaining. "Fighting Dick" Richardson, normally pugnacious, had been spanked by McDowell for being too aggressive three days earlier, and he had learned his lesson. He would later tell the Joint Committee that he replied, "Colonel Miles, I have a positive order in my pocket for this brigade not to attack at all." He showed it to Miles, who concurred with its clarity, saying, "That is positive." Miles was, however, still not completely satisfied. He ordered Richardson to send skirmishers out as a probe. Richardson sent five companies toward the stream. They came under fire, and he recalled them. Miles departed and went to visit Davies.

Under Miles's prodding, Davies also ordered four companies to check out things in front of his position. They started off, cautiously entering some woods. They had not gone far when they, too, bumped into some Confederate troops. The two sides exchanged shots, and the Union companies scampered back. Miles left. It was about three o'clock.[192]

The Confederates and Miles's Outposts

Meanwhile, Ewell and D. R. Jones had received new orders. They were to plunge across Bull Run in a smaller version of Beauregard's earlier plan. Bonham and Longstreet were told the same but then received a follow-up message just before starting that they were *not* to move. (Headquarters had heard that a Yankee force was approaching Manassas Junction from some direction and feared this meant the long-anticipated arrival of Patterson. The rumor was inaccurate; someone had jumped to the wrong conclusion when seeing Elzey's men near the station.) Since neither Jones nor Ewell received re-call orders at that time, the two commanders, moving from different places, started forward with their brigades. Ewell pushed his three regiments across the stream. The "roads" on the other side were mere paths. One of his soldiers described them as "narrow, winding, and precipitous" — only wide enough to allow two men on horseback to ride side by side. The going was slow. At the front of Ewell's brigade was the Fifth Alabama. (It was these Alabamians that Davies's reconnaissance bumped into.)

Ewell now received an order from Beauregard to return *immediately* and hurry toward the stone bridge. (This message had been sent much earlier when the fighting in that area had been at a critical and uncertain stage.) One of Ewell's aides asked his superior what the meaning of the message was. "It means," Ewell snapped, "we are whipped!" As Ewell wrote his wife a few days later, "My feelings then were terrible, as such an order could only mean that we were defeated and I was to cover the retreat." He turned his tired men around and started trudging north. As it turned out, his men and Holmes's brigade that was preceding them were still in transit when the battle passed its climax. The fighting on Henry House Hill had caused Beauregard to weaken his right wing. This decision had important consequences.[193]

D. R. Jones felt lousy. He was suffering a pounding headache and had not fully recovered from a bout with both pneumonia and pleurisy. The men of his three regiments were tired. They had spent all morning fruitlessly marching about. It was his understanding he was going to be part of a broad sweep by several brigades. He believed that Ewell was somewhere off to his right and that Longstreet was on his left. As he imagined it, he was participating in an attack involving 5,000 men. But in fact he was all alone — and was moving directly into Davies's position. His regiments — undisciplined and weary — were about to challenge almost two full batteries of artillery and four well-rested Yankee infantry regiments, nicely positioned atop a hill.

Davies's Position

For once this day, the Union army had its own "masked battery." And they were in a defensive posture while the enemy was on the attack. Although the Union troops were almost taken by surprise when the rebels appeared on their left flank, the enemy was far enough away that the gunners had time to swing their cannon around. Davies put one infantry regiment on each side of the guns — to keep his volunteers from getting excited and mistakenly shooting into the backs of the artillerists. The guns were unlimbered slightly back from the crown of the hill, and the infantrymen were ordered to lie down. Let the artillerymen do the work.

Just as the action was about to open, Davies received an order from Miles: He and Richardson were to withdraw to Centreville. A messenger from McDowell had arrived at Miles's headquarters to say that General McDowell was returning to Centreville with his army and wanted Miles to cover the move. Davies told the courier he could not change his position just now and indicated the approaching rebels.

The officer commanding the Union guns was Brevet Major Henry J. Hunt. He and his men had been together only a few days, and he worried about their pluck under fire. He told them he wanted them to fire canister and they must work quickly. They should not stop to swab out their barrels between each shot. His gunners waited.

The Confederate "Attack"

The ground in front of Hunt's battery was wooded and cut by ravines so deep that some reports called them "gorges." To reach this spot, D. R. Jones's men had tramped through five miles of dense forest and up and down rugged terrain. They felt tortured by the oppressive heat. Jones put the Fifth South Carolina in the middle and placed his Mississippi regiments on either side. But the terrain did not permit such a neat arrangement. The Fifth led the way, shouting and shooting wildly as they galumphed down into the laurel-filled ravine, the branches dragging at their feet. A fairly deep creek ran through the base of the gorge, and the South Carolinians splashed across it. The Eighteenth Mississippi followed, confused by the nature of the landscape and the dense foliage. Then came the Seventeenth Mississippi. The Yankee artillery opened fire, filling the air with hundreds of deadly pellets, whizzing at them like hornets. Men went down. The Confederates fired back as well as they could, but the Yankee infantrymen lay safely behind the crest, and the Yankee cannon continued to belch out death. Worse, as the South Carolinians started to climb up the far side of the ravine, some Mississippians thought they were retreating Yankees and opened fire on them. It was too much. The South Carolinians turned around and started back.

The disaster continued. One Mississippian, still in the gorge, asked a comrade, "Hal, how do you feel." "Quite warm," his friend replied. Personally, he was convinced they were under attack by eight cannon and at least *seven thousand* riflemen. The Mississippians turned to go, but as they exited the ravine, some of them excitedly shot at each other. The whole affair lasted perhaps half an hour.

It proved at least two things: Attackers anywhere near Bull Run were at a disadvantage, and green troops, while often brave, fell apart rapidly when confused. In a sense the stunning collapse of Jones's brigade was far worse than the setback that Richardson had suffered in the battle of Blackburn's Ford three days earlier, or even the defeat of Howard's brigade. But the implications of this incident would be swallowed up and forgotten because of other events.

Near Centreville

Richardson, following Miles's orders, moved back a bit toward the village and placed his regiments to block the road from Blackburn's Ford. Miles rode up and looked at Richardson's position. He did not like it. He ordered one regiment to a new spot, saying, "You are now where I want you. Stay there, damn you, and die there." He went to another of Richardson's regiments. He was dissatisfied with its placement, too, and began moving it about. Its commander sent a messenger to find Colonel Richardson to inform him of the change. The news displeased "Fighting Dick." By this time Miles's demeanor had deteriorated. He was now quite obviously drunk. Even McDowell heard of this situation and sent word to Richardson to act independently of Miles, to do as he saw fit. Richardson was in the process of rearranging his regiments to their original positions when Miles rode up, unsteady in his saddle. He blustered that he could not understand how Richardson could disobey his wishes.

"Colonel Miles," Richardson replied, "I will do as I please. I am in command of these troops."

"I don't understand this," Miles repeated.

"Colonel Miles, you are drunk."

Miles threatened to have him arrested. Richardson ignored his sputtering. Miles found Major Barry, McDowell's chief of artillery, and appealed to him, but Barry also ignored him. Then McDowell appeared, and when Miles applied to him for support, McDowell said, "Colonel Miles, I find you have everything here in great confusion. You are relieved of the command of your troops."

One problem had been solved. Others remained.[194]

VESPERS

Cowardice, as distinguished from panic,
is almost always simply a lack of ability to suspend
the functioning of the imagination.
—ERNEST HEMINGWAY

Courage is not the absence of fear but the mastery of it.
—JAMES M. McPHERSON

Union soldiers had been leaving the battlefield for hours. Some were wounded, swathed in bloody bandages. Others had simply lost whatever psychological mechanism that keeps a soldier fighting. They crossed Bull Run by one route or other and found their way to the Warrenton pike, then up the hill past the watching civilians. By midafternoon this occasional drip-drip of soldiers had become a steady trickle. It was a human reaction. These men were weary beyond words. Their thirst had become genuinely unbearable. And they were volunteers—native-born Americans or immigrants, accustomed to deciding their fate for themselves. This marked a different dynamic between volunteers and regular soldiers. When the going got tough, regulars stuck together. They had been taught that safety lay with the group—their "pack," if you will. Volunteers, on the other hand, civilians a few weeks, or even days, earlier, still had trouble accepting a group mentality. A certain disintegration, therefore, was inevitable.

But the actual retreat, the one officially ordered by General McDowell, began in a fairly orderly way. Upon learning of the new orders, the regiments and the brigades, once they heard of the change, began moving toward Centreville, often returning by the route they had taken in the morning. When the first retreating body of troops that crossed Bull Run, near or by the stone bridge, were asked what was going on, some of them told their listeners that the whole army had been defeated. Most of these naysayers were officers on horseback, and this news had an effect on the wagon drivers, lined up for two miles or more along the turnpike. These teamsters, almost all civilians, had been edging their vehicles forward since noon, waiting impatiently for the abatis to be cleared from the stone bridge or the erection of a parallel bridge. Now, a few teamsters nearest the stream decided to turn around. Others behind them did, too. Weighted down with barrels and boxes, rope and shovels and pickaxes, their wagons were slow and clumsy. To lighten their loads, drivers began flinging things out. Debris quickly built up on the road, blocking it. The teamsters, now feeling trapped, increasingly crazed by fear, whipped their horses mercilessly. Wagons crashed into each other or against the debris. Some flipped over. At least one soldier was crushed when a heavy artillery wagon went over him. A few drivers become so panicky they cut the traces holding the horses to the wagons, mounted a horse, and raced away, leaving the wagon stranded. The pandemonium worsened. The onrush of speeding wagons arrived at the spot where most of the civilian carriages were. The civilians who had come to observe a battle had no desire to participate in one. They began fleeing from this danger zone. All this had its own dynamic of hysteria—caused by fear, triggering fear. Exhausted soldiers saw the moving vehicles as their salvation and clambered aboard, and, to make room, they, too, tossed things out. Some even paid hard cash to drivers to take them.

Several civilians refused to be spooked and were outraged by the terror they saw in some volunteers. (To be fair to the soldiers, the civilians who shouted, "Cowards!" had slept and eaten fairly well during the past twenty-four hours and had not had to march many miles in the sun or fight.) Half a dozen armed politicians joined tough Ben Wade to form a human wall to stop the early stampede. The only result was that a representative from Detroit was shot in the wrist by a crazed teamster.

One New York congressman, Alfred Ely, forty-six, from Rochester had previously wandered far down until he was near Bull Run. He lingered too long. He was captured and nearly shot by Colonel E. B. C. Cash of South Carolina. Cash was normally a hothead and had probably been drinking. When he recognized Ely as a Yankee politician, he pulled his pistol. "You infernal sonofabitch! You came to see the fun, did you? God damn your white-livered soul! I'll show you! I'll blow your brains out on the spot!" It took several Confederates to persuade Cash not to carry out his threat. (Ely would spend the next five months a prisoner of the Confederacy.)

How many of McDowell's troops — as opposed to teamsters or other civilians — participated in this first panicky wave? It is impossible to know. But their numbers do not seem that significant. Major Barnard, the army's chief engineer, was with McDowell when the general and his staff returned to Centreville. They observed this paroxysm on the pike and considered it, Barnard said, "But brief in time and limited as to locality." When that incident took place, moreover, most of the army was still well back and unaffected. It should be kept in mind, therefore, that the "civilian" or "teamster" panic was different from the military retreat, though the stuff strewn across the pike made it appear to Confederates the next day that the two events were the same. The bubble of fear that really unsettled many of the retreating soldiers came later.[195]

The Confederates

One might ask why the Confederates did not, at this time, launch a major assault on the retreating Yankees. The reasons were twofold. Although the Federals seemed to be moving from the field, it was not obvious what McDowell had in mind. Because of the trees and the terrain, most of the Union army was not in view. Those Yankees who were visible seemed fairly well organized. When men like Beauregard first celebrated, it was because they felt relief that the pressure was off. They had obviously repelled their enemy from Henry House Hill and Chinn's farm, but a military repulse was not the same as a defeat. They themselves had suffered two repulses during the past few hours. In fact, not much earlier, Johnston and Beauregard, concerned about a complete collapse of their army, had been formulating plans for a general withdrawal from Manassas Junction.

Also, the Confederates were as battered as their foes. With the exception of two or three regiments, the brigades that had fought much of the battle—Evans's, Bee's, Bartow's, Jackson's—had been pulverized beyond recognition. It would take them a while—a day, a week—to regain the capacity to march long distances and fight. Like the Yankees, the Confederates needed to eat, to quench their burning throats, to rest, to sleep, to regroup. Even Elzey's brigade and Early's were worn to a frazzle by the exertions of the past day or two. They still retained their cohesion, but their physical stamina flickered low.

In the very first moments after fighting ceased, Beauregard and some officers held their own ad hoc conference on the field to discuss what the Yankees might be up to. Were the Federals retreating or was it another ruse, an attempt to swing around and attack from a different direction? As the Confederates watched, those Yankees they could see "were moving in beautiful style." (These were Sykes's regulars.) Beauregard stared, then mistakenly concluded, "It is a movement on our right." He ordered Eppa Hunton to take his Eighth Virginia regiment and stymie this "attack."

Hunton began trotting his men in the direction Beauregard indicated. He came to a knoll and realized Beauregard was wrong; the Yankees were actually moving back toward Centreville. In fact, as Hunton saw it, they "were running like dogs."

By itself, for the moment that Federal withdrawal seemed sufficient. To attack a Yankee force of unknown strength at Centreville—assuming the enemy retreated that far—seemed out of the question. To reach the Yankee outer line there, they would have to march five or six miles. And they would have to travel that distance without much, or any, artillery support. Or food. Or sufficient water. Or wagons. The sun was starting to set. Full darkness would arrive soon. The idea of an all-out Confederate charge at this moment was absurd, the wishful thinking of critics of a later date.[196]

———

On the other hand, the Confederates did attempt three different probes—with mixed results.

Longstreet had had his brigade ready for hours, awaiting orders to advance against Richardson. Longstreet's scouts had examined the enemy's position and drawn maps. Although, half a mile away, D. R. Jones had failed in his attack on Davies and retreated, Longstreet stood fast, increasingly frustrated as he listened to the sounds of battle from behind him. Then, at 4:40, Joe Johnston sent a messenger to Bonham. The South Carolinian should take his two remaining regiments across Bull Run and lead a joint assault with Longstreet against the Yankee left. If McDowell really was pulling back to Centreville, it was possible the Yankees were withdrawing troops from their forward positions. If so, Bonham and Longstreet might catch them off balance. Once again, Johnston was thinking clearly; McDowell's entire flank might collapse—with who knew what results? (In fact, when McDowell arrived at Centreville—just as Bonham and Longstreet were starting to move—he was startled to hear that Richardson had pulled back and angrily confronted him about abandoning his critical post. Richardson replied he had only done so under orders from Miles—which was likely the main reason McDowell now relieved Miles of his command. That decision, however, did not solve the problem of the sudden gap on his left flank, and McDowell scrambled for a solution.)

Longstreet crossed the stream and marched his men quickly up the road toward Centreville. On the way his troops learned the Yankees were in a general retreat. Longstreet's Virginians cheered over and over, throwing their caps into the air. This happy news energized them. They pressed forward so quickly that their officers had trouble controlling their ardor. They came to Richardson's abatis, hesitated a moment, then passed around it, and found the other side vacant, coffee boiling atop campfires. Clearly, the enemy had departed only moments before. Longstreet's men concluded that the cowardly Yankees had fled at the sight of their approach. This thought redoubled their enthusiasm. "The more scared we found the enemy to be," one recalled, "the more brave we became."

Bonham, in overall command of this advance, was less sanguine. His orders were to try to reach the turnpike and intercept the retreating army, if it was collapsing—but Bonham's scouts and his own observations convinced him that McDowell's army had not fallen apart. He could see that the Yankees (Richardson and Davies) had merely moved back a way and had placed themselves in a strong position next to the road he would be moving up. Also, from what he could discern on the turnpike to his left, the Federals were far from "routed." Their lines seemed orderly enough, and his orders from Johnston had said he and Longstreet should only attack if "practicable." Night was coming on. Bonham contemplated the situation without enthusiasm.

Longstreet felt far more confident. Perhaps he made the same mistake his men did when examining Richardson's camp, and he assumed the entire enemy force was in disarray. He brought his guns up and prepared to open fire on the Yankee position. Just then, Johnston's chief of staff, Chase Whiting, rode up, glanced at the lay of the land, and told Longstreet not to fire. Longstreet demanded to know if this was Johnston's explicit order, and Whiting said, no, that this was his decision. In that case, said Longstreet, he would take full responsibility. He turned back to his guns. Then Bonham himself appeared and said he agreed with Whiting, Longstreet must not fire. Bonham returned to his regiments to await developments.

For the next hour Bonham's and Longstreet's attack force lingered, not far from the Union lines. Then a courier from Bonham galloped to Longstreet and announced Bonham's troops were going to move back. General Bonham had decided his men and horses needed water and ought to return to Bull Run to get it. "Retreat!" Longstreet yelled, throwing his hat on the ground. "Hell! The Federal army has broken to pieces." He stamped his foot in rage. He and Bonham were, he was convinced, missing a wonderful opportunity. His men were equally outraged. They cursed when they heard the news. Some even started sobbing with frustration. Longstreet stubbornly refused to leave. Several hours later, another messenger rode in, this time with an even more insistent order: Longsheet must come back. He was deeply angry but obeyed. Portions of his brigade had gone back and forth across Bull Run six times in the past twenty-four hours.

What would have been the result if Bonham and Longstreet and their six "fresh" regiments had attacked, backed by some artillery? They would have crashed against Richardson, Davies, and Blenker, who had far more men and cannon. Not far away were many other Union troops, who might have been exhausted but who could still pull triggers. One thing the day had shown: In general it was better to be on the defensive than the offensive. One can admire Longstreet's bulldog pugnacity, but in all likelihood an assault here would only have led to much more bloodshed with no other result.[197]

A second Confederate probe resulted from Colonel Kershaw's boldness. After pushing his demibrigade from Bonham's original position all the way around to Chinn's farm and joining the general onslaught on Howard's men, Kershaw (unlike Elzey and Early) remained unsatisfied. He pressed on. He had over a thousand troops, including the remarkable handful of the Hampton Legion who still refused to stop. Using the turnpike, Kershaw trailed after the Yankees. It is unclear what he hoped to accomplish, probably to snare "targets of opportunity." He did not want to walk into a trap, so he was moving cautiously, but he found the way to the stone bridge surprisingly open.

He crossed the bridge — now, ironically, completely cleared by McDowell's engineers — and somewhere past it he saw in the distance a strong enemy force with artillery. He did not want to be too reckless and sent a messenger back for instructions. A few minutes later he was told Beauregard authorized him to pursue the Yankees but not to bring on a major battle. He edged forward again, picking up occasional prisoners. By this time the large Yankee force was out of sight. A small unit of Confederate cavalrymen, then two guns, joined his pack of pursuers.

So did Edmund Ruffin. Up to this moment the old man had contributed little to the battle. His age was catching up with him. His gimpy left hand made it hard to load and fire a rifle, and his leg was sore. He could no longer keep up with soldiers fifty years younger than himself. He had become an observer, and he found this disappointing. But he could not resist joining Kershaw's South Carolinians. When the men of Hampton's Legion saw him, they cheered. For soldiers from South Carolina, who recalled his efforts against Fort Sumter, he was part mascot, part good-luck charm.

Kershaw's force moved slowly forward, with skirmishers ahead of them on both sides of the turnpike. The pike here went uphill for a bit and through some woods. His troops crept past Mrs. Spindle's house that had been used as a hospital and picked up a few more prisoners. Then they came to the top of a ridge. In front of them, some distance away, were perhaps two thousand Yankees, many of whom were slogging down the pike away from them, while others were arriving from the left (at the blacksmith's shop). A long string of wagons and ambulances and artillery stretched into the distance toward Centreville. From where Kershaw was, he could see that one thing held all this together like a brooch: the narrow, rickety bridge across Cub Run. He could not resist that wonderful target. The enemy was too far away for infantry rifles, but he thought his artillery could reach the spot. He ordered his two guns to unlimber on the road. One was to aim at the Yankees on the left path, the other at the bridge.

The officer in charge of the guns, Del Kemper, turned to Ruffin and asked if the old man would like the honor of the first shot. (Throughout the South it was believed that Ruffin had fired the first artillery shell against Fort Sumter.) Kemper's right-hand gun, loaded with spherical case, was aimed directly at the wagons crossing the bridge. Ruffin yanked its lanyard. During this entire day of fighting, up to this moment, few artillerists had distinguished themselves by their accuracy, but on this occasion, through a breathtaking fluke, the aim was perfect. The deadly pieces of metal crashed into the lead horses of a large wagon just crossing Cub Run.

Ruffin's diary described the effect: "In their pain & fright they suddenly turned, upset the wagon so as to barricade the whole breadth of the bridge & effectually precluded any other wheel-carriage or horse, from moving on. The whole mass of fugitives immediately got out of the track, & all escaped who could, on foot & as quickly as possible." For McDowell's army, the jam on the bridge was a disaster. Cub Run was narrow and its water waist high. Men and horses could scramble across, but its banks were too steep to permit vehicles to make it. As a result, the Union army was forced to abandon wagon loads of provisions and cartridges. Worse, they also had to leave behind nine more cannon — guns that would eventually be used against them in other battles.

Kemper's two cannon kept up their fire — ten or twelve shots in all. Presumably, they then ran out of ammunition. Soon after this, Colonel Kershaw received an order to return to the stone bridge. Night was coming on. Besides, Confederate headquarters had learned that McDowell was pushing part of his army over Bull Run several miles downstream, attempting a surprise assault on Manassas Junction. When Beauregard had heard this, he acted quickly. He not only recalled Kershaw; he rode off and found Holmes and Ewell, whose brigades had almost arrived at the battlefield, turned them around, and started them back to the new danger zone. These turnabouts turned out to be unnecessary. The report was a mistake. Someone had seen D. R. Jones's bedraggled troops recrossing Bull Run after their disastrous attack on Davies's battery and assumed they were a major Yankee attack force. By the time the mistake was recognized, Kershaw had long since retired from the turnpike.[198]

The third Confederate assault on the Yankee withdrawal was not a single action. Confederate cavalry units of various sizes, but most of them small, acting like swarms of hornets, attacked different parts of McDowell's army. A well-organized infantry could wreak havoc on massed horsemen — a lesson medieval knights had painfully learned centuries earlier. One technique men on foot could use against cavalry was to "form a square," with their guns and bayonets facing outward. Sykes applied this tactic late that afternoon when bringing up the rear. Even Sherman had tried it when his brigade left the field, with somewhat less crispness, but with fair success. A military axiom stated that a cavalry's most useful role came when an enemy was in retreat. An army in retrograde motion was vulnerable. A cavalry attack on its flanks or rear tended to scatter foot soldiers, breaking down cohesion. Cavalry could also pick off slow-moving vehicles and round up stragglers.

A lieutenant from Maine later wrote his father. His regiment, the Fifth Maine, was in disarray, and he found himself trudging along in a daze. He heard someone shout that cavalry was coming and looked around. He could see no immediate danger but was determined to reach a patch of woods a mile away where he might be safe. He found himself too tired to move fast enough. His terror soared. He felt as though the Headless Horseman was behind him, gaining ground, an unseen, terrifying presence. "I confess, dear Father, at that moment I felt the sensation of fear." He tottered toward the trees. "The idea of going as far as I had been that day and getting out so far and so well, and then having my head cut of[f] was anything but pleasant." Somehow, he reached the copse. "I sat down on a stump to pull off my boots in order to help me along, but I was so weak I could not get one leg over the other without taking hold and lifting it up, but I managed to get them of[f] somehow." He stood up and continued to lurch toward Centreville. He never actually saw any enemy cavalry.

During that evening Jeb Stuart's cavalrymen performed fairly well, but, surprisingly, without notable élan. He led two squadrons toward Sudley, and they picked up scores of prisoners. They also captured the hospital at the stone house, then the one at Sudley. There he settled his men down for the night. They had done mop-up work — important enough, but not vital.

Several miles away, other Confederate cavalrymen were charging the enemy near Cub Run. Unlike Stuart's activities, these attacks, in combination with Kershaw's two cannon, had major consequences. Coming just at the same moment the Cub Run bridge was closed, they created a ripple of hysteria among the retreating soldiers that was far more significant than the teamsters' earlier panic.

Late in the afternoon, Beauregard's young aide, Alexander Chisolm, was still making himself useful. After spending a while on Henry House Hill assisting Jackson, he had returned to Portici, arriving there just after the retreat began. He was asking General Johnston what he could do when Colonel R. C. W. Radford cantered up to offer the services of his troopers. He had with him his own Thirtieth Virginia Cavalry and assorted other troopers who had spontaneously joined him. (Beauregard's army had included almost 900 cavalrymen, but the Creole had never properly organized them into regiments, and many acted as virtually independent companies. At this moment Radford's so-called Thirtieth Cavalry Regiment probably consisted of about 50 men. Counting those who linked themselves to him, he seems to have had with him, under his loose command, fewer than 200 men.) General Johnston suggested that he harry the enemy's rear — if he could find it. Chisolm, standing there, piped up. He said that during the past few weeks, acting as one of Beauregard's aides, he had ridden around the region extensively; he knew the area and would show Radford's troopers the best route. There was a ford, he said, across Bull Run not far from there, and an ancient wagon path went from Portici straight across it and continued until it linked up with the turnpike about a mile and a half away. Radford was pleased with this news, and Chisolm guided the troopers across the stream, then through some fields and woods. As they finally emerged through the tree line, riding two or three abreast, they saw, spread out before them, a long line of Yankees, stretching as far to the right as they could see. Some of the cavalrymen were awed by the large number of their foes and started to pull back. Chisolm, officially a colonel, told them they were acting craven and got them moving again.

The nearest Federal troops to Radford's troopers were the Sixty-ninth New York, bringing up the rear of Sherman's brigade, and at least one of Schenck's regiments. Although Schenck's men had done little fighting, once a retreat begins, anyone turning his back on the enemy feels a natural itchiness between his shoulder blades. Schenck's troops believed they formed the tail end of McDowell's army. This thought made them want to hurry — particularly as they caught sight of Radford's cavalrymen coming from their right through the trees. They started to run and crashed into the Sixty-ninth, who had just stepped onto the turnpike from the path that had taken them over the farm ford. The New Yorkers were instantly churned into disorder. Their colonel, Michael Corcoran, tried to rally them. He dismounted and went to his color-bearer. He screamed at his men to halt, to rally 'round this flag, to turn and face the horsemen almost upon them. But just as he shouted, the rebel cavalrymen opened fire with their carbines. His words were swallowed in the noise, and less than a dozen of his men heard him — or, at least, stopped to join him. In seconds he and these few men and his banner were captives.

One of the frightening things about these rebel horsemen was the name Union soldiers had been giving them, "the Black Horse Cavalry." Throughout the whole battle, whenever Federal troops spied any body of horsemen, they yowled that phrase. During the past two months, the name had become synonymous with fearsome fighters — almost equivalent to "Mongol hordes" or "Attila's Huns." The volunteers back at their camps near Washington, like children around a campfire telling ghost stories, had often spoken in awe about the mysterious "Black Horse Cavalry," swarming somewhere outside their lines. Northern newspapers picked up the tale and added to the legend. Most of these rumors were entirely false. There was indeed a "Black Horse Cavalry," but it was only a single mounted militia company made up of young men from the Warrenton region. Their celebrity had grown more from their tough-sounding name than their exploits, which had not been very noteworthy. (They had originally been mentioned in newspapers in late 1859, when they had guarded the prisoner, John Brown.) But reality made no difference. At Bull Run, every time a Union soldier yelled that phrase, men glanced around nervously.

So when Radford and his troopers materialized from the woods, the exhausted volunteers were preconditioned to see them almost as apparitions. Schenck's men ran first, followed by Corcoran's Sixty-ninth, shouting the dreaded name over and over. This chorus spread a contagion of fever up the turnpike. Radford's band should never have caused such a reaction. They were not very numerous when assembled together, and they now broke into smaller segments, each with no more than thirty troopers. Wherever Union infantrymen now stood firm and fought back, these horsemen were forced to retreat. When some rebel cavalrymen attacked two guns whose artillerymen refused to quail, who stuffed canister into their barrels and fired three times

at close range, the slaughter of Confederates and horses was terrific. On the other hand, when the Federal volunteers turned and
ran, scattering through the fields, they were easy prey.

By chance, other rebel cavalry units, coming from two different directions, hit parts of McDowell's retreating army within
minutes of the arrival of Radford. The horsemen who had been
traveling with Kershaw's demibrigade as it crossed the stone
bridge had kept going when Kershaw stopped. They espied the
long line of Yankees up the turnpike (Keyes's men who had
crossed Bull Run behind Sherman). These cavalrymen numbered
less than fifty men, but they charged Keyes's infantry, many of
whom turned and fled. Their elderly general, Daniel Tyler, his
long white hair whipping about his face, tried rallying them.
Tyler and Keyes and a few other officers, standing in a field, were
able to persuade fifty or sixty volunteers to stay and fight. It
worked; the troopers rode off, looking for easier pickings. At
almost this same moment, other cavalry companies that had
crossed Bull Run far upstream pounced on Burnside's brigade,
which had been moving in a fairly organized way on the path
from Sudley. (By chance, this cavalry charge—of about a hundred horsemen—did include the real Black Horse company.)
Again, the Union soldiers ran.

In summary, between six and seven o'clock, a few hundred
Confederate horsemen, coming from three directions, began hitting isolated parts of the retreating line. These attacks were not
coordinated in any way, and they took place several miles from
each other. Some were costly failures. Not one succeeded in
slaughtering significant numbers of the enemy. But, although
mere pinpricks, the attacks initiated a collapse of entire sections
of McDowell's army. The bottleneck on the Cub Run bridge,
caused by Kemper's shots, ratcheted up the tension even more.
The horsemen's efforts had required much audacity. But the
horsemen were also very lucky.[199]

The Retreat

Up to this point, McDowell's army had not been *beaten*. They
had been *repulsed* from their attempt to take the train station at

Manassas Junction, but they were hardly vanquished. Physically and emotionally, however, they had been badly drained. Even Napoleon once said: "After fighting six hours a soldier will seize on any pretext to quit, if it can be done honorably." In general, McDowell's men had been retreating toward Centreville in fairly good order — especially when one considers how fatigued they were and that most were volunteers with only a slight patina of military discipline. They were faint from hunger as well. When entering the battlefield hours earlier, most regiments had set aside their haversacks containing their provisions, expecting to pick them up later, but in their retreat few units had retraced their steps precisely. Their abandoned haversacks were lost. Many of McDowell's troops had not eaten in twenty-four hours.

The cavalry attacks and Kershaw's guns proved too much for such men. Even after the assorted rebel attacks had long ceased, many volunteers had stopped being "soldiers" and had become "individuals," whose only purpose was survival. When troops are advancing, they tend to feel part of an "army." Now in retreat, their mood was like that of dispirited theatergoers leaving a disappointing show or that of factory workers after a long day, intent on getting home and putting their feet up. Many troops were aware they had reached the end of their official enrollment. They had volunteered to fight. They *had* fought, and now in their minds they were civilians again. The uniforms they wore were simply a temporary covering of their civilian nakedness. Hundreds of McDowell's troops went straight home without stopping. They walked to Washington, got on trains, and left.

The army had a rule — Article 52 — that the punishment for throwing away one's weapon in battle could be execution. But thousands of soldiers now found the ten-pound weight not only cumbersome but unnecessary, and the roads and fields around Bull Run were soon strewn with cast-off weapons and ammunition. A young enlisted man from New Hampshire, dropping his gun, would recall: "I did not feel able to carry it any farther, and felt sure it would be of no use to anyone if I left it there, for by this time I was so tired." Men like him had — at least for this moment — lost the will to fight. After any battle there often follows a feeling of letdown, a period of deep lassitude, that can last for days, somewhat triggered by emotions but quite physical and very real. The chemistry of the body is altered. The battle-induced adrenaline is dissipated.[200]

Despite all this, however, it should be noted that more than half McDowell's army never saw enemy cavalry and were not shot at by Kemper's two guns. The majority of Federals were exhausted, of course, but were unaffected by the second phase of hysteria. After the half-hour stampede across Cub Run, things settled down somewhat. In the twilight, lined up beyond the bridge, was Blenker's brigade: three regiments of confident Germans — along with more than three batteries. (McDowell had wanted Blenker and Davies to move their brigades to the *stone* bridge, but, once again, Miles had misunderstood or messed up his orders. It was perhaps just as well for the Union cause.) To the left of Blenker were Davies's and Richardson's brigades, and, just arriving at Centreville, were the first elements of Runyon's division. Most of the retreating soldiers returned to their bivouacs of the night before. Many had abandoned their blankets back where they had deposited their haversacks, but the absence of such comforts made little difference. They dropped to the ground and fell asleep. Some, however, continued to shuffle, zombielike, through the little village and kept going down the road toward Washington. When Runyon's New Jersey troops tried to stop them, the exhausted soldiers flowed past, using the fields and woods on either side, inexorably heading for "home." To these men, any horse or mule seemed a positive salvation. They pulled themselves aboard those they encountered, two or three at a time, and rode away from Centreville.

Tyler arrived at the village, the last Union general to do so, well after dark. Clouds were rolling in and hid the moon. He tracked down McDowell and asked what ought to be done. As Tyler recalled it, McDowell wearily said, "I don't know." Tyler decided the younger man was "completely exhausted mentally and physically." He proposed a council, and McDowell wearily acquiesced. During the council's discussion, McDowell, sitting near the fire, fell asleep, then roused himself and announced he wanted a vote on whether they ought to return to Washington or stay here. Both options had pros and cons. Staying at Centreville would avoid the appearance of a genuine retreat, and they would remain in control of all of Fairfax County, which they had taken on their way to this spot. Also, asking the troops to march twenty more miles under the circumstances could be considered unnecessary and cruel. By the time the soldiers reached their camps near Washington, they would be used up, and good for nothing for weeks. On the other hand, artillery ammunition was low, and so were provisions. Their supply line from Washington was long and narrow, a magnet for Confederate cavalry. It was unclear how many men Beauregard and Johnston had. Perhaps 60,000, some thought. Weighing all these factors, therefore, the council voted to go back. And to start immediately. It was after ten o'clock.

Then began a nightmare march.

Tyler left the conference, went and found Sherman asleep, woke him, and told him to get his brigade started. Sherman was powerfully angry, about everything—the defeat, the lack of discipline, an attitude he saw in the volunteers he considered whininess. A few hours later he saw a young officer who looked depressed. "Ever been whipped before, Captain?" "Not since I left school," the younger man replied. "Well, Captain, it's my private opinion, publicly expressed, that it's a damned disagreeable thing to be whipped!"

Some units stuck together during the long night. Blenker's Germans not only kept their cohesion but sang marching songs along the way. Keyes's three Connecticut regiments were not so boisterous, but they remained well-enough organized that they preserved not only their own stuff but also the equipment that the Ohio regiments had simply abandoned at their camp near Arlington. The Rhode Island troops also stayed together rather well, even though they had lost many of their officers in the battle. Partly this resulted from William Sprague's constant energies, and partly from their own excellent morale entering the fight. For other volunteers, however, that night's march was ghastly. An officer in Sherman's brigade later wrote his sister. "The mere loss of the men," he said, "is nothing compared to the demoralization caused by the retreat. O that retreat! I shall never forget that night. It was worse than the battle."

During the daylight hours the roads were rough — pitted and rocky. In the darkness they were far worse. Men with blistered feet would take off their shoes for relief, then find their feet too swollen to put them back on and were forced to walk barefoot. Inevitably, they bashed their raw and bleeding toes into rocks or obstructions tossed into the road by teamsters or soldiers.

Most individuals moved at whatever pace their bodies could maintain. Some tried to stay with buddies. "Over here, Rhode Island," they would shout. "Here, Seventy-ninth!" In the darkness a man would mumble to a soldier, shuffling along next to him, the two sharing their misery for whatever comfort such conversations wrought. Then they would lose track of each other and plod on in silence. Men literally dropped dead from exhaustion and dehydration. Many had convulsions. One could hear a constant muttering, "Water! Water, for God's sake! Please! Anybody have any water?"

How some of them made it all the way back cannot be explained. The report of the Sanitary Commission was shocking. One soldier whose arm had just been amputated walked the entire way. So did another with a hole through both cheeks and with his tongue nearly severed. Another poor wretch somehow found his way back, probably on a wagon, "with a large hole through both thighs and the scrotum." Yet the Commission could find no case where any of the wounded reached camp in ambulances — which, instead, were packed only with unwounded men.[201]

The Confederate Decision

About the time McDowell was holding his council at Centreville, on the far side of Bull Run the Confederate leadership was discussing what they should do. The main participants in this conversation were three weary but happy individuals: Beauregard, Johnston, and Jefferson Davis.

For days, President Davis had been impatient to go to Manassas Junction. On Saturday he had attended the official Richmond opening of the Confederate congress, then made arrangements to take a train early Sunday morning. It chugged into the depot late in the afternoon. The battle, three miles away, was just reaching its crescendo. Davis found a horse and started toward the sound. He did not like what he saw. Stragglers, many of them unwounded, with beaten countenances and slumped shoulders, lined the road. This could only mean, he thought, a desperate defeat. But when he arrived at Portici, Joe Johnston assured him the opposite was true, McDowell's army was retreating. Davis said he wished to see for himself and began to ride about the battlefield. He gave little speeches to groups of soldiers: "Brave Louisianans, I thank you from the inmost recesses of my heart." Troops huzzahed him. At some point he concluded that any immediate assault on the Yankee line at Centreville was unfeasible. His educated eyes told him the troops around him were too tired and hungry. This fact was disappointing, but its reality was palpable. He bumped into Jubal Early, who asked what he ought to do now, and Davis told him to rest his brigade. Finally, Davis returned to Beauregard's headquarters and sent a brief telegram announcing the victory.

It was well after ten o'clock before both Beauregard and Johnston arrived. Johnston had been out seeing to it that provisions were distributed to the troops. Sometime before midnight the three men were chatting when they received a report that McDowell had not settled down in Centreville, as they had presumed, but had picked up stakes and was faltering toward Washington, his army in tatters. They immediately discussed whether to haunt the Federal army, perhaps all the way to the capital, starting at first light. (Doing so at night would be risky, at the very least, because of the possibility of ambuscades.) Davis asked whether it was "possible" to launch an attack in the morning, whether any units were available. He was advised that Bonham and Longstreet were nearest to Centreville. Okay, said Davis, how about using them? Johnston and Beauregard were unresponsive. If the president insisted, they indicated, it would be done, but they were unenthusiastic. Tom Jordan, who was in the room, asked if President Davis wished to dictate to him the necessary orders. All right, said Davis, and started. He had not gotten far when Jordan noted quietly that the report about the collapse of the Yankees came from a dubious source, Captain

Robert C. Hill, whose nickname at West Point had been "Crazy Hill." The three leaders, all graduates of West Point, knowing about such nicknames, began to laugh. Clearly, Hill was still not well balanced. Following more discussion, they agreed on a simple probe just after dawn.

The Confederate reconnaissance the next morning returned with word that McDowell had indeed abandoned Centreville and left behind a plethora of guns and equipment, demonstrating the haste of his departure. Davis again suggested action. Beauregard and Johnston still resisted. It had started to rain during the night, and the dusty roads had turned to quagmires. The army lacked food and transportation. Assuming a Confederate force did reach the Alexandria-Arlington line of Federal fortifications, they had few siege guns. The Potomac was about a mile wide in front of the District, and heavily armed naval vessels would patrol its waters. The bridges north of the city for forty miles had all been burned.

Some men, like Longstreet, and even Sherman, would always maintain that the Confederacy had just lost a great opportunity, perhaps even to end the war. Joe Johnston, on the other hand, would later insist the Confederate army was more scrambled by victory than the Federals had been by defeat, but it was Johnston's wont to be cautious.

Those who admire pugnacity, who are drawn to gritty fighters like George Patton and Stonewall Jackson, agree with Longstreet. The war, they think, could now have been won by immediate aggressiveness, and to prove it they have a story. Many years after the war, Jackson's friend, the army surgeon Hunter McGuire, told an anecdote about the late afternoon of the battle. In his account, Jefferson Davis was riding through a hospital area on the battlefield, urging men to follow him into the fray. Dr. McGuire was there, and so was Jackson, having his wounded finger worked on. Stonewall had never seen Davis before and asked who that fellow was. When told, he stood up, faced the president and—according to McGuire—said, "We have whipped them; they ran like dogs. Give me ten thousand men and I will take Washington City tomorrow." Did Jackson say these words? Possibly, but unlikely. In the presence of authority figures, he was seldom so assertive, and such swaggering braggadocio was hardly his style. But if he did say it, he was wrong — even assuming Davis could find 10,000 men for him. McDowell had several fresh brigades like Blenker's, and Winfield Scott had at least another 25,000 troops near Washington. And many more were on their way toward the city. Almost certainly, taking Washington in July 1861 was as far-fetched as Lincoln's notion of grabbing Richmond had proved to be.[202]

ENVOI

Stumbling is not falling.
— PORTUGUESE PROVERB

The Union

On July 22, as morning arrived, the pitiful soldiers of McDowell's "grande armée," as Northern newspapers had been calling it, were trudging toward their camps — or just to "safety." They were filthy and ragged, defeated somewhat by rebels and very much by exhaustion. The pouring rain only added to their misery. A staff officer rode past McDowell's headquarters in Arlington. "As I approached Arlington House there was no life nor sound except that of the birds twittering in the dripping branches." A few weary horses stood nearby, their heads hanging low. Some orderlies lay asleep on the bare ground. The officer caught sight of McDowell himself. "On the portico was the solitary figure of a large man sitting on a chair with his arm hanging over the back and his bare head bowed on his breast. His flushed face and stentorian breathing indicated profound slumber. At his feet lay a soiled helmet that had once been white and the metal lance-head on top of it was broken off."

One citizen of Alexandria had had no inkling of the retreat until that morning when two soldiers came to his door to cadge a breakfast. As he looked at them and others passing by outside, he could not help sympathizing with them; they were such a miserable lot: "They sat on the door steps and curb stones from one end of the street to the other."

Not a single District newspaper that morning provided any news of the disaster. (Nor did the papers of the rest of the country. Winfield Scott's censors saw to that. Across the North, morning newspapers spoke only of McDowell's great "victory." Fort Sumter, some journals declared, had been avenged.) The soldiers who reached Washington, therefore, startled the population by their physical appearance. Walt Whitman described them. "They drop down anywhere," he wrote, "on the steps of houses, up close by the basements or fences, on the sidewalk, aside on some vacant lot... and on them sulkily drips the rain."

Few Americans had ever seen such a sight. "Wars" were distant things, abstractions. So were "defeats" and "routs." The bloody bandages, the blistered feet, the haggard cheeks and raw, sunken eyes, the stinking uniforms—these seemed the stuff of Valley Forge. Americans were ill-equipped to absorb it—or to understand that such an army, given time, can recuperate. Some Washingtonians could not believe such wraiths would ever be capable of fighting again. The exhausted troops themselves had no way to deal realistically with their own condition, so they added to the notion that they could never henceforth go off to battle. Beauregard, many of them insisted hysterically, would be here soon, his Black Horse Cavalry clattering through the streets. Citizens of the capital packed and left town. It was three or four days before the arrival of new troops provided some calm. The appearance of General George B. McClellan would also be steadying when he came to replace McDowell as commander of the army. McClellan's youth, good looks, and self-confidence provided optimism.

But not everyone felt immediate reassurance. Frederick Law Olmsted, secretary of the Sanitary Commission, was beside himself. On July 29 he wrote his wife. "We are in a frightful condition here, ten times as bad as anyone dare say publickly. I think we are getting better, but are also growing nearer a crisis—an attack. Why Beauregard does not attack I cannot imagine ... The demoralization of a large part of our troops is something more awful than I ever met with." He thought the only thing that could save them was a revolution. "You will see," he admitted, "that I am overwhelmed." Luckily for the state of his confidence, Olmsted did not know what McClellan himself thought after reviewing the camps. "I found no preparations whatever for defense," the young general would write, "not even to the extent of putting troops in military positions. Not a regiment was properly encamped, not a single a venue of approach guarded. All was chaos, and the streets, hotels, and barrooms were filled with drunken officers and men, absent from their regiments without leave — a perfect pandemonium."

General McClellan was right about the lack of discipline. The initial appearance of McDowell's bedraggled troops had been shocking to the untutored eye, but worse, in many ways, was the semilawlessness that ran through the army over the following week. A few regiments erupted into half mutinies that required a firm hand from commanders like Sherman. More often, individual soldiers left their camps and wandered through the area in search of booze or bordellos. A civilian from Alexandria wrote in his diary: "Our city is overrun with the drunken vagabonds who, being without discipline, are a terror to our people." One soldier would recall: "In every grog shop and low place were crowds, drunk, vomiting, and rolling in their filth. The hotels were crammed with mobs of officers." Some soldiers simply hoped to find food because their camps lacked provisions and cooking utensils. A private from Massachusetts wrote home: "I begged for a piece of bread, and was given some hoecake and butter; I sat down on the fence of the White House while eating it, and enjoyed it, for I was hungry."[203]

Observers found it hard to see any silver lining in all this. But they were too close to the situation. McClellan quickly brought an end to the chaos inside Washington. He named General Porter head of the Provost Guard and commanded him to bring order. Porter used the regulars as his fist — the cavalry and Sykes's men. On July 26 an enlisted man from the Second New Hampshire shot and killed a young woman, Mary Butler, on the streets of

Alexandria. He was drunk and apparently had never met her. A military tribunal met within hours and sentenced him to be executed. They wanted the lesson to be clear. A gallows was erected on a nearby parapet, and all available regiments were ordered to stand at attention and watch the hanging. Private William F. Murray was the first Union soldier executed for attacking a civilian.

Olmsted and his Sanitary Commission investigated the army's condition and concluded, in some surprise, that many regiments actually had not fallen apart during the battle or the retreat. To Olmsted himself, the pattern was clear: "As a rule, the best officered, the best disciplined, and the best fed regiments, were obviously the least demoralized." During the next few weeks, about two hundred officers resigned to avoid public embarrassment; others left quietly before boards of investigation could humiliate them. As a result, perhaps a third of McDowell's officers were soon gone. In general this was a blessing.

(Almost no one understood that McDowell's soldiers had actually fought very well. It took half a century before a statistician, analyzing casualties at the battle, noted that the aim of Union infantrymen at Bull Run was better than that of the Confederates. Using a complex mathematical formula, he showed that the fire from every thousand Union infantrymen hit a hundred rebels, whereas each thousand Confederates hit only eighty. The accuracy of the Union soldiers' fire was therefore "superior," despite the assumption that Southern boys had had more experience with guns. This revelation also indicates something else. Since properly using a rifle or a musket in that battle meant standing firm against enemy fire, grit was required, and Lincoln's soldiers had therefore shown that their courage was equal to that of the Confederates. Unfortunately, this fact had been muddied out of all recognition by the physical appearance of the soldiers after their retreat.)

During the weeks after the battle, there was a noticeable decline in enthusiasm for the war. It became harder to fill military quotas—in both North and South. This was especially true in the Northeast—though partly that was due to an improved job market there. The war was less romantic now, and soldiers had less ardor. They also had more respect for their enemy. "We have learned," a private from Wisconsin wrote home, "that they are not a miserable rabble, half-clothed and half-armed, but a well-armed, powerful army." If the war had turned out to be of short duration, Bull Run would have been a disaster for the Union. But if, as now seemed more plausible, a long and nasty war was inevitable, that battle had a curiously salutary effect for the Union side. It proved a wake-up call for those optimists—like Seward and even Lincoln—who had hoped for or counted on a quick result.[204]

Horace Greeley, whose newspaper, the *New York Tribune,* had shouted the slogan "On to Richmond," felt wretched. He could not sleep. "This is my seventh sleepless night," he wrote the president. "You are not considered a great man, and I am a hopelessly broken one." As Greeley saw it, everywhere there was "black despair." He concluded, "If it is best for the country and mankind that we make peace with the Rebels at once and on their own terms, do not shrink even from that." Lincoln read this and sighed. He did not reply. He had no intention now of backing down. Besides, he was rather confident Greeley was wrong about "public sentiment"; he sensed little "black despair."

On the afternoon of the battle, about the time McDowell decided to withdraw from the field, President Lincoln was still out riding, thinking the Union army had won. At six o'clock, while Lincoln was away, Seward arrived at the White House. The secretary of state looked haggard. He told Nicolay in confidence the battle had been lost and said, "Find the President and tell him immediately to come to General Scott's." A few minutes later Lincoln returned. Nicolay told him what Seward had said. Lincoln listened in silence. He showed no expression. He walked to the War Department, where he read the following message from McDowell: "The day is lost. Save Washington and the remnants of this army. The routed troops will not re-form." Soon after that, a few politicians dropped in to see what news the War Department had. The president told them he was not at liberty to say, but when one of them pressed him, he gripped the man on the arm and whispered, "It's damned bad." That night Lincoln slept little. He stayed at the War Department until after two o'clock, then retreated to his office, where he continued to receive reports as they filtered in. Telegrams were sent out by Winfield Scott and his staff to various military headquarters, telling them the news, urging them to send reinforcements. Lincoln made notes.

Victor Hugo once asked, "Is the shipwreck due to the pilot?" In this case the correct answer is: Yes, partly. It was, after all, the president's insistence that had pushed the army to Bull Run against the advice of Winfield Scott. But Lincoln was not broken by this defeat. In the ensuing days he sent orders to stiffen the blockade and strengthen his forces in northern Virginia. A week after Bull Run he wrote a memo. He wanted his four main armies to press forward—the one at Cairo, Illinois (soon to be under the command of Ulysses S. Grant), the one centered at Cincinnati (which would in a few months be led by William Tecumseh Sherman), the third at Harpers Ferry (which had been commanded by General Patterson and would eventually have a long list of undistinguished leaders), and the fourth at the Arlington-Alexandria line (with George B. McClellan in charge). Those orders to his navy and this memo pretty much summarized the rest of the Civil War.

On the surface the change in Lincoln was not dramatic. Before the battle he had maintained an outward calm—though at some cost in sleeplessness and a nervous stomach. The loss at Bull Run made him stronger. This country lawyer had a marvelous capacity for growth, and he now grew. Not in his resolve, which remained as steely as ever. Nor in his humanity or compassion, for these qualities of his seemed almost without depth. The change came in his acceptance of part of the heavy price the nation would have to pay—though it would be more than a year before he embraced emancipation, and even then only as a military necessity. During the war's first hundred days, he had shown a spasmodic willingness to apply a certain *toughness*—especially in Maryland—but after Bull Run, he was far firmer. As one of Lincoln's biographers, Stephen B. Oates, has said, in the war's early days, Lincoln was opposed to turning the war into what the president called a "remorseless revolutionary struggle." His early policies had been both limited and cautious. Bull Run goaded this conservative politician toward the "revolution" that the war eventually became.[205]

Francis Scott Key's famous poem that became the national anthem was not about winning battles. It was about character, not victory. Did America, Key's poem might be asking, have the moral fiber it took to get off the mat when knocked down? Courage is a fine quality, but losses are inevitable. A nation shows its backbone when it shrugs off losses. What neither side in the Civil War had taken into account is that Americans, North and South, had heard repeatedly of Lexington and Concord, of Cowpens and Bunker Hill, of Valley Forge. But those were not tales of gallantry and victory. They were stories about fortitude. George Washington was the great national model because he had stuck it out, for eight long years of war. By 1861 his type of determination had been taught to every child for three full generations. Given this, how could Northerners now give up? They would have failed the great test; they would have had to turn George Washington's picture to the wall. In Providence, Rhode Island, two days after Bull Run, a local newspaper carried an editorial: "To the brave man defeat is only an argument for new effort. Our banner, which has been trailing in the dust, must be lifted up towards the stars... Let no man lisp the word discouragement." The editor then asked, "What is to be done? Everything... Let us begin today. Let not an hour be lost." *Frank Leslie's Illustrated Weekly*, one of the most popular magazines in the country, said the loss at Bull Run would "rouse the whole North as one man, and cause an army of overwhelming proportions to be thrown upon Virginia, where a bloodier and more terrible conflict will ensue."

The day following the battle, as the exhausted, muddy volunteers were still streaming into the capital, a resolution was introduced in the House, "declaring that the maintenance of the Constitution and the preservation of the Union are paramount duties, and that no disasters shall discourage us from their performance." This measure passed overwhelmingly. Interestingly, on that same day both houses of Congress also passed Senator Crittenden's resolution that the war was not intended to "subjugate" Southerners nor interfere with slavery. (Slaveholders, however, would have felt more nervous had they noted that the Senate Judiciary Committee that day added a clause to a bill it was considering, permitting the confiscation of the "property" of rebels.)

A certain rage was creeping across the North. Four days after Bull Run, a Northern Democrat announced, "I go for liberating the niggers. We are fighting on a false issue. The negro is at the bottom of the trouble. The south is fighting for the negro, and nothing else." To that man at least, emancipation would be an act of vengeance.[206]

The Confederacy

On the day of the Battle of Bull Run, Varina Davis, in Richmond, attended the funeral of a friend's child. She then returned to the Spotswood — and waited. The hours dragged. The members of Davis's cabinet also cooled their heels, spending much time at the War Department, hoping to receive bulletins from the battlefield. By evening most of them had a sour feeling that a terrible disaster had taken place up at Manassas Junction. One cabinet member went to the Spotswood to see if Varina Davis had heard anything. A few minutes later he returned to his colleagues, beaming. Mrs. Davis, he said, had just received a telegram from her husband. Their army had won a "glorious victory."

It is touching, but curious, that Jefferson Davis's first message to Richmond was a short note to his wife, followed for many hours by no official word from him. If Varina had not immediately shared his wire, the cabinet would not have known. As it was, not until the following morning did many citizens of Richmond hear the news. Yet there was little public celebration. Unlike the hours just after Virginia's secession, the city engaged in no parades, no bonfires, no military salutes. A gloomy sky, high winds, and torrents of rain kept most folks indoors. Also it dawned on people that a "great battle" meant great losses, no matter which side won.

The official records of the Confederacy listed 387 killed and 1,582 wounded — a total of 1,969. These figures are certainly wrong. Among other things, many of those listed as "wounded" died within a few days of the battle. Also, record keeping before the battle had been haphazard, so it would have been impossible to calculate the real losses. Furthermore, during the next month a great many Confederate soldiers near Manassas Junction sickened and died. Disease accounted for most of these deaths, but certainly some were the result of the physical demands of the battle. Of the casualties—on either side—it is also impossible to know how many were the direct result of enemy fire. A large percentage, of course, had been killed by "friendly fire." Others died from accidents—crushed by wagons, for example, or drowned in Bull Run. An unknown number died of heatstroke. Federal losses, not counting prisoners or those listed as "missing," were lower: the official number was 1,584. This, too, was an understatement, though by how much it is impossible to know.

One can safely estimate that about a thousand Americans were killed at Bull Run and perhaps three thousand more were wounded. (Putting this in a frame of reference that American citizens in 1861 could relate to: Only 1,733 American soldiers had been killed during the *entire* Mexican War, so more than half as many Americans were killed in eight hours at Bull Run than were killed in two years of the previous conflict.) As a percentage of those who actually fought on the battlefield, these losses would have been about 15 percent, dreadful by any definition. There had never been a day like it in the history of the nation. Later in this war, and after other wars, some would declare the losses at Bull Run almost "insignificant." Such a notion is ludicrous. Thousands of American families had just been permanently scarred. The deaths affected communities in eleven Northern states and nine Southern—though about half were from towns in Virginia and New York. The country would never again be the same. As one Virginian said, "War was no longer funny."

A tobacco warehouse on Main Street in Richmond, Harwood's, was designated to house Yankee prisoners. It would prove insufficient. The Confederacy had to find places to stuff 1,421 prisoners, many of whom were wounded soldiers found in battlefield hospitals. Eventually, some prisoners would be sent farther south—to North Carolina, to New Orleans, to Charleston. During the winter, under a system of prisoner exchange, the survivors began to return home. The Joint Committee interviewed a few of them. The treatment they had received, they said, varied. Several guards in Richmond were unnecessarily cruel, medical care was scanty, food was minimal. None of this was surprising. The Confederacy had been unprepared for such a deluge. The testimony of the ex-prisoners did show that tales that had been floating around were exaggerated or false. There were no cases of uncontrollable civilian mobs. A handful of individual Confederate soldiers had acted barbarically — on the battlefield, and after — but most Northerners understood that that was to be expected.

In towns throughout Virginia, homeowners volunteered to take in wounded Confederates because there were too many of them for the state's few hospital facilities. These towns soon had more than their share of soldiers with bandaged heads or of limping veterans clumsily swinging along on crutches, their amputated legs waving like bloody banners. Meanwhile, throughout the South could be heard the dour notes of the "Dead March" from *Saul*. All this made it hard to rejoice. A married woman, a refugee from Alexandria, kept a diary. On July 22, when she first heard the news about victory, she jotted quickly, "The victory is ours! The enemy was routed! The Lord be praised for this great mercy." A few hours later, after hearing of the fate of two young boys she knew, she added these words: "How can I record the death of our young friends, the Conrads of Martinsburg?"

At Manassas there was much grim work. The dead had to be buried. Usually this task would have been turned over to slaves, but there were far too many bodies. And besides, comrades often wanted to perform the task themselves. One Virginian decided it was his sworn duty to bury his friend Blue. He looked around for a shovel but could only find a hoe and a spade; these would have to do. He started digging in the orchard next to Mrs. Henry's house. A Georgian came up and asked if he could borrow the tools afterward, since he wished to bury his brother. The two agreed to work together, to dig one hole large enough for both corpses. "So we buried them that way," the Virginian recalled, "and gathered up some old shingles to put over the bodies."

Not everyone in Virginia had such woeful experiences. In Lynchburg it was raining hard on July 22. Inside the house of the

Blackford family, many anxious people waited, including numerous women and children. During the afternoon the head of the household, the father of three sons at Manassas, went to town to see if he could learn any news. He returned, through the downpour, in an hour. "At last we heard his footsteps on the front porch," one of the women recalled, "and our hearts stopped beating." Everyone rushed to the door, where the old man stood, trying to catch his breath. Then he shouted, "All safe!" The women sobbed for joy as the old man "offered up thanks to God for having spared [their] loved ones." (That same day one of the father's sons was riding across the battlefield. He passed a dead Yankee and noticed that next to the body was a baby doll with only one leg. He stopped and stared down a moment. He decided it was a memento of someone dear to this poor fellow. He dismounted, picked up the doll, and gently stuffed it inside the dead man's coat.)

In Centreville on July 22, crowds of local whites and slaves gathered around the abandoned Federal wagons, scooping up such victuals as flour that might well have been lost in the rain.

Also on that date General Jackson wrote a letter to the Reverend Dr. White of Lexington, Virginia. "My dear pastor, in my tent last night, after a fatiguing day's service, I remembered that I had failed to send you my contribution for our colored Sunday-school. Enclosed you will find my check."

That day's downpour meant the ground was too soggy to farm anywhere in northern Virginia. It was still too damp on Tuesday, but on Wednesday the weather improved. John Wheeler, a farmer near Washington, cut his oats. In his diary he pronounced this crop the best he had seen. The following day he noted that his corn was also quite fine. Life went on.

On Tuesday evening, July 23, Amos Benson and his wife, Margaret, who lived in the community of Sudley, noticed a still form in a blue uniform lying in the weeds near their fence. Cautiously, they approached it and found the man alive, barely. He turned out to be Private John L. Rice of the Second New Hampshire. He had a bullet embedded in his lung. A Confederate surgeon came by and glanced at him and announced that the Yankee stood no chance. The Bensons, devout Christians who attended the Methodist church not far away, tried to make the enemy's last hours comfortable. They knew he was too injured to move, so they built a tent to cover him. They dressed his wound, they fed him, they brought him water. Ten days they spent caring for Private Rice. He lived. In time he was officially declared a prisoner of war and sent to Richmond. When he was later exchanged, he reenlisted and rose eventually to the rank of colonel.

In 1886 John Rice returned to the battlefield, as a tourist, just to see it. There, by chance, he met the Bensons. Amos had joined a cavalry unit early in 1862, had fought, and survived. John Rice found it impossible to think of Amos Benson as an enemy. The Bensons — the whole Sudley community — were not well-off. The war and the postwar years had been harsh. Colonel Rice thanked them for saving his life, for all their kindnesses. Nonsense, they said, they had only been following common decency, the "dictates of humanity." Was there anything, Rice asked, he could do for them? No, they said, but their church had fallen on hard times, so if he could contribute anything to help refurbish the structure — a dollar or two — it would be much appreciated.

He returned home to Springfield, Massachusetts, and wrote this story in his local newspaper and asked for contributions for the little church in Virginia. Within days, enough money was raised to rebuild the place. The building that served as a hospital on July 21, 1861, had become part of the healing process between North and South. Racism would prove deep and long-lived, but secession and slavery, at least, were dead. Citizens of Massachusetts and Virginia had just joined together in a common endeavor, to build something lasting. It was fitting.[207]

ACKNOWLEDGMENTS

I am pleased to thank many people. Without the tireless assistance of Joanne Elpern, expert tracker of ILL materials, I would still be scrambling about the bowels of a hundred libraries. My friend George Combs opened my eyes to the richness of Alexandria's history, and no doubt he ought to accept the consequences of that act. David Ward and Vesta Lee Gordon both shared their vast bibliographic knowledge with me. Rich Gallagher and J. Randolph Cox advised me about the reading matter of Civil War soldiers. Michael Ball at West Point and Gary Gallagher at the University of Virginia answered my tiresome questions. So did Jim Burgess and Tim Nosal of the Manassas National Battlefield Park, and Lydia Rapoza of the Cranston (Rhode Island) Historical Society. The staffs at countless libraries assisted me, most particularly, Southern Mississippi State University, Maryland Historical Society, the Library of Congress, the Connecticut State Archives, and the USMHI at Carlisle Barracks, Pennsylvania.

And in this computerized world, it is important to thank all those individuals who have taken the time to place obscure manuscript materials on their Web sites. Tom Hayes, in Massachusetts, for example, has performed a magnificent service to all of us who study the Civil War. Hundreds of others have shared with us their private collections of letters or their knowledge about local military units; thus they have enriched our understanding.

NOTES

Throughout this book I have occasionally altered quotations in slight matters involving punctuation and spelling, but only to modernize nineteenth-century usage.

For the sake of brevity, I have used the following shorthand notations in the endnotes:

AL   *The Collected Works of Abraham Lincoln,* 9 vols., New Brunswick, NJ: Rutgers University Press, 1953–55.

BAL   *Battles and Leaders of the Civil War,* 4 vols.

CCW   37th Con., 3d sess., *Report of the Joint Committee on the Conduct of the War,* Washington, 1863.

CWTI   *Civil War Times Illustrated.*

CV   *Confederate Veteran.*

ER   Edmund Ruffin, *The Diary of Edmund Ruffin,* edited by William Kauffman Scarborough, 3 vols., Baton Rouge, Louisiana: Louisiana State University Press, 1972–1980.

JD   Jefferson Davis, *The Papers of Jefferson Davis,* eds. Lynda Lasswell Crist et al., Baton Rouge, Louisiana: Louisiana State University Press, 1971–.

LSUP   Louisiana State University Press (Baton Rouge, Louisiana).

MNBP   Manassas National Battlefield Park, Archives.

MIL   H. L. Scott, *Military Dictionary,* 1861.

MO   Alfred Roman, *The Military Operations of General Beauregard,* 2 vols, New York, 1884.

MOLLUS   Military Order of the Loyal Legion of the United States.

OR   The War of the Rebellion: A Compilation of the Official Records of
      the Union and Confederate Armies, 1880–1901.
ORN   Official Records of the Union and Confederate Navies in the War of
      the Rebellion, 1897–1927.
SCL   South Carolina Library, University of South Carolina
      (Columbia).
SHSP Southern Historical Society Papers.
UNC   Archives, University of North Carolina.
UNCP University of North Carolina Press (Chapel Hill).
USCP University of South Carolina Press (Columbia).
UVA   University of Virginia.

The Sacred Soil

1. OR, ser. 1, II, 43–44. Singing: Alexander Hunter, *Johnny Reb and Billy Yank* (New York, 1905), 40–41. Hugh Henry letter, May 30, 1861, MNBP. For exodus: John B. Zimmerman, Diary, Archives, Alexandria Library; Edgar Warfield, *A Confederate Soldier's Memoirs* (Richmond, 1936), 32; George Wise, *History of the Seventeenth Virginia Infantry, C.S.A.* (Baltimore, 1870), 13–15; John Ogden, "The Town Is Took," *Alexandria History* (1981), III, 10; T. Michael Miller, *Pen Portraits* (Alexandria, 1987), 231–32.

2. Mary Chesnut's lunch: C. Vann Woodward (ed.), *Mary Chesnut's Civil War* (New Haven, 1981), 62.

3. Davis: see, especially, William C. Davis, *Jefferson Davis: The Man and His Hour* (New York, 1991) and Steven E. Woodworth, *Davis and Lee at War* (Lawrence, Kansas, 1995). "I have an infirmity": Carl Sandberg, *Abraham Lincoln: The War Years* (New York, 1939), I, 247. Varina Davis in Richmond: Alfred Hoyt Bill, *The Beleaguered City: Richmond, 1861–1865* (New York, 1946), 53–55.

4. On railroads in general: George Edgar Turner, *Victory Rode the Rails* (New York, 1953); Angus James Johnston, Jr., *Virginia Railroads in the Civil War* (UNCP, 1961). British correspondent: William Howard Russell, *My Diary North and South* (New York 1988), 208. South Carolina traveler: Richard Lewis, *Camp Life of a Confederate Boy* (Charleston, 1883), 9–10. Sabbath: letter to the *Charleston Courier*, July 3, 1861.

5. Robert E. Lee: Everyone must begin with Douglas Southall Freeman's magisterial four-volume biography, *R. E. Lee: A Biography* (New York, 1934–35); refreshing correctives to the Lee hagiography include Thomas L. Connelly, *The Marble Man* (New York, 1977) and Alan T. Nolan, *Lee Reconsidered* (UNCP, 1991)—see, especially, for this period, Nolan, 31–43. Davis: "we seek no conquest" in William C. Davis, *Jefferson Davis: The Man and His Hour* (New York, 1991), 329. CSA assertiveness: see, e.g., Joseph L. Harsh, *Confederate Tide Rising: Robert E. Lee and the Making of Southern Strat-*

egy, 1861–1862 (Kent, Ohio, 1998). Lee and railroads: Turner, 68; order to Cocke: OR, series 1, II, 806. "strictly defensive": ibid., 1, II, 865.

6. Cocke: physician's remarks: Robert Enoch Withers, *Autobiography of an Octogenarian* (Roanoke, 1907), 134–35; see also Charles Minor Blackford, III (ed.), *Letters from Lee's Army* (New York, 1947), 12. Bonham: Max Wyckoff, *A History of the 2nd South Carolina Infantry, 1861–1865* (Fredericksburg, Virginia, 1994), 3; Edward G. Longacre, "On the Staff of the Dictator," *Manuscripts*, 36 (Summer 1984), 224–227; Thomas W. Cutrer, *Longstreet's Aide: The Civil War Letters of Major Thomas J. Goree* (Charlottesville, 1995), 25. Flurry of official messages: OR, series 1, II, 42–43, 817–19, 841–42, 845, 865; series 1, LI/2, 108–09. May 29 rumor and march at Manassas Junction: Charles T. Loehr, *War History of the Old First Virginia Infantry Regiment* (Richmond, 1884), 8.

7. MO, I, 66–67; Woodworth, 22–25.

8. Beauregard's arrival: Roman, I, 71; William Presley McKnight, letter to mother, May 28, 1861, Papers, Alexandria Library; William Frierson Fulton, *Family Record and Reminiscences* (Livingston, Alabama, 1919), 45. Beauregard report and proclamation: OR, series 1, II, 901, 907; see also *Richmond Enquirer,* May 7, 1861, *Charleston Courier,* May 8 and June 7, 1861; see also William Fisher Plane to Helen, June 1, 1861, in S. Joseph Lewis, Jr., "The Letters of William Fisher Plane, C.S.A. to His Wife," *The Georgia Historical Quarterly,* 48 (1964), 217.

Untenable Position

9. The best recent biography of Jackson is by Byron Farwell, *Stonewall* (New York, 1992). Sifting through the hagiography, one can derive various insights from certain primary sources: Hunter McGuire, "Stonewall Jackson," SHSP, 19 (1891), 291–319; D. B. Conrad, "History of the First Battle of Manassas," ibid., 82–91; J. William Jones, "Stonewall Jackson," ibid., 145–64; Thomas Jackson Arnold, *Early Life and Letters of General Thomas J. Jackson* (New York, 1916), especially 310–38; George Cary Eggleston, *A Rebel's Recollections* (New York, 1874), especially 132–34; and Mary Anna Jackson, *Memoirs of Stonewall Jackson* (Louisville, 1895), which contains his letters to her. "well-nigh morbid devotion": Eggleston, 133. "that's the reason I don't drink it": McGuire, 315. "halves of his body": Conrad, 83.

10. "He made me sick": quoted in Farwell, 150.

11. "Who is this Colonel Jackson?": Jones, 146. whiskey barrels: Opie, 19–20.

12. OR, 1, II, 824–25.

13. The two best biographies of Johnston differ: Gilbert Eaton Govan and James Weston Livingood, *A Different Valor: The Story of Joseph E. Johnston, C.S.A.* (New York, 1956) has a higher opinion of the general than Craig L. Symonds, *Joseph E. Johnston* (New York, 1992). See also Joseph E.

Johnston, *Narrative of Military Operations* (New York, 1874); Bradley T. Johnson (ed.), *A Memoir of the Life and Public Service of Joseph E. Johnston* (Baltimore, 1891). Alexander, "looks, carriage & manner": Gary W. Gallagher (ed.), *Fighting for the Confederacy: The Personal Recollections of General Edward Porter Alexander* (UNCP, 1989), 48. Wadsworth, "ablest officer": JC, II, 48.

14. "undisciplined of course"; "natural fortress": Johnston, 16, 17.

15. The best biography of Stuart is Emory M. Thomas, *Bold Dragoon: The Life of J. E. B. Stuart* (New York, 1986). For the story about him and Howard at West point, see Thomas, 23–25; cf., O. O. Howard's autobiography (New York, 1908). "you don't want to go back to camp" and "remembering our names and faces": Eggleston, 123, 124. "galloped down to us laughing": W. W. Blackford, *War Years with Jeb Stuart* (LSUP reprint, 1993), 18. Stuart to Flora, July 4, 1861, Stuart Papers, Robert W. Woodruff Library, Emory University.

The School of the Soldier

16. George H. Carmical, "Reminiscence," typescript, MNBP.

17. The sources on Civil War military life and thought form a vast library, but the following were quite helpful: John D. Billings, *Hardtack and Coffee* (Boston, 1888); Bell Irvin Wiley's classics, *The Life of Billy Yank* (LSUP, 1952) and *The Life of Johnny Reb* (LSUP, 1943); Joseph Allen Frank and George A. Reaves, *'Seeing the Elephant': Raw Recruits at the Battle of Shiloh* (New York, 1989); James M. McPherson, *For Cause and Comrades: Why Men Fought in the Civil War* (New York, 1997), and also *What They Fought For* (LSUP, 1994); Reid Mitchell, *Civil War Soldiers* (New York, 1988), and *The Vacant Chair: The Northern Soldier Leaves Home* (New York, 1993); Earl J. Hess, *The Union Soldier in Battle* (Lawrence, Kansas, 1997). It is also useful to compare Civil War military experiences with those of other eras: See, e.g., Richard Holmes, *Acts of War: The Behavior of Men in Battle* (New York, 1985); F. M. Richardson, *Fighting Spirit* (London, 1978); Anthony Kellett, *Combat Motivation* (Boston, 1982); and William L. Hauser, "The Will To Fight," in *Combat Effectiveness*, ed. Sam C. Sarkesian (Beverly Hills, 1980), 186–211; Brent Nosworthy, *The Bloody Crucible of Courage: Fighting Methods and Combat Experience of the Civil War* (New York, 2003). On mid-nineteenth-century history textbooks: Ruth Miller Elson, *Guardian of Tradition: American Schoolbooks of the Nineteenth Century* (Lincoln, 1964), especially 324–27.

18. "elected First Sergeant": Elisha Hunt Rhodes, *The First Campaign of the Second Rhode Island Infantry* (Providence, 1878), 13. "Ike": *Roxbury City Gazette*, July 5, 1861. "drunk on dress parade": Gustavus Sullivan Dana, "'Bully for the First Connecticut' The Recollections of a Three-Month Volunteer," ed. Lester L. Swift, *Lincoln Herald*, Summer, 1965, LXVII, 76; see also Andrew McClintock to his sister Jane, July 6, 1861, in *Waterbury* (Connecticut) *Republican*, February 12, 1989. "deferential politeness":

Charles B. Haydon, *For Country, Cause & Leader: The Civil War Journal of Charles B. Haydon*, ed. Stephen W. Sears (New York, 1993), 7. "selling rations": William Howard Russell, *My Diary North and South* (New York, 1988), 233. "shoulder-straps": George Cary Eggleston, *A Rebel's Recollections* (New York, 1874), 72. "popskull": Jesse Walton Reid, *History of the Fourth Regiment of S. C. Volunteers* (Charleston, 1891), 8.

19. John S. French, "'We Have Got a Noble Set of Fellows,'" CWTI (October 1975), XIV, 15.

20. Cudworth, 32; William Greene Roelker, "Civil War Letters of William Ames," *Rhode Island Historical Society Collections* (October 1940), XXXIII, 83–84; C. Vann Woodward, ed., *Mary Chesnut's Civil War* (New Haven, 1981), 90; D. G. Crotty, *Four Years Campaigning in the Army of the Potomac* (Grand Rapids, 1874), 19. "pretys girls": Chester McArthur Destler, "The Second Michigan Volunteer Infantry Joins the Army of the Potomac," *Michigan History* (December 1957), XLI, 395–96.

21. Bookstore: *Richmond Dispatch*, July 8, 1861. On the various manuals, see especially Grady McWhiney and Perry D. Jamieson, *Attack and Die: Civil War Military Tactics and the Southern Heritage* (University, Alabama, 1982), 25–79.

22. "run in disorder": MIL, 401–02.

23. Making cartridges: *Harper's Weekly*, June 20, 1861, 449–50. "considered ourselves": John M. Gould, *History of the First-Tenth-Twenty-ninth Maine Regiment* (Portland, 1871), 49. "a barrel": Jesse Walton Reid, *History of the Fourth Regiment of S. C. Volunteers* (Charleston, 1891), 15. "sharp drill": Charles B. Haydon, *For Country, Cause & Leader*, ed. Stephen W. Sears (New York, 1993), 14. Mississippi practice: Augustus L. P. Vairin, Diary, June 29, 1861, ed. Andrew Brown, <www.rootsweb.com>. Sentinel: "Hal," *Chelsea* (Massachusetts) *Telegraph and Pioneer*, July 20, 1861.

24. "Bullfroggs": Walker G. Twyman, letter to Billy, June 15, 1861, Twyman Papers, UVA. "green boy": David E. Johnston, *The Story of a Confederate Boy in the Civil War* (Portland, Oregon, 1914), 50–51. "I don't know 'beans'": Richard Moe, *The Last Full Measure: The Life and Death of the First Minnesota Volunteers* (New York, Henry Holt and Company, 1993), 16. Maine letters: J. H. Bacon to mother, July 4, 1861, and W. F. Bacon to mother, July 7, 1861, MNBP. "whiskie": William P. Holland to Papa, July 7, 1861, Holland Papers, UVA.

25. "men are only children": Billings, 38. Sanitary Commission's Report: "Report of a Preliminary Survey of the Camps of a Portion of the Volunteer Forces," July 9, 1861. See also the extensive interview with Dr. John C. Peters of the Commission, *New York Tribune*, July 20, 1861 (which is the source about the robes and slippers); Frederick Law Olmsted, *The Papers of Frederick Law Olmstead*, ed. Jane Turner Censer (Baltimore, 1986), IV; the delightfully accurate and ignorant military advice of Dr. J. Walter Booth, *The Soldier's Pocket Health Companion* (New York, 1861), which

suggested that bad cooking was harmful, as was any bathing over three minutes or drinking water during a march. George Worthington Adams, *Doctors in Blue* (New York, 1952), is an excellent summary, and page 12 is the source for the estimate of about 400 women who enrolled in the army. Sarah Emma Edmonds: Patricia Lee Holt, "Female Spy, Male Nurse," *Military History* (August, 1988), V, 8ff.

26. Fourth Maine: Edward K. Gould, *Major-General Hiram G. Berry* (Rockland, Maine, 1899), 47–48. First Massachusetts: Warren Cudworth, *History of the First Regiment* (Boston, 1866), 29; "Hal," *Chelsea Telegraph and Pioneer,* June 29, 1861; *Roxbury City Gazette,* June 27, 1861 ("unidentified," is the source for "negro boy"). Southern marching: Culpeper's journal is among the holdings at the McCain Library and Archives, University of Southern Mississippi; some of it is paginated, and the quotations here appear on page 64 and page 78. The last quotation is from an unpaginated section, but dated July 13; Hanger's "Diary" is drawn from "Valley of the Shadow," on the Virginia Center for Digital History's Web site.

27. A soldier's uniform and accouterments: Benjamin Apthorp Gould, *Investigations in the Military and Anthropological Statistics of American Soldiers* (New York, 1869); William Watson, *Life in the Confederate Army* (London, 1887), 183–84; Frederick P. Todd, *American Military Equipage, 1851–1872* (New York, 1974).

28. The best single source on Civil War "grub" is Billings, especially 72–95, but also see William C. Davis, *A Taste for War* (Mechanicsburg, Pennsylvania, 2003). Olmsted: "Report No. 17," 8–11, 21–23. "instinctively a cook": *Charleston Courier,* June 26, 1861. "yellow-man-cook" and "first-rate cook": William King to wife, Annie Leftwich King, July 12 and 14, 1861, King Papers, UVA. Connecticut's contraband cook: McClintock to Jane, June 20, 1861, *Waterbury Republican,* February 5, 1989. "exploring expedition": John S. French, "'We Have Got a Noble Set of Fellows,'" CWTI (October, 1975), XIV, 21. twenty-five cent meal: "H. F. R.," *Chelsea Telegraph and Pioneer* (June 8, 1861). "cherries we have": Charles H. Thurston to mother, July 2, 1861, Thurston Papers, UVA. "whortle berries": unnamed member of the Second Wisconsin, July 8, 1861, on the Web site <www.secondwi.com>. "damned flies": John Henry Burrill to mother, July 12, 1861, Burrill Papers, State Historical Society of Wisconsin, Madison. "thimbleberries": Allen Alonzo Kingsbury, "Journal," June 27, 1861, in *Hero of Medfield* (Boston, 1862). "a-skirmishing": July 30, 1861, in "A Biography of Col. William Henry Walling," unpaginated typescript, Carlisle Barracks. "double handfuls": Haydon, 42.

Tentative Warriors

29. "to investigate"; "principal cause": CCW, I, 1, 5. For an excellent analysis, see Bruce Tap, *Over Lincoln's Shoulder* (Lawrence, Kansas, 1998).

30. Bruce Catton, *The Coming Fury* (New York, 1961), 445; Shelby Foote, *The Civil War: A Narrative* (New York, 1958), I, 57; James McPherson (New York, 1988), 335; Allan Nevins, *The War of the Union* (New York, 1959), I, 58; and Ethan S. Rafuse, *A Single Grand Victory* (Wilmington, Delaware, 2002), 37.

31. "you are green": McDowell's recollection of Lincoln's statement at the meeting, given to the Joint Committee in December 1861: CCW, II, 36, 38. OR, 1, II, 118, 672.

32. Ibid., 680–81.

33. "timid": Ibid., 934. "panic": JD, VII, 208–09. "altered muskets" and "never marched a day": John O. Casler, *Four Years in the Stonewall Brigade* (Girard, Kansas, 1906), 17, 16.

34. Nor was Scott alone in his panic at this juncture; Cameron wired New York on June 18, pleading for more troops, immediately. Scott's notes are in the OR, 1, II, 691, 694–6; Cameron's on page 700. In 1862 General George Cadwalader, who commanded the brigade that the regulars were part of, told the CCW that Johnston's pullback from Harpers Ferry had made Washington believe he was about to join Beauregard in a combined attack on Washington, but Cadwalader offered no evidence: CCW, II, 235. The best source is Patterson, 33–47, simply because here one can also sense his befuddlement. "threatened advance": George Templeton Strong, *Diary of the Civil War, 1860–1865* (New York, 1962), I, 158.

35. Maynard J. Shier, "The Battle of Falling Waters" CWTI 15 (February 1977), 16–26; James O. Pierce, "The Skirmish at Falling Waters," *Glimpses at the Nation's Struggle*, MOLLUS (St. Paul, Minnesota, 1890), II, 289–313; William Henry Locke, *The Story of the Regiment* (Philadelphia, 1868), 14–24. "climbed upon the fences": Opie, 21–22.

To Carry the War into Africa

36. "an act of faith" and "excellent intentions": Louis M. Starr, *Bohemian Brigade: Civil War Newsmen in Action* (New York, 1954), 16–17. Among the local newspapers that reprinted the *Tribune*'s headline was, e.g., the medium-circulation *Hartford Courant*, but its rival, the *Hartford Daily Times* refused and took issue with it over the issue (see July 24, 1861); a casual survey of scores of Northern newspapers confirms such a pattern — see J. Cutler Andrews, *The North Reports the Civil War* (Pittsburgh, 1955), 98–99. "the popular mood": Richard S. Sewell, *A House Divided* (Baltimore, 1988), 93. John G. Nicolay and John Hay, *Abraham Lincoln: A History* (New York, 1904–07), IV, 321.

37. Scott's late-May meeting: Charles T. Stone, "Washington in 1861," *The Magazine of American History*, 12 (July 1884), 56–61. Chase and McDowell: Russel H. Beatie, *Army of the Potomac: Birth of the Command, November 1860 to September 1861* (New York, 2002), 145–46; see also ibid., 205–7, for McDowell's evolving thinking by late June. McDowell explained his

plan: Letter to Chase, May 16, 1861, Chase Papers, microfilm, University Publications of America.

38. "Delmonico chef" and "sylph-like grace": John Tidball, "War Journal," typescript, United States Military Academy, 226a, 227. McDowell's promotion: Whitelaw Reid, *Ohio in the War* (New York, 1868), I, 658–59; James Henry Stine, *History of the Army of the Republic* (Philadelphia, 1892), 2–3; Nicolay and Hay, IV, 323, say that Lincoln actually offered McDowell the rank of major general, but that McDowell turned it down: "It would be unjust to his brother officers, he said." McDowell's assignment: Cf., his testimony, CCW, II, 37; Stine, 6–8, quotes Schuyler Hamilton as saying that Scott tried to induce McDowell to take command of the Anaconda Plan's Mississippi venture, and when McDowell said he could not and left, Scott said to Hamilton: "Did you ever see such a stone? He was not moved by any of my appeals" (8). Mansfield's comment to Chase: Robert Bruce Warden, *An Account of the Private Life and Public Services of Salmon Portland Chase* (Cincinnati, 1864), 466. Sandford testimony: CCW, II, 54–55. It is possible Scott had hoped to appoint General William Sandford, a militia general with important New York connections.

39. George Templeton Strong, *Diary of the Civil War, 1860–1865* (New York, 1962), I, 164–65. "your distress": OR, 1, II, 664.

40. A Confederate soldier, R. F. Graham, wrote his wife on June 25 that they watched Lowe's balloon go up each day "to look after us": in William Curry Harllee (comp.), *Kinfolks* (New Orleans, 1934), 583. "do this, or do that": CCW, I, 145. "I saw him do things": Adam Gurowski, *Diary* (Boston, 1862), I, 61. Villard's reactions: Henry Villard, *The Memoirs of Henry Villard* (New York, 1904), I, 179–80, 182. "He seemed oppressed": John Bigelow, *Reflections of an Active Life* (New York, 1913), II, 360.

41. The assorted plans can be found in OR, especially McDowell's detailed plan: OR, 1, II, 719–21. The Committee testimony: CCW, II, 35–38. "greatest coward": see the letter Representative Elihu Washburne wrote his wife on July 22, describing the scene of that "morning" (perhaps in the wee hours of the night before), Gaillard Hunt, *Israel, Elihu & Cadwallader Washburne: A Chapter in American Biography* (New York, 1925), 203; compare it with a rehash of that scene described in the *Congressional Globe*, July 24, 246, followed by numerous newspapers during the days thereafter. "people are impatient": *Providence* (Rhode Island) *Daily Journal*, July 11, 1861.

42. CCW, II, 55.

Sonar

43. Jordan: Clement Evans, *Confederate Military History* (Atlanta, 1899), II; G. Moxley Sorrell, *Reflections of a Confederate Staff Officer* (New York, 1905), 22; Beauregard, "The First Battle of Bull Run," BAL, I, 196–200. Punishment of "spies": *Richmond Dispatch*, May 25, 1861; Walter G.

Twyman, Papers, May 28, 30, 1861, University of Virginia; *Baltimore Sun,* July 4, 1861; *National Republican,* July 13, 1861; Charles Carleton Coffin, *Drum-Beat of the Nation* (New York, 1888), 89. There are innumerable sources for Rose Greenhow, mostly confectionary, but, in addition to OR, 2, II, series 115, 561ff. and Greenhow's own account—Rose O. Greenhow, *My Imprisonment and the First Year of Abolition Rule at Washington* (London, 1863)—Ishbel Ross, *Rebel Rose* (St. Simons Island, Georgia, 1954), Harnett T. Kane, *Spies for the Blue and Gray* (Garden City, New York, 1954), 27–36, and Louis A. Sigaud, "Mrs. Greenhow and the Rebel Spy Ring," *Maryland Historical Magazine* (September, 1946), XLI, are solid; see also MO, I, 89; James D. Horan, *The Pinkertons* (New York, 1967), 83–89. Bettie Duvall: Milledge L. Bonham to Beauregard, August 27, 1877, Bonham Papers, USC; OR, 1, LI, pt. 2, 688. See also *Mary Chesnut's Civil War,* edited by C. Vann Woodward (New Haven, 1981), 92; the Harllee letter: William Curry Harllee (comp.), *Kinfolks* (New Orleans, 1934), 661–62.

44. "Alabama negro": several Northern newspapers carried this story; the *Richmond Dispatch* reprinted it, sardonically, July 15, 1861. Women sellers: ibid., July 19, 1861. "harmless and inefficient" were the words of Thomas Goree, just in from Texas: Thomas W. Cutrer, *Longstreet's Aide: The Civil War Letters of Thomas J. Goree* (Charlottesville: University Press of Virginia, 1995), 20. Union reconnaissance: OR, 1, II, 299.

45. "unconscious assistance": Roman, I, 75. "valuable information": *Richmond Dispatch,* July 2, 1861. "condition and location": OR, 1, LI/2, 152. "both, simultaneously": *Mercury,* July 15, 1861.

46. Beauregard, *A Commentary on the Campaign and Battle of Manassas of July, 1861 (together with a summary of the Art of War)* (New York, 1891), 140, 160, 166–7.

47. "A decided change": Alexander Hunter, *Johnny Reb and Billy Yank* (New York, 1905), 45. Beauregard's June 12 letter and Davis's reply: JD, VII, 197–200. "strike a blow": MO, I, 79. "Special Order No. 100": OR, 1, II, 447–48. "act with extreme caution": JD, VII, 234–35. "I write in haste" and "who can forget": MO, I, 87. Mary Chesnut: *Mary Chesnut's Civil War,* ed., C. Vann Woodward (New Haven, 1981), 69, 72, 75, 80. "stupid fool": John L. Manning, aide to Beauregard, letter to Mrs. Manning, July 7, 1861, Williams-Chesnut-Manning Papers, SCL. James Chesnut's meeting in Richmond and "lost the South": MO, I, 85–89.

Scapegoat

48. The thinking at Patterson's headquarters about the size of Johnston's army and how best to meet it can be found in: Robert Patterson, *A Narrative of the Campaign in the Valley of the Shenandoah in 1861* (Philadelphia, 1865), especially 58ff.; CCW, passim; William Henry Locke, *The Story of the Regiment* (Philadelphia, 1868), 28–33; W. W. H. Davis, "The Campaign

of 1861 in the Shenandoah Valley," *Military Essays and Recollections*, MOL-LUS: Pennsylvania (Philadelphia, 1893), I, 163–70; Daniel H. Strother, "Personal Recollections of the War," *Harper's New Monthly Magazine* (July 1866), XXXIII, 137–60. For the correspondence between Scott and Patterson: OR, 1, II, 157–71. See also Thomas L. Livermore, "Patterson's Shenandoah Campaign," in Theodore F. Dwight, ed., *Papers of the Military Historical Society of Massachusetts* (Boston, 1881); Letter, Fitz-John Porter to Livermore, November 28, 1992, LC. Russel H. Beatie, *Army of the Potomac: Birth of Command, November 1860–September 1861* (New York, 2002), especially 222–24, makes the interesting argument that Fitz-John Porter played the most important role in making Patterson cautious. Beatie, however, is far less sympathetic about Patterson than I am.

49. On impressment, see, e.g.: *New York Herald*, June 5, 1861; *Baltimore American*, July 6, 1861; *New York Tribune*, July 20, 1861. See also the *Richmond Dispatch*, July 15–20, 1861. "fowling pieces": ER, II, 42.

50. *A Rebel Cavalryman with Lee, Stuart and Jackson* (Chicago, 1899), 23.

Jostling to the Starting Line

51. James McPherson, *For Cause & Comrades: Why Men Fought in the Civil War* (New York: Oxford University Press, 1997) is an excellent example of how to make historical generalizations — primarily by extensive research and an honest expression about limitations. "flat, stale": "Canonicus" in *Providence* (Rhode Island) *Daily Journal*, July 1, 1861. "state prison": Ezra Greene, in <www.brownwaternavy.com/diaries/>. "tuff as any ox": John S. Bartlett to sister, June 14, 1861, Bartlett Papers, Connecticut Historical Society. "dog's life": *Roxbury* (Massachusetts) *City Gazette*, July 5, 1861. "I confess": Walter Stone Poor to George Fox, June 30, 1861, in James J. Hamlin, "A Yankee Soldier in a New York Regiment," *New York Historical Society Quarterly* (April 1966), L, 116. "misguided brethren": Richard Moe, *The Last Full Measure: The Life and Death of the First Minnesota Volunteers* (New York, 1993), 29.

52. "hearty good will": John G. Nicolay, *The Outbreak of the Rebellion* (New York, 1881), 173. "test my machinery": CCW, II, 38.

53. C. B. Fairchild (comp.), *History of the 27th Regiment, N. Y. Vols.* (Binghamton, 1888), 3–9.

54. Biographical information about Tyler: *Daniel Tyler: A Memorial Volume* (privately printed, 1883). "unpopular": *Hartford Press*, undated, reprinted in *Norwich* (Connecticut) *Morning Bulletin*, July 18, 1861. "finest men": Andrew McClintock to Jane, June 16, 1861, *Waterbury Republican*, February 5, 1989. "courtier": *Tyler*, 50.

55. Heintzelman: The best source would be his lengthy diary and other papers, LC. Hunter: Edward A. Miller, Jr., *Lincoln's Abolitionist General: The*

Biography of David Hunter (UNCP, 1997). There is no adequate biography of Dixon Miles.

56. McDowell's orders: OR, 1, II, 303–05. Masked battery: definition: MIL, 83; "consummate skill": Judith White Brockenbrough McGuire, *Diary of a Southern Refugee during the Wa*r (New York, 1867), 31; "stupid press": Adam Gurowski, *Diary* (Boston, 1862), I, 58. E. P. Alexander, "The Battle of Bull Run," *Scribner's Magazine* (1907), XLI, 84, thought that the phrase and the initial concerns about "masked batteries" originated with stories written about Fort Sumter, but he seems to have been wrong, since the hullabaloo began after Big Bethel, and the phrase long preceded the Civil War. Franklin's letter: quoted in Mark A. Snell, *From First to Last: The Life of Major General William B. Franklin* (New York, 2002), 61.

57. Russell: William Howard Russell, *My Diary North and South* (New York, 1998), 240. "are a-gowing": quoted in Chester McArthur Destler, "The Second Michigan Volunteer Infantry Joins the Army of the Potomac," *Michigan History* (December 1957), XLI, 397. "determined stand": quoted on <www.secondwi.com>. Ballou letter: on many Web sites, and also in *Brown University Alumni Quarterly* (November 1990), 38–42.

Each Journey Begins with a Single Step

58. Staples, "Reminiscences of Bull Run," *War Papers*, Maine MOLLUS (Portland, 1898), III, 130; Sherman, *Memoirs of William Tecumseh Sherman* (New York, 1875), I, 198.

59. "loud hurrahs": "G" to the *New Haven Daily Morning Journal and Courier*, July 19, 1861. "so uncomfortable": "At the Battle of Bull Run with the Second New Hampshire Regiment," *The New England Magazine* (October, 1894), XVII, 155. Sixty-ninth New York: D. P. Conyngham, *The Irish Brigade and Its Campaigns* (New York, 1867), 26. "looks like war": Charles B. Haydon, *For Country, Cause & Leader*, ed. Stephen W. Sears (New York, 1993), 47–48.

60. William Howard Russell, *My Diary North and South* (New York, 1988), 250–51; cf., Russell, *William Howard Russell's Civil War: Private Diary and Letters, 1861–1862* (Athens, Georgia, 1992), 86, 88.

61. Death of soldier: "Lex" in *Norwich* (Connecticut) *Morning Bulletin*, July 31. music: Augustus Woodbury, *A Narrative of the Campaign of the First Rhode Island* (Providence, 1862), 76–77. "starry heavens": Joseph Marshall Favill, *The Diary of a Young Officer* (Chicago, 1909), 27.

62. "miserable country": quoted in Richard Moe, *The Last Full Measure: The Life and Death of the First Minnesota Volunteers* (New York, 1993), 44–45. arduous trek: Henry N. Blake, *Three Years in the Army of the Potomac* (Boston, 1865), 8–9. Single-file: George W. Bicknell, *History of the Fifth Regiment Maine Volunteers* (Portland, 1871), 22; George Grenville Benedict, *Vermont*

in the Civil War (Burlington, 1888), Chapter V, unpaginated; Edward K. Gould, *Major-General Hiram G. Berry* (Rockland, Maine, 1899), 57. Sherman letter: William Tecumseh Sherman, *Sherman's Civil* War, eds., Brooks D. Simpson and Jean V. Berlin (UNCP, 1999), 116–17.

63. "perfect silence": Richard Wright Simpson to aunt, July 14, 1861, in *"Far, Far from Home": The Wartime Letters of Dick and Tally Simpson, Third South Carolina Volunteer*s, eds., Guy R. Everson and Edward W. Simpson (New York, 1994), 25–27. *vivandières:* Charles Minor Blackford to Susan Leigh Blackford, July 10, 1861, in Charles Minor and Susan Leigh Blackford, *Letters from Lee's Army* (New York, 1947), 23. 6th Alabama: Thomas R. Lightfoot to the Reverend Moody, July 14, 1861, in "Letters of the Lightfoot Brothers," *Georgia Historical Quarterly* (1941), XXV, 394–95; Michael Holmes to (wife) Martha Eliza Roberts Holmes, July 13, 1861, on Web site: <home.att.net/~al_6th_inf/>. Nineteenth Virginia: Joseph A. Higginbotham, July 14–16, 1861, "Diary," UVA. Bonham brigade: Thomas Henry Pitts to Lizzie Craig, July 17, 1861, Pitts-Craig Letters, Emory University.

64. Movement by Confederates: Higginbotham, July 17, 1861; Richard Irby, *Historical Sketch of the Nottoway Grays* (Richmond, 1878), 10–11. McDowell to Committee: CCW, II, 39. "avidity": *Supplement to the OR*, I, 148. Skirmishing: "Dominus," *Hartford Daily Times*, July 24, 1861; *The Connecticut War Record* (Hartford, 1863–64), I, 116. Paying for water: letter to "Friend Willie" written by an anonymous member of the Second New Hampshire, July 24, 1861, MNBP. Blackberries: Elisha Hunt Rhodes, *All for the Union* (Lincoln, Rhode Island, reprint, 1985), 24.

65. The time of Tyler's departure: "J. R. H." (Joseph R. Hawley), *Hartford Evening Press*, August 5, 8, 1861. "a great army": Washburne to wife, July 18, 1861, in Gaillard Hunt, *Israel, Elihu, & Cadwallader Washburne: A Chapter in American Biography* (New York, 1925), 196–97. Returning fatigued soldiers: a letter datelined Camp Sprague, July 19, 1861, speaks of eight men from just the two Rhode Island regiments having been sent back on the seventeenth, *Providence Daily Evening Press*, July 22, 1861.

66. "keep your intervals": Gustavus Sullivan Dana, "'Bully for the First Connecticut!' The Recollections of a Three-Month Volunteer," ed., Lester L. Swift, *Lincoln Herald* (Summer 1965), LXVII, 77. Hunter's arrival: Thomas M. Aldrich, *The History of Battery A: First Regiment Rhode Island Light Artillery* (Providence, 1904), 15; Rhodes, 24. Seven o'clock: Richard Wright Simpson to "Pa," July 20, 1861, in Everson and Simpson, 29. "morning wash": a letter from an unnamed member of the Second South Carolina, dated July 26, 1861, *Charleston Courier*, August 2, 1861. "about daylight": James Butler Suddath to "friends," July 24, 1861, in Frank B. Williams, Jr., ed., "From Sumter to the Wilderness: Letters to Sergeant James Butler Suddath, Co. E, 7th Regiment, S.C.V.," *South Carolina Historical Magazine* (1962), LXIII, 5. "8 o'clock" and "soon after sunrise": OR, 1, II, 450, 459.

"sea of silver": Simpson to "Pa," op. cit. "bristling bayonets": Thomas Henry Pitts to wife, Lizzie, July 20, 1861, Pitts-Craig Letters, Emory University. "500,000": Goree to "Uncle Pleas," August 2, 1861, in Thomas W. Cutrer, *Longstreet's Aide: The Civil War Letters of Major Thomas J. Goree* (Charlottesville, 1995), 25.

67. Goree's opinion: ibid.

68. Kershaw's ruse: Robert Wallace Shand, "Diary," July 17, 1861, Shand Papers, SCL; *Charleston Courier,* August 2, 5, 1861; A. Augustus Dickert, *History of Kershaw's Brigade,* reprint of the 1899 edition (Wilmington, North Carolina, 1990), 56; OR, 1, II, 451. "perfect order": ibid., 450. Panicky pace: ER, II, 71–72; letter, William H. Goodlett to his father, July 19, 1861, F. M. Goodlett Papers, Perkins Library, Duke; Everson and Simpson, 28–31.

69. First Union arrivals: *Hartford Courant,* July 19, 1861; *Orleans* (New York) *Republican,* August 14, 1861. Depredations: all three major New York newspapers contain good accounts by eyewitnesses: *Herald, Times, Tribune.* "dirty, straggling little village": Joseph Marshall Favill, *The Diary of a Young Officer* (Chicago, 1909), 28.

70. Passage of the Sixty-ninth: Thomas Francis Meagher, *The Last Days of the 69th in Virginia* (New York, 1861), 6; and see 6–7 for examples of the thievery. "two houses, one pigsty": "C. E. P.," in *Winsted* (Connecticut) *Herald,* July 26, 1861. "to fight against invasion": Warren Cudworth, *History of the First Regiment (Massachusetts Infantry)* (Boston, 1866), 37–38. "we will get all the water": William Todd, *The Seventy-ninth Highlanders* (Albany, 1886), 20. Examples of shame: "J. R. H.," op. cit; William Thompson Lusk, *War Letters of William Thompson Lusk* (New York, 1911), 52–53. "Goths and Vandals": Letter, Sherman to Ellen, July 28, 1861, *Sherman's Civil War,* 125.

71. Tyler's movement from Flint Hill: "J. R. H.," op. cit. McDowell's report: OR, 1, II, 305.

First Blood

72. "attack the entrenched camp": Scott to George B. McClellan, July 18, 1861, Lincoln Papers, LC. "I think they are": OR, 1, II, 306. "Nothing to eat": *John H. Stevens: Civil War Diary,* eds., Gladys Stuart and Adelbert M. Jakeman, Jr. (Acton, Maine, 1997), 27. Commissary problems: OR, 1, II, 336–44; "refractory" and "utterly unfit": ibid., 341, 343.

73. Order: ibid., 1, II, 312. McDowell and Heintzelman: Heintzelman, *Journal,* July 19, 1861, LC. Wadsworth: Henry Greenleaf Pearson, *James S. Wadsworth of Geneseo* (New York, 1913).

74. Plan, including Beauregard's July 8 orders: OR, 1, II, 439–48; note about Johnston: 980. Arrival of the Eighth Virginia: letter, "Florence" to sister, July 23, 1861, in *Southern Magazine* (May 1874), unpaginated typescript, MNBP.

75. McLean's farm: Edward Porter Alexander, *Fighting for the Confeder-acy*, ed., Gary W. Gallagher (UNCP, 1989), 45–47. Longstreet: James Longstreet, *From Manassas to Appomattox* (Philadelphia, 1896). Move to Blackburn's Ford: James Franklin, Jr., "Incidents at the First Manassas Battle," CV (October 1894), 292; Alexander Hunter, *Johnny Reb and Billy Yank* (New York, 1905), 50–54.

76. Cf. Kershaw's report, OR, 1, II, 451–53, which states that the man's name was O'Brien and that he was connected in some manner to the Union quartermaster department, with the diary entry for July 18, 1861, of Robert Wallace Shand, SCL. Since Shand was one of the pickets, I've adopted his interpretation. The precise position of "Butler's farm" is un-known; in fact the 1860 census doesn't even list a "Butler," though it does list a "Pierce Bulton." My decision that the farm belonged to Pierce Butler is based on tax records collected by Edith Moore Sprouse, "Fairfax County in 1860: A Collective Biography" (an unpublished manuscript among the holdings at the Alexandria, Virginia, library), II, 251. Closer to the stream lived the families of the farmers William Rough, Daniel G. Roberts, and Joseph Holden.

77. On types of reconnaissance maneuvers, see MIL, 488–90. Analyz-ing Tyler's "motives": see, e.g., William C. Davis, *Battle at Bull Run* (LSUP, 1977), 114–15. First artillery duel: OR, 1, II, 451–53, 458–59.

78. Richardson's recent improved manner: Charles B. Haydon, *For Country, Cause & Leader: The Civil War Journal of Charles B. Haydon*, ed., Stephen W. Sears (New York, 1993), 13. Advance of Brethschneider's skir-mishers: John T. Setright, letter to cousin, July 28, 1861, Bentley Histori-cal Library, University of Michigan. Barnard's report: OR, 1, II, 328–30; his testimony to Joint Committee: CCW, II, 162. Newspapermen: in addi-tion to the major newspapers, see Henry Villard, *The Memoirs of Henry Villard* (New York, 1904), I, 184–86; "most exciting experience": Charles Loring Brace, *The Life of Charles Loring Brace* (New York, 1894), 242–43; Charles Carleton Coffin, *The Boys of '61* (Boston, 1899), 42; J. Cutler Andrews, *The North Reports the Civil War* (Pittsburgh, 1955), 85–86. Civil-ians: Daniel McCook, letter to son, July 26, 1861, MNBP.

79. "sweep the woods": Ezra Walrath, letter, *Washington Star*, July 29, 1861. Twelfth New York: "Ed," letter to father, dated July 19, in *Rochester Democrat and American*, July 27, 1861. First Massachusetts: George H. Johnston, undated letter to wife, MSS Division, East Carolina University (although he was in this regiment and fought, he may have been one of Brethschneider's original skirmishers—he speaks of taking a house on the battlefield that had a number of Confederates in it; if his statement is accurate, these may have been part of Kershaw's forward pickets, and the house may have been the Butler place or perhaps the Rough or the Roberts farms); Charles A. Jackson, letter to editor, *Chelsea Telegraph and Pioneer*, July 27, 1861; "J. G. P.," letter home, in *Roxbury City Gazette*, August 8, 1861, "Hal," letter to editor,

Chelsea Telegraph and Pioneer, July 27, 1861; Warren Cudworth, *History of the First Regiment (Massachusetts Infantry)* (Boston, 1866), 41–47. "sons of bitches": Allen Alonzo Kingsbury, letter to parents, undated, *Dedham* (Massachusetts) *Gazette,* August 3; see also his expurgated letter to parents, July 25, 1861, and journal entry of July 19, 1861, both in *Hero of Medfield* (Boston, 1862). Second Michigan and blackberries: D. G. Crotty, *Four Years Campaigning in the Army of the Potomac* (Grand Rapids, 1874), 22.

80. "impertinent woods": "J. R. H." (Joseph R. Hawley) to editor, *Hartford Evening Press,* August 6, 1861. "cut to pieces": Thomas S. Allen, "The Second Wisconsin at the First Battle of Bull Run," MOLLUS (Milwaukee, 1891), 383. "you may dodge": William Todd, *The Seventy-ninth Highlanders* (Albany, 1886), 25. See also George W. Wilkes, *History of the 71st Re, N.G., N.Y.* (New York, 1919), 168–70; Thomas Francis Meagher, *The Last Days of the 69th in Virginia* (New York, 1861), 8–10; William Tecumseh Sherman, *Memoirs* (New York, 1875), I, 198–204; and *Sherman's Civil War,* eds., Brooks D. Simpson and Jean V. Berlin (UNCP, 1999), 119–21. See also Albert C. Brackett, "Battle at Blackburn's Ford," *Philadelphia Weekly Times,* December 27, 1884.

81. "first hostile shot": Alexander, 46. "every man imagined": Hunter, 55–60. Wrestling match: Edgar Warfield, *A Confederate Soldier's Memoirs* (Richmond, 1936), 49–50. Longstreet: Longstreet, 38–41; Thomas W. Cutrer, *Longstreet's Aide: The Civil War Letters of Major Thomas J. Goree* (UVA Press, 1995), 25–27; W. H. Morgan, *Personal Reminiscences of the War of 1861–5* (Lynchburg, Virginia, 1911), 51–63. Opera glasses: Alexander Robert Chisolm, *Recollections,* The New-York Historical Society, Chapter 4, 6.

82. Richardson's pugnacity: his official report, OR, 1, II, 313; his testimony, CCW, II, 21; see also John B. Barnard, *The C.S.A. and the Battle of Bull Run* (New York, 1862), 49. The kiss: Haydon, 54. McDowell's reactions: ibid., 39; James B. Fry, "McDowell's Advance to Bull Run," BAL, I, 179. "rather sober": Todd, 75. Mayor Fay's letter: *Chelsea Telegraph and Pioneer,* August 10, 1861; see also his first report home on July 25.

83. The quandary over names: *Richmond Enquirer,* July 27, 1861, discusses various names and concludes "Bull Run" is okay; the *Richmond Dispatch,* however, thinks "the Battle of Stone Bridge" is far better; but the *Wilmington* (North Carolina) *Journal* proposes "Manassas" because it is a "Scriptural" word, and on July 30, the *Richmond Dispatch,* quoting this undated editorial, agrees. "confidence in themselves": Cutrer, 27. "inspiring effect": Jubal Anderson Early, *Jubal Early's Memoirs* (Baltimore, 1989), 10.

Valley Boys

84. A waspishness intruded early into Confederate military reports, as individuals used this venue to take credit for successes and blame others for failures. After the war the sniping grew louder as participants began to

publish memoirs. Among the most vigorous practitioners of these techniques were Jefferson Davis, P. G. T. Beauregard, and Joseph Johnston, all three prickly about their reputations. The messages involved here are a case in point; much ink would be wasted carping about the smallest details. In general it does not seem worth killing more trees to replow the same ground. See OR, 1, II, 478–79, 515, 976–77, 982. Cf. Jefferson Davis, *Rise and Fall of the Confederate Government* (New York, 1881), I, 346; MO, I, 91. See also John D. Imboden, "Incidents of the First Bull Run," BAL, I, 229; Joseph E. Johnston, "Responsibilities of the First Bull Run," ibid., 243–44; Gilbert Eaton Govan and James Weston Livingood, *A Different Valor: The Story of Joseph E. Johnston, C.S.A.* (New York, 1956), 46–48.

85. Shenandoah Sharpshooters: John O. Caswell, *Four Years in the Stonewall Brigade* (Girard, Kansas, 1906), 21. gleeful: Robert T. Coles, *From Huntsville to Appomattox*, ed., Jeffrey D. Stocker (Knoxville, 1996), 18; James G. Hudson, "A Story of Company D, 4th Alabama Infantry Regiment, C.S.A.," *Alabama Historical Quarterly* (Spring 1961), XXIII, 163.

86. "totally ignorant": quoted in Steven H. Stubbs, *Duty, Honor, Valor: The Story of the Eleventh Mississippi Infantry Regiment* (Philadelphia, Mississippi, 2000), 85. Gardner's speech: John Wesley Culpeper, *Journal*, mistakenly dated July 17, McCain Library and Archives, University of Southern Mississippi. Crossing the river: B. M. Zettler, *War Stories* (New York, 1912), 53–55; Hudson, 165; Coles, 19; Michael Reid Hanger, *Diary*, July 18, 1861, "Valley of the Shadow," Virginia Center for Digital History, Charlottesville; letters, Robert L. Grant to mother, July 24, 1861, and Ferdinand Dallas McMillan to family, August 18, 1861, MNBP; A. T. Barclay, "The Liberty Hall Volunteers," reprint, *Historical Papers* (1904), VI, 129.

87. Desertion: Dennis E. Frye, *2nd Virginia Infantry* (Lynchburg, 1984), 11. The physical breakdown: see, e.g., John P. Hite, *Diary*, July 19, 1861, MNBP.

88. Cf. P. G. T. Beauregard, *A Commentary on the Art of War and Battle of Manassas of July, 1861* (New York, 1891), 30–32, as well as MO, I, 91; Joseph Eggleston Johnston, *Narrative of Military Operations* (New York, 1874), 36–37. See also Jeffrey N. Lash, "Joseph E. Johnston and the Virginia Railways," *Civil War History* (March 1989), XXXV, 13–14. Chisolm's ride: Alexander Robert Chisolm, *Recollections*, The New-York Historical Society, Chapter 5, 1–3.

89. "good things": letter, William B. Gallagher to mother, July 20, 1861, Gallagher Papers, Virginia Tech. "pompous gravity": W. W. Blackford, *War Years with Jeb Stuart* (New York, 1945; LSUP reprint, 1993), 23. Movement of artillery: Clement Daniel Fishburne, "Memoirs," UVA; James M. Garnett, "Harpers Ferry and First Manassas," SHSP (1900), XXVIII, 62–63; Susan P. Lee, *Memoirs of William Nelson Pendleton, D.D.* (Philadelphia, 1897), 148; report of John D. Imboden, *Richmond Dispatch*, July 26, 1861.

90. Curiously, given the importance of the events at Piedmont, confidently stitching together a crisp narrative about them is impossible. It is unclear why certain regiments were sent and others were not; apparently, several did not arrive in Piedmont in time, though where they were is unclear. The train "accident" and the "execution" are often discussed, but not by eyewitnesses. It is not even known exactly how many different trains were involved. "black hole of Calcutta": Zettler, 58. John P. Hite, a member of Jackson's brigade, kept a diary, MNBP; his entry for the nineteenth states that, although their train (the second one out of Piedmont) arrived at Manassas Junction at 2:00 A.M., they stayed on the cars "until morning." Scene at Beauregard's headquarters: Jubal Anderson Early, *Jubal Early's Memoirs* (Baltimore, 1989), 10–11.

91. Davis's order: OR, 1, II, 985; Joseph E. Johnston, "Responsibilities," 244; Bradley T. Johnson, *A Memoir of the Life and Public Service of Joseph E. Johnston* (Baltimore, 1891), 49.

Initial Inertia

92. "vilige": Joseph A. Higginbotham, *Diary*, June 23, 1861, UVA. "done its business": Thomas Francis Meagher, *The Last Days of the 69th in Virginia* (New York, 1861), 10.

93. William Shakespeare King, Report, *Supplement to the OR*, I, 146–56. See also Frank Hastings Hamilton, *A Treatise on Military Surgery and Hygiene* (New York, 1865), 192–94, 301–02, 324.

94. "Bush Camp": Thomas M. Aldrich, *The History of Battery A: First Regiment Rhode Island Light Artillery* (Providence, 1904), 17; "Tockwotton," *Providence Daily Evening Press*, July 25, 1861. "initial inertia": Charles Carroll Gray, *Diary*, July 19, 1861, UNC.

95. Jackson's close call: Samuel Wragg Ferguson, "Memoirs" (typescript, 1900), 2, MNBP. "raw vols.": Heintzelman, *Journal*, July 19, 1861, LC. Sound of axes: Richard Irby, *Historical Sketch of the Nottoway Grays* (Richmond, 1878), 11. Bathing Sixty-ninth: *New York Times*, July 21, 1861. Cocke's two regiments: OR, 1, II, 549. "reached the Run": quoted in Alan D. Gaff, *If This Is War* (Dayton, Ohio, 1991), 182.

96. Hanging: letter, "Geo" to editor, *Boston Herald*, July 22, 1861; letter, A. E. Bronson to editor, *Danbury* (Connecticut) *Times*, July 25, 1861. Whipping: letter, "C" to "Friend Beach," printed in *Orleans* (New York) *Republican*, August 14, 1861; Daingerfield Parker, "The Battalion of Regular Infantry at the First Battle of Bull Run," MOLLUS (Washington, 1900), 8; William B. Westervelt, *Lights and Shadows of Army Life* (Marlboro, New York, 1886), 2–3; *History of the 27th Regiment N.Y. Vols.* (Binghamton, 1888), 10–11.

97. Barnard's report: OR, 1, II, 330–31 (emphasis added to the phrase, "various quarters"). "mere country path": Barnard's testimony: CCW, II,

160. One of the sources may have been a local gentleman, Mathias C. Mitchell, reputedly a Union man: Robert Goldthwaite, *Four Brothers in Blue* (Washington, 1913), 22.

98. McDowell's report: OR, 1, II, 308. His testimony to the committee: CWW, II, 39.

99. Barnard's noon report and McDowell's plan: ibid., 39, 41.

100. Ibid., 22, 40, 162; see also Robert Patterson, *A Narrative of the Campaign in the Valley of the Shenandoah in 1861*, 2d ed. (Philadelphia, 1875), 88. The wagon train: *Providence* (Rhode Island) *Daily Evening Press*, July 22, 1861. "responded derisively": *New York Times*, July 21, 1861.

101. "low spirits": letter, Elihu Washburne to his wife, 4:00 P.M., July 20, 1861, in Gaillard Hunt, *Israel, Elihu & Cadwallader Washburne: A Chapter in American Biography* (New York, 1925), 198. First Connecticut: *Hartford Courant*, July 29, 1861; Gustavus Sullivan Dana, "'Bully for the First Connecticut!',", ed., Lester L. Swift, *Lincoln Herald* (Summer 1965), LXVII, 77. Seventy-first New York: George W. Wilkes, Recollections, in *History of the 71st Re, N.G., N.Y.* (New York, 1919), 200–01. The units that left: OR, 1, II, 745. Crickets, et al.: Robert Ardrey, *The Territorial Imperative* (New York, 1970), 106–09. Cameron's sudden return to Washington: An anonymous ten-page essay titled "Historical Notes on 1st Bull Run" was found among the papers of Governor Sprague and was originally published as part of Elisha Hunt Rhodes, *All for the Union* (Lincoln, Rhode Island, 1985), 35. The essay was written either by Sprague or someone close to him, and Sprague did speak during the day to Cameron.

102. McDowell-Burnside meeting: Hunt, 198. Edmund Clarence Stedman, the correspondent for the *World*, was at Centreville. His report a few days later mentioned the last minute change of plans but said the main reason was that McDowell realized he needed more ammunition on hand, and he sent back to Fairfax Court House for a supply. Although this was a possible factor in McDowell's decision, it seems doubtful: see Stedman, *The Battle of Bull Run* (New York, 1861), 12.

103. CCW, II, 30, 33, 131, 151, 207; see also the July 20, 1861, diary entry of Orlando B. Willcox in Robert Garth Scott, *Forgotten Valor* (Kent, Ohio, 1999), 289. "stampede": William Tecumseh Sherman, *Sherman's Civil War* (UNCP, 1999), 119, MNBP.

104. Crittenden's resolution: *Congressional Globe*, 37th Cong., 1st sess., 222–223. Russell: William Howard Russell, *My Diary North and South* (New York, 1988), 257, 259.

105. Laura Fletcher, *Recollections*, typescript (1936).

106. Father O'Reilly: Meagher, 12. "Oh, Lord": Joseph A. Higginbotham, *Diary*, July 20, 1861, UVA. "I pray": Charles B. Haydon, *For Country, Cause & Leader*, ed., Stephen W. Sears (New York, 1993), 53. Graffiti: *Richmond Dispatch*, August 2, 1861. "forgive me": Hamilton Branch to mother, July 20, 1861, in Edward G. Longacre, "Three Brothers Face

Their Baptism of Battle, July 1861," *The Georgia Historical Quarterly* (1977), LXI, 163. "forget my faults": Thomas B. Barker to brother, July 20, 1861, Barker Papers, Maine Historical Society. "be in Richmond": "W. H. H. C." to sister, July 20, 1861, quoted in *Richmond Dispatch*, August 2, 1861. Amputated foot: John O. Casler, *Four Years in the Stonewall Brigade* (Girard, Kansas, 1906), 24. "rail breastwork": Joseph A. Higginbotham, *Diary*, UVA. "dam Rebel coats": Charles R. Fisk to Wilbur Fisk, July 16, 1861, quoted in *Richmond Dispatch*, July 29, 1861. "Loading and firing": letter, Henry F. Ritter to uncle, July 23, 1861, MNBP. Campfire scenes: D. G. Crotty, *Four Years Campaigning in the Army of the Potomac* (Grand Rapids, Michigan, 1874), 23; John Taylor, "The Story of a Battle," (1893; reprinted in Trenton, 1939), 5; H. Seymour Hall, "A Volunteer at the First Bull Run," *War Talks in Kansas* (Kansas City, Missouri, 1906), 152. Raymond's report: *New York Times*, July 24, 1861.

Stumbling

107. Edward Henry Clement, *The Bull-Run Rout* (Cambridge, 1909), 13n; Edmund Clarence Stedman, *The Battle of Bull Run* (New York, 1861), 14; McDowell's testimony: CCW, II, 41–42.

108. Semimutiny: *New York Times*, July 23, 1861. Propping up bridge: Augustus Woodbury, *A Narrative of the Campaign of the First Rhode Island Regiment* (Providence, 1862), 88–89. Skirmishers and first shots: George M. Finch, "The Boys of '61," *G.A.R. Papers* (Cincinnati, 1891), 255–56; "Our Corporal," *Yorkville* (South Carolina) *Enquirer*, August 1, 1861. "pottering": CCW, II, 212. "Bully for you!": Hiram Eddy, journal, typescript, 3, Connecticut Historical Society.

109. CCW, II, 24, 178; OR, 1, II, 373–74, 377–78, 381–82, 423–24, 428–29.

110. Hains: Peter Conover Hains, "The First Gun at Bull Run," *Cosmopolitan* (August 1911), LI, 388–99; John Taylor, "The Story of a Battle" (1893; reprinted in Trenton, 1939), 7; some recollections of that morning recall only two shots, but Hains seems the best witness. "5 a.m.": OR, 1, II, 362. Raymond: *New York Times*, July 22.

111. Withers: Robert Enoch Withers, *Autobiography of an Octogenarian* (Roanoke, 1907), 145; OR, 1, II, 546. Preston: ibid., 549. Kirkland's report: OR, 1, II, 518, 521.

112. Thornton: "An English Combatant," *Battle-Fields of the South* (London, 1863), 55–56. "Cousin Welby": Robert Carter, Papers, Federal Writers' Project, LC. Evans's report: OR, 1, II, 559. Hunton's message: Eppa Hunton, *The Autobiography of Eppa Hunton* (Richmond, 1933), 33.

113. Beauregard's military advice: *A Commentary on the Campaign and Battle of Manassas of July 1861 (together with a summary of the Art of War)* (New York, 1891), 166, 176–77. Plans and messages: ibid., 65–69; OR, 1, II,

473–74, 479–80, 487, 518–29, 555, 565, and CVIII, 199; Beauregard, "The First Battle of Bull Run," BAL, I, 203; Johnston, "Responsibilities of the First Bull Run," ibid., 245–46; MO, I, 447–48. The courier: Campbell Brown, "General Ewell at Bull Run," BAL, I, 260; Henry Francis Lyster, "Reflections of the Bull Run Campaign after Twenty-seven Years," MOL-LUS (Detroit, 1888), 10–11. Evans's movements: B. B. Beazeale, *Co. J, 4th South Carolina Infantry at the First Battle of Manassas* (Manassas, 1912), 6–8. Longstreet's movements: *Charlotte* (North Carolina) *Western Democrat,* August 6, 1861; Edgar Warfield, *Manassas to Appomattox: The Civil War Memoirs of Pvt. Edgar Warfield, 17th Virginia* (McLean, Virginia, 1996, a reprint of *A Confederate Soldier's Memoirs*), 51; Thomas W. Cutrer, *Longstreet's Aide: The Civil War Letters of Major Thomas J. Goree* (Charlottesville, 1995), 24, 27; Alexander Hunter, *Johnny Reb and Billy Yank* (New York, 1905), 62; OR, 1, II, 543–44, and 1, LI, 32–33.

114. "quietly laughing": J. C. Nott to "Harleson," *Mobile Evening News,* July 30, 1861. "good solid meal": Charles A. Jackson to parents, *Chelsea* (Massachusetts) *Telegraph and Pioneer,* July 25, 1861. Hardy letter: July 21, 1861, MNBP.

En Garde

115. March to Sudley Ford: Martin A. Haynes, *History of the Second Regiment New Hampshire Volunteers* (Manchester, New Hampshire, 1865), 19; "At the Battle of Bull Run with the Second New Hampshire Regiment," *The New England Magazine* (October 1894), XVII, 155–56; *Providence* (Rhode Island) *Daily Evening Press,* July 31, 1861; Augustus Woodbury, *A Narrative of the Campaign of the First Rhode Island Regiment* (Providence, 1862), 88–92; Woodbury, *The Second Rhode Island Regiment* (Providence, 1875), 31; Elisha Hunt Rhodes, *All for the Union* (reprint, Lincoln, Rhode Island, 1985), 36; Edward P. Doherty, *History of the 71st Re, N.G., N.Y.* (New York, 1919), 809–10; Edwin S. Barrett, *What I Saw at Bull Run* (Boston, 1886), 116–17. Scraped bark: William A. Burwell, journal, Burwell Papers, UVA. Concerns about the pace: King's report, *Supplement to the OR,* I, 151–52.

116. Officers of the Second: *Memorial of John Stanton Slocum* (Providence, 1886); Woodbury, *Second*; William Greene Roelker, "Civil War Letters of William Ames," *Rhode Island Historical Society Collections* (October 1940), XXX, 73–93. Elisha Hunt Rhodes: Rhodes, ix, 11–25. Sprague: Thomas Graham Belden and Marva Robins Belden, *So Fell the Angels* (Boston, 1956), 41–45. On the morale of the Second: Frederick Law Olmsted, *The Papers of Frederick Law Olmsted* (Baltimore, 1986), IV, 168–69.

117. Evans: Douglas Southall Freeman, *Lee's Lieutenants* (New York, 1943), I, 87; Eugene C. Tidball, "The View from the Top of the Knoll," *Civil War History* (September 1998), XLIV, 185. Fourth South Carolina

("droughty"): Jesse Walton Reid, *History of the Fourth Regiment of S. C. Volunteers* (Charleston, 1891), 8, 12–13; B. B. Beazeale, *Co. J, 4th South Carolina Infantry at the First Battle of Manassas* (Manassas, 1912), 3–5; J. B. E. Sloan, "Notes," MNBP. Wheat's Battalion: "Personne" (F. G. De Fontaine), *Richmond Courier*, June 12, 1861; Thomas Cooper De Leon, *Four Years in Rebel Capitals* (Mobile, 1890), 71–73 [curiously, he claimed he first saw them in Pensacola]; Reid, 19–20; Beazeale, 4–5. Wheat ("beloved by all"): Elliot Ashkenazi (ed.) *The Civil War Diary of Clara Solomon* (LSUP, 1995), 88; "Major Chatham Roberdeau Wheat," CV, (September 1911), XIX, 425–28; Charles L. Dufour, *Gentle Tiger: The Gallant Life of Roberdeau Wheat* (LSUP, 1957; reprint, 1985).

118. Confederate cavalry: OR, 1, II, 564. Beazeale, 8–9. Sherman: William Tecumseh Sherman, *Sherman's Civil War*, eds., Brooks D. Simpson and Jean V. Berlin (UNCP, 1999), 123.

119. Alexander: Maury Klein, *Edward Porter Alexander* (Athens, Georgia, 1971); Alexander, "The Battle of Bull Run," *Scribner's Magazine* (1907), XLI, 87–90; Alexander, *Fighting for the Confederacy*, ed., Gary W. Gallagher (UNCP, 1989), 37–50. Signal system: John D. Billings, *Hardtack and Coffee* (Boston, 1888), 279–85; Alexander, *Fighting*, 13–14. "so stupid": Klein, 33. Evans's decision: OR, 1, II, 558–59. I wish to thank Jim Burgess of the Manassas National Battlefield Park for persuading me that Alexander did not erect any actual towers there.

First Glimpse of the Elephant

120. Holsinger, "How Does One Feel Under Fire?" Kansas Commandery, MOLLUS, *War Talks in Kansas* (Leavenworth, 1898), I, 3.

121. Evans's movements: OR, 1, II, 559–64; B. B. Beazeale, *Co. J, 4th South Carolina Infantry at the First Battle of Manassas* (Manassas, 1912), 11; *Supplement to the OR*, I, 194–95. Uniforms: *New York Times*, July 1, 1861; *Richmond Dispatch*, July 8, 1861. "dress parade": J. B. E. Sloan, undated memorandum, MNBP.

122. The time: Thomas M. Aldrich, *The History of Battery A: First Regiment Rhode Island Light Infantry* (Providence, 1904), 19. "whir of the bullets": Elisha Hunt Rhodes, *All for the Union* (reprint, Lincoln, Rhode Island, 1985), 26–28. Lieutenant and cane: Letter from John P. Shaw, July 22, 1861, in *Providence Daily Journal*, July 27, 1861. "hideous scream": "Sergeant" to editor, *Providence Daily Evening Press*, July 31, 1861. "three or four thousand": Samuel J. English to mother, July 24, 1861, in ibid., 33.

123. "made him laugh": letter, Anonymous to "Friend Willie," July 24, 1861, MNBP. "O, libby": Philo H. Gallup, "The Second Michigan Volunteer Infantry Joins the Army of the Potomac," ed., Chester McArthur Destler, *Michigan History* (December 1957), XLI, 398. "earth has burst": James B. Ligon, undated note, MNBP. "mine eyes": Jesse Walton Reid to

wife, July 24, 1861, in Reid, *History of the Fourth Regiment of S. C. Volunteers* (Charleston, 1891), 25–26.

124. David Hackworth, *About Face* (New York, 1989), 76. World War II, then Vietnam, led to a number of analyses of battlefield motivation. Some encompass all wars: see, e.g., John Baynes, *Morale: A Study of Men and Courage* (London, 1967); Peter Watson, *War on the Mind: The Military Uses and Abuses of Psychology* (New York, 1978); Charles Moran, *The Anatomy of Courage* (London, 1966); William L. Hauser, "The Will to Fight," in *Combat Effectiveness*, ed., Sam C. Sarkesian (Beverly Hills, 1980); Anthony Kellett, *Combat Motivation: The Behavior of Soldiers in Battle* (Boston, 1982); F. M. Richardson, *Fighting Spirit: A Study of Psychological Factors in War* (London, 1978). Some excellent studies focus on the Civil War: see, e.g., Joseph Allen Frank and George A. Reaves, *'Seeing the Elephant': Raw Recruits at the Battle of Shiloh* (New York, 1989); Grady McWhiney and Perry D. Jamieson, *Attack and Die* (University, Alabama, 1982); Michael Barton, *Goodmen: The Character of Civil War Soldiers* (University Park, 1981); Earl J. Hess, *The Union Soldier in Battle: Enduring the Ordeal of Combat* (Lawrence, Kansas, 1997).

125. CV, XIX, 427.

126. "your hands": Augustus Woodbury, *The Second Rhode Island Regiment* (Providence, 1875), 33.

Carnage

127. "hardest work": letter, Shelby to editor, August 5, 1861, *Huntsville Democrat*, August 7, 1861. "my duty": letter to family, July 23, 1861, in *Providence Daily Evening Press*, July 27, 1861.

128. Jackson's movements: OR, 1, II, 481. Beauregard's view: Pierre Gustave Toutant Beauregard, "The First Battle of Bull Run," BAL, I, 205–6; Beauregard, *A Commentary on the Campaign and Battle of Manassas of July, 1861* (New York, 1891), 71; MO, I, 100; A. R. Chisolm, Report to Beauregard, August 1, 1861, National Archives (M331, Roll 54) [Chisolm, an aide to Beauregard, here describes his mission for Beauregard]. Johnston's view: His report: OR, 1, II, 474; Johnston, "Responsibilities of the First Bull Run," BAL, I, 246; "every order": Johnston to Bradley Johnson, September 30, 1887, Johnson Papers, Perkins Library, Duke University.

129. Portici: Edmund Raus, "The Voices of Portici," *Civil War* (September 1988), XIV, 43–52. Cocke's role: OR, 1, LI/1, 28.

130. "beau-ideal": Robert Garth Scott (ed.) *Forgotten Valor: The Memoirs, Journals & Civil War Letters of Orlando B. Willcox* (Kent, Ohio, 1999), 60. "long hair": B. B. Beazeale, *Co. J, 4th South Carolina Infantry at the First Battle of Manassas* (Manassas, 1912), 17. Imboden's arrival: John D. Imboden, "Incidents of the First Bull Run," BAL, I, 230. Imboden mistook the first shot from Richardson's guns for Hains's (earlier) signal gun.

131. Bee's orders and map: Samuel Wragg Ferguson, "Memoirs," typescript, 1900, MNBP. Bee and Imboden: Imboden, Report, July 22, 1861, *Richmond Dispatch*, July 26, 1861; Report of S. R. Gist, R. A. Howard, and A. Vander Horst [all Bee's aides], *Supplement to the OR*, I, 192–93; Henry Chase Whiting, Report, ibid., 185–86; Imboden, "Incidents," 232; Richard Watson York (ed.) "The 'Old Third' Brigade and the Death of General Bee," *Our Living and Our Dead* (Raleigh, 1875), I, 662–64; Cary Ingram Crockett, "The Battery That Saved the Day," *The Field Artillery Journal* (January 1940), XXX, 30; Harold Woodward, Jr., *Defender of the Valley: Brigadier General John Daniel Imboden, C.S.A.* (Berryville, Virginia, 1996); Spencer C. Tucker, *Brigadier General John D. Imboden* (Knoxville, 2002).

132. Evans-Bee conversation and Bee's following maneuvers: Reports of both Bee's aides and of Whiting, *Supplement*, 186–87, 193. Second Mississippi: "slovenly": OR, 1, II, 868–69; Hugh R. Miller, "The Great Battle of Manassas," the (Pontotoc, Mississippi) *Examiner*, September 13, 1861; letter, John M. Stone to mother, undated, Mississippi Department of Archives and History (No. Z265). Fourth South Carolina cheers Bee: J. B. E. Sloan, undated memorandum, MNBP.

133. Letter, Ai Baker Thompson to father, July 24, 1861, MNBP. Burnside's and Fiske's reports: OR, 1, II, 396, 401.

134. *New York Times*, July 31, 1861. First Rhode Island: *Providence Daily Evening Press*, July 28, 1861; Henry A. DeWitt, letter to editor, *Providence Daily Journal*, July 25, 1861; see ibid., July 26–31, 1861, for numerous reports from anonymous correspondents, including "H," who told the story of the man who fired between his legs; Charles Carroll, *Rhode Island: Three Centuries of Democracy* (New York, 1932), III, 601; Sprague's remarks in Senate, April 8, 1869, *Congressional Globe*, 618; OR, 1, II, 399–400. Seventy-first New York: Josiah Marshall Favill, *The Diary of a Young Officer* (Chicago, 1909), 32–34; George W. Wilkes, Journal, in *History of the 71st Re, N.G., N.Y.* (New York, 1919), 183–84; see also other recollections of members of the Seventy-first, passim; OR, 1, LI/I, 23–24.

135. There is a large knob almost halfway up Matthews Hill. Locals called it Buck Hill, but I have not mentioned it to avoid confusion. General accounts: Robert T. Coles, *From Huntsville to Appomattox*, ed., Jeffrey D. Stocker (Knoxville, 1966), 20–22; Thomas J. Goldsby, report, *Richmond Dispatch*, August 17, 1861; OR, 1, II, 561; Joe P. Angell, CV (March 1910), XVIII, 133; Kenneth W. Jones, "The Fourth Alabama Infantry First Blood," *Alabama Historical Quarterly* (Spring 1974), XXXVI, 35–53; James G. Hudson, "A Story of Company D, 4th Alabama Infantry Regiment, C.S.A.," ibid., (Spring 1961), XXIII, 166–67; Gregory J. Starbuck, "'Up, Alabamians!' The Fourth Alabama Infantry at First Manassas," *Military Images Magazine* (July/August 1986), 24–29; William A. Robbins, "How the Fourth Alabama Received Its 'Baptism of Fire'," *Philadelphia Weekly Times*, February 26, 1881. "seemed very much excited": W. O. Hudson to

Richard Watson York, February 17, 1867, in York, 562. Overalls and straw hats: "J. H. G." to editors, *New York Mercury,* August 3, 1861. Conecuh Guards: *Richmond Dispatch,* July 31, 1861. Private Anderson's brother: *Huntsville Democrat,* August 7, 1861. "what they would say at home": Robbins. "a bede": in David M. Sullivan (ed.) "Fowler the Soldier, Fowler the Marine," CWTI (February 1988), XXVI, 30. "the horrors": quoted in Starbuck, 28.

"Victory! Victory!"

136. Clouts to family, July 29, 1861, Georgia Archives.

137. "Get ready, men!" and "My! how tired": B. M. Zettler, *War Stories* (New York, 1912), 61. Preparations: Joel S. Yarborough, "Recollections," unpaginated, Georgia Department of Archives. "shock was stunning": Thomas D. Gilham, "Oglethorpe Rifles: A Full History of This Celebrated Company," in *This They Remembered* (Columbus, Georgia, 1986), 45.

138. "mother earth": Vardy P. Sisson, "Close Calls," *Atlanta Journal,* February 2, 1901. "shot bears" and "This is unfair": Zettler, 62, 63. Burrowing: George S. Barnsley, *Diary,* Barnsley Papers, UNC. Brass band: Warren Wilkinson and Steven E. Woodworth, *A Scythe of Fire: A Civil War Story of the Eighth Georgia Infantry Regiment* (New York, 2002), 65. "glad to see you": Yarborough. "have your range": Zettler, 64. Both speeches: Letter, in *Rome* (Georgia) *Courier,* August 6, 1861; Zettler, 64. See also Henry Clay Harper, *Diary,* Robert Woodruff Library, Emory University. The sources differ about where they lay down. Behind Mrs. Henry's house seems most likely, though John C. Reed, "Journal," Alabama Department of Archives and History, includes a map indicating the cornfield was well past the pike.

139. Story of Jesse Dalton: Reed, 19–20. Branch brothers: Edward G. Longacre, "Three Brothers Face Their Baptism of Battle, July 1861," *The Georgia Historical Quarterly* (1977), LXI, 165–68; see also *Charlotte's Boys: Civil War Letters of the Branch Family of Savannah* (Berryville, Virginia, 1996). "kneeled at a sapling": Zettler, 66. "hot a place": Reed, 22.

140. Sykes and his battalion: Daingerfield Parker, "The Battalion of Regular Infantry at the First Battle of Bull Run," MOLLUS (Washington, 1900), II; Timothy J. Reese, *Sykes' Regular Infantry Division, 1861–1864* (Jefferson, North Carolina, 1990); OR, 1, II, 390–91. "let me have the regulars": William Woods Averell, *Ten Years in the Saddle* (San Rafael, California, 1978), 297. "too hasty vigor": OR, 1, II, 384. "Good God!": Reese, 35.

141. The order to Howard: OR, 1, II, 418. McDowell's thinking: CCW, II, 42–44. Order to Tyler: Barnard's report (OR, 1, II, 331–32) says McDowell saw the dust clouds while he was on the path, and Barnard, writing eight days later, was very specific about it. McDowell told the Joint Committee in December he was still at the blacksmith shop when he gave

the order (CCW, II, 43), but since Barnard's recollections were closer to the event, they seem more likely to have been correct. The history of the Second Rhode Island by Augustus Woodbury (Providence, 1873), 31, states that McDowell arrived at Sudley Ford *before* Burnside crossed and urged him to speed up because of the dust clouds; the report of Surgeon William Shakespeare King, on McDowell's staff and with him all day, agrees: *Supplement to the OR* (Wilmington, North Carolina, 1994), I, 152 — but if so, one wonders where McDowell was between 9:30 and 11:00.

142. "cheering like madmen": Martin A. Haynes, *History of the Second Regiment of New Hampshire Volunteers* (Manchester, New Hampshire, 1865), 22. Sherman's move: OR, 1, II, 368.

143. "as if by magic": Sisson. "get these men out of here": Reed, 22. "I did not hear it": Virgil A. Stewart, Recollections, in George M. Battey, Jr., *A History of Rome and Floyd County* (Atlanta, 1969), 143. "all up": Zettler, 67. The small group that rallied: letter, James Hamilton Couper to sister, Maggie, July 25, 1861, in James Emmet Bagwell, "James Hamilton Couper, Georgia Rice Planter" (Ph.D. diss., University of Southern Mississippi, 1978), 309–11; *Savannah Republican,* July 29, 1861. "honor of the State": Letter, Couper to father, July 23, 1861, Couper Papers, Coastal Georgia Historical Society, St. Simon Island (Georgia) Lighthouse Museum. "Who is that officer": Reed, 24. "Georgians are running": ibid. Bee vs. Bartow: Stewart.

144. "strange troops": John Coxe, "The Battle of First Manassas," CV (January 1925), XXIII, 26. "My men are nearly": David Green Fleming, *The Hawkinsville* (Georgia) *Dispatch,* July 24, 1879. "They have killed me": *Savannah Republican,* August 1, 1861. See also John Reed, *Journal,* 25, Alabama Department of History.

145. ER, II, 83–84.

146. The scene: Henry F. Ritter, letter to uncle, July 23, 1861, MNBP; Edward P. Doherty, *History of the 71st Re, N.G., N.Y.* (New York, 1919), 810. "Victory!": Henry N. Blake, *Three Years in the Army of the Potomac* (Boston, 1865), 16.

Intermezzo

147. "worst material": *Supplement to the OR* (Wilmington, North Carolina, 1994), I, 146. "My impression": ibid., 153. Mrs. Spindle: *Providence* (Rhode Island) *Daily Evening Press,* July 24, 1861. Transformation of the church: Magruder's report: ibid., 157; cf. King's report, OR, 1, II, 344, in which he claimed that using the church had been his idea and that he ordered Magruder to do so — but Magruder's opposing recollections are quite explicit and more convincing. Thornberry's house: Laura Fletcher, recollection, typescript, 1936, MNBP. "ice cart": Edwin S. Barrett, *What I Saw at Bull Run* (Boston 1886), 25.

148. Hospitals at Bull Run: Joseph Mills Hanson, *Bull Run Remembers* (Manassas, 1953), 23. See also letter from Dr. J. C. Nott, *Mobile* (Alabama) *Evening News*, July 30, 1861; Thomas Cooper De Leon, *Four Years in Confederate Capitals* (Mobile, 1890), 121. "resolute, matronly": "J. R. H." (Joseph R. Hawley), *Hartford Evening Press*, August 7, 1861.

149. Frank Hastings Hamilton, *A Treatise on Military Surgery and Hygiene* (New York, 1865) is highly informative; see 564–68 for his comments about infections. Among many modern treatments, see especially Horace Herndon Cunningham, *Doctors in Gray* (LSUP, 1986 reprint of 1958); Cunningham, *Field Medical Services at the Battles of Manassas* (Athens, Georgia, 1968); George Worthington Adams, *Doctors in Blue* (New York, 1952). Minister's estimate of wounded: Cunningham, *Field*, 15. "Under a small table": "With the Fire Zouaves at First Bull Run: The Narrative of Private Arthur O. Alcock," edited by Brian C. Pohanka, *Civil War Regiments* (1997), V, 91.

150. Mathew Brady: quoted in J. Cutler Andrews, *The North Reports the Civil War* (Pittsburgh, 1955), 89. William Croffut, a professional reporter with the *New York Tribune*, did cross Bull Run at Sudley Ford with the army: Louis M. Starr, *Bohemian Brigade: Civil War Newsmen in Action* (New York, 1954), 45. No single source lists all the politicians who were there, but Samuel Sullivan Cox, *Union — Disunion — Reunion* (Washington, 1885), 150, took a stab at it. Wilson at Willard's: Arba N. Waterman, "Washington at the Time of the First Bull Run," Military Essays and Recollections, MOLLUS, II (Chicago, 1894), 29. Thomasson: *Providence* (Rhode Island) *Daily Evening Press*, August 2, 1861; Josiah Marshall Favill, *The Diary of a Young Officer* (Chicago, 1909), 34. McCooks: Daniel McCook to R. L. McCook, July 26, 1861, MNBP. Two adolescents: Edward Henry Clement, *The Bull-Run Rout* (Cambridge, Massachusetts, 1909), 7–9; one of them was probably John Batchelder.

151. Joel S. Yarborough, *Recollections*, Georgia Department of Archives; Hamilton, 308; *Providence* (Rhode Island) *Daily Journal*, July 26, 1861; Charles Woodward Hutson to parents, July 22, 1861, Hutson Papers, UNC.

152. William Howard Russell, *My Diary North and South* (New York, 1988), 265. The parents at Centreville: letter, "Sam" to friend, July 23, 1861, in *Rochester Democrat and American*, July 30, 1861. Jane Hinsdale: *Hartford Courant*, July 29, 1861.

153. Civilians on "Douglas Heights": letter, "Florence" to sister, July 23, 1861, in *Southern Magazine* (May, 1874), from typescript, MNBP; Laura Fletcher, *Recollections* (1936), typescript, MNBP. Henry family: Hanson, 88–89; and the research skills of the MBNP "Museum Specialist," Jim Burgess.

154. *Courier*, August 2, 1861. Edward Farley: John Esten Cooke, *Wearing of the Gray* (New York, 1867), 408. Loreta Janeta Velazquez, *The Woman in Battle* (Richmond, 1876). Eppa Hunton, *The Autobiography of Eppa Hunton* (Richmond, 1933), 42. Mrs. Saunders: Charles Minor and Susan Leigh

Blackford, *Letters from Lee's Army* (New York, 1947), 36. Alexandria: John Ogden, "The Town Is Took," *Alexandria History* (1981), III, 11. Listening in Washington: "W. S. W." to editor, *Herkimer* (New York) *County Journal*, August 1, 1861. Lincoln: William Bender Wilson, "News from Bull Run," *Philadelphia Weekly Times*, April 16, 1881.

Building Stone Walls

155. Hampton Legion: letter, J. E. Poyas to sister, July 24, 1861, in *Charleston Courier*, July 30, 1861; letter, "Laurens" to editor, *Laurensville* (South Carolina) *Herald*, August 9, 1861; letter, Charles Woodward Hutson to parents, July 22, 1861, Hutson Papers, UNC; letter, James Singleton to "Mattie," July 26, 1861, Singleton Papers, UVA; Hampton's report, OR, 1, II, 566–67; Judith N. McArthur and Orville Vernon Burton, *"A Gentleman and an Officer": A Military and Social History of James B. Griffin's Civil War* (New York, 1996), 49–53. "a large body": letter, James Conner to mother, July 22, 1861, Conner Papers, SCL. "My first shot": letter, Richard W. Habersham to mother, July 26, 1861, Habersham Papers, LC. "fought in squads": Coxe, 26.

156. Chisolm's wanderings of the morning: His report to Beauregard, dated August 1, 1861, National Archives (M331, Roll 54); his journal, July 21, 1861, Chisolm Papers, The New-York Historical Society. (It is unclear when or how Chisolm maintained this journal, but he has it divided by "chapters," each chapter paginated separately. See his "Bull Run" chapter, 5–6.) Reporters: *Richmond Dispatch*, July 25, 1861; *Charleston Courier*, July 30, 1861; J. Cutler Andrews, *The South Reports the Civil War* (Princeton, 1970), 81–84. "My heart": OR, 51, pt. 2, 689.

157. "a better heart": John B. Gordon, *Reminiscences of the Civil War* (New York, 1903), 38. "profanity which might be parsed": George Cary Eggleston, *A Rebel's Recollections* (New York, 1875), 136.

158. Alexander: Gary W. Gallagher, ed., *Fighting for the Confederacy: The Personal Recollections of General Edward Porter Alexander* (UNCP, 1989), 52–53. "set out together": Beauregard, *A Commentary on the Campaign and Battle of Manassas of July, 1861* (New York, 1891), 87. Who made the decision to leave Lookout Hill?: Cf. Joseph E. Johnston, "Responsibilities of the First Bull Run," BAL, I, 247–48; OR, 1, II, 474–75; Beauregard, *Commentary*, 76–85; Douglas Southall Freeman, *Lee's Lieutenants* (New York, 1943), 59–62.

159. "every segment": Beauregard, "The First Battle of Bull Run," BAL, I, 210. Johnston's move to Portici: Cf. Beauregard, *Commentary*, 95–96; OR, 1, II, 475.

160. John D. Imboden, "Incidents of the First Bull Run," BAL, I, 232–36; Imboden's official report, dated July 22, 1861, in *Richmond Dispatch*, July 26, 1861; John Gibbon, *Artillerist's Manual*, 2nd ed. (New York, 1863).

161. "He did not know": Samuel Wragg Ferguson, "Memoirs," type-script, written in 1900, MNBP. Bee's death: Supplement to the OR, I, 173–74, 193; John Cheeves Haskell, *The Haskell Memoirs* (New York, 1960), 36n; Samuel Will John, "The Importance of Accuracy," CV, (August 1914), XXII, 343; James G. Hudson, "A Story of Company D, 4th Al. Infantry Regt., C.S.A.," *Alabama Historical Quarterly,* (Spring 1961), XXIII, 169–70; letter, W. O. Hudson to Richard Watson York, February 17, 1867, in "The 'Old Third' Brigade and the Death of General Bee," *Our Living and Our Dead* (Raleigh, 1875), I, 562–65. Nickname: Edward Porter Alexander, "The Battle of Bull Run," *Scribner's Magazine* (1907), XLI, 90n; Asher Harman, MSS, MNBP; J. B. E. Sloan, draft of notes, undated, MNBP; William M. Robbins, "The Sobriquet 'Stonewall': How It Was Acquired," SHSP (1891), XIX, 166–67; Harmon's undated recollection was given to MNBP in 1961 and contains a note saying it was taken from the Harman-Garber Record, 91, "compiled by Mrs. Virginia Armistead"; see also countless reverential accounts, drawing on the newspapers; the most perceptive recent analysis is that of John Hennessy, "Stonewall Jackson's Nickname," *Civil War* (March/April, 1990), XXII, 5–13.

162. Letter, Casler to parents, July 24, 1861, in John O. Casler, *Four Years in the Stonewall Brigade* (Girard, Kansas, 1906), 25–45.

Take the High Ground

163. "Now, you Yankee devils": Edmund Clarence Stedman, "The Battle of Bull Run," a reprint of his extended eyewitness account in the *New York World,* July 23, 1861 (New York, 1861), 22. Mutiny: Anonymous letter from a member of the Second New York to *New York Mercury,* July 28, 1861; George W. Wilkes, diary, reprinted in *History of the 71st Re, N.G., N.Y.* (New York, 1919), 180–81.

164. Tyler's motivation and movements: John Hennessey, *The First Battle of Manassas* (Lynchburg, 1989), 74; based entirely on Hennessey's book, Ethan Rafuse, "The Man Who Could Have Knocked Off Stonewall," CWTI (August 2001), XL, 30 ff., and his *A Single Grand Victory* (Wilmington, 2002), 154–55; cf. Tyler's report, OR, 1, II, 348–49; Tyler's testimony: CCW, II, 201.

165. "smiling and happy" and "do your duty": "J. R. H." (Joseph R. Hawley), *Hartford Evening Press,* August 8, 1861. "Pandemonium" and "sing about": Elnathan B. Tyler, *'Wooden Nutmegs' at Bull Run* (Hartford, 1872), 68. "take that bayonet": ibid., 70. Upton speech: Letter, "G" to editor, *New Haven Morning Journal and Courier,* July 31, 1861. "Oh, Father": letter, Benjamin F. Smart to father, July 23, 1861, MNBP. Tyler's message to McDowell: CCW, II, 201. Descriptions of Keyes's charge and the follow-up march: *New Haven Morning Journal and Courier,* July 26, 1861; *Hartford Courant,* August 7, 1861; Jameson's and Keyes's reports: OR, 1, II, 353–

356; William E. S. Whitman and Charles H. True, *Maine in the War for the Union* (Lewiston, 1865), 41–43; Horatio Staples, "Reminiscences of Bull Run," MOLLUS (Portland, 1898), 133–35; *The Connecticut War Record* (Hartford, 1863), I, 81; George S. Burnham (commander of the First Connecticut), report, July 24, 1861, Connecticut State Library; also his "History of the First Connecticut Volunteers (Three Months)," typescript, MNBP; Gustavus Sullivan Dana, "'Bully for the First Connecticut!' The Recollections of a Three-Month Volunteer," *Lincoln Herald* (Summer 1965), LXVII, 78–79; Henry Villard, *The Memoirs of Henry Villard* (New York, 1904), I, 188–89.

166. Averell's testimony: CCW, II, 213–15; see also his *Ten Years in the Saddle* (San Rafael, California, 1978), 289. Marines: OR, 1, II, 391–92.

167. Placement of the batteries: OR, 1, II, 394; CCW, II, 142–44, 168–69, 218–20, 242–46; J. Albert Monroe, *The Rhode Island Artillery at the First Battle of Bull Run* (Providence, 1878), 20–23; letter from unnamed officer in Rhode Island battery, *Providence Daily Journal*, July 31, 1861; *Hartford Courant*, July 30, 1861; letters, Adelbert Ames to John C. Ropes, May 14 and 28, 1894, MNBP. "pretty thick": quoted in David M. Sullivan, *The United States Marine Corps in the Civil War: The First Year* (Shippensburg, Pennsylvania, 1997), I, 135.

168. "I do not think": ibid., 174.

169. Heintzelman: Compare his diary entries for September 2, 4, 1861, Heintzelman Papers, LC; his report in OR, 1, II, 402–05; and his testimony to the Committee, CCW, II, 30. Capture of Boone: William Colvill, "Narrative of the First Regiment," in William Lochren, *Minnesota in the Civil and Indian Wars, 1861–1865* (St. Paul, 1890), 9; "Return Ira Holcombe," *History of the First Regiment Minnesota Volunteer Infantry, 1861–1864* (Stillwater, Minnesota, 1916), 47–48. Actually, the Union army also captured General George Steuart of Maryland, but he was freed late in the day before he could be taken back to Washington.

170. Stuart's march to position: W. W. Blackford, *War Years with Jeb Stuart* (LSUP, 1993), 27–29. Griffin's decision not to attack: CCW, II, 144, 169, 175–76. The debate: McDonald, *"We"* (Shippensburg, Pennsylvania), 105–06; Hennessey, *First* (Lynchburg, Virginia), 80–85; also see Mark Snell's "First Manassas; An End of Innocence: A Conversation with Historian John Hennessey," *Civil War Regiments* (n.d.), V, 105–19; Rafuse, *Single* (Wilmington, Delaware), 166–67. Stuart's reaction: Report, OR, 1, II, 482–83; his letter to Flora, July 27, 31, 1861, Stuart Papers, Perkins Library, Duke University. Charge from Confederate view: Blackford, 29–31; "O. P. Q.," report, *Richmond Dispatch*, July 31, 1861; "Southern Lady," ibid., August 5, 1861; "J. S. B.," "Confederate Cavalry at the First Manassas," *The Southern Bivouac* (August 1884), II, 529–30. Charge from the Union viewpoint: Lewis Herbert Metcalf, "'So Eager Were We all . . .'," *American Heritage* (June 1965), XVI, 37–38; "The New York Zouaves in Battle," *New*

York Leader, August 3, 1861. The exact timing of the cavalry charge, compared to that of the Thirty-third, has been in dispute. Griffin and Barry, for example, say it came beforehand. But none of the members of the Eleventh concur, and if they, in fact, had faced a cavalry charge on the way *to* the hill, that memory would have been vivid. The clue may be in Stuart's after-action report, where he says that he saw the Second Mississippi arrive *after* the cavalry charge: OR, 1, II, 483. Since we know that Colonel Boone of the Second Mississippi was apparently captured by Irvine, traveling with the First Minnesota, this would indicate the scenario laid out here. But nailing down times and the placement of events for the next two hours is hazardous. (Officially, cavalrymen were divided into *troops,* but in 1861 most cavalrymen still referred to their units as "companies," and I have followed their practice.)

171. Griffin's guns: Cf. the testimony of Barry, Griffin, and Ricketts in CCW, II, 142–44; 168–77; 242–46. Heintzelman's wound: Heintzelman, diary, September 2, 4, 1861; William Woods Averell, *Ten Years in the Saddle* (San Rafael, California, 1978), 298–99. There is some possibility Griffin actually brought three of his guns to the new position, but the weight of evidence leans strongly to two.

172. Artillery losses: Ralph W. Donnelly, "Federal Batteries on the Henry House Hill, Bull Run, 1861," in *Military Analysis of the Civil War* (Millwood, New York, 1977), 310–14. "nearer to heaven": George W. Baylor, *From Bull Run to Bull Run; or Four Years in the Army of Northern Virginia* (Richmond, 1900), 20. Willcox: Robert Garth Willcox, *Forgotten Valor: The Memoirs, Journals, & Civil War Letters of Orlando B. Willcox* (Kent, Ohio, 1999), 291–92.

173. The marine battalion: Sullivan, I, 135–38. "three attacks": Letter, H. M. Link to father, July 30, 1861, in *Herkimer* (New York) *County Journal,* August 8, 1861; anonymous Fire Zouaves officer in undated *New York Tribune,* quoted in Frank Moore (ed.) *The Rebellion Record* (New York, 1862), II, 18.

Entropy

174. "more dirt": quoted in Alan D. Gaff, *If This Is War: A History of the Campaign of Bull's Run by the Wisconsin Regiment Thereafter Known as the Ragged Ass Second* (Dayton, Ohio, 1991), 230. "it's true": Henry Kyd Douglas, *I Rode with Stonewall* (reprint, 1961), 22.

175. Thirty-third: Arthur C. Cummings, "Thirty-third Virginia at First Manassas," SHSP (1906), XXXIV, 363–71; Randolph Barton, "Stonewall Jackson at Louisville," CV (November 2000), VIII, 481–85; John H. Grabill, "Diary of a Soldier of the Stonewall Brigade" (Woodstock, Virginia, 1909), unpaginated, July 21, 1861.

176. Fourteenth's charge: John A. Wells, Memorandum, undated, MNBP. Allen's report, *Supplement to the OR,* I, 189–90; Cleon Moore, "The Civil War Recollections of Cleon Moore," *Magazine of the Jefferson County Historical Society* (December 1988), LIV, 89 ff. "cut to pieces": A. R. Chisolm, Report, August 1, 1861, National Archives (M331, Roll 54).

177. "Yesterday we fought": Mary Anna Jackson, *Memoirs of Stonewall Jackson* (Louisville, Kentucky, 1895), 177–78. Report: OR, 1, II, 482. "have mercy": Letter, Alexander Tedford Barclay to mother, July 27, 1861, Washington and Lee. "All's well" and "I was scared": quoted in Byron Farwell, *Stonewall: A Biography of General Thomas J. Jackson* (New York, 1992), 179. "Me, too, Lord": J. B. Caddall, *Richmond Times-Dispatch,* November 27, 1904. "Up, Fourth and Twenty-seventh": Letter, unnamed lieutenant to "Charlie," August 19, 1861, Cabell-Ellet Papers, UVA. "drive them to Washington": J. Gray McAllister, *Sketch of Captain Thompson McAllister, Co. A, 27th Virginia Regiment* (Petersburg, 1896), 18. "yell like furies": *Lexington Gazette,* August 1, 1861.

178. Shooting from behind tree: Letter to "Charlie." McAllister: J. McAllister, 14–18, which contains Captain McAllister's own account and the recollections of some of his men; Letter, John C. Carpenter to William M. McAllister, December 26, 1902, MNBP. The charge: Allen's report, *Supplement,* 190; Clarence Albert Fonerden, *A Brief History of the Military Career of Carpenter's Battery* (New Market, Virginia, 1911), 8–12; Charles Copland Wight, "Recollections of Charles Copland Wight," Wight Papers, Virginia Historical Society. "happiest day": Elisha Franklin Paxton, *Memoir and Memorials* (privately printed, 1905), 12.

179. "called a coward": William Todd, *The Seventy-ninth Highlanders* (Albany, 1886), 51. Seventy-ninth's ethnic make-up: Ella Lonn, *Foreigners in the Union Army and Navy* (LSUP, 1951), 130. "O Lordy!": John N. Opie, *A Rebel Cavalryman with Lee, Stuart and Jackson* (Chicago, 1899), 32. Bayoneted foot: Richard Moe, *The Last Full Measure: The Life and Death of the First Minnesota Volunteers* (New York, 1993), 51. Soldier knocked out by flying gun: Gaff, 226–67. Fifth Massachusetts: Edwin C. Bennett, *Musket and Sword* (Boston, 1900), 17–20; Alfred S. Roe, *The Fifth Regiment Massachusetts Volunteer Infantry* (Boston, 1911), 81; *Chelsea* (Massachusetts) *Telegraph and Pioneer,* August 10, 1861.

180. Sherman: *Memoirs of William Tecumseh Sherman* (New York, 1875), I, 209; OR, 1, II, 369–70; *Sherman's Civil War,* eds., Brooks D. Simpson and Jean V. Berlin (UNCP, 1999), 124. "the woods in front of us": "N. R.," (Wisconsin) *State Journal,* July 25, 1861. "guns were discharged": quoted in Gaff, 155–56. See the fascinating Web site, <www.secondwi.com>, which contains numerous letters written by members of the Second Wisconsin. "Isn't it terrible": Joseph Mills Hanson, *Bull Run Remembers* (Manassas, 1953), 91. Withers's Eighteenth Virginia: Benjamin Irby Scott, "Horrors of Manassas Battle," the (Culpeper) *Virginia Star,* August 27, 1936, at MBNP;

Richard Irby, *Historical Sketch of the Nottoway Grays* (Richmond, 1878), 10n, 12. Firing guns at retreating Union soldiers: Several claimed that honor, but among the most convincing is Samuel Wragg Ferguson, "Memoirs," (typescript, 1900), 3, in MNBP.

181. "you have no idea": James Overcash to Joseph Overcash, August 11, 1861, Joseph Overcash Papers, Perkins Library, Duke. "I myself" and "turned over the command": P. G. T. Beauregard, "The First Battle of Bull Run," BAL, I, 213, 215. "veteran-like": MO, I, 106. "Day is ours!": Scott, op. cit.

The End of the Day

182. "ganed the battle": quoted in Terrance V. Murphy, *10th Virginia Infantry* (Lynchburg, 1989), 10. "turn of the tide": Abner R. Small, *The Road to Richmond* (Berkeley, 1939), 23.

183. Custer: Frederick Whittaker, *A Popular Life of Gen. George A. Custer* (New York, 1876), 66–68; OR, 1, II, 393.

184. "dying limp": Small, 21. "intirely existed": Michael McFadden to "Libby," July 28, 1861, MNBP. Numbers: Howard's report estimated his brigade as half-filled, OR, 1, II, 418; cf. 15 in company: letter to *Brunswick* (Maine) *Telegram*, August 2, 1861; 8 in company: Frank L. Lemont to father, August 24, 1861, MNBP.

185. Fire Zouaves: Augustine E. Costello, *Our Firemen: A History of the New York Fire Departments* (New York, 1887), 726; letter, Alfred A. Doby to Elizabeth M. Kennedy, July 25, 1861, MNBP. "There they are": "The Sumter Volunteers" (unidentified scrap, probably from the *Sumter* (South Carolina) *Watchman*, late summer, 1861), MNBP. Hampton Legion: Letter, James Conner to mother, July 24, 1861, Conner Papers, SCL. Broken canteen and "mashed when it hit me": Robert Wallace Shand, Shand Papers, SCL.

186. Arrival of the Smith/Elzey brigade: Elzey's report, in *Supplement to the OR*, I, 179–80; Nina Kirby Smith, "Blucher of the Day at Manassas," CV (March 1899), VII, 108–09; McHenry Howard, *Recollections of a Maryland Confederate Soldier and Staff Officer* (Baltimore, 1914), 34–36. "guided by the shouts": quoted in *Richmond Dispatch*, August 5, 1861. Whiting's statement to Smith about planning a retreat comes from Smith's diary: Smith, 109.

187. Early's march: OR, 1, II, 555–57; Jubal Anderson Early, *Jubal Early's Memoirs* (Philadelphia, 1912), 16–22. "Go, it boys!": quoted by J. McLean, "The 13th Miss. Infantry. Regt. Men and their Battle Flag," <www.misscivilwar.org>. "Glory!": David E. Johnston, *The Story of a Confederate Boy in the Civil War* (Portland, Oregon, 1914), 74; cf. Early, 22. "any condition to fight": Letter, T. D. Nutting to wife, July 23, 1861, in *Weekly* (Jackson, Mississippi) *Mississippian*, August 14, 1861.

188. "My glass" and "abundant crop of blackberries": Howard, 38. Colonel Whiting hiding: Letter, William Henry Bond to friends, July 22, 1861, on "First Vermont Brigade" Web site. "wild uproar": Small, 22. "an attack of illness": Oliver O. Howard, *Autobiography* (New York, 1908), I, 159–60; cf. his report, OR, 1, II, 418–19. "It beat a circus": P. F. Ellis, CV (December 1897), IX, 624.

189. "it seems evident" and "we are not whipped": William Woods Averell, *Ten Years in the Saddle* (San Rafael, California, 1978), 299–300. "noble regiment": Charles Elihu Slocum, *The Life and Services of Major-General Henry Warner Slocum* (Toledo, 1913), 15–16. "fatigue and thirst": OR, 1, II, 316.

190. Mail delivery: Warren Cudworth, *History of the First Regiment (Massachusetts Infantry)* (Boston, 1866), 64; CCW, II, 25, 179; Thomas M. Vincent, "The Battle of Bull Run, July 21, 1861," MOLLUS (Washington, 1905), 223. Davies's personality: Letters, William Henry Walling to family, dated June 13 and July 30, 1861, in "A Biography of William Henry Walling" (unpaginated typescript), USMHI, Carlisle Barracks, Pennsylvania.

191. "Get away!": Gordon, 41–42. "Why are you obstructing": Newton Martin Curtis, *From Bull Run to Chancellorsville: The Story of the Sixteenth New York Infantry* (New York, 1906), 48. The girl's identity: Curtis was part of Davies's brigade and may have seen her at the abatis; he thought she was Oceola Mason, a descendant of the well-known Masons of Virginia; more likely, it was Sally Summers, who was seventeen and who lived at "Level Green," a farm not far from where Davies's brigade was. Story about two "heroines": see, e.g., *Charleston Courier,* June 24, 1861.

192. CCW, II, 25, 77. Miles's hearing: Mark A. Snell, *From First to Last: The Life of Major General William B. Franklin* (New York, 2002), 69–70.

193. Davies's probe: Curtis, 42–43. Ewell's return: Campbell Brown, "Colonel Campbell Brown's Reply to General Beauregard," SHSP, XIII, 4; George F. Harrison, reply, ibid., XIV, 357; OR, 1, II, 536. "we are whipped": Terry L. Jones, *Campbell Brown's Civil War* (LSUP, 2001), 30n. "My feelings then": Percy Gatling Hamlin, *The Making of a Soldier: Letters of R. S. Ewell* (Richmond, 1935), 106.

194. OR, 1, II, 377–82, 433–37, 537–41; W. S. Nye, "Action North of Bull Run: An Often Overlooked Phase of Battle of First Manassas," CWTI (April 1965), IV, 48–49. Union side: Henry J. Hunt, "Sketch of Lieutenant Samuel A. Benjamin, 2d Art'y" (June 14, 1886), National Archives, Record Group 391; "J. J. S.," in *Malone* (New York) *Frontier Palladium*, August 1, 1861. Confederate side: Letter, Halt McGehee to Louisa McGehee Burrus, August 8, 1861, J. C. Burrus Papers, Archives, Jackson, Mississippi; "Personne," *Charleston Courier,* August 1, 1861; the (Jackson, Mississippi) *Mississippian,* August 2, 1861; (Yorkville, South Carolina) *Enquirer,* August 1, 1861; George Alphonso Gibbs, "With a Mississippi Private in a Little Known Part of the Battle of First Bull Run and at Ball's Bluff,"

CWTI (April 1965), IV, 42–50; Asbury Coward, *The South Carolinians: Colonel Asbury Coward's Memoirs* (New York, 1968), 16–18. Miles: OR, 1, II, 375–76. "Burke," at the Provost Marshal's office in Washington, however, wrote a friend about Richardson: "He disgraced himself, I think, & has shown he is not a true man & gentleman in his attack on poor Miles": Letter to John C. Ropes, August 8, 1861, original at Boston University Library, MNBP.

Vespers

195. Panic: John Tidball, *War Journal*, USMA, 277–83; H. B. Jackson, "From Washington to Bull Run and Back Again in the Second Wisconsin Infantry," MOLLUS (Wisconsin, 1910), 242; *Providence Daily Evening Press*, July 24, 27, 186; letter, Elihu Washburne to wife, July 22, 1861, in Gaillard Hunt, *Israel, Elihu & Cadwallader Washburne* (New York, 1925), 201–02. Ely: Alfred Ely, *Journal of Alfred Ely* (New York, 1862), 15–16; Edward Porter Alexander, *Fighting for the Confederacy*, edited by Gary W. Gallagher (UNCP, 1989), 55. "brief in time": John G. Barnard, *The C.S.A. and the Battle of Bull Run* (New York, 1862), 121.

196. Eppa Hunton, *The Autobiography of Eppa Hunton* (Richmond, 1933), 37–38.

197. OR, 1, II, 543–44; Longstreet, *From Manassas to Appomattox* (Philadelphia, 1896), 51–52; Johnston, *Narrative of Military Operations* (New York, 1874), 52–53; Johnston, "Responsibilities of the First Bull Run," BAL, I, 249. "the more scared" and "broken to pieces" and "burst into tears": Alexander Hunter, *Johnny Reb and Billy Yank* (New York, 1905), 63–65; see also G. Moxley Sorrel, *Recollections of a Confederate Staff Officer* (New York, 1905), 26.

198. ER, I, 87; OR, 1, II, 524–25, 535–36.

199. Chisolm: *Journal*, Chapter 5, 9–11, A. R. Chisolm Papers, The New-York Historical Society. "I confess": Letter, Frank L. Lemont to Samuel R. Lemont, August 24, 1861, MNBP. Cavalry attacks: OR, 1, II, 532–33, 552–53, 562, 564–65; William Fitzhugh Randolph, SHV, XXIII, 263–64; *Richmond Dispatch*, July 29, 1861; "J. S. B.," "Confederate Cavalry at the First Manassas," *The Southern Bivouac* (August 1884), II, 529–34; W. W. Blackford, *War Years with Jeb Stuart* (LSUP, 1993), 34–41; Peter Conover Hains, "The First Gun at Bull Run," *Cosmopolitan* (August 1911), LI, 395–99. Corcoran's stand: Letter, Michael Corcoran to wife, July 26, 1861, in the *Irish-American*, August 17, 1861. Tyler's stand: *New York Times*, July 28, 1861; *Hartford Evening Press*, August 9, 1861.

200. Napoleon: quoted in R. M. Johnston, *Bull Run: Its Strategy and Tactics* (New York, 1913), 244. "I did not feel": John Henry Burrill, unpaginated memoir, 1902, Burrill Papers, State Historical Society of Wisconsin, Madison. Disintegration: Stephen D. Wesbrook, "The Potential for

Military Disintegration," in *Combat Effectiveness: Cohesion, Stress, and the Volunteer Military* (Beverly Hills, 1980), 244–78; Anthony Kellett, *Combat Motivation: The Behavior of Soldiers in Battle* (Boston, 1982); John Keegan, *The Face of Battle* (New York, 1976), 136.

201. McDowell's council: *Daniel Tyler: A Memorial Volume* (privately printed, 1883), 62–63. "damned disagreeable": George M. Finch, "The Boys of '61," *G.A.R. War Papers* (Cincinnati, 1891), 261. "O that retreat!": Letter, Charles Brown to Caroline Lansing, July 29, 1861, MNBP. Nightmare march: See contemporary newspapers, e.g., *Providence Daily Evening Press*, July 24, 1861. Commission: cited in George Worthington Adams, *Doctors in Blue* (New York, 1952), 26.

202. "Brave Louisianans": quoted in William C. Davis, *Jefferson Davis: The Man and His Hour* (New York, 1991), 351. "Crazy Hill": Gary W. Gallagher (ed.) *Fighting for the Confederacy: The Personal Recollections of General Edward Porter Alexander* (UNCP, 1989), 58. "I will take": Hunter McGuire, "Stonewall Jackson," SHSP, XIX, 303. Conference: Jefferson Davis, *Rise and Fall of the Confederate Government* (New York, 1881), I, 349–56; Joseph H. Johnston, "Responsibilities of the First Bull Run," BAL, I, 245, 252; MO, I, 108–14. On taking Washington: OR, 1, II, 1004; Robert Enoch Withers, *Autobiography of an Octogenarian* (Roanoke, 1907), 152; Edward Henry Clement, *The Bull-Run Rout* (Cambridge, 1909), 12; W. H. Morgan, *Personal Reminiscences of the War of 1861–5* (Lynchburg, 1911), 78–79; Jubal Anderson Early, *Autobiographical Sketch* (Philadelphia, 1912), 27–46; John D. Imboden, "Incidents of the First Bull Run," BAL, I, 239; William T. Sherman, *Sherman's Civil War* (UNCP, 1999), 125.

Envoi

203. "solitary figure": William Woods Averell, *Ten Years in the Saddle* (San Rafael, California, 1978), 302. "they sat on the door steps": John Ogden, "The Town Is Took," *Alexandria History* (1981), III, 11. "sulkily drips": Walt Whitman, *Complete Prose Works* (Boston, 1907), 24–25. "a frightful condition": Olmsted, *The Papers of Frederick Law Olmsted* (Baltimore, 1986), IV, 130–31. "a perfect pandemonium": Jed Hotchkiss, *Confederate Military History* (Atlanta, 1899), III, 120. "every grog shop": John M. Gould, *History of the First-Tenth-Twenty-ninth Maine Regiment* (Portland, 1871), 60–61. "I sat down on the fence": Letter, "J. G. P." to "Folks," in *Roxbury City Gazette*, August 8, 1861. "Our city is overrun": Henry Whittington, *Diary*, Box 11, Alexandria Library.

204. "As a rule": Olmsted, 162 (from the Commission's "Report on the Demoralization of the Volunteers"). Shooting statistics: Thomas Leonard Livermore, *Numbers & Losses in the Civil War in America, 1861–65* (New York, 1901), 77. Military quotas: Fred Albert Shannon, *The Organization and Administration of the Union Army, 1861–1865* (Cleveland, 1928), I, 259–60.

"miserable rabble": quoted in Alan D. Gaff, *If This Is War* (Dayton, 1991), 298–99.

205. "sleepless night": Greeley to Lincoln, July 29, 1861, Lincoln Papers, LC. "Find the President": Letter, Nicolay to wife, July 27, 1861, LC. Scene at War Department: William B. Wilson, "News from Bull Run," *Philadelphia Weekly Times*, April 16, 1881. Lincoln's plans: John G. Nicolay and John Hay, *Abraham Lincoln: A History* (New York, 1904–17), IV, 368–69. Revolution: Stephen B. Oates, *Abraham Lincoln: The Man behind the Myths* (New York, 1984), 92.

206. *Providence Daily Journal,* July 23, 1861; *Frank Leslie's Illustrated Magazine*, July 27, 1861, 162. Resolutions: *Congressional Globe,* July 22, 1861, 218–22. "I go for liberating": Charles Carleton Coffin, *The Boys of '61* (Boston, 1884), 26.

207. "no longer funny": Charles T. Loehr, *War History of the Old First Virginia Infantry Regiment* (Richmond, 1884), 12. Prisoners: CCW, II, 449, 457–79. "Lord be praised": Judith White Brockenbrough McGuire, *Diary of a Southern Refugee during the War* (New York, 1867), 42. Burying "Blue": John O. Casler, *Four Years in the Stonewall Brigade* (Girard, Kansas, 1906), 32. Blackfords: Charles Minor Blackford and Susan Lee Blackford, *Letters from Lee's Army* (New York, 1947), 33, 36–37. "My dear pastor": Mary Anna Jackson, *Memoirs of Stonewall Jackson* (Louisville, 1895), 182. Farming: John H. Wheeler, Diary, LC. Sudley Church: *Springfield Republican,* November 24, 1886.

INDEX